LINUX NETWORK ADMINISTRATOR'S

INTERACTIVE WORKBOOK

JOE KAPLENK

ISBN 0-13-020790-X

Prentice Hall PTR
Upper Saddle River, NJ 07458
http://www.phptr.com/phptrinteractive

Editorial/Production Supervision: *Wil Mara*
Acquisitions Editor: *Mark Taub*
Development Editor: *Ralph Moore*
Marketing Manager: *Kate Hargett*
Manufacturing Manager: *Alexis Heydt*
Editorial Assistant: *Michael Fredette*
Cover Design Director: *Jerry Votta*
Cover Designer: *Anthony Gemmellaro*
Art Director: *Gail Cocker-Bogusz*
Technical Editor: *Sam Shamsuddin*

Prentice-Hall, Inc.
Upper Saddle River, New Jersey 07458

Prentice Hall books are widely used by corporations and government agencies for training, marketing, and resale. The publisher offers discounts on this book when ordered in bulk quantities.
For more information, contact: Corporate Sales Department, Phone: 800-382-3419;
FAX: 201-236-7141; email: corpsales@prenhall.com

Or write: Corp. Sales Dept., Prentice Hall PTR, 1 Lake Street, Upper Saddle River, NJ 07458

Printed in the United States of America
10 9 8 7 6 5 4 3 2 1

ISBN 0-13-020790-X

Prentice-Hall International (UK) Limited, *London*
Prentice-Hall of Australia Pty. Limited, *Sydney*
Prentice-Hall Canada Inc., *Toronto*
Prentice-Hall Hispanoamericana, S.A., *Mexico*
Prentice-Hall of India Private Limited, *New Delhi*
Prentice-Hall of Japan, Inc., *Tokyo*
Pearson Education Asia P.T.E., Ltd.,
Editora Prentice-Hall do Brasil, Ltda., *Rio de Janeiro*

DEDICATION

This book is dedicated to my loving wife, Ramona, who has been very patient, supportive, and helpful in the writing of my first three books and throughout our marriage.

CONTENTS

From the Editor ix

About the Author xi

Introduction xv

CHAPTER 1 Basic TCP/IP Networking 1

LAB 1.1 The Current System TCP/IP Values 2
- 1.1.1 Use `ifconfig` 11
- 1.1.2 Use `netstat` 12

LAB 1.2 Accessing Other TCP/IP Hosts 18
- 1.2.1 `ping` 22
- 1.2.2 `traceroute` 23
- 1.2.3 `nslookup` 25

CHAPTER 1 Test Your Thinking 37

CHAPTER 2 Configuring Your TCP/IP Network 39

LAB 2.1 Setting Up TCP/IP 40
- 2.1.1 Determine Your Current Network Characteristics 47
- 2.1.2 Bring Down the Network Interface 51
- 2.1.3 Bring Up the Network Interface 53
- 2.1.4 Set Up Your Host Table 60
- 2.1.5 Enable Client Name Resolution 61

CHAPTER 2 Test Your Thinking 87

CHAPTER 3 Setting Up a Nameserver 93

LAB 3.1 Your Current Nameserver Configuration 95
- 3.1.1 Determine Your Current Nameserver Configuration 98

LAB 3.2 Setting up a Primary Nameserver 104
- 3.2.1 `resolv.conf` 106

3.2.2 `named.ca` 108
3.2.3 `named.local` 108
3.2.4 `named.hosts` 110
3.2.5 `named.rev` 111
3.2.6 `named.boot` 112
3.2.7 `named.conf` 113
3.2.8 Test Your Configuration 114

CHAPTER 3 Test Your Thinking 121

CHAPTER 4 Sharing Data in a Windows World 123

LAB 4.1 Determine Your Current Windows Network Configuration 125

4.1.1 Determine Your Current Windows Network Configuration 126
4.1.2 Set up and Log into Your PC as a Windows Network User 131
4.1.3 Verify Your Windows Network Environment 133

LAB 4.2 Getting Samba 143

4.2.1 Get the Latest Samba 144

LAB 4.3 Getting Samba Running 160

4.3.1 Determine Your Current Version of Samba 161
4.3.2 Remove Samba 162
4.3.3 Install Samba 164
4.3.4 Upgrade Samba 166
4.3.5 Set up and Test Samba 167
4.3.6 Connect from MS Windows to Samba 170
4.3.7 Connect from Samba to MS Windows 171

CHAPTER 4 Test Your Thinking 188

CHAPTER 5 Sharing Data in an NFS World 191

LAB 5.1 Setting Up NFS 192

5.1.1 Set up Your `/etc/exports` File to Allow Mounting 193
5.1.2 Do a Remote NFS Mount 196

CHAPTER 5 Test Your Thinking 212

APPENDIX A Answers to Self-Review Questions **215**

APPENDIX B Using Minimal Linux **219**

APPENDIX C Building Your Linux Home Network **223**

APPENDIX D Samba Documentation **235**

Appendix D.1 The GNU License 235
Appendix D.2 The Samba FAQ 243
Appendix D.3 Just what is SMB? 274

APPENDIX E Samba Man Pages **287**

Appendix E.1 lmhosts(5) 288
Appendix E.2 nmbd 290
Appendix E.3 samba(7) 294
Appendix E.4 smb.conf 297
Appendix E.5 smbclient(1) 408
Appendix E.6 smbd(8) 422
Appendix E.7 smbpasswd(5) 431
Appendix E.8 smbpasswd(8) 435
Appendix E.9 smbstatus(1) 441

APPENDIX F TCP/IP Documentation **443**

Appendix F.1 TCP/IP Network Resources List 443
Appendix F.2 Private IP Network Addresses 473

APPENDIX G Nameserver Documentation **483**

Appendix G.1 DNS How-To 483

APPENDIX H NFS Documentation **525**

Appendix H.1 NFS How-To 525

INDEX **545**

FROM THE EDITOR

Prentice Hall's Interactive Workbooks are designed to get you up and running fast, with just the information you need, when you need it.

We are certain that you will find our unique approach to learning simple and straightforward. Every chapter of every Interactive Workbook begins with a list of clearly defined Learning Objectives. A series of labs make up the heart of each chapter. Each lab is designed to teach you specific skills in the form of exercises. You perform these exercises at your computer and answer pointed questions about what you observe. Your answers will lead to further discussion and exploration. Each lab then ends with multiple-choice Self-Review Questions, to reinforce what you've learned. Finally, we have included Test Your Thinking projects at the end of each chapter. These projects challenge you to synthesize all of the skills you've acquired in the chapter.

Our goal is to make learning engaging, and to make you a more productive learner.

And you are not alone. Each book is integrated with its own "Companion Website." The website is a place where you can find more detailed information about the concepts discussed in the Workbook, additional Self-Review Questions to further refine your understanding of the material, and perhaps most importantly, where you can find a community of other Interactive Workbook users working to acquire the same set of skills that you are.

All of the Companion Websites for our Interactive Workbooks can be found at `http://www.phptr.com/phptrinteractive`.

Mark L. Taub
Editor-in-Chief
Pearson PTR Interactive

ABOUT THE AUTHOR

Everyone has a story to tell. Some tell it in person, some in pictures and some in words. Every person is an individual. Every story is different and every situation is unique. So the number of stories is infinite.

—*Joe*

Education

Joe Kaplenk graduated from the University of Utah with a B.S. in physics. He also studied mathematics, chemistry, biology, and journalism on an undergraduate and graduate level. His first writing experience was in college where he served as science editor and reporter for the *Daily Utah Chronicle*. He started his college education while still in High School with college mathematics courses at Orange County Community College in Middletown, NY. He continued there for a year where he majored in Physical Science. This was followed by a Mathematics major at Rensselaer Polytechnic Institute (RPI) in Troy, NY. From there he went to University of Utah where he graduated and did his graduate studies.

He has also studied computer science at the University of Illinois at Chicago, College of Dupage, Joliet Junior College and a number of non-credit seminars. His first experience with computers was in 1967 with an IBM mainframe in college at RPI that did not even have a disk or tape drive, and the Operating System was loaded from punch cards. He is actively involved in the computer world through postings on various newsgroups and discussion areas.

Work Experience

Joe's experience includes working in physics and computer science for Argonne National Labs, Fermi National Accelerator Lab, the University of Illinois at Chicago Physics Department, Motorola, Loyola University

Chicago, R.R. Donnelley, and Comdisco. He currently works for IBM Global Services as a senior systems management integration professional. He has been working with UNIX since 1980 and as a UNIX administrator since 1984.

Teaching Experience

Joe has been teaching part-time at the College of Dupage in Glen Ellyn, Illinois, for over 14 years. His experience includes teaching classes such as Introduction to Computers, Program Logic and Design, Pascal, FORTRAN, Basic, Introduction to UNIX, and Advanced UNIX. He has been teaching Advanced UNIX for seven years. He is always looking for new, easier, and better ways to teach computer science.

Like his previous book, *UNIX System Administrator's Interactive Workbook,* this book is based on his experience in teaching those classes and is the outcome of his constant search for a good textbook to teach UNIX administration and networking. His first book, published by Prentice Hall (1999), was written because he could not find a good text. This text is a continuation of the concepts covered in the first text. His other published works include primary authorship on the IBM Redbook Series book *Netfinity and TurboLinux Integration Guide,* and contributing authorship to portions of the other IBM Redbook Netfinity Integration Guides on RedHat, Caldera, and Suse Linux.

Research Interests

Joe has been interested in a number of topics related to learning computers. Some of the topics he has been looking at include:

- The process that is used by an individual to learn about computers when they are outside of a formal learning environment
- Process analysis—whereby the minimum number of steps necessary are performed to accomplish a given task, including learning. This is based on his many years of experience in learning and teaching computer science and various skills from ice, roller, and inline skating, as well as teaching guitar.
- Versions of Linux and UNIX that can be run from RAM and independent of a hard disk. There are a number of minimal or tiny Linux versions that can be run totally from diskette. These versions can be used for embedded controllers as well as for classes where it is not possible to give students administrative

access. The diskettes themselves can be run independent of the current security environment.

- Anything that strikes his fancy at the moment.

Outside Life

Joe's enjoys spending time with his wife Ramona and daughter Anisa, likes to visit museums, and enjoys skating and the outdoors.

Joe has achieved some notoriety in the skating world. He has been an active ice, roller, and inline skater. He served as the first Chair of the United States Figure Skating Association (USFSA) Adult Skaters Advisory Committee from 1992 to 1995 and as the chair of the Adult Nationals Task Force. He was actively involved in getting the first adult figure skating national championships started in 1995. At the age of 48, his first year of competition in roller skating, he went to the Junior Olympics in Sacramento, California, where he placed eleventh in figures. He was also a charter member of the International Inline Skating Association. He has studied skating under some of the top skating coaches in the Chicago area and was an active competitor in roller, ice, and figure skating for a number of years.

Joe enjoys country music. He plays guitar and keyboard and has written many songs, some of which have been rated as very good by other professional songwriters. He has studied voice under an instructor in Nashville, who has been the instructor for many top country and pop singers.

INTRODUCTION

To really connect you need a network.

—*Joe*

It is difficult to learn Linux or UNIX networking in today's security-conscious, technical, business, and academic environments. You need to be able to try new ideas without having to worry about what or who you are going to impact. Fortunately, Linux is available at a low or minimal cost. In addition, the cost of hardware for Linux systems is considerably less than equivalent MS Windows or commercial UNIX systems.

In this book, I will try to guide you on the road to building an environment that you can use to learn Linux networking and expand your horizons. This book is a continuation of my first book—the *UNIX System Administrator's Interactive Workbook,* also by Prentice Hall (1999). In both books, I have tried to make it simple enough that you won't even realize how difficult and frustrating it can be for someone to learn the same information without books similar to this one.

This is not without some sacrifice. This book is **not** a comprehensive discussion of networking principles. In the first book, some people were looking for more detailed discussions. Because of time, space, and learning considerations, much material must be left out. There are many excellent books that cover Linux networking in detail. There is no need to cover the same material as these other books.

The approach I have taken is to present a methodology and way of thinking that you can use to continue the learning process. Once your network is up and running, you should have more confidence as you continue on the learning process. If you successfully finish this book, you will have a working network that you can use to continue the process.

This book is very usable in a commercial or academic training environment. As an educator, I have tried to present material that I can use in class and that can be used to help the student learn as much as possible on their own. You will want to examine the Notes to the Student and the Notes to the Instructor sections to see how you can use this in your training environment. You may also want to look at the other books in this series to see how they can be used for classes.

Much emphasis is placed on using the man pages and other online help. The man pages are a very important tool for students and administrators. This book tries to include information you can't find online or in the required textbooks. It also tries to avoid duplicating information that would be in your texts.

Good luck, and I hope you have an excellent learning experience.

—Joe

NOTES TO THE STUDENT

The main focus of education is the student. However, there are many kinds of students and perhaps just as many ways of learning.

—Joe

Welcome to the *Linux Network Administrator's Interactive Workbook*. You're about to embark on a unique learning experience, one that we hope will be a good starting point for learning Linux networking. Much like learning to repair an automobile, it's one thing to read about procedures in a book and answer questions about what you read. But it's another thing entirely to lift up the hood and dig right in.

Let me make one thing perfectly clear. This is not a comprehensive training manual on Linux networking. Before you run, you have to learn to walk. You should consider this book your walking manual for networking. You will need to have a good Linux networking reference manual that you can refer to as you learn. Hopefully, you will feel much more confident about learning and experimenting with networking once you are finished with this text.

WHO THIS BOOK IS FOR

Frankly, this book is for anybody who wishes to learn Linux networking, *no experience necessary*. If you are learning Linux networking on your own, it is essential that you have a system that you can totally control. In the traditional corporate or academic training environment, it is difficult to find a box that you can experiment with. When you do networking, you will need two boxes to test your configuration. Only one of these will need to be modified to any extent.

Linux makes learning networking a lot easier than traditional approaches. Linux runs on your PC and can be added to your existing Windows environment. You will see in several of the chapters how you can use Linux to share your PC and disks with other operating systems. You can even run Linux totally from a diskette or CD-ROM if necessary.

If you are in an academic environment with a teacher in a class, you may not have system administrative access to a Linux system. There are sometimes concerns about security in such an environment. In these cases, you have access to a Linux box as a regular user only.

Fortunately, Linux is a very open environment. Things are not hidden unless it is absolutely essential. So you can look at most of the system files and even copy them and edit them as a regular user. You just can't modify the critical system files in their original location, or copy your modified files back, as a regular user. Therefore, there is also an emphasis in this text on you looking at files, modifying them, and then seeing if the changes would give the desired effect, if they were implemented.

A commercial training environment gives us perhaps the best group-training environment for learning administration. You generally have a system that is totally under your control. At worst, you will be sharing the box with one or two others. When you start the class, the system will usually have been totally rebuilt from scratch. This is like having a blank canvas ready to be painted on. So now you can change the system, install software, remove software, make mistakes, and so forth, all without having to worry about the long-term effects.

Learning network administration is very much a self-directed activity. It requires persistence, courage, and sometimes a bit of abandon to try new ideas and see the effects.

HOW THIS BOOK IS ORGANIZED

The Interactive Workbook series offers an extraordinary opportunity to learn Linux networking through a journey of discovery. In this book, you are presented with a series of interactive Labs that are intended to highlight certain aspects of administration. Each Lab, which is designed to stand alone as much as possible, begins with Learning Objectives that show you what Exercises (or tasks) are covered in that Lab. This is followed by an overview of the concepts that will be further explored through the Exercises, which are the heart of each Lab.

There is no way that all the networking topics can be covered in detail. So emphasis is placed on developing a way of thinking and developing of your skills. There is some duplication from one Lab to another in order to emphasize the concepts learned up to that point. This is an attempt to repeat something from a different angle that might be harder to learn or may have given a number of people problems.

Each Exercise consists of a series of steps that you will follow to perform a specific task, along with questions that are designed to help you discover the important things on your own. The answers to these questions are given at the end of the Exercises, along with more in-depth discussion of the concepts explored.

At the end of each Lab is a series of multiple-choice Self-Review Questions. If you feel certain that you already understand a certain Objective, you are free to skip that Exercise, but are still encouraged to take the Self-Review quiz at the end of the Lab, just to make sure. The answers to these questions appear in Appendix A. There are also additional Self-Review Questions at this book's companion Web site, found at `http://www.phptr.com/phptrinteractive/`. But more on that in a moment. . . .

Finally, at the end of each chapter you will find a Test Your Thinking section, which consists of a series of projects designed to solidify all of the skills you have learned in the chapter. If you have successfully completed all of the Labs in the chapter, you should be able to tackle these projects with few problems. There are not always "answers" to these projects, but where appropriate, you will find guidance and/or solutions at the companion Web site.

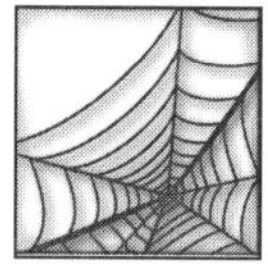

The final element of this book actually doesn't appear in the book at all. It is the companion Web site, and it is located at:

`http://www.phptr.com/phptrinteractive/`

This companion Web site is closely integrated with the content of this book, and we encourage you to visit often. It is designed to provide a unique interactive online experience that will enhance your Linux networking education. As mentioned, you will find guidance and solutions that will help you complete the projects found in the Test Your Thinking section of each chapter.

You will also find additional Self-Review Questions for each chapter, which are meant to help solidify your understanding of the topics, with instant results for each quiz. Take these quizzes after you have completed the Lab work in the book, taken the book's quizzes, and completed the Test Your Thinking sections. These online quizzes will help you gauge how much you have learned, and what areas you may need to revisit in the book.

In the Author's Corner, you will find additional information that we think will interest you, such as Linux news, book updates, and any errata that didn't make it into the book before publication.

Finally, you will find a Message Board, which you can think of as a virtual study lounge. Here, you can interact with other *Linux Network Administrator's Interactive Workbook* readers, share and discuss your projects, and perhaps even pick up a professional tip or two.

CONVENTIONS USED IN THIS BOOK

There are several conventions that we've used in this book to try and make your learning experience easier. These are explained here.

This icon is used to flag notes or advice from the authors to our readers. For instance, if there is a particular topic or concept that you really need to understand, or if there's something that you need to keep in mind while working, you will find it set off from the main text like this.

This icon is used to flag tips or especially helpful tricks that will save you time or trouble. For instance, if there is a shortcut for performing a particular task or a method that the author has found useful, you will find it set off from the main text like this.

Computers are fickle creatures and can easily be configured incorrectly. This icon is used to flag information and precautions that will not only save you headaches in the long run, they may save you from messing up your entire network.

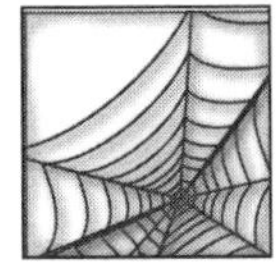

This icon is used to flag passages in which there is a reference to the book's companion Web site, which once again is located at:

`http://www.phptr.com/phptrinteractive/`

SOME SEASONED ADVICE

Those who are serious about learning Linux networking will dedicate whatever time is required to properly prepare for the task. As mentioned earlier, this should not be your only reference to Linux networking. This

The Whole Truth

Sometimes due to the Interactive Workbook format, some information is simplified for learning's sake. When that's the case, we have used this sidebar element to alert you that "it's not exactly as simple as that," and to offer a more detailed explanation.

book teaches you actual hands-on practices and procedures—it's a practical guide to getting your hands dirty. Another book will get into the nitty-gritty of all the technical details that cannot possibly be covered here. That said, you will find that the discovery method employed by the *Linux Network Administrator's Interactive Workbook* will surely enlighten and educate you unlike any other resource. However clever or comprehensive another resource might be, the discovery method is a proven training technique that is employed in classrooms and training centers around the world. This hands-on approach is the cornerstone of the International Workbook series, and we are sure that you will find it an engaging and productive way to learn. *There is no better way!*

NOTES TO THE INSTRUCTOR

The challenge for the instructor is to teach in the quickest and most effective way. Different teachers have different approaches, but each must work within constraints that are often outside of their control.

—*Joe*

The teacher of computer science topics is often faced with constraints caused by budget, security, time, or politics. Teaching network administration is not one of those traditional topics that come immediately to mind when we think of an academic environment. Yet there are many colleges, community colleges, technical institutes, corporate and commercial training environments where network administration is a very important part of the curriculum.

There are a number of different training environments that you can be involved in. But they fall into two basic categories, with variations in each:

1. An academic credit course—This usually runs for a full term, is assigned a number of credits, and the student is given a grade.
2. A commercial, corporate, or non-credit college training program—This is short-term, usually several days to a week, and

does not involve college credit or grades, and the students whole attention is focused on the class.

Each one of these approaches has its own particular concerns.

AN ACADEMIC CREDIT ENVIRONMENT

This is a college, university or community college where the class is set up so that college credit is granted to students taking the class. These classes typically run for a full term or more. Their environment usually has PCs set up to access a network. Only the fortunate students will actually have access to dedicated Linux boxes. The PCs are typically Microsoft Windows-based PCs. Sometimes they don't have a hard drive at all, but boot entirely off the network! However, since Windows software has become more demanding, the PCs often do have disk drives.

The concerns in such an environment focus around two issues:

1. *Computer Integrity*—In such an environment there are many concerns about security. Students oftentimes download software with viruses. Such PCs oftentimes get other software accidentally or intentionally loaded onto them. Therefore anything, such as a live, full-blown Linux operating system on a PC that the students can fully administer, gives nightmares to the administrators of the network and PCs. Even doing a dual boot system still leaves the PC open to abuse.

   Some solutions include:

   a. Running Linux from a CD-ROM, as is possible with Yggdrasil Linux, which will boot off a diskette first. SuSE Linux and several others have bootable CD-ROMs
   b. Running Linux from diskettes. There are a number of minimal versions of Linux that that be run from diskette. The enclosed CD-ROM includes a number of versions that you can install to diskette and boot from.
   c. Putting two hard drives on a system and making one write-protected via hardware configuration or jumpers, and the other writeable and easy to rebuild via the network and a boot disk. The write-protected disk can contain important information and programs that do not require write access. You could also use a second drive to contain an image of the first drive that can easily be restored by the original drive.
   d. Having a separate computer lab for Linux. This is oftentimes difficult to achieve and may not make the most use

of the available systems. In many cases, the PCs are used for Windows applications, and classroom space is sometimes at a premium. However, if the school is upgrading their 486, or even 386, PCs to new Pentiums, they can find new life as Linux boxes since Linux can run very happily with a single user on a 386 box. A 486 in this case would be a luxury. There are also a number of vendors that make Linux versions that smoothly run on a 486 PC with 16 megs of memory.

2. *Network Integrity*—There is a concern that if a student can have root access on such a system, they can perhaps compromise the network. This is because the root user in Linux has access to many network tools that are not present on the Windows PC. A student may accidentally or intentionally do something that can bring down the network.

There are a number of solutions to the network security problem. The classroom or user area where Linux is being run can easily be isolated from the rest of the network. A router blocks TCP/IP traffic except traffic that meets certain criteria. It can block indiscriminate packets from getting through and damaging the network integrity.

An even better way of isolating the network would be to use a firewall, which would protect the campus network's integrity even further. A firewall does add additional processing over what a router would do, so performance needs should be looked at also. Fortunately, Linux provides router and firewall capabilities either with the OS or via the Internet. Another option would be to totally isolate the network used to teach network administration from the rest of the campus network.

Thus, putting together a system that can be administered in an academic environment may require many special steps. So your mileage may vary.

A SHORT-TERM, NON-CREDIT TRAINING ENVIRONMENT

Putting together a Linux training environment for a commercial or short-term, non-credit academic program is a lot simpler. These are classes that usually run for several days to a week. The systems are dedicated to the training process currently being done. Students either have a system of their own or share it with one or two other students. The boxes are usually reloaded with software whenever a new class is started. Thus, system integrity is not a major concern. Also, network integrity is not as much of an issue, since each classroom can totally be isolated from the others if needed.

Since the focus is on Linux training, any Linux servers can be put on that network, or they can have a separate access point or network interface card to other, more central, servers that may be needed. This way, everyone else can be isolated from that network. The students need not see any other networks. If the classroom is needed for a different type of class afterward, cables can easily be moved in a wiring closet to put the classroom on a new network. This method of teaching Linux is a lot simpler to manage because of its dedicated function of doing one thing at a time.

FURTHER DISCUSSION FOR THE INSTRUCTOR

Each chapter in this text is broken down into sections. In addition, all questions and projects have the answers readily available. This text is designed to supplement whatever other training materials you may be using. Therefore, you should choose those materials with this in mind. Any comments, ideas, or suggestions would be greatly appreciated. You can send email to jkaplenk@aol.com.

CHAPTER 1

BASIC TCP/IP NETWORKING

When you communicate to someone or something else, you need to be able to speak a language that the listener understands. Networking requires that both the sender and receiver use the same networking protocols and languages.

—Joe

CHAPTER OBJECTIVES

In this chapter, you will learn about:

- ✔ The Current System TCP/IP Values — Page 2
- ✔ Accessing Other TCP/IP Hosts — Page 18

When you first set up your UNIX system, it may automatically attempt to set up networking. Most newer versions of UNIX work this way. The earlier versions of UNIX were more oriented toward terminals than networking. Networking packages were often an afterthought. This chapter introduces you to the concepts of networking and will help you to understand some of the steps that are done by your system during installation.

LAB 1.1

THE CURRENT SYSTEM TCP/IP VALUES

LAB OBJECTIVES

After this Lab, you will be able to:

- Use `ifconfig`
- Use `netstat`

This Lab discusses `netstat` and other commands used to determine your basic network characteristics. You will need access to an existing network. You will determine the values discussed in the introductory network discussion.

You can set up your network in one or more of the following ways:

1. **Manual**—You need to edit UNIX files (enter commands from a prompt) and then restart the various network daemons or reboot your system.
2. **Install**—During the install process, you are prompted to set up or change the networking features.
3. **Menu**—You can use a menu to set up the system parameters needed.

In this Lab, you will be introduced to the simplest way of setting up your network. Later discussions will build upon this and show you how to set up your network parameters automatically by using other servers. The most common manual methods and concepts are discussed. Because your system will probably allow you to set up networking when you install the operating system, much of the discussion also involves how to change your system values.

Look in the man pages for the following: `/etc/hosts hostname telnet ifconfig tcp/ip ethernet netstat traceroute ping ifconfig`

TCP/IP

By far the most common way to connect your UNIX box to a network is with ethernet and TCP/IP. While other networking schemes will work and are often used, your system will practically always start off with these two. TCP/IP stands for Transmission Control Protocol/Internet Protocol. The name refers to the two layers of the networking protocol that are used and are discussed very well in many books about the Internet and networking. The Internet is a TCP/IP-based network, so an understanding of networking will help you to better understand how your system will work on the Internet. The standard version of TCP/IP is called IPv4. There is a newer version of TCP/IP that allows for many more hosts and is called IPv6. This text will only talk about IPv4 networks.

TCP/IP ADDRESS

The TCP/IP network address can be broken down into the following grouping:

WWW.XXX.YYY.ZZZ

This is made up of 4 groups of 3 numbers. Each group of numbers can vary from 0 to 255—not 0 to 999—because this number is actually based on a series of binary numbers. These numbers can be either 0 or 1, and each group can only have 8 binary numbers. In mathematical terms, this is 2^8, which equals 256. Because there are 256 numbers from 0 to 255, this gives us our addresses.

■ *FOR EXAMPLE:*

The following are TCP/IP addresses:

9.7.254.117

172.16.1.3

210.1.19.99

However, in practice, the numbers 0 and 255 are not used for the address of a host. The number 0 is typically reserved for the *network address.* This is the address used by routers and other hosts to access the network.

■ FOR EXAMPLE:

The following are network addresses:

9.0.0.0

172.16.0.0

210.1.19.0

BROADCAST ADDRESS

The number 255 is used as part of the *broadcast address.* This is the address that is used to send general information from a server to other servers on the network. All servers will, in turn, listen on this address for information that is being sent out. Basically, wherever you have a 0 in the network address, you can replace it with a 255.

■ FOR EXAMPLE:

9.255.255.255

172.16.255.255

210.1.19.255

NETWORK CLASSES

TCP/IP networks are broken up into three classes in order to set the maximum number of hosts per network and the maximum number of networks. The value used for WWW (the first group of three numbers) will determine its network class. The classes will differ in the number of possible networks and the number of hosts per network. In Table 1.1, the values for XXX, YYY, and ZZZ will vary from 1 to 254. The table summarizes the features of the various classes of networks.

The remaining values for XXX, ranging from 224 to 254, are used for special types of networks. You will note that the XXX value of 127 is not listed in Table 1.1. This is a special address called the *loopback* or *local address*; it is used by the host to connect to itself and can be used even if you have not set up a Network Interface Card (NIC). The only address that is used in this range is 127.0.0.1.

Table 1.1 ■ TCP/IP Address Ranges and Characteristics

Class	WWW	XXX	YYY	ZZZ	Number of Possible Networks	Number of Possible Hosts	Standard Network Address	Standard Broadcast Address
A	Net 1–126	Host 1–254	Host 1–254	Host 1–254	126 = 126	254x254x254 = 16,387,064	WWW.0.0.0	WWW.255.255.255
B	Net 128–191	Net 1–254	Host 1–254	Host 1–254	64x254 = 16,256	254x254 = 64,516	WWW.XXX.0.0	WWW.XXX.255.255
C	Net 192–223	Net 1–254	Net 1–254	Host 1–254	32x254x254 = 2,064,512	254 = 254	WWW.XXX.YYY.0	WWW.XXX.YYY.255

Table 1.2 ■ Sample Network Characteristics

Class	Address	WWW	XXX	YYY	ZZZ	Network Address	Broadcast Address
A	9.7.254.117	9	7	254	117	9.0.0.0	9.255.255.255
B	172.16.1.3	172	16	1	3	172.16.0.0	172.16.255.255
C	210.1.19.99	210	1	19	99	210.1.19.0	210.1.19.255

■ *FOR EXAMPLE:*

Table 1.2 is an example of how you might set up networks in the various classes.

PUBLIC ADDRESS RANGES

There is a range of IP addresses for each class that is available for use by anyone, without registration. This information is shown in Table 1.3. These IP addresses are not routed to the Internet and can be used internally. You can use them on the internal intranet side of a router or firewall without a problem. Your router or firewall can be set up to route traffic easily to the Internet from your LAN or WAN. However, your hosts that use these addresses cannot be accessed directly from the Internet; they need a more sophisticated gateway to access your internal WAN or LAN.

NETMASK

The `netmask` signifies the part of the address used for the network and the part used for the host address. Here you need to convert the information to a binary format. If you think about the TCP/IP addresses in a binary format, the number will become a series of 4 groups of 8 numbers of 0 or 1. The number 255.255.255.255 would look like the following:

11111111.11111111.11111111.11111111

Table 1.3 ■ Public Unregistered Network Ranges

Class	Start IP Address	Last IP Address	Default `subnet` Mask
A	10.0.0.0	10.255.2255.255	255.0.0.0
B	172.16.0.0	172.31.255.255	255.255.0.0
C	192.168.1.0	192.168.255.255	255.255.255.0

The number 0.0.0.0 becomes:

00000000.00000000.00000000.00000000

The `netmask` will vary from 0.0.0.0 to 255.255.255.255.

By default, each network class has a standard `netmask`. In Table 1.4, the 1's represent the space used for the network address. The 0's represent the space used for the host address. The values are summarized in Table 1.4.

SUBNET

It is possible to take some of the digits that are used for the host address and create what is called a *subnet*. This allows you to do routing to create many smaller networks by splitting up the address range that is assigned to host addresses. In Table 1.4, every 0 that is changed to a 1 is used to create a new network and `subnet`.

■ *FOR EXAMPLE:*

An example of setting up a `subnet` mask for a class A is:

11111111.11111111.00000000.00000000

This is a `netmask` of 255.255.0.0 and would create 2^8, or 256, additional subnetworks under whatever class A network this is applied to. Note that for simplicity, you will change the 0's to 1's going from left to right. Otherwise, the network becomes very complicated. A good example is:

11111111.11111111.100000000.00000000 or 255.255.128.0

This is 2^9, or 512, subnetworks in a class A network. But the following `netmask` is not proper because there is a 1 between the 0's:

11111111.11111111.00000001.00000000 or 255.255.1.0

Table 1.4 ■ Default Binary Representation of the Netmasks

Class	`Netmask`	`Netmask` in binary format
A	255.0.0.0	11111111.00000000.00000000.00000000
B	255.255.0.0	11111111.11111111.00000000.00000000
C	255.255.255.0	11111111.11111111.11111111.00000000

> **The Whole Truth**
>
> Note that a `netmask` of 255.255.255.0 for a class A `subnet` is not exactly the same as a class C `subnet`, although the `netmask` is the same, and the number of hosts on this `subnet` are the same as on a class C network. Some of the network addresses may not be valid combinations or routable because of the way that the `netmask` works. You will need to apply your `netmask` to your addresses and examine the resulting network address. Further discussion of this is beyond the scope of this text.

ROUTING

The last important concept to consider is *routing,* which is sending a packet of information from one `network` or `subnet` to another. A router has at least two `networks` or `subnets` attached to it. Each network is identified by:

1. A unique IP address on the Network Interface Card (NIC)
2. A `netmask`

By applying the `netmask` to the IP address, both the network address and the range of addresses available for the network can be determined.

■ *FOR EXAMPLE:*

Consider the following:

IP address 172.16.1.1

`Netmask` 255.255.255.0

If you take the 0's in the netmask and replace the corresponding number in the IP address with 0's, you will have the network address. If you replace all the same numbers with 255, or all 1's you will have the broadcast address. So a netmask of 255.255.255.0, applied to a network of 172.16.1.3, creates a network of 172.16.1.0, with 254 hosts and a broadcast address of 172.16.1.255. The possible addresses of a host on the network with this `netmask` will vary from 172.16.1.1 to 172.16.1.254.

Both the address of the network interface card and the `netmask` *must be chosen so that there is no possibility that a particular address can be on two different networks or* `subnets`*. Otherwise, the router will not*

know where to route the packets and will probably ignore those packets or send them to the first address that is available.

THE IFCONFIG COMMAND

The `ifconfig` command returns the status of the network interfaces. By using the `-a` option, you can find the status all the network interfaces.

FOR EXAMPLE:

```
# ifconfig -a

lo0: flags=849<UP,LOOPBACK,RUNNING,MULTICAST> mtu
8232 inet 127.0.0.1 netmask ff000000

eth0  Link encap:Ethernet  HWaddr 00:AA:00:27:33:38
inet addr:172.16.1.1  Bcast:172.16.1.255
Mask:255.255.255 UP BROADCAST RUNNING MULTICAST
MTU:1500  Metric RX packets:133005 errors:0 dropped:0
overruns:0 frame TX packets:3572 errors:0 dropped:0
overruns:0 carrier collisions Interrupt:10 Base
address:0x300
```

The `ifconfig` command returns the information about the ports. Some of the items above will be discussed later or can be looked up on your own. If you look at the above display, the most important things to look at are:

- `lo0, eth0`—These are the network interfaces that have TCP/IP activated for them.
- `UP`—This means that the interface is up. If it is down, then it is `DOWN`.
- `BROADCAST`—The broadcast address is enabled.
- `inet addr`—This is the Internet address; for `eth0` it is 172.16.1.1.
- `Mask`—This was described earlier; for `eth0` it is 255.255.255.0.
- `HWaddr`—This is the hardware address of the network interface card. Every NIC has a unique hardware address assigned to it by the manufacturer. For this card the hardware address is 00:AA:00:27:33:38.
- `Interrupt` is the Interrupt Request value and is commonly called the IRQ. For `eth0` the IRQ is 10.
- `Base address` is the base address of the hardware device and is the address that the computer uses to talk to the hardware for basic communications. For `eth0` it is 0x300.

The `ifconfig` *will not give the same results in all versions of UNIX. In AIX, an error is actually produced with some options of* `ifconfig` *that are normally used in other versions of UNIX.*

THE NETSTAT COMMAND

The `netstat` command will return basic information about your network. The following results will be seen from running the `netstat -nr` command:

```
Kernel IP routing table
Destination  Gateway       Genmask        Flags  MSS   Window  irtt  Iface
172.16.1.0   0.0.0.0       255.255.255.0  U      1500  0       0     eth0
127.0.0.0    0.0.0.0       255.0.0.0      U      3584  0       0     lo
0.0.0.0      10.131.173.1  0.0.0.0        UG     1500  0       0     eth0
```

This is broken down as follows:

- `Destination` is the name of the network to which you are sending information. As you get more familiar with `netstat`, you will see that this can help you get to a remote network. You will notice the default route goes through a host with the address 10.131.173.1.
- `Gateway` is the port or network interface card that is used to pass the information to the destination.
- `Flags, Ref and Use` refer to characteristics of the network and can be ignored for now.

If your network has no access to other networks, then the default route line may not exist in your results. You may also see several lines for the default entry. Your system will try the first default route entry, then the second default route, and so on, until it exhausts the list of default routes.

You will notice that there are three lines that begin with:

- 172.16.1.0—This is the network that is set up for your Network Interface Card, which in this case is 172.16.1.1.
- 127.0.0.1—This is the loopback address for the localhost.
- 0.0.0.0—In the first position on the line, it indicates the entry for the default route. In the second position on the line, it means that there is no defined gateway, and the card itself is

the actual gateway. This may be different from other versions of UNIX that you are used to.

LAB 1.1 EXERCISES

1.1.1 USE IFCONFIG

Log in with your normal user id. For this Exercise, you will use the `-a` option. Do the following command:

```
ifconfig -a
```

This returns information about your ports.

a) What are the results of the `ifconfig -a` command?

____

____

b) What is the address of your network interface card?

____

____

c) What is the broadcast address of your network interface card?

____

____

d) What is the ethernet hardware address of your network interface card?

____

____

You can enter the command to get results for a particular port just by specifying the device name. Do the following command:

```
ifconfig lo0
```

e) How does this differ from the results in Question a?

1.1.2 Use netstat

For this Exercise, you will use an option to `netstat` in order to more clearly display the network information. Do the following:

```
netstat -nr
```

a) What are the results from the `netstat -nr` command?

b) What is the network that your system is on?

c) What is your loopback result line?

Now do the following:

```
netstat -r
```

d) What are the results from the `netstat -r` command?

e) How do the results from the `netstat -r` command in Question d differ from the `netstat -nr` command?

____

____

LAB 1.1 EXERCISE ANSWERS

1.1.1 ANSWERS

a) What are the results of the `ifconfig -a` command?

Answer: You should see something similar to the following:

```
# ifconfig -a

lo0: flags=849<UP,LOOPBACK,RUNNING,MULTICAST> mtu
8232 inet 127.0.0.1 netmask ff000000

eth0  Link encap:Ethernet  HWaddr 00:AA:00:27:33:38
inet addr:172.16.1.1  Bcast:172.16.1.255
Mask:255.255.255 UP BROADCAST RUNNING MULTICAST
MTU:1500  Metric RX packets:133005 errors:0 dropped:0
overruns:0 frame TX packets:3572 errors:0 dropped:0
overruns:0 carrier collisions Interrupt:10 Base
address:0x300
```

b) What is the address of your network interface card?

Answer: Using the sample results in Question a, you would determine from the following output that the network interface card address is 172.16.1.12:

```
eth0  Link encap:Ethernet  HWaddr 00:AA:00:27:33:38
inet addr:172.16.1.1  Bcast:172.16.1.255
Mask:255.255.255 UP BROADCAST RUNNING MULTICAST
MTU:1500  Metric RX packets:133005 errors:0 dropped:0
overruns:0 frame TX packets:3572 errors:0 dropped:0
overruns:0 carrier collisions Interrupt:10 Base
address:0x300
```

c) What is the broadcast address of your network interface card?

Answer: In this Exercise's example, you would see 172.16.1.255.

d) What is the ethernet hardware address of your network interface card?

Answer: In this Exercise's example, you would see 0:10:4b:8c:91:79.

e) How does this differ from the results in Question a?

Answer: In question a you saw the results for all your network interfaces. ifconfig lo0 will return the results for the local loopback interface only.

1.1.2 ANSWERS

a) What are the results from the `netstat -nr` command?

Answer: You should see results similar to the following:

```
$ netstat -nr
Kernel IP routing table
Destination  Gateway        Genmask          Flags   MSS  Window   irtt   Iface
172.16.1.0   0.0.0.0        255.255.255.0    U       1500 0        0      eth0
127.0.0.0    0.0.0.0        255.0.0.0        U       3584 0        0      lo
0.0.0.0      10.131.173.1   0.0.0.0          UG      1500 0        0      eth0
```

b) What is the network that your system is on?

Answer: Your results will vary, but in this Exercise's example, your network is 172.16.1.0, because that is the network to which your port is attached.

c) What is your loopback result line?

Answer: Your loopback address is 127.0.0.1, as seen on the third line in Question a's answer.

d) What are the results from the `netstat -r` command?

Answer: The results are as follows:

```
[root@tux /root]# netstat -r
Kernel IP routing table
Destination  Gateway            Genmask          Flags   MSS    Window   irtt   Iface
172.16.1.0   *                  255.255.255.0    U       1500   0        0      eth0
127.0.0.0    *                  255.0.0.0        U       3584   0        0      lo
default      remote1.mynet.net  0.0.0.0          UG      1500   0        0      eth0
[root@tux /root]#
```

e) How do the results from the `netstat -r` command in Question d differ from the `netstat -nr` command?

Answer: The `netstat -r` *command uses the DNS or network names of hosts or devices. When you enter the command, it will go to your local nameserver (which we will discuss later) and resolve the IP address with a name whenever possible. If the nameserver does not return a name, then you will just see an IP address.*

Note that if your nameserver or access to your nameserver is down, then the `netstat` command may just sit there and hang until it times out.

LAB 1.1 SELF-REVIEW QUESTIONS

In order to test your progress, you should be able to answer the following questions.

The command `netstat -nr` was executed. Use the following results to answer the first five questions that follow.

Destination	Gateway	Flags	Ref	Use	Interface
10.1.1.0	10.1.1.12	U	3	1	eth1
224.0.0.0	10.1.1.12	U	3	0	eth1
default	10.1.1.1	UG	0	0	eth1
default	10.1.1.2	UG	0	0	eth1
127.0.0.1	127.0.0.1	UH	0	6	lo0

1) The Interface reference `lo0` refers to the loopback interface.
  a) _____True
  b) _____False

2) Which of the following is the address of the network interface card?
  a) _____0.1.1.0
  b) _____10.1.1.12
  c) _____10.1.1.1
  d) _____10.1.1.2
  e) _____127.0.0.1

3) There is only one default route for this host.
  a) _____True
  b) _____False

4) When the host cannot find a specified hostname or IP address on the local network, which address will it access next to continue the search?
  a) _____10.1.1.0
  b) _____10.1.1.12
  c) _____10.1.1.1

d) _____10.1.1.2
e) _____127.0.0.1

5) If the host fails to find the host after accessing the address in Question 4, which address will it then access?
a) _____10.1.1.0
b) _____10.1.1.12
c) _____10.1.1.1
d) _____10.1.1.2
e) _____127.0.0.1

The command `ifconfig -a` was executed. Use the following results to answer the next five questions:

```
# ifconfig -a

lo0:  flags=849<UP,LOOPBACK,RUNNING,MULTICAST> mtu
8232 inet 127.0.0.1 netmask ff000000

eth0:  flags=863<UP,BROADCAST,NOTRAILERS,RUNNING,
MULTICAST> mtu 1500  inet 10.1.1.11 netmask ffffff00
broadcast 10.255.255.255 ether 0:10:4b:8c:91:80

eth1:  flags=863<UP,BROADCAST,NOTRAILERS,RUNNING,MUL-
TICAST> mtu 1500  inet 10.1.1.12 netmask ffffff00
broadcast 10.255.255.255 ether 0:10:4b:8c:91:79
```

6) How many network interface cards does the host have?
a) _____0
b) _____1
c) _____2
d) _____3
e) _____4

7) What is the IP address of the loopback interface?
a) _____127.0.0.1
b) _____0:10:4b:8c:91:80
c) _____0:10:4b:8c:91:79
d) _____10.1.1.11
e) _____10.1.1.12

8) What is the IP Network Class of the host?

a) _____A
b) _____B
c) _____C
d) _____D
e) _____E

9) What is the ethernet hardware address of the first NIC card on the host?

a) _____127.0.0.1
b) _____0:10:4b:8c:91:80
c) _____0:10:4b:8c:91:79
d) _____10.1.1.11
e) _____10.1.1.12

10) What is the `netmask` of the NIC cards expressed as a grouping of four decimal numbers?

a) _____255.255.255.0
b) _____255.0.0.0
c) _____255.255.0.0
d) _____0.0.0.0
e) _____255.255.255.255

Quiz answers appear in Appendix A, Section 1.1.

LAB 1.2

ACCESSING OTHER TCP/IP HOSTS

LAB OBJECTIVES

After this Lab, you will be able to use:

- `ping`
- `traceroute`
- `nslookup`

This Lab discusses `ping`, `traceroute`, `nslookup`, and other commands to determine your access to other TCP/IP hosts. You will need access to a network that is already in existence. You will learn how to determine the values that were discussed in the introductory network discussion in Lab 1.1.

THE PING COMMAND

The `ping` command can be used to test whether you have a route to, and can access, a host. It does not show the actual network route, which is the purpose of `traceroute`. You can use the command with various options, so you just send one packet and see if it is returned. You can also send packets in fixed intervals of time, such as every five seconds, and test the average length of time for a packet to travel to the destination. Different versions of UNIX will have different options set as the default. Some will `ping` once and some will ping continuously.

The `ping` command has the format:

```
ping -options destination_host
```

FOR EXAMPLE:

The `-I` option followed by a number, for example 5, says to ping on a continual basis with each ping separated by 5 seconds. You can vary the rate just by changing the number. In Linux, by default, ping will continuously ping approximately every second.

The `destination_host` in this example is either the IP address or hostname of a destination host.

THE TRACEROUTE COMMAND

The `traceroute` command can be used to show the actual network route. When you send information from a source location to a destination, the packets of computer data will move from one system or router to another, then another, until it reaches its destination. You can think of it as hopping like a rabbit. In fact, the term *hop* tells you how many locations the data will go through.

The `traceroute` command will give you the time that it takes to get to each location. The time to reach the destination will be a lot longer than it takes for the `ping` command to reach the destination. This is because it expects a response from each location along the way, and it will also try to do a name resolution on each location instead of just an IP address. You can think of it as doing a `ping` from each location along the way.

You can see a representation of the process in Figure 1.1.

Figure 1.1 ■ A sample TCP/IP network

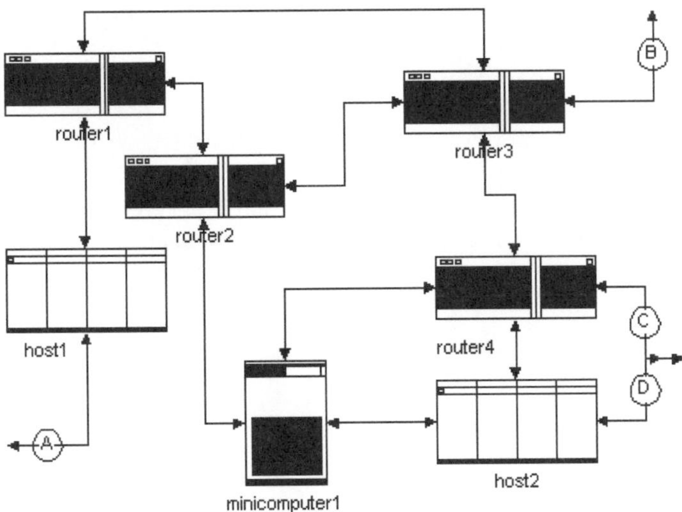

In order to analyze what `traceroute` does, and to understand routing concepts, take a look at Figure 1.1. Notice that each line has arrows pointing both directions. This means that each link is bi-directional and that the data can flow in both directions. In addition, assume for now that **host1, minicomputer1,** and **host2** can all act as routers, which means they can send packets of information to other ports to which they are connected. We will now discuss several possible routes for packet.

A packet of data going from `point A` to **router1** it must go through **host1.** There is one possible route. For a packet to go from `point A` to **router2,** it will go through **host1** and **router1.** However, if the link from **router1** to **router2** is down, it can also follow this path:

`point A` → **router1** → **router3** → **router2**

Another possible route would be:

`point A` → **router1** → **router3** → **router4** → **minicomputer1** → **router2**

(Remember **minicomputer1** can route in this example.)

This is one of the useful features of a router: If a route is either down or saturated, the data can be routed through a different route. In this example, the hosts are acting as routers (this is one of the features of the host software—Linux and most versions of UNIX have this feature built in).

Using `traceroute`, we can get the time that it takes to get to each point in the route and return from that point. We can also get the name of the host along the way. This allows us to trace the packets and can be a useful diagnostic tool if one of the connections in the route goes down.

FOR EXAMPLE:

Let's do a `traceroute` from **host1** to **host2.** One route is:

host1 → **router1** → **router3** → **router4** → **host2**

For the purposes of determining the time to each point, you can break this down into the following steps:

host1 → **router1** → **host1**

host1 → **router3** → **host1**

host1 → router4 → host1

host1 → host2 → host1

Let's execute the `traceroute` command. An example output of the command executed on host1 is:

```
# traceroute host2

traceroute to host2 (10.97.13.95)
1   router1 (10.25.35.17) 6ms   5ms   5ms
2   router3 (10.115.45.19) 15ms 12ms 10ms
3   10.15.35.98 (10.15.35.98) 28ms  25ms 20ms
4   host2 (10.97.13.95) 38ms 28ms 26ms
```

Notice that as you get further away from **host1,** the longer it takes for the packet to return, which is consistent with the earlier description. You will also notice that the third line has 10.15.35.98 and no network name. This means that **host1** could not determine the DNS or network name for **router4,** so it just returns the IP address. The second and third columns are additional checks for each point, since the first check or column is always slowed down by searching for the name on the nameserver.

THE NSLOOKUP COMMAND

Before you start making changes or setting up a new system, it is important to know how the nameservices are being handled. The `nslookup` command can be used to help you determine how your system is resolving names. It will not tell you whether the `/etc/hosts`, nameservices or NIS are consulted first. But it is a quick way to look at your system and to start to get a feel for how nameservices is set up.

When you enter the `nslookup` command, you will see results similar to the following:

```
# nslookup

Default Server:  nuprxy01.my.myisp.net

Address:  172.16.1.15


>
```

Generally, this gives the name of the nameserver that you are using. If it comes back with a `Default Server` entry, it means your system has the proper initial file set up for DNS, or Domain Name Services, to handle name-to-IP address conversion. These results mean your nameservices are being done by another server and that your box is referring all unresolvable names to that box. If this entry returns the loopback address, this means that your local server is either the nameserver or you are not using nameservices at all and just the files are there. If DNS is running, you can still use the `/etc/hosts` file for the names of other hosts; however, you may need to adjust some files to determine whether the `/etc/hosts` or DNS are consulted first for anything other than the local hostname. Further discussion of DNS, other than `nslookup`, will be done in Chapter 4.

LAB 1.2 EXERCISES

1.2.1 PING

This Exercise shows you how to use the `ping` command, and it will also show you an option that allows you to ping a remote host at regular intervals. You should login with your normal user id.

Your `ping` command may not be in the same place as in other versions of UNIX or Linux. The most common directories will be `/bin`, `/usr/bin`, `/sbin`, `/usr/sbin`, `/usr/ucb` and `/etc`. If you have a public domain version of the command, it may be in the `/usr/local/bin` directory. You may need to execute the command with the absolute pathname or change your search path to include those directories.

a) Where is the `ping` command located on your system?

____

____

b) How did you find the `ping` command?

____

____

Keeping in mind the command's location, do the following command:

```
ping hostname
```

where hostname is the name of an IP device on your network. It can be a server, workstation, router, or even a network printer. You can also ping yourself at 127.0.0.1 or use your own hostname.

c) What kind of results do you get from the `ping` command?

____

____

Now do the following in Linux:

```
/bin/ping -i5 hostname
```

where hostname is the name of a host on your network.

d) Now what are the results of the `ping` command with the `option -i5`?

____

____

1.2.2 TRACEROUTE

This Exercise shows you how to use the `traceroute` command, and it will also show you how to determine the route to get to a destination host. You should login with your normal user id.

Note that `traceroute` may not be available at all on your version of UNIX. There are, however, a number of freeware versions of `traceroute`. You might consider downloading and installing these versions. You can do a search for `traceroute` with a number of Web tools. Sometimes there are binary versions ready to be installed and run.

A good Internet host to check a route to is `rs.internic.net`. This host is always up. If your network does not have Internet access, or you want to check the route to local hosts first, then you can use a local host first.

The first thing you should do is `ping` the host to see if it is up and is accessible from your host. Do the following command with the appropriate absolute path location of the `ping` command if necessary:

```
ping rs.internic.net
```

a) What kind of results did you get from the `ping rs.internic.net` command?

b) Did you see "host unreachable" or a similar message?

c) What do you think is the cause of "host unreachable" or a similar message?

If you got a "host unreachable" message, choose another host or one on your local network. (You can always ping yourself, but `traceroute` won't be very useful.)

Now you are ready to check the route to the host. Run the following command:

```
traceroute rs.internic.net
```

d) Where is the `traceroute` command located on your system?

e) What kind of results did you get from the `traceroute` command?

f) If your `ping` command works, but `traceroute` either fails or takes a long time, what would be a possible cause?

---

g) How would you solve the problem in Question f?

1.2.3 NSLOOKUP

This Exercise shows you how to use the `nslookup` command, and it also helps you to determine what nameservices you are running.

You will again need to determine the location of the `nslookup` command. Most versions of UNIX allow a regular user to use `nslookup`, but do not have the file in the normal user search path. Therefore, you will again need to search for it on your system. Log in with your normal user id.

a) Where is the `nslookup` command is located on your system?

---

b) What kind of results do you get from the `nslookup` command?

---

c) If you got an error from the `nslookup` command in Question b, what do you think is the cause?

---

d) How would you fix any errors from the `nslookup` command in Question b?

____

____

e) If you didn't get any errors after typing the `nslookup` command in Question b, what is your prompt?

____

____

Now enter the following at the `nslookup` prompt:

`rs.internic.net`

f) What are your results after typing `rs.internic.net`?

____

____

g) If you got an error from entering `rs.internic.net` in Question f, what do you think is the cause?

____

____

h) How would you fix any errors from the `nslookup` command in Question f?

____

____

i) If you didn't get any errors after typing the `nslookup` command in Question f, what is your prompt on the screen?

____

____

Now enter the following at the `nslookup` prompt:

`quit`

j) What are your results after typing `quit`?

k) Based on what you know about UNIX, how would you then exit from `nslookup`?

LAB 1.2 EXERCISE ANSWERS

1.2.1 ANSWERS

a) Where is the `ping` command located on your system?

Answer: It can be in `/bin, /usr/bin, /sbin, /usr/sbin, /usr/ucb, /usr/local/bin, /etc`, *or some other directory.*

b) How did you find the `ping` command?

Answer: The `whereis` *command is a useful command to look for files, but it may only find files that are in your search path already, so you may need to look manually for the file.*

You can do this by going to the directory with the `cd` command. As an example, type the command `cd /usr/sbin` to go to the `/usr/sbin` directory. When you get there, type the command `ls ping`. This will show whether the file is there or not.

c) What kind of results do you get from the `ping` command?

In Linux, the `ping` *command will ping every second, which will look something like this:*

```
[myid@wheels myid]$ ping myserver
PING myserver (172.16.1.12): 56 data bytes
64 bytes from 172.16.1.12: icmp_seq=0 ttl=255 time=4.1 ms
64 bytes from 172.16.1.12: icmp_seq=1 ttl=255 time=2.8 ms
...
-- myserver ping statistics --
10 packets transmitted, 10 packets received, 0% packet loss
round-trip min/avg/max = 2.8/2.9/4.1 ms
[myid@wheels myid]$
```


Note that this command will ping repeatedly until it is stopped. You can stop it by pressing `Ctrl+C`.

d) Now what are the results of the `ping` command with the `option -i5`?

Answer: In Linux, the `ping` command with the `option -i 5` will repeatedly ping every second.

```
 [myid@wheels myid]$ ping -i5 myserver
PING myserver (172.16.1.2): 56 data bytes
64 bytes from 172.16.1.2: icmp_seq=0 ttl=255 time=4.3 ms
64 bytes from 172.16.1.2: icmp_seq=1 ttl=255 time=2.9 ms
64 bytes from 172.16.1.2: icmp_seq=2 ttl=255 time=2.9 ms

-- myserver ping statistics --
3 packets transmitted, 3 packets received, 0% packet loss
round-trip min/avg/max = 2.9/3.3/4.3 ms
[myid@wheels myid]$
```

1.2.2 ANSWERS

a) What kind of results did you get from the `ping rs.internic.net` command?

Answer: You should see results similar to the following:

```
[myid@wheels myid] ping rs.internic.net
Pinging rs.internic.net [198.41.0.6] with 32 bytes of data:
Reply from 198.41.0.6: bytes=32 time=67ms TTL=243
Reply from 198.41.0.6: bytes=32 time=48ms TTL=243
Reply from 198.41.0.6: bytes=32 time=46ms TTL=243
Reply from 198.41.0.6: bytes=32 time=55ms TTL=243
[myid@wheels myid]
```

b) Did you see "host unreachable" or a similar message?

Answer: You may or may not get this message. If you do get this message, see the answer to the next question.

c) What do you think is the cause of "host unreachable" or a similar message?

Answer: A "host unreachable" message would be caused by the fact that the host is either actually unreachable, or it takes so long for the packet of information to get to the destination that the `ping` *process will timeout. In the second case, it is possible to set some parameters or options to allow for extra time to reach the destination.*

d) Where is the `traceroute` command located on your system?

Answer: It canbe in `/bin`, `/usr/bin`, `/sbin`, `/usr/sbin`, `/usr/ucb`, `/usr/local/bin`, `/etc`, *or some other directory.*

e) What kind of results did you get from the `traceroute` command?

Answer: A partial display of the results of the `traceroute` *command is as follows:*

```
traceroute to rs.internic.net (6.0.41.198), 30 hops max, 12 byte packets
1  10.131.129.206 (24.131.129.206)  12 ms  15 ms  9 ms
2  h2-0.mynextnet.net (10.0.192.253)  32 ms  24 ms  22 ms
3  f0-0-0.mynextnet.net(10.0.48.1)  20 ms  24 ms  13 ms
4  h2-0.mynextnet.net (10.0.2.10)  29 ms  23 ms  19 ms
5  a1-0-1.cleveland1-br2.mynextnet.net (10.0.2.6)  35 ms  19 ms  36 ms
6  h4-0.nyc1-br2.mynextnet.net (10.0.2.14)  29 ms  35 ms  81 ms
7  h1-0.nynap.mynextnet.net (10.0.1.26)  41 ms  63 ms  28 ms
8  sprint-nap.disa.mil (192.157.69.45)  39 ms  51 ms  42 ms
9  137.209.200.205 (137.209.200.205)  34 ms  51 ms  59 ms
```

. . . and so forth.

f) If your `ping` command works, but `traceroute` either fails or takes a long time, what would be a possible cause?

Answer: There may be a failure of nameservices for some hosts along the way. If you look at the display for Question d, you will see that some addresses resolve to names and some remain only as addresses. If the name resolution takes too long, the `traceroute` *command may timeout.*

g) How would you solve the problem in Question f?

Answer: You can allow additional time with some versions of `traceroute` *by using an option to control this value. You can also use the* `traceroute -n host` *command to prevent the* `traceroute` *command from trying to resolve the IP addresses to names.*

1.2.3 ANSWERS

a) Where is the `nslookup` command located on your system?

Answer: It can be in `/bin, /usr/bin, /sbin, /usr/sbin, /usr/ucb, /usr/local/bin, /etc,` *or some other directory.*

b) What kind of results do you get from the `nslookup` command?

Answer: You should see some results similar to the following:

```
# nslookup

Default Server:  nuprxy01.my.myisp.net

Address:  172.16.1.15



>
```

c) If you got an error from the `nslookup` command in Question b, what do you think is the cause?

Answer: There are several kinds of errors that could result. Some of the errors could be as follows:

- `default server not found`—This usually means that the proper files are not set up or that the server IP address is not correct.
- `unable to execute the command`—Either the file doesn't exist, its rights are not set properly, or you don't have rights to execute it.
- `file not found`—It can't find the file. This can happen—even if you specify the proper path—if there are some attribute issues, wrong terminal settings, or some environment set up problems.

d) How would you fix any errors from the `nslookup` command in Question b?

Answer: Some possible fixes for the above problems are:

- `default server not found`—Correct the proper files. Because we will talk about DNS later, you will want to refer back here later on to make sure things are set okay.

- `unable to execute the command`—You need to examine all the file attributes of the `nslookup` command and look at the attributes of the directories where it is located and those above it.
- `file not found`—You need to be sure that `nslookup` is in your search path. You can determine your search path by the command `echo $PATH`.

Besides looking for and fixing those items in the previous messages, you might want to look at your environment by executing the `stty -a` command and looking at your terminal settings. If things don't look right, you can type `stty sane` to reset the terminal attributes. You can also type `set` from the Korn shell or `printenv` from the C shell and look for anything abnormal. You can also type `alias` to see if the command has been aliased in the C or Korn shells.

e) If you didn't get any errors after typing the `nslookup` command in Question b, what is your prompt?

Answer: You should see the following prompt:

```
>
```

f) What are your results after typing `rs.internic.net`?

Answer: You should see the following on the screen:

```
> rs.internic.net

Server:   mynameserver.mydomain.com

Address:   172.16.1.45



Name:     rs.internic.net

Address:   198.41.0.6

>
```

g) If you got an error from entering `rs.internic.net` in Question f, what do you think is the cause?

Answer: There are several kinds of errors that could result. Some of the errors could be as follows:

- `unable to access server`—The nameserver is not available. This is usually accompanied by a timeout message.
- `hostname not found`—The hostname could not be resolved to an IP address.

h) How would you fix any errors from the `nslookup` command in Question f?

Answer: Some possible fixes for the problems are:

- `unable to access server`—Be sure that the default server is set properly. This will be discussed in the chapter on DNS, but be sure that it is the correct one. If you are not certain, you might contact your network administrator for the correct name.
- `hostname not found`—You need to be sure that you entered a valid name. You should also check for typing errors.

i) If you didn't get any errors after typing the `nslookup` command in Question f, what is your prompt on the screen?

Answer: You should see the following prompt again:

```
>
```

j) What are your results after typing `quit`?

Answer: You should see results similar to the following:

```
hostname not found
```

Unfortunately, you cannot use `quit`, `exit`, or any of the standard UNIX commands to exit from `nslookup`. It interprets any strings that are not part of the `nslookup` options as being names of IP hosts and tries to interpret them.

k) Based on what you know about UNIX, how would you then exit from `nslookup`?

Answer: You would need to press either `Ctrl+C` *or* `Ctrl+D` *to exit from the command.*

LAB 1.2 SELF-REVIEW QUESTIONS

In order to test your progress, you should be able to answer the following questions.

The command to ping another host was executed. Use the following results to answer the first five questions that follow.

```
[myid@wheels /home/myid]$ ping mohawk
PING mohawk (172.16.1.2): 56 data bytes
64 bytes from 172.16.1.2: icmp_seq=0 ttl=255 time=2.7 ms
64 bytes from 172.16.1.2: icmp_seq=1 ttl=255 time=2.9 ms
64 bytes from 172.16.1.2: icmp_seq=2 ttl=255 time=2.9 ms
64 bytes from 172.16.1.2: icmp_seq=3 ttl=255 time=2.9 ms

-- mohawk ping statistics --

4 packets transmitted, 4 packets received, 0% packet loss
round-trip min/avg/max = 2.7/2.8/2.9 ms
```

1) The ping message is being responded to by a server called `mohawk`.
  a) _____True
  b) _____False

2) The address of the network interface card on mohawk is 172.16.1.2.
  a) _____True
  b) _____False

3) The time to get a response from the remote host is approximately how long?
  a) _____0
  b) _____2.9
  c) _____4
  d) _____64
  e) _____255

4) What was the number of packets sent?
  a) _____0
  b) _____2.9
  c) _____4
  d) _____64
  e) _____255

5) The `ttl` value refers to the IP packet time to live.
  a) _____True
  b) _____False

Look at Figure 1.1 to answer the following 3 questions.

6) The *shortest* route to go from the circled points A to B involves going through how many different IP devices?

a) _____0
b) _____1
c) _____2
d) _____3
e) _____4

7) Assuming that all the hosts can route, how many different routes are there from the circled point A to point B without circling back over the same point?

a) _____0
b) _____2
c) _____4
d) _____5
e) _____6

8) Assuming that all the hosts can route except **minicomputer1,** how many different routes are there from the circled point A to point B without circling back over the same point?

a) _____0
b) _____2
c) _____4
d) _____5
e) _____6

Use the following results to answer the next two questions.

```
traceroute to host2 (10.97.13.95)
1  router1              (10.25.35.17)     6ms    5ms     5ms
2  router3              (10.115.45.19)    15ms 12ms   10ms
3  10.15.35.98 (10.15.35.98)   28ms      25ms 20ms
4  host2         (10.97.13.95)   38ms      28ms 26ms
```

9) What is the IP address of the destination IP device?

a) _____10.97.13.95
b) _____10.25.35.17
c) _____10.115.45.19
d) _____10.15.35.98
e) _____10.1.1.12

10) How many IP devices, hosts, routers or other devices will a packet travel through to get to the destination? (You can ignore the source and destination devices.)

a) _____0
b) _____2
c) _____3
d) _____4
e) _____5

Use the following results to answer the next four questions.

```
# nslookup

Default Server: ropxy01.my.myisp.net

Address: 172.16.1.3

> www.myserver.com

Server:  ropxy01.my.myisp.net

Address:  172.16.1.3


Name:     wwwwabc123.myserver.com

Address:  192.9.49.33

Aliases:  www.myserver.com

>
```

11) What is the IP address of `www.myserver.com`?
a) _____172.16.1.3
b) _____192.9.49.33
c) _____`wwwwabc123.myserver.com`
d) _____`ropxy01.my.myisp.net`
e) _____none of the above

12) `www.myserver.com` is really an alias for what server name?
a) _____172.16.1.3
b) _____192.9.49.33
c) _____`wwwwabc123.myserver.com`
d) _____`ropxy01.my.myisp.net`
e) _____none of the above

13) What is the *hostname* of the DNS nameserver in the above list?

a) _____172.16.1.3
b) _____192.9.49.33
c) _____`wwwwabc123.myserver.com`
d) _____`ropxy01.my.myisp.net`
e) _____none of the above

14) What is the *IP address* of the DNS nameserver in the above list?

a) _____172.16.1.3
b) _____192.9.49.33
c) _____`wwwwabc123.myserver.com`
d) _____`ropxy01.my.myisp.net`
e) _____none of the above

Quiz answers appear in Appendix A, Section 1.2.

Table 1.5 ■ Project Results

Network Class	IP Address	Netmask	Network Address	Broadcast Address
	10.35.15.25	255.255.255.0		
	172.16.1.15		172.16.1.0	
	192.168.1.35			192.168.1.255
	5.15.95.16		5.15.0.0	
	192.168.235.45	255.255.255.0		
	172.31.25.25	255.255.0.0		
	10.21.35.15		10.21.0.0	
	10.15.3.35			10.255.255.255
	192.168.35.35		192.168.35.0	

CHAPTER 1

TEST YOUR THINKING

1) Fill in the Table 1.5 with network characteristics that are missing. You can assume default values only if absolutely required.

2) Design a network based on the IP addresses. Be sure to consider:

   a) Network Class

   b) `NIC IP` address

   c) `netmask`

   d) network address

   e) broadcast address

   f) Any additional characteristics you might need to give answers to the commands you will have learned in this chapter.

3) What will be the results of executing the following commands:

   a) `ifconfig` command

   b) `netstat -nr`

CHAPTER 2

CONFIGURING YOUR TCP/IP NETWORK

When you construct a building you start with the foundation and then work your way up. To do otherwise would just not work.

—Joe

Chapter Objectives

In this chapter, you will learn about:

Exercises for the Great and Super User

 Setting Up TCP/IP Page 40

This chapter will help you understand how to build up your network. You will determine your current network characteristics. Then you will use this to help you build your own network configuration. Because of this, you will need root access on some Linux box. You might find the minimal Linuxes on the included CD-ROM very useful for this.

LAB 2.1

SETTING UP TCP/IP

LAB OBJECTIVES

After this Lab, you will be able to:

- Determine Your Current Network Characteristics
- Bring Down the Network Interface
- Bring Up The Network Interface
- Set up Your Host Table
- Enable Client Name Resolution

This Lab discusses how to set up your TCP/IP on your box. Because of the various kinds of UNIX, it is impossible to cover all versions of UNIX and the various ways of setting up your networking and your addresses. This Lab focuses on using the command line to set up your TCP/IP networking in Linux. However, your system may have a very acceptable way of setting up the addressing using a menu. It is important to understand the command-line way of doing things in UNIX and Linux, because it is much faster than a menu and sometimes you can resolve issues much quicker with the command line. The Lab Exercises here assume you have root access on your Linux box. If you don't have root access, you can still run some of the commands, but you will not be able to change system characteristics.

THE DEVICE DRIVER

A device driver allows your Linux kernel to talk to the actual hardware. Device drivers are usually written at very low levels of coding and are often good candidates for writing in assembler language. Because of this, they tend not to port very well from one version of UNIX to another and from one processor to another. The device driver is loaded when your machine is booting up. You can see what it looks like in Figure 2.1.

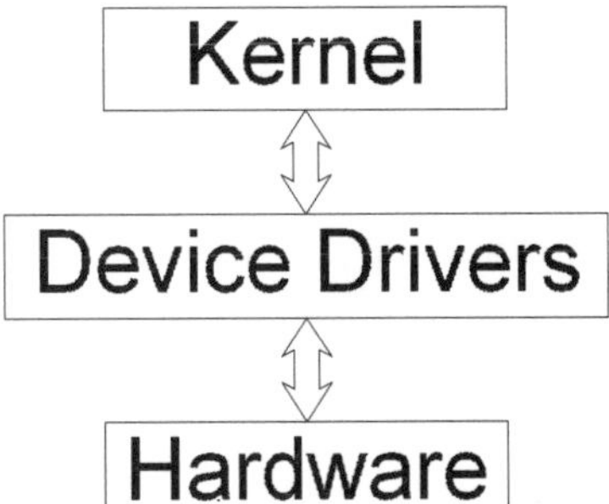

Figure 2.1 ■ The UNIX Device Driver

When your Linux system boots up, it will attempt to determine the various hardware devices that are attached to it. This is part of the autoconfiguration process. However, this takes time, and once your system is properly set up, you will want to eliminate much of the probing. This book does not attempt to teach you how to modify the autoconfiguration process and assumes that whatever version of UNIX or Linux you are using will automatically determine the necessary drivers.

THE DMESG COMMAND

Your system will record the bootup information, including devices found and not found, in a file. You can find out the contents of the file by using the `dmesg` command. This is a standard Linux command. A partial listing of the `dmesg` command can be seen in the following display from Red Hat Linux 5.2. The results of finding the network cards on bootup are selected and shown as follows:

```
wd.c: Presently autoprobing (not recommended) for a single card.

wd.c:v1.10 9/23/94 Donald Becker (becker@cesdis.gsfc.nasa.gov)

eth0: WD80x3 at 0x280,  00 00 C0 06 6F 2D WD8003, IRQ 5, shared
memory at 0xd0000-0xd1fff.

eexpress.c: Module autoprobe not recommended, give io=xx.

eth1: EtherExpress at 0x300, IRQ 10, Interface 10baseT, 32k

eexpress.c: v0.10 04-May-95 John Sullivan <js10039@cam.ac.uk>

 v0.14 19-May-96 Philip Blundell <phil@tazenda.demon.co.uk>

            v0.15 04-Aug-98 Alan Cox <alan@redhat.com>
```

It is important to know which devices the system finds so that you can set up the networking. In the above display, you will see there are two lines that begin with eth. They are eth0 and eth1. These are actually the names of the device drivers that are being loaded by Linux. The devices shown above are a Western Digital 8003 ethernet card and an etherexpress ethernet card.

THE IFCONFIG COMMAND

We discussed the ifconfig command earlier in chapter one when we used it to determine the current characteristics of your network card. We will now see how to use the command to configure the network characteristics of the box. There are a number of options to the ifconfig command. For our purposes, the ifconfig command can take on the following format for configuring a NIC card:

```
ifconfig <interface>  [<address>] [ up ] [ down ] [ netmask
<mask> ] [ broadcast <broad_addr> ]
```

where:

1. interface is the interface, which in the above discussion is eth0 or eth1.
2. address is the IP address of the NIC.
3. up or down will bring the networking up or down on the card.
4. netmask <mask> will set the netmask according to the value of <mask>.
5. broadcast <broad_addr> will set the broadcast address according to the value <broad_addr>.

There are other options that will not be discussed, but you might find them useful in certain circumstances.

■ *FOR EXAMPLE:*

You might establish the TCP/IP parameters for the eth1 card with the following:

```
ifconfig eth1 172.16.1.3 up netmask 255.255.255.0
broadcast 172.16.1.255
```

ROUTING

The default route is discussed in Lab 1.1 and is the IP address that is accessed for all IP addresses not on the local network. The local network is determined by the IP address on the NIC card of the router and by the `netmask` that is used. So if you have the following characteristics:

```
Router IP address: 172.16.1.3
Netmask:   255.255.255.0
```

any addresses that are less than 172.16.1.0 or greater than 172.16.1.255 are sent to the router address 172.16.1.3. The router will accept those packets. If it is directly connected to the network that the destination is on, it will pass the packet out on the NIC on that network. If it is not directly connected to this address on the network, it will pass it onto its own defined default router until either the packet is received by the destination or the packets dies out, in which case you would get a "no response" or "host unreachable" message.

FOR EXAMPLE:

Let's examine the following network layout in Figure 2.2.

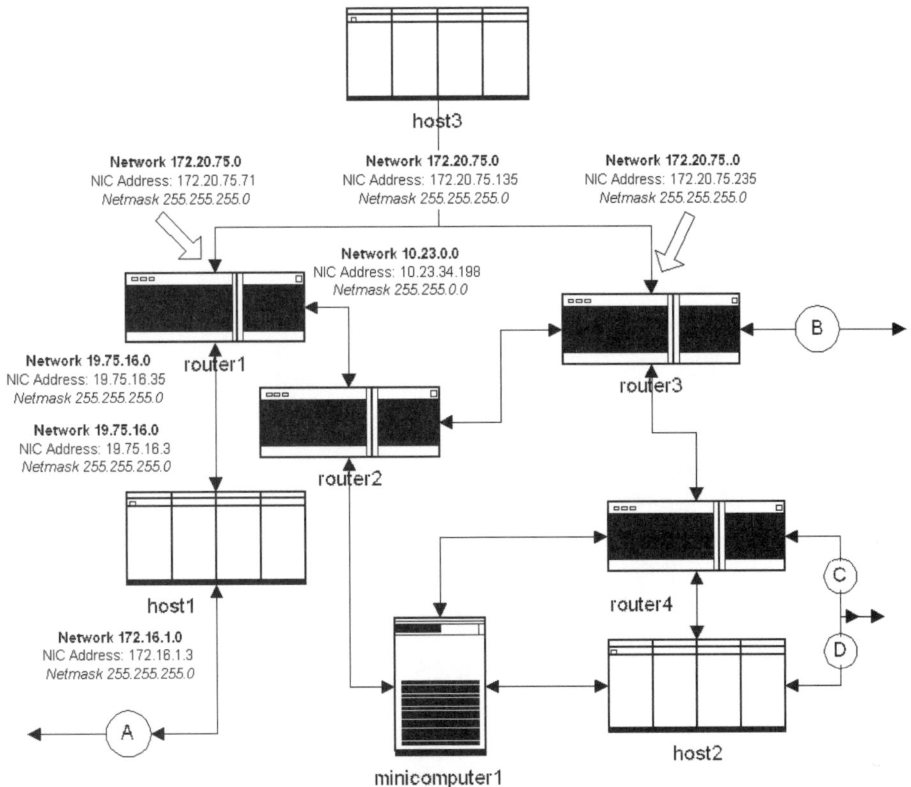

Figure 2.2 ■ An Example Routing Scheme

Look at **router1.** It has 3 NIC cards:

172.20.75.71

10.23.34.198

19.75.16.3

Note that while other address ranges may be possible and usable, it is not recommended that you choose any addresses with 255 or 0, because you may find that those addresses may not be accessible, or if you subdivide your network later, those addresses may become not accessible.

A further analysis of this network will find that when a packet comes to the router, it decides which port to go out based on the characteristics shown in Table 2.1. A packet destined for an IP address of 10.23.15.69 will go out the port with the address 10.23.34.198. Let's say, in Figure 2.2, you want to send a packet from **host1** to **host3.** The address for **host3** is 172.20.75.135. The packet first enters **router1.** The router then looks in its tables and sees that the address 172.20.75.135 is accessible from its NIC card with the address 172.20.75.71. It then sends the packet to **host3.**

However, if the router receives a packet destined for an address of 192.16.17.15., it does not initially know what to do with it. Either it can return the packet with a message saying that the destination is unknown, or it can pass the packet to the `default router`. The `default router` is where you send a packet of data when you don't know where else to send it. **Host1** must first establish **router1** as a `default router`, and then **router1** will search its tables. If the network is not a local network, the packets are passed on.

Table 2.1 ■ IP Analysis of a router.

NIC Address	Netmask	Network Address	Network's Starting Address	Network's Ending Address
172.20.75.71	255.255.255.0	172.20.75.0	172.20.75.1	172.20.75.254
10.23.34.198	255.255.0.0	10.23.0.0	10.23.1.1	10.23.254.254
19.75.16.35	255.255.255.0	19.75.16.0	19.75.17.1	19.75.16.254

FOR EXAMPLE:

Let's say that you want to send a packet from **host1** to point B in Figure 2.2. The path it must follow would be:

host1 → router1	**(this is a default route for host1)**
router1 → router3	**(this is a default route for router1)**
router3 → point B and beyond	**(this is a default route for router3)**

ROUTE COMMAND

Sometimes in Linux, if you manually establish TCP/IP on the NIC, you also need to manually start up the routing. You can do this as follows:

```
route add -net network_address network_port
```

so an example would be:

```
route add -net 19.75.16.0 eth0
```

You establish a default route with the `route` command. The actual syntax is:

```
route add default gw network_address netmask
netmask_value network_port
```

where `network_address` is the address of the default route or, specifically, the address of the NIC card on your network that will pass the IP packets to the next network; `netmask_value` is the `netmask`; and `network port` is the port name returned by the `ifconfig` command. In Figure 2.2, for **host1** to access **host3** it must pass through **router1.** In this case, you would enter the command:

```
route add default gw 19.75.16.35 netmask
255.255.255.0 eth0
```

Packets from **host1** that are not on the network 19.75.16.0 will be sent to the NIC card with the address 19.75.16.35—the NIC card on **router1.**

HOSTS FILE

By default, your UNIX computer will first access the file `/etc/hosts` to determine the IP address for hosts that you have a name for. The syntax of the file is as follows:

```
127.0.0.1 localhost
172.16.13.96    myhost    myhost.mydomain.net    mybox
tux
```

The first field gives the IP address for names in the second column.

The second field contains the primary name and any aliases that there may be for the host. The first name in the second field is the main name of the host. The remaining names are aliases that can also be used to access the host. The aliases will usually also be found in the `/etc/hosts` file on the corresponding remote host.

NSLOOKUP

Once you have your system up and running, there are several options for doing nameservices as we have discussed earlier. After the initial IP address is set up in `/etc/hosts`, your UNIX box can then use nameservices to get the IP addresses for names that need to be resolved. If your nameserver cannot resolve a name, it will usually point to another nameserver that can be queried. If this nameserver doesn't have the information, then it will pass the query on to another nameserver, and so on, until either the name is resolved or a message is returned saying that the name cannot be resolved.

In order to establish access to DNS nameservices, it is necessary to modify the file `/etc/resolv.conf`. This file has the format:

```
domain        domainname
nameserver    name_server_address
nameserver    name_server_address
..
```

where `domain` is the name of your domain.

■ *FOR EXAMPLE:*

Some examples of domain names are: `aol.com`, `ibm.com`, `sun.com`, `cod.edu`, `mediaone.net`, and so forth. So a good example would be:

```
domain        mydomain.net
```

```
nameserver  172.16.17.34
nameserver  172.16.17.35
```

Your UNIX or Linux server will access the nameservers to determine the IP address of a hostname. Your software can first check `/etc/hosts` and then check DNS services, or the order can be switched by modifying `/etc/nsswitch.conf`. This can usually be configured on your box. It is a good policy to have at least two nameservers on your network: If one goes down, you have a fallback. Linux is an ideal nameserver because it can run nameservices very well on an Intel 486, or even on a 386-based PC. The overhead of nameservices is very low. Nameservers are often referred to as DNS servers because the service they run is called `Domain Name Services`, or DNS for short.

LAB 2.1 EXERCISES

2.1.1 DETERMINE YOUR CURRENT NETWORK CHARACTERISTICS

This Exercise will show you how to determine what network devices you have on your system, to drop the associated module, and then to set it up again.

If your system does not yet have networking enabled, you first should do Exercise 2.1.2, in which you establish the networking. You can then return to this Lab and practice bringing the port down and then back up again.

To do this Exercise, you must log in from either the console, serial port via a modem or terminal, or a network port that you will not be affecting by this Exercise. Otherwise, you will lose communications when you bring down the network port.

This Exercise is also dependent on your system loading the network drivers as modules into memory while the system is coming up. It is also possible to compile modules into the kernel in Linux. If your system uses the kernel method, you can still do many of the Exercises.

You can use the `dmesg` command to see what network adapters were discovered on bootup.

Log in with your root id or become superuser.

Execute the following command and see if you can determine the network adapters on your system:

```
dmesg | more
```

a) What kind of network adapters did you discover from the `dmesg` command?

____

____

When you find the network card, it will often be preceded by a file with the `.c` extension. This is the actual source code file in Linux that is used to create the file for the device driver. For an ne2000 card, the device driver source code would be `ne.c`. The system will assign its own name to the network card, that is usually `eth0`, which means the first network card using a particular style of communications, or `protocol` such as TCP/IP. The second card in the same box using the same `protocol` would be `eth1`, and so forth. Some NIC cards may be given different name such as `tr0` and so forth.

b) Fill in the information for the following characteristics for your network card using the `dmesg` command:

- base address
- interrupt or IRQ
- device driver module
- protocol device name

____

____

The `ifconfig -a` will list all the network adapters that are configured or ready to be configured for your system.

Execute the following command:

```
ifconfig -a
```

c) What are the results of the `ifconfig -a` command?

____

____

You need to choose a network card or NIC that you will be setting up networking on. If you only have one network card, then the choice is easy.

Before doing anything to the device definitions, you need to record the information about the network card so that you can bring it back to its original state.

d) Choose the network card that you want to bring down and collect the following information for that port from the `ifconfig -a` command:

`IP address`	(often labeled as `inet` address)
`broadcast address`	(often labeled as `Bcast`)
`netmask`	(often labeled as `Mask`)
`interrupt`	(usually labeled as `Interrupt`)
`base address`	(labeled base address)

____

____

e) Does the base address and the interrupt agree in the answers to Questions b and d? If not, then stop here and determine why not.

____

____

You can determine the device driver modules that are loaded with the command:

```
lsmod
```

f) What are the results of your `lsmod` command?

____

____

You should also see the device driver that you determined in Question b of this Exercise.

g) What is the entry for the driver module for your network card in the answer to Question f?

---

h) Do the device drivers from Questions d and g agree? If not, why not?

The next step is to determine the network routing characteristics. You can do this with the `netstat` command. A recommended format is:

```
netstat -nr
```

i) What kind of results did you get from the `netstat -nr` command?

You need to examine the results of the `netstat -nr` command. Keep in mind the default routes and other gateways. You will need to understand this in order to bring the network card and networking back up.

j) How would you explain the results of the `netstat -nr` command?

Do not continue on until you have determined the proper device driver and have ensured that the common answers from Questions b and d and the answers to Questions d and g agree. You must analyze your system to determine the proper device drivers and hardware characteristics. If you are not sure, then consult your instructor, if you have one, or one of the many online Linux documentation sites, or use your reference text.

2.1.2 Bring Down the Network Interface

If you answered yes to Questions e and h in Exercise 2.1.1, you can now bring down the network card. The diagram in Figure 2.3 summarizes the steps you need to take when you bring down your network interface. These steps are done for you or are not needed during shutdown.

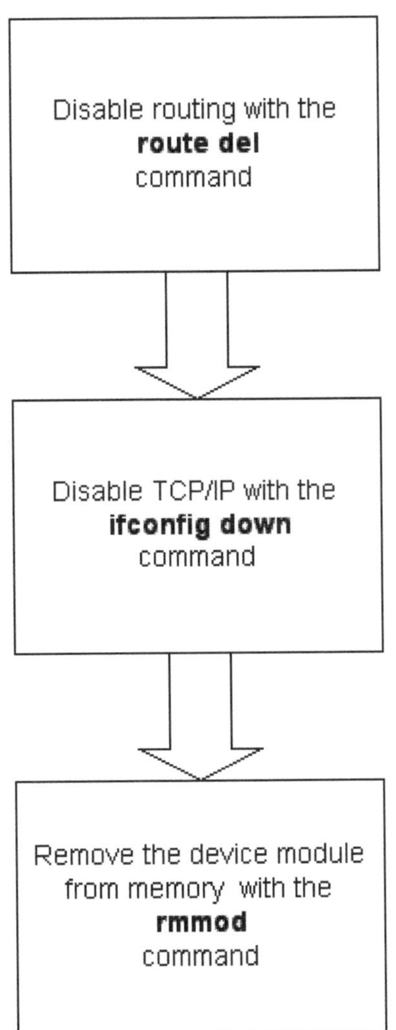

Figure 2.3 ■ Bringing Down the Network Interface Card

First you need to bring down the network services that are running on the card. You can do this with the following command:

```
ifconfig net_device down
```

where `device` is the system name that is assigned to the network interface card. An example would be:

```
ifconfig eth0 down
```

a) What are the results of the `ifconfig down` command on the network interface card?

Now type the following command:

```
ifconfig -a
```

b) What are the results of the `ifconfig -a` command after bringing down the network interface card?

Now you could remove the device driver module from memory for the network interface card that you found in Question g of Exercise 2.1.1. But first, you should verify that the driver is still loaded, in case bringing down the network interface card removed it from memory.

Enter the following command:

```
lsmod
```

c) What were your results from running `lsmod`?

If you still show the network interface card device drivers as being loaded in memory, then you need to enter the following command:

```
rmmod device_driver_module
```

In the case of the ne2000 module, that would be:

```
rmmod ne
```

d) What kind of results did you get from entering the `rmmod device_driver_module` command?

____

____

Now you should verify the modules that are loaded with `lsmod`.

e) What are the results of running the `lsmod` command after removing the module from memory?

____

____

You should now have a system that does not have the network driver loaded or configured.

2.1.3 Bring Up the Network Interface

Now that you have brought down the network interface card, you want to bring it back up again. If you skipped Exercise 2.1.1, then you first want to establish the current status of your network connections.

Figure 2.4 summarizes and compares the steps used in manually bringing up the network interface card and shows what happens on bootup. This figure summarizes the steps you will be following. It also shows the files that are normally run when you boot up. You should note that in some versions of Linux the network startup scripts are in rc3.d and rc5.d.

If the system did not bring up the network interface card when it first came up, then you need to determine the type of the network interface card. As described earlier, enter the following command:

```
dmesg | more
```

Loading Network Interface Card Information During Bootup

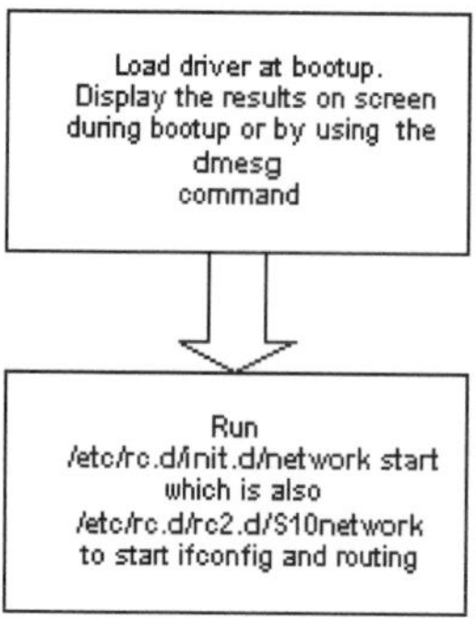

ManuallyLoading Networ
Interface Card Informatio

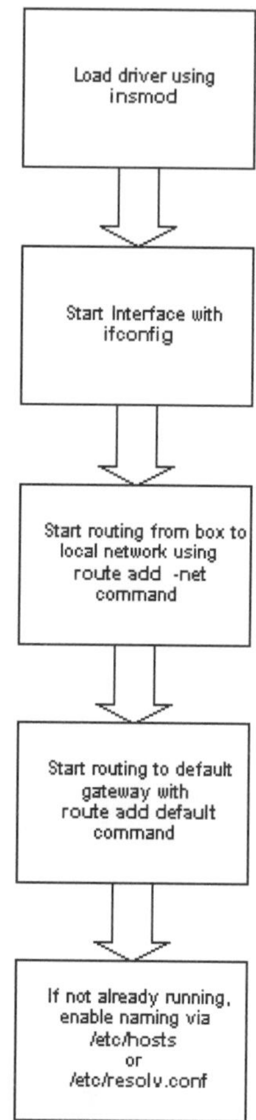

Figure 2.4 ■ Starting up TCP/IP Networking on a Network Interface Card

a) Using the `dmesg | more` command, what did you determine to be the network interface cards on your system?

____

____

You need to verify that the network interface card is down or nonexistent. You do this with the following command:

```
ifconfig -a
```

b) What did you find out about the network interface card from the `ifconfig -a` command?

____

____

You need to determine whether the network interface card driver module is loaded into memory, so enter the following command:

```
lsmod
```

c) What did you find out about the network interface modules that are loaded from the `lsmod` command?

____

____

The results of Questions a, b, and c should show that your networking is disabled on the card with which you will be working. If it is not disabled totally, then repeat Exercise 2.1.2 and make sure that all the steps are followed.

Note that in some versions of Linux, particularly some of the minimal versions, you need to load the module into memory manually. However, other versions of Linux will load the module automatically when you do the `ifconfig` *command to set up the networking on the card or they will load it at bootup. The network module can be compiled into the kernel. Also, if you have just removed the module from memory, the system may still remember the module's information. If you get an error on the following Exercise, just continue on with the* `ifconfig` *command. Then, if that doesn't work, you will need to examine what is going on.*

Now you need to load the network card module.

d) What is the module name for your network card?

Now use this module name or use the name from your documentation to load the module into memory. Enter the following command:

```
insmod device_driver_module
```

where `device_driver_module` is the name of the device driver for your network interface card. In the case of the ne2000 card, you would enter the following command:

```
insmod ne
```

e) What are the results of the `insmod` command?

You can verify this with the `lsmod` command. You should see the device driver listed.

f) What are the results of running the `lsmod` command?

g) Is there a listing for the device module for your card when you run the `lsmod` command? If not, what do you think are the reasons?

Now you need to set up the TCP/IP parameters. Use the `ifconfig` command to do this. You need to get the necessary parameters from Exercise 2.1.1 or 1.3.1. If this is the first time you are setting up your network card, then you may need to get those parameters from your network administrator or your instructor. If you are running your own network, then just choose values that are reasonable for your network.

h) What are the values for the following parameters, which you want to set for the network interface?

```
network_interface_name
IP address
Broadcast Address
Netmask
```

The next step is to set up your `ifconfig` command. You do this by using the following format:

```
ifconfig network_interface_name ip_address broadcast
broadcast_address netmask netmask_value
```

where:

- `network_interface_name` is the name of the network interface we saw earlier in this text, such as `eth0`.
- `ip_address` is the IP address that you found earlier.
- `broadcast_address` is the broadcast address from earlier.
- `netmask_value` is the value of the `netmask` that was used earlier.

■ *FOR EXAMPLE:*

```
ifconfig eth0 172.16.1.3 broadcast 172.16.1.255
netmask 255.255.255.0
```

Now set up your network card with your desired values.

i) What is the command that you will be using to set up your network interface card?

j) What are the results of executing the command in Question i?

Now you need to verify that your network interface is up. Simply enter the following command that we saw earlier:

```
ifconfig -a
```

k) What are the results of running the `ifconfig -a` command?

You now need to reestablish your initial routing. First, you need to verify that your routing is back to where it was before. To do this, just reenter the `netstat -nr` command.

l) What kind of results do you get from the `netstat -nr` command?

m) How does this compare to the results you had in Exercise 2.1.1?

If you do not see the route to your local network, then you need to use the `route` command. You can do this as follows:

```
route add -net network_address network_interface
```

An example would be:

```
route add -net 172.16.1.0 eth0
```

Add the route if you do not see it.

n) What happens when you add the route to your network address?

____

____

You now need to set up your default routing if it is not running. As explained in the introductory discussion, you can use the following command:

```
route add default gw router_address {options}
network_port
```

where the `router_address` is the address of the network interface card that you will use to leave your local network and go to the next network.

■ *FOR EXAMPLE:*

Here is an example from Figure 2.2 for **host3,** where the first default route would be:

```
route add default gw 172.20.75.235 netmask
255.255.255.0 eth0
```

and a second default route for **host3** would be:

```
route add default gw 172.20.75.71 netmask
255.255.255.0 eth0
```

o) What commands did you use to start the default routing features, if necessary?

____

____

p) Now what are the results of running the `netstat -nr` command?

____

____

Your network interface card should now be running like it was in the beginning of this Lab. If not, then step back through the Exercises and verify that you have not made any mistakes.

q) What happens when you ping an IP address or a host that is not on your network but is accessible to you from other systems?

____

____

2.1.4 SET UP YOUR HOST TABLE

The next step is to set up your `/etc/hosts` file. This Exercise assumes that your host does not have DNS, NIS, or NIS+ enabled. If you are not sure, you should see your instructor or network administrator. DNS will be discussed in Chapter 3. The `/etc/hosts` file will allow you to access other hosts by name instead of by IP address. Use the example in Figure 2.2 for discussion purposes.

Let's assume for discussion's sake that you are on the private IP address network 172.20.75.0, which is subnetted with the `netmask` of 255.255.255.0. Your host is called **host3** and has an IP address of 172.20.75.135. Now modify or create the `/etc/hosts` file with the following entries (you should customize this file with entries from your own network, and you should include the name of at least one other host that you can access):

127.0.0.1 **localhost**
172.20.75.135 **host3 loghost**
172.20.75.71 **router1**
172.20.75.235 **router3**
172.16.1.3 **host1**

a) What do you see when you try to `telnet` by name to a host that is in the `/etc/hosts` file?

____

____

b) What do you see when you try to `telnet` by name to a host that is on your network but is not in the `/etc/hosts` file?

---

c) What happens when you try to do a `traceroute` to a host in the `/etc/hosts` file?

---

d) What happens when you try to do a `traceroute` by name to an existing host that is not in the `/etc/hosts` file?

2.1.5 ENABLE CLIENT NAME RESOLUTION

This Exercise assumes that you have DNS nameservices running but do not have NIS or NIS+ running. In this Exercise, you will set up your host so that you will not need to have any entries in your `/etc/hosts` file other than the loopback address and the address of the host where you are working. It also assumes that your nameservers are aware of the addresses of other hosts outside your local network. If your nameserver is not aware of hosts outside your network, the exercises will still work for hosts in your local network.

Create the `/etc/resolv.conf` file as described in the introductory text for this Lab using the following format, but change the values for the domain to your own domain and the values of the nameservers to the ones on your network. If you are not sure what those values should be, then you should contact your network administrator or instructor. An example `/etc/resolv.conf` file is as follows:

```
domainname     mydomain.com
nameserver     172.16.1.10
nameserver     172.16.1.11
```

Now backup your /etc/hosts file to /etc/hosts.bak, then create a /etc/hosts using the following example, replacing the values for **host3** with the values of the host you are working on:

```
127.0.0.1       localhost
172.20.75.135   host3 loghost    # This is my local
host that I am working on.
```

There should be no other entries in the /etc/hosts file.

You can now verify that your host is using nameservices by using the nslookup command. This command is usually located at /usr/sbin/nslookup, in case you get an error about the file not being found.

a) What happens when you enter the nslookup command? Explain what you see.

____

____

b) If you received any errors from the nslookup command, what do you think caused them?

____

____

c) Now you should use the nslookup command to find the information about the host rs.internic.net. Explain what you see.

____

____

d) What happens when you do a telnet to a known host on your network by using the host's name and not the IP address? Explain the results.

____

____

Find the name of a server that is not resolved by the nslookup command.

e) What kind of results do you get from the `nslookup` command for a nonexistent server?

---

f) What happens when you do a `telnet` by name to a host that is not resolved by the nameservices? Explain the results.

---

g) What happens when you do a `telnet` by name to a host that is outside your network by using the host's name and not the IP address? Use the server `rs.internic.net` if you don't know of any such hosts. Explain the results.

---

h) What happens when you do a `telnet` to a nonexistent host by using the host's name and not the IP address? Explain the results.

---

i) What happens when you do a `traceroute` to a known host on your network by using the host's name and not the IP address? Explain the results.

---

j) What happens when you do a `traceroute` to an existing host that is not on your network by using the host's name and not the IP address? You can use the host `rs.internic.net` if you don't have any other names to use. Explain the results.

---

k) What happens when you do a `traceroute` to a nonexistent host that is not on your network by using the host's name and not the IP address? Explain the results.

____

____

LAB 2.1 EXERCISE ANSWERS

2.1.1 ANSWERS

a) What kind of network adapters did you discover from the `dmesg` command?

Answer: When you run the `dmesg` *command, you will get results similar to the following:*

```
[root@tux /root]#dmesg
Memory: sized by int13 088h
Console: 16 point font, 400 scans
Console: colour VGA+ 80x25, 1 virtual console (max 63)
pcibios_init : BIOS32 Service Directory structure at
0x000f6f10
pcibios_init : BIOS32 Service Directory entry at
0xf6f20
pcibios_init : PCI BIOS revision 2.10 entry at
0xf6f41
Probing PCI hardware.
Calibrating delay loop.. ok - 66.36 BogoMIPS
Memory: 30624k/32768k available (748k kernel code,
384k reserved, 840k data)
This processor honours the WP bit even when in super-
visor mode. Good.
Swansea University Computer Society NET3.035 for
Linux 2.0
NET3: Unix domain sockets 0.13 for Linux NET3.035.
Swansea University Computer Society TCP/IP for
NET3.034
IP Protocols: IGMP, ICMP, UDP, TCP
Linux IP multicast router 0.07.
VFS: Diskquotas version dquot_5.6.0 initialized
Checking 386/387 coupling... Ok, fpu using exception
16 error reporting.
```

```
Checking 'hlt' instruction... Ok.
Linux version 2.0.36 (root@porky.redhat.com) (gcc
version 2.7.2.3) #1 Tue Oct 13
 22:17:11 EDT 1998
Starting kswapd v 1.4.2.2
Serial driver version 4.13 with no serial options en-
abled
tty00 at 0x03f8 (irq = 4) is a 16550A
tty01 at 0x02f8 (irq = 3) is a 16550A
Real Time Clock Driver v1.09
Ramdisk driver initialized : 16 ramdisks of 4096K size
hda: WDC AC34300L, 4104MB w/256kB Cache,
CHS=1042/128/63
hdd: CS-R36 1, ATAPI CDROM drive
ide0 at 0x1f0-0x1f7,0x3f6 on irq 14
ide1 at 0x170-0x177,0x376 on irq 15
Floppy drive(s): fd0 is 1.44M
FDC 0 is an 8272A
md driver 0.36.3 MAX_MD_DEV=4, MAX_REAL=8
scsi : 0 hosts.
scsi : detected total.
Partition check:
 hda: hda1 hda2 < hda5 hda6 >
RAMDISK: Compressed image found at block 0
VFS: Mounted root (ext2 filesystem).
Configuring Adaptec (SCSI-ID 7) at IO:330, IRQ 11,
DMA priority 5
scsi0 : Adaptec 1542
scsi : 1 host.
  Vendor: TOSHIBA   Model: CD-ROM XM-6201TA   Rev:
1030
  Type:   CD-ROM                              ANSI
SCSI revision: 02
Detected scsi CD-ROM sr0 at scsi0, channel 0, id 5,
lun 0
Vendor: RICOH     Model: MP6200S            Rev: 2.00
  Type:   CD-ROM                              ANSI
SCSI revision: 02
Detected scsi CD-ROM sr1 at scsi0, channel 0, id 6,
lun 0
VFS: Mounted root (ext2 filesystem) readonly.
Trying to unmount old root ... okay
Adding Swap: 128988k swap-space (priority -1)
Swansea University Computer Society IPX 0.34 for
NET3.035
```

```
IPX Portions Copyright (c) 1995 Caldera, Inc.
Appletalk 0.17 for Linux NET3.035
wd.c: Presently autoprobing (not recommended) for a
single card.
wd.c:v1.10 9/23/94 Donald Becker
(becker@cesdis.gsfc.nasa.gov)
eth0: WD80x3 at 0x280,  00 00 C0 06 6F 2D WD8003, IRQ
5, shared memory at 0xd000
0-0xd1fff.
eexpress.c: Module autoprobe not recommended, give
io=xx.
eth1: EtherExpress at 0x300, IRQ 10, Interface
10baseT, 32k
eexpress.c: v0.10 04-May-95 John Sullivan
<js10039@cam.ac.uk>
            v0.14 19-May-96 Philip Blundell
<phil@tazenda.demon.co.uk>
            v0.15 04-Aug-98 Alan Cox
<alan@redhat.com>
Swansea University Computer Society IPX 0.34 for
NET3.035
IPX Portions Copyright (c) 1995 Caldera, Inc.
Appletalk 0.17 for Linux NET3.035
[root@tux /root]#
```

If you look at this output, you will see that there are actually two ethernet cards on this box. You can determine this by the entries that begin with `wd.c`, which is `eth0`, and `eexpress.c`, which is `eth1`. For the purposes of this Exercise, we will work with only the first interface, which is `eth0`. If you have a second card, you may also want to experiment with setting that one up.

b) Fill in the information for the following characteristics for your network card using the `dmesg` command:

Answer: Let's look at the previous results for `eth0` *from the* `dmesg` *comand. The results you get will be different in details, but will generally look like the following:*

```
wd.c: Presently autoprobing (not recommended) for a
single card.
wd.c:v1.10 9/23/94 Donald Becker
(becker@cesdis.gsfc.nasa.gov)
eth0: WD80x3 at 0x280, 00 00 C0 06 6F 2D WD8003, IRQ
5, shared memory at 0xd000 0-0xd1fff.
```

Table 2.2 summarizes some of the values that you would see for the device driver that is loaded for an ethernet card.

c) What are the results of the `ifconfig -a` command?

Answer: You should see some results similar to the following:

```
[root@tux /root]# ifconfig -a
lo Link encap:Local Loopback
  inet addr:127.0.0.1 Bcast:127.255.255.255
  Mask:255.0.0.0
  UP BROADCAST LOOPBACK RUNNING MTU:3584  Metric:1
       RX packets:45 errors:0 dropped:0 overruns:0 frame:0
       TX packets:45 errors:0 dropped:0 overruns:0
       carrier:0  collisions:0

eth0 Link encap:Ethernet  HWaddr 00:00:C0:06:6F:
  inet addr:172.16.2.95 Bcast:172.16.2.255
  Mask:255.255.255.
  UP BROADCAST NOTRAILERS RUNNING MULTICAST  MTU:1500
  Metric:1
  RX packets:198548 errors:0 dropped:0 overruns:0 frame
  TX packets:2657 errors:0 dropped:0 overruns:0 carrier:0
  collisions:0
  Interrupt:5 Base address:0x280 Memory:d0000-d2000

eth1 Link encap:Ethernet  HWaddr 00:AA:00:27:33:
  inet addr:172.16.1.1  Bcast:172.16.1.255
```

Table 2.2 ■ Ethernet Card Device Driver Load Information

Description	Value	Comment
base address	`0x280`	
interrupt or IRQ	5	
device driver module	`wd.o`	`wd.c` is the C source code. The driver module is `wd.o`, since it is a loadable module to another C program.
Protocol device name	`eth0`	

```
          Mask:255.255.255.0
          UP BROADCAST RUNNING MULTICAST  MTU:1500  Metric:1
          RX packets:2596678 errors:0 dropped:0 overruns:0 frame
          TX packets:5179693 errors:0 dropped:0 overruns:0 carrier
          collisions:351
          Interrupt:10 Base address:0x300

[root@tux /root]#
```

We will choose the characteristics for `eth0` because that is the card we are using for this Exercise. The results for your system will vary.

d) Choose the network interface card that you want to bring down and collect the following information for that port from the `ifconfig -a` command:

Answer: Based on the previous results in this Exercise, the answers would be as follows in Table 2.3. Your system will vary, so your results will differ.

e) Does the base address and the interrupt agree for the answers to Questions b and d? If not, then stop here and determine why not.

Answer: In the previous example output, the answers do agree. In actuality, the base address found by the two methods might differ by 10 (i.e., you might get 0x280 from one command and 0x290 from the other). In this case, do not worry about the value differences. You might revisit it later if your network card does not start up. Otherwise, all the other values should agree. The difference is due to the way the card is probed.

Table 2.3 ■ Summary of Ethernet Values from `ifconfig`

Description	Value	Actual output
IP address	172.16.2.95	`inet addr: 172.16.2.95`
broadcast address	172.16.2.255	`Bcast:172.16.2.255`
`netmask`	255.255.255.0	`Mask:255.255.255.0`
interrupt	5	`Interrupt:5`
base address	0x280	`Base address:0x280`

f) What are the results of your `lsmod` command?

Answer: On the example system, the following values were displayed:

```
[root@tux /root]# lsmod
Module            Pages     Used by
eexpress              3            1 (autoclean)
wd                    2            1 (autoclean)
8390                  2     [wd]   0 (autoclean)
nls_iso8859_1         1            1 (autoclean)
nls_cp437             1            1 (autoclean)
vfat                  4            1 (autoclean)
aha1542               3            0
[root@tux /root]#
```

Do not worry about the values in any columns other than the first. You may find those values useful later.

g) What is the entry for the driver module for your network card in the answer to Question f?

Answer: You will see that both ethernet cards are showing up in the answer to Question f. The one we are looking for is the entry for `wd`*, which is:*

```
wd                    2            1 (autoclean)
```

h) Do the device drivers from Questions b and g agree? If not, why not?

Answer: The answers should agree. If they don't, then more than likely the system found the card on bootup, but did not start up the network module. In this case, you can manually load the network module, which we will be doing later when we bring up the network. (If you are anxious to try this, you might try the `lsmod module_name` *command described in Exercise 2.1.3 later.)*

i) What kind of results did you get from the `netstat -nr` command?

Answer: On the example system, the following values were displayed:

```
 [root@tux /root]# netstat -nr
Kernel IP routing table
Destination Gateway Genmask   Flags MSS Window irtt Iface
172.16.2. 0 0.0.0.0  255.255.255.0  U  1500 0     0 eth0
172.16.1. 0 0.0.0.0  255.255.255.0  U  1500 0     0 eth1
0.0.0.0   172.16.2.1 255.255.255.0  UG 1500 0     0 eth0
127.0.0.0 0.0.0.0    255.0.0.0      U  3584 0     0 lo
[root@tux /root]#
```

j) How would you explain the results of the `netstat -nr` command?

Answer: On the example system, consider the following output in Table 2.4.

2.1.2 ANSWERS

a) What are the results of the `ifconfig down` command on the network interface card?

Answer: On the example system, you would bring down the network interface card with the following command:

```
[root@tux /root]# ifconfig eth0 down
[root@tux /root]#
```

You should not get any error messages, and you should just get a command line prompt back. This is an example of the UNIX philosophy "no news is good news."

Table 2.4 ■ Summary of Ethernet NIC Information

Destination	Gateway	Genmask	Flags	Iface	Description
172.16.2.0	0.0.0.0	255.255.255.0	U	eth0	The interface we are working with in this exercise
172.16.1.0	0.0.0.0	255.255.255.0	U	eth1	The second ethernet interface, which we will not be discussing in this exercise
0.0.0.0	172.16.2.1	255.255.255.0	UG	eth0	The default interface, which says that if there are any packets that are not on the local network they will be sent to this interface
127.0.0.0	0.0.0.0	255.0.0.0	U	lo	The localhost or loopback interface

b) What are the results of the `ifconfig -a` command after bringing down the network interface card?

Answer: You should see results similar to the following:

```
[root@tux /root]# ifconfig -a
lo Link encap:Local Loopback
   inet addr:127.0.0.1  Bcast:127.255.255.255
Mask:255.0.0.0
   UP BROADCAST LOOPBACK RUNNING  MTU:3584  Metric:1
   RX packets:45 errors:0 dropped:0 overruns:0 frame:0
   TX packets:45 errors:0 dropped:0 overruns:0 carrier:0
   collisions:0

eth1 Link encap:Ethernet  HWaddr 00:AA:00:27:33:38
     inet addr:172.16.1.1  Bcast:172.16.1.255
Mask:255.255.255.0
     UP BROADCAST RUNNING MULTICAST  MTU:1500  Metric:1
     RX packets:2598751 errors:0 dropped:0 overruns:0
frame:0
     TX packets:5180428 errors:0 dropped:0 overruns:0
carrier:0
     collisions:351
     Interrupt:10 Base address:0x300

[root@tux /root]#
```

Notice that the interface for `eth0` is no longer running, but the other interfaces have not changed.

c) What were your results from running `lsmod`?

Answer: You would now see something similar to the following:

```
[root@tux /root]# lsmod
Module           Pages     Used by
eexpress             3              1 (autoclean)
nls_iso8859_1        1              1 (autoclean)
nls_cp437            1              1 (autoclean)
vfat                 4              1 (autoclean)
aha1542              3              0
[root@tux /root]#
```

Notice that the `wd` module is now dropped from memory. In this particular case, bringing down the ethernet interface card also removed the driver from memory. This will not always happen, particularly in some of the minimal Linux versions, so the additional steps of removing the module are discussed here.

d) What kind of results did you get from entering the `rmmod device_driver_module` command?

Answer: On the example system, the module was already removed, but if the module was still loaded, you could do the following command:

```
[root@tux /root]# rmmod ne
[root@tux /root]#
```

If there are no results or error messages, then you will know that the command has successfully completed.

e) What are the results of running the `lsmod` command after removing the module from memory?

Answer: On the example system, you should see the results that were expected for the answer to Question c in section 1.3.3.

Note that module listing for the `ne` driver is gone. It should also be gone from your system. If not, you need to examine why.

2.1.3 ANSWERS

a) Using the `dmesg | more` command, what did you determine to be the network interface cards on your system?

Answer: The results should be the same as the answer to Question a in section 1.3.1.

b) What did you find out about the network interface card from the `ifconfig -a` command?

Answer: Your results should be the same as the results for Question b in section 1.3.2.

c) What did you find out about the network interface modules that are loaded from the `lsmod` command?

Answer: Your results should be the same as the results for Question e in section 1.3.2.

d) What is the module name for your network interface card?

Answer: Look at the results to Question 2.1.1 f and determine your network card module from the results. All the "You have mail . . ." comments should be deleted.

e) What are the results of the `insmod` command?

Answer: You would now see something similar to the following:

```
[root@tux /root]# insmod ne
[root@tux /root]#
```

You should not get any messages or errors. If you do, try to examine them.

```
[root@tux /root]# insmod wd
```

You may get errors similar to the following:

```
/lib/modules/preferred/net/wd.o: unresolved symbol
ei_open
or
No PCI device found. For ISA devices use io=0xNNN
values for ISA
```

These are usually resolved by ignoring this step and bringing up the actual networking on the card with `ifconfig` in the steps we will cover later.

f) What are the results of running the `lsmod` command?

Answer: You would now see something similar to the following:

```
[root@tux /root]# lsmod
Module          Pages    Used by
eexpress            3            1 (autoclean)
wd                  2            1 (autoclean)
8390                2    [wd]     0 (autoclean)
nls_iso8859_1       1            1 (autoclean)
nls_cp437           1            1 (autoclean)
vfat                4            1 (autoclean)
aha1542             3            0
[root@tux /root]#
```

Answer: This should be the same or similar to the results from Lab 2.1.1.

g) Is there a listing for the device module for your card when you run the `lsmod` command? If not, what do you think are the reasons?

Answer: If there is, then you have successfully loaded the module. If the module is not loaded, you want to examine any error messages. You also want to be sure that you have typed the module names correctly.

h) What are the values for the following parameters, which you want to set for the network interface?

Answer: You would now see something similar to the results in Table 2.5.

i) What is the command that you will be using to set up your network interface?

Answer: The command would be something similar to the following:

```
ifconfig eth0 172.16.2.95 netmask 255.255.255.0
broadcast 172.16.2.255
```

This will bring up the network interface.

j) What are the results of executing the command in Question i?

Answer: You would now see something similar to the following:

```
[root@tux /root]# ifconfig eth0 172.16.2.95 netmask
255.255.255.0 broadcast 172.16.2.255

wd.c: Presently autoprobing (not recommended) for a
single card.

wd.c:v1.10 9/23/94 Donald Becker
(becker@cesdis.gsfc.nasa.gov)

eth0: WD80x3 at 0x280,  00 00 C0 06 6F 2D WD8003, IRQ
5, shared memory at 0xd000

0-0xd1fff.
```

You will notice that except for the first line, this is the same message that you saw from the `dmesg` command when the system was first brought up.

Table 2.5 ■ NIC Ethernet Values

Description	Value
`network_interface_name`	`eth0`
IP address	`172.16.2.95`
broadcast address	`172.16.2.255`
`netmask`	`255.255.255.0`

k) What are the results of running the `ifconfig -a` command?

Answer: The answer should be the same as what you saw in Question a in section 1.1.1.

l) What kind of results do you get from the `netstat -nr` command?

Answer: You would now see something similar to the following:

```
[root@tux /root]# netstat -nr
Kernel IP routing table
Destination Gateway Genmask Flags MSS Window  irtt Iface
172.16.1.0 0.0.0.0 255.255.255.0 U  1500 0        0 eth1
127.0.0.0  0.0.0.0 255.0.0.0     U  3584 0        0 lo
[root@tux /root]#
```

m) How does this compare to the results you had to Question a in Exercise 1.1.2?

Answer: It is missing the entry for the local network and the default route. Those whose missing values should be similar to the following:

```
Destination Gateway Genmask  Flags MSS Window irtt Iface
172.16.2.0  0.0.0.0    255.255.255.0 U  1500 0    0 eth0
0.0.0.0    172.16.2.1 255.255.255.0 UG 1500 0    0 eth0
```

n) What happens when you add the route to your local network?

Answer: You should not see any error messages and would just get a command-line prompt back. You should use the following command:

```
route add -net 172.16.2.0 eth0
```

o) What command(s) did you use to start the default routing features, if necessary?

Answer: You should do a command similar to the following:

```
route add default gw 172.16.2.1 netmask 255.255.255.0
eth0
```

This will tell the TCP/IP software that the network 172.16.2.0 is attached to the `eth0` port.

p) Now what are the results of running the `netstat -nr` command?

Answer: You would now see something similar to the following:

```
[root@tux /root]# netstat -nr
Kernel IP routing table
Destination Gateway      Genmask          Flags  MSS  Window irtt Iface
172.16.2.0  0.0.0.0      255.255.255.0    U      1500 0      0    eth0
172.16.1.0  0.0.0.0      255.255.255.0    U      1500 0      0    eth1
0.0.0.0     172.16.2.1   255.255.255.0    UG     1500 0      0    eth0
127.0.0.0   0.0.0.0      255.0.0.0        U      3584 0      0    lo
[root@tux /root]#
```

q) What happens when you ping an IP address or a host that is not on your network but is accessible to you from other systems?

Answer: You would now see something similar to the following:

```
[root@tux /root]# ping 172.45.98.79
PING 172.45.98.79(172.45.98.79): 56 data bytes
64 bytes from 172.45.98.79: icmp_seq=0 ttl=19 time=56.4 ms
64 bytes from 172.45.98.79: icmp_seq=1 ttl=19 time=41.9 ms
<enter control-c>
– 172.45.98.79 ping statistics —
2 packets transmitted, 2 packets received, 0% packet loss
round-trip min/avg/max = 41.9/49.1/56.4 ms
[root@tux /root]#
```

Because the default routing is now established, it is possible to connect to a host that is not on your network.

2.1.4 ANSWERS

a) What do you see when you try to `telnet` by name to a host that is in the `/etc/hosts` file?

Answer: You would now see something similar to the following:

```
[root@tux /root]# telnet host1
Trying 172.16.1.3...
Connected to host1.
Escape character is '^]'.
SunOS 5.7
login:
```

This indicates that the `telnet` to the host was successful.

b) What do you see when you try to `telnet` by name to a host that is on your network but is not in the `/etc/hosts` file?

Answer: You would now see something similar to the following:

```
[root@tux /root]# telnet myhost
myhost: Unknown host
[root@tux /root]#
```

Remember that you should not have DNS, NIS or NIS+ nameservices currently working. If you do, then you need to disable them to get these results.

c) What happens when you try to do a `traceroute` to a host in the `/etc/hosts` file?

Answer: You would now see something similar to the following:

```
[root@wheels /root]# traceroute host1
traceroute to host1(172.16.1.3), 30 hops max, 40 byte
packets
 1  solstice (172.16.1.3)  6.651 ms *  2.963 ms
[root@wheels /root]#
```

d) What happens when you try to do a `traceroute` by name to an existing host that is not in the `/etc/hosts` file?

Answer: You would now see something similar to the following:

```
  [root@wheels /root]# traceroute host3
traceroute: unknown host host3
[root@wheels /root]#
```

2.1.5 ANSWERS

a) What happens when you enter the `nslookup` command? Explain what you see.

Answer: You would now see something similar to the following:

```
[root@tux /root]# nslookup
Default Server: ns1.mynet1.mynet.net
Address: 172.16.1.10
>
```

This shows that the default nameserver is `ns1.mynet1.mynet.net` and the address of the server is 172.16.1.10

b) If you received any errors from the `nslookup` command, what do you think caused them?

Answer: There are several possible errors. Some of them are:

```
[root@wheels /root]# nslookup
*** Can't find server name for address 172.16.1.3: No
response from server
*** Default servers are not available
[root@wheels /root]#
```

These errors are caused by the fact that the nameserver that is listed in the `/etc/resolv.conf` file, whose address is 173.16.1.3, is not responding to a request for nameservices. Another error you might get is:

```
[root@wheels /root]# nslookup
Default Server:  wheels
Address:  0.0.0.0
>
```

This can be caused by the fact that you do not have a `/etc/resolv.conf` file or it is improperly set up.

c) Now you should use the `nslookup` command to find the information about the host `rs.internic.net`. Explain what you see.

Answer: You will see results similar to the following:

```
[root@tux /root]# nslookup rs.internic.net
Default Server: ns1.mynet1.mynet.net
Address: 172.16.1.10
Non-authoritative answer:
Name:    rs.internic.net
Address:  198.41.0.6
[root@tux /root]#
```

Here, you see the name of the local nameserver, its address, the name of the host you are trying to get information about, and its address. The fact that it says the answer is non-authoritative just means that the name cannot be verified to be absolutely true. This is important if you are concerned about security, but is beyond this current discussion. This server is chosen because it is one of the most important servers on the Internet. It keeps track of or has access to a lot of information about various servers on the Internet. When you register your network on the Internet, this is one of the first servers that gets your information.

d) What happens when you do a `telnet` to a known host on your network by using the host's name and not the IP address? Explain the results.

Answer: Your results should be the same as in Question a, section 1.3.4, which are as follows:

```
[root@tux /root]# telnet host1
Trying 172.16.1.3...
Connected to host1.
Escape character is '^]'.
SunOS 5.7
login:
```

Whether you get nameservices from the `/etc/hosts` file or from the network nameservices, the screen will look the same in this case.

e) What kind of results do you get from the `nslookup` command for a nonexistent server?

Answer: You can check to see that the existing host is not resolved by the `nslookup` *command. Let's assume that the host's name is* ***host3.*** *You can check the name with the following command:*

```
nslookup host3
[root@tux /root]# nslookup host3
Default Server: ns1.mynet1.mynet.net
Address: 172.16.1.10
*** ns1.mynet1.mynet.net can't find host3: Non-
existent host/domain
[root@tux /root]#
```

f) What happens when you do a `telnet` by name to a host that is not resolved by the nameservices? Explain the results.

Answer: You should use the name that you used in the previous Exercise. Let's assume that the host's name is ***host3.*** *You should see results similar to the following:*

```
[root@wheels /root]# telnet host3
traceroute: unknown host host3
[root@wheels /root]#
```

g) What happens when you do a `telnet` by name to a host that is outside your network by using the host's name and not the IP address?

Use the server `rs.internic.net` if you don't know of any such hosts. Explain the results.

Answer: You will get results similar to the following:

```
 [root@tux /root]# telnet rs.internic.net
Trying 198.41.0.6...
Connected to rs.internic.net.
Escape character is '^]'.
UNIX(r) System V Release 4.0 (rrs5)
*****************************************************
**********************
* — InterNIC Registration Services Center  —
*
* For the *original* whois type:     WHOIS [search
string] <return>
* For referral whois type:           RWHOIS [search
string] <return>
*
* For user assistance call (703) 742-4777
# Questions/Updates on the whois database to HOSTMAS-
TER@internic.net
* Please report system problems to
ACTION@internic.net
*****************************************************
**********************
The InterNIC Registration Services database contains
ONLY
non-military and non-US Government Domains and con-
tacts.
Other associated whois servers:
       American Registry for Internet Numbers -
whois.arin.net
       European IP Address Allocations        -
whois.ripe.net
       Asia Pacific IP Address Allocations    -
whois.apnic.net
       US Military                            -
whois.nic.mil
       US Government                          -
whois.nic.gov
Cmdinter Ver 1.3 Sun Feb 21 22:17:08 1999 EST
[ansi] InterNIC >
```

You will notice that even though this server is outside your local network, there is no clear indication of this. The fact that you had to specify the domain name is the only thing that would be different from accessing a host on your local network.

h) What happens when you do a `telnet` to a nonexistent host by using the host's name and not the IP address? Explain the results.

Answer: You will see the following error:

```
[root@wheels /root]# telnet host3
host3: Host name lookup failure
[root@wheels /root]#
```

This means that you were unable to get the name resolved by using the nameservices. You may also get the following error:

```
[root@wheels /root]# telnet host3
host3: Host name lookup failure
[root@wheels /root]#
```

In the second case, it is not clear whether the failure was due to the `/etc/hosts` file or the nameservices being unable to provide the IP address from the name.

i) What happens when you do a `traceroute` to a known host on your network by using the host's name and not the IP address? Explain the results.

Answer: You should see the following results:

```
[root@wheels /root]# traceroute tux

traceroute to tux (172.16.1.1), 30 hops max, 40 byte
packets

 1  tux (172.16.1.1)  6.836 ms  3.789 ms  3.496 ms

[root@wheels /root]#
```

You see that the name is resolved to an IP address. In this case, because they are both on the same network, there is only one hop between the two hosts.

j) What happens when you do a `traceroute` to an existing host that is not on your network by using the host's name and not the IP address? You can use the host `rs.internic.net` if you don't have any other names to use. Explain the results.

```
[root@tux /root]# traceroute rs.internic.net

traceroute: Warning: Multiple interfaces found; using
172.16.1.1 @ eth0

traceroute to rs.internic.net (198.41.0.6), 30 hops
max, 40 byte packets

 1  route1.mynet.net (172.16.1.1)  22.094 ms  12.079
ms  17.254 ms

..

 [root@wheels /root]#
```

This will give a listing of every IP device that it passes through until it reaches the destination. Note the multiple interface message. It means that the system chose this interface.

k) What happens when you do a `traceroute` to a nonexistent host that is not on your network by using the host's name and not the IP address? Explain the results.

```
 [root@wheels /root]# traceroute host3
host3: Host name lookup failure
[root@wheels /root]#
```

Because your system is unable to convert the name to an address, the `traceroute` command cannot even attempt to make a connection.

LAB 2.1 SELF REVIEW QUESTIONS

In order to test your progress, you should be able to answer the following questions.

The following information was created by the `dmesg` command. Using this information, answer the questions that follow. Note that some of the questions ask for information that is not discussed in the book. Further details can be found by using the `man` command on various topics discussed in this chapter.

```
Memory: sized by int13 088h
Console: 16 point font, 400 scans
Console: colour VGA+ 80x25, 1 virtual console (max
63)
pci_init: no BIOS32 detected
Calibrating delay loop.. ok - 5.73 BogoMIPS
Memory: 14480k/16384k available (748k kernel code,
384k reserved, 600k data)
This processor honours the WP bit even when in super-
visor mode. Good.
Swansea University Computer Society NET3.035 for
Linux 2.0
NET3: Unix domain sockets 0.13 for Linux NET3.035.
Swansea University Computer Society TCP/IP for
NET3.034
IP Protocols: IGMP, ICMP, UDP, TCP
Linux IP multicast router 0.07.
VFS: Diskquotas version dquot_5.6.0 initialized^M
Checking 386/387 coupling... Ok, fpu using exception
16 error reporting.
Checking 'hlt' instruction... Ok.
Linux version 2.0.36 (root@porky.redhat.com) (gcc
version 2.7.2.3) #1 Tue Oct 13
 22:17:11 EDT 1998
Starting kswapd v 1.4.2.2
Serial driver version 4.13 with no serial options en-
abled
tty00 at 0x03f8 (irq = 4) is a 16550A
tty01 at 0x02f8 (irq = 3) is a 16550A
Real Time Clock Driver v1.09
Ramdisk driver initialized : 16 ramdisks of 4096K
size
hda: Conner Peripherals 1080MB - CFA1080A, 1032MB
w/256kB Cache, CHS=524/64/63
hdd: CS-R36 1, ATAPI CDROM drive
```

```
ide0 at 0x1f0-0x1f7,0x3f6 on irq 14
ide1 at 0x170-0x177,0x376 on irq 15
Floppy drive(s): fd0 is 1.44M
FDC 0 is a post-1991 82077
md driver 0.36.3 MAX_MD_DEV=4, MAX_REAL=8
scsi : 0 hosts.
scsi : detected total.
Partition check:
 hda: hda1 hda2 < hda5 hda6 >
RAMDISK: Compressed image found at block 0
VFS: Mounted root (ext2 filesystem).
VFS: Mounted root (ext2 filesystem) readonly.
Trying to unmount old root ... okay
Adding Swap: 66492k swap-space (priority -1)
sysctl: ip forwarding off
Swansea University Computer Society IPX 0.34 for
NET3.035
IPX Portions Copyright (c) 1995 Caldera, Inc.
Appletalk 0.17 for Linux NET3.035
ne.c:v1.10 9/23/94 Donald Becker
(becker@cesdis.gsfc.nasa.gov)
NE*000 ethercard probe at 0x300: 00 40 05 1a 3c 19
eth0: NE2000 found at 0x300, using IRQ 5.
eexpress.c: Module autoprobe not recommended, give
io=xx.
eth1: EtherExpress at 0x300, IRQ 10, Interface
10baseT, 32k
eexpress.c: v0.10 04-May-95 John Sullivan
<js10039@cam.ac.uk>
            v0.14 19-May-96 Philip Blundell
<phil@tazenda.demon.co.uk>
            v0.15 04-Aug-98 Alan Cox
<alan@redhat.com>
```

1) How much memory is in this system?
- **a)** _____8 K
- **b)** _____8 Meg
- **c)** _____16 Meg
- **d)** _____64 Meg
- **e)** _____16 Gig

2) The IP protocols include TCP and UDP.
- **a)** _____True
- **b)** _____False

3) The network protocols shown do not include IPX and Appletalk.
a) _____True
b) _____False

4) IP forwarding is enabled.
a) _____True
b) _____False

5) Which of the following network card modules are loaded on bootup?
a) _____`wd.o`
b) _____`eexpress.o`
c) _____`ne.o`
d) _____a and b
e) _____b and c

6) Which of the following was the IRQ for the first ethernet card found?
a) _____5
b) _____10
c) _____1
d) _____13
e) _____15

7) Which of the following was the IRQ for the second ethernet card found?
a) _____5
b) _____10
c) _____11
d) _____13
e) _____15

Use the results of the following `netstat -nr` command to answer the questions that follow:

```
Kernel IP routing table
Destination Gateway  Genmask   Flags MSS Window irtt Iface
25.131.173.0 0.0.0.0       255.255.255.0 U  1500 0    0 eth0
172.16.1.0    0.0.0.0       255.255.255.0 U  1500 0    0 eth1
127.0.0.0     0.0.0.0       255.0.0.0     U  3584 0    0 lo
0.0.0.0       25.131.173.1 0.0.0.0       UG 1500 0    0 eth0
```

8) The IP address 127.0.0.0 refers to the localhost or loopback port.
a) _____True
b) _____False

9) The default route uses what address to connect out of the network?

a) _____172.16.1.0
b) _____0.0.0.0
c) _____255.255.255.0
d) _____25.131.173.1
e) _____25.131.173.0

10) Which command would you use to load the device driver module into memory **before** setting up the TCP/IP?

a) _____`insmod`
b) _____`rmmod`
c) _____`lsmod`
d) _____`chmod`
e) _____`ifconfig`

Quiz answers appear in Appendix A, Section 2.1.

CHAPTER 2

TEST YOUR THINKING

1) You are to design a network with the characteristics found in Figure 2.5:

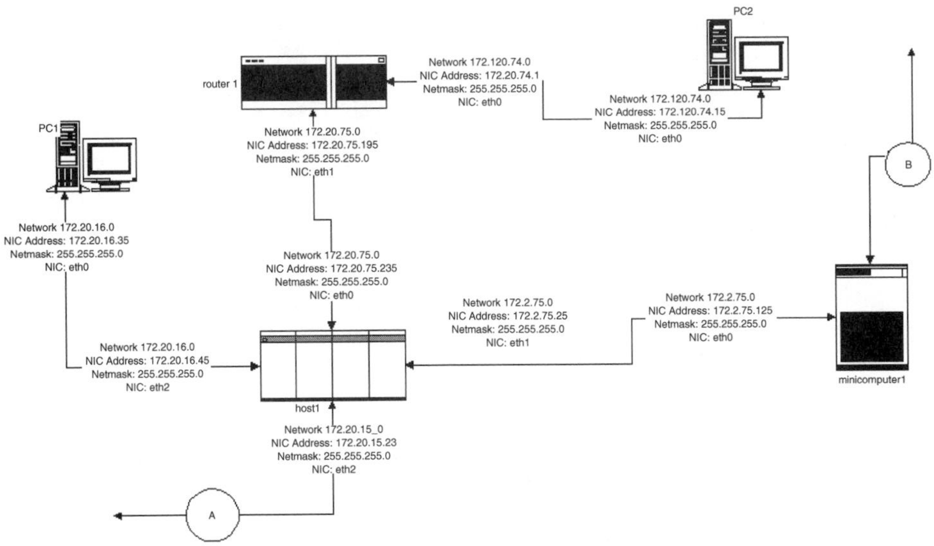

Figure 2.5 ■ Network Design

Figure out what UNIX commands you would use to establish the network characteristics for each of the following:

a) PC1 (assume you are running Linux)

b) PC2 (assume you are running Linux)

c) **host1**

d) **minicomputer1**

This includes the routes to get from one system to another. Be sure to include the following commands:

a) `ifconfig`

b) route to the local network

c) default route from your host to another network

Fill in the results in Table 2.5:

Table 2.5 ■ Project Results

Source Host	Destination Host	Type of command	Command Syntax
PC1	PC2	`ifconfig`	
		local route	
		default route	
	host1	`ifconfig`	
		local route	
		default route	
	minicomputer1	`ifconfig`	
		local route	
		default route	
PC2	PC1	`ifconfig`	
		local route	
		default route	
	host1	`ifconfig`	
		local route	
		default route	
	minicomputer1	`ifconfig`	
		local route	
		default route	
host1	PC1	`ifconfig`	
		local route	
		default route	
	PC2	`ifconfig`	
		local route	
		default route	
	minicomputer1	`ifconfig`	

		local route	
		default route	
minicomputer1	PC1	ifconfig	
		local route	
		default route	
	PC2	`ifconfig`	
		local route	
		default route	
	host1	`ifconfig`	
		local route	
		default route	

2) In Figure 2.5, what kind of results would you expect when using each host in project 1 to connect to every other host listed in project 1 for the following commands:

a) `ping`

b) `traceroute`

c) `telnet` assuming the PCs are running Linux

d) `ftp` assuming the PCs are running Linux

Fill in the Table 2.6 with your answers.

Table 2.6 ■ Project Results

Source Host	Destination Host	Command	Command Syntax	Expected Results
PC1	PC2	`ping`		
		`traceroute`		
		`telnet`		
		`ftp`		
	host1	`ping`		

		traceroute	
		telnet	
		ftp	
	minicomputer1	ping	
		traceroute	
		telnet	
		ftp	
PC2	PC1	ping	
		traceroute	
		telnet	
		ftp	
	host1	ping	
		traceroute	
		telnet	
		ftp	
	minicomputer1	ping	
		traceroute	
		telnet	
		ftp	
host1	PC1	ping	
		traceroute	
		telnet	
		ftp	
	PC2	ping	
		traceroute	
		telnet	
		ftp	
	minicomputer1	ping	
		traceroute	
		telnet	
		ftp	
minicomputer1	PC1	ping	
		traceroute	
		telnet	

		ftp	
	PC2	ping	
		traceroute	
		telnet	
		ftp	
	host1	ping	
		traceroute	
		telnet	
		ftp	

CHAPTER 3

SETTING UP A NAMESERVER

"I'm glad to have met you. Please tell me your name"
"The name that they call me, it's not fancy, just plain
How am I known? It just is My Name"
"Well, my name is Your Name. If your name is My Name
Then how will either of us ever be known?"

—Joe

CHAPTER OBJECTIVES

In this chapter, you will learn about:

Exercises for the Masses

✔ Your Current Nameserver Configuration Page 95

Exercises for the Great and Super User

✔ Setting up a Primary Nameserver Page 104

When you first install your Linux system, you are often given the choice of installing nameservices. This may be installed automatically, installed as part of a much larger package, or you may be able to choose the package to install. This is usually referred to as DNS for Domain Name Services.

DNS takes the place of the `/etc/hosts` file and allows you to get the information as you need it—and not have to store it locally. DNS allows you to take a name and return an IP address, take an IP address and find the name associated with it, find a sites mail server, or even track information about various computers on your network. The Internet is based on DNS. A DNS server is often the first Linux box on a site, because DNS on Linux has almost no system overhead, can be run on a slow 486, and never crashes. In this chapter, you will build and run a nameserver.

LAB 3.1

YOUR CURRENT NAMESERVER CONFIGURATION

LAB OBJECTIVES

After this Lab, you will be able to:

- Determine Your Current Nameserver Configuration

Look in the man pages for the following: named, named.boot, named.conf, named.hosts, named.rev, named.local, named.ca, resolv.conf, bind, dns

TOP-LEVEL DOMAINS

Nameservers are built on the idea that one nameserver can talk to another nameserver, which in turn can talk to other nameservers, and so forth. Look at Figure 3.1 to get a picture of the domain tree.

You can think about an inverted tree with its roots at the top. This is the way the Internet works and is the way the directory structure is laid out also. You will see that there can be many levels of host and domain naming that exist. The only standards are at the root and domain level. Everything below that is site-specific.

There are a number of root nameservers. The names are stored in the cache file on your nameserver. This file is often called `named.ca`, `db.cache`, or some other name. The name really doesn't matter as long as you have the proper reference to the cache file in either

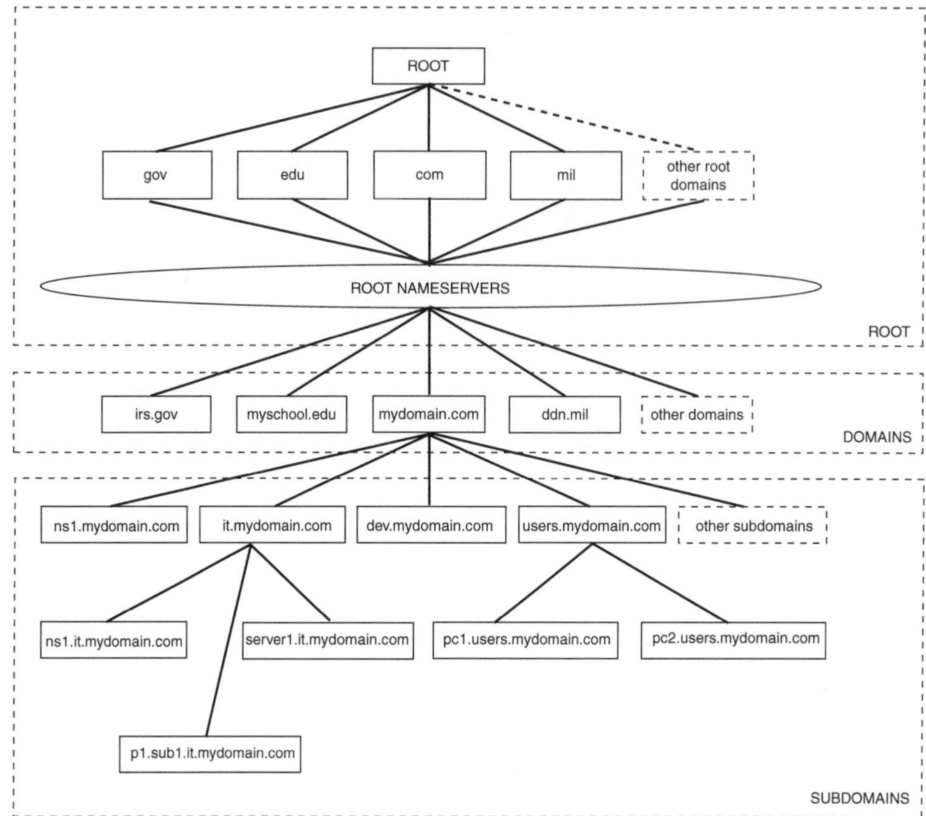

Figure 3.1 ■ The Nameserver and Domain Name Inverted Tree

`/etc/named.boot` or `/etc/named.conf`. We will discuss those files in a moment.

You should regularly update the file that is the cache file used to store the names of the root servers. This can be `named.ca`, `db.cache`, *or some other filename. This file can be obtained by accessing* `ftp.rs.internic.net` *and grabbing the file* `/domain/named.root` *for your nameserver. You should regularly update this file on your nameservers because addresses and names do change. If you have problems getting to a site, you might try updating this file. Be sure you rename or copy this file to your nameserver with the proper filename.*

NAME TO ADDRESS RESOLUTION

Figure 3.2 illustrates the process of resolving a name to an IP address.

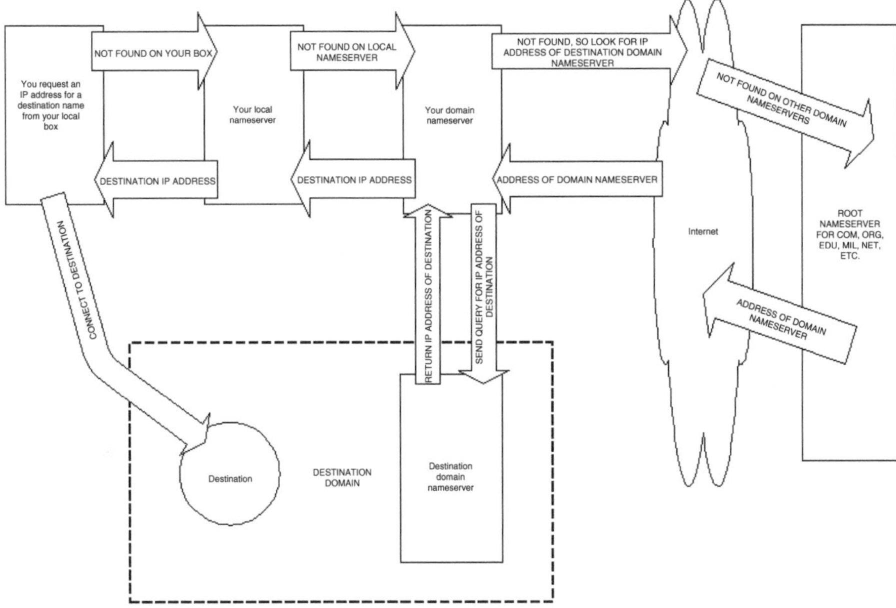

Figure 3.2 ■ The Detailed Process of Resolving a Name to an IP Address

The name-to-address-resolution process goes as follows:

1. A query is first sent to your local box to see if the address is stored either in `/etc/hosts`, a DNS file, or cache. If it is found, then it is returned to the process, and the process uses this IP address to connect to the destination.
2. If the address is not found, then a query is sent to the local nameserver, which is usually a department nameserver. If the IP address is found, then it is returned to your local box, which then passes it to the process.
3. If it is not on the local nameserver, the request goes to the domain nameserver, which then attempts to resolve either the domain nameserver or the actual IP address.
4. If the domain nameserver can't find either the domain nameserver or the IP address, the request is sent out to the Internet and eventually will get to the root nameserver if the addresses are not found somewhere along the way.
5. The root nameserver will then return the address of the nameserver for the domain where the destination is located.

6. The address is returned to the domain nameserver, which then queries the nameserver of the destination domain.
7. The destination domain nameserver will then return the IP address of the destination to your domain nameserver. The destination domain nameserver may have to query other nameservers in its domain.
8. Your domain nameserver will return the IP address of the destination to your local nameserver.
9. This address will then be passed on to your local box.
10. The process then uses that IP address to connect to the destination.

LAB 3.1 EXERCISES

3.1.1 DETERMINE YOUR CURRENT NAMESERVER CONFIGURATION

If you know that you do not currently have a nameserver set up, you should build one. Appendix B shows how you load Trinux from three diskettes to memory. Trinux includes the ability to run a nameserver totally from RAM. We will be building upon the standard Linux, Trinux, and the Red Hat 5.2 models in this chapter. We will be using Trinux and other minimal versions of Linux throughout this book.

In this Exercise, we will determine the current characteristics of your nameserver. The command you would use is the familiar :

```
nslookup
```

We will be adding to your understanding of this command as we move through the various chapters of this book.

a) What do you get when you enter the `nslookup` command?

____

____

If you get an error about the server not being found, or the server address not being resolved to a name, then you will need to either build your simple nameserver or go to a box that has access to a nameserver. We will discuss later in this chapter about how to build the nameserver. Then you can finish this Exercise.

b) What is the Default Server that shows up when you enter the `nslookup` command?

c) What is the address of the Default Server that you get from the `nslookup` command?

You can find out what the default values for your nameserver are by using the following command when you are at the `nslookup >` prompt:

```
set all
```

d) What are the results from entering the `set all` command while you are in `nslookup`?

e) Looking at the results from the `set all` command, what is your root `nameserver`?

f) Looking at the results from the `set all` command, what is your domain?

The searchlist is the sequence of the domain search that your nameserver will follow when it searches for the nameserver information when given a host name.

You should choose a host that is on your network. In the following example, replace `host_name` with the name of the host on your network. Now enter the name of the host from the `nslookup` > prompt as follows:

```
>  host_name
```

g) What kind of results do you get when you enter the host's name by itself?

---

h) What is the domain that was appended to the host's name when you entered just the host's name?

---

i) What is the IP address of the host when you entered just the host's name?

LAB 3.1 EXERCISE ANSWERS

3.1.1 ANSWERS

a) What do you get when you enter the `nslookup` command?

Answer: You should see something similar to the following:

```
[root@tux /root]# nslookup
Default Server:  mynameserver.mydomain.com
Address:  172.16.1.45
```

If you get "no default server," then it means that your nameservices have not yet been set up. If you get some other error, you then need to make sure that you entered the command properly. Otherwise, you don't need to dwell on this because this is for information purposes, and you will be building your own nameserver.

b) What is the Default Server that shows up when you enter the `nslookup` command?

Answer: The second line in the results of Question a shows the default server:

```
Default Server: mynameserver.mydomain.com
```

So the default nameserver is `mynameserver.mydomain.com`.

c) What is the address of the Default Server that you get from the `nslookup` command?

Answer: The address is given by the third line, which is:

```
Address:   172.16.1.45
```

This is the address that `mynameserver.mydomain.com` *resolves to, which is 172.16.1.45.*

d) What are the results from entering the `set all` command while you are in `nslookup`?

```
> set all
Default Server:   mynameserver.mydomain.com
Address:   172.16.1.45

Set options:
  nodebug          defname      search          recurse
  nod2             novc         noignoretc      port=53
  querytype=A      class=IN     timeout=5       retry=4
  root=a.root-servers.net.
  domain=mydomain.com
  srchlist=mydomain.com

>
```

If you do not get results that are similar, be sure you entered the `nslookup` command by itself and have a > prompt.

e) Looking at the results from the `set all` command, what is your `root nameserver`?

Answer: The following line gives the root nameserver:

```
root=a.root-servers.net.
```

f) Looking at the results from the `set all` command, what is your domain?

Answer: The domain in the example is `mydomain.com.` *Your domain will be different.*

g) What kind of results do you get when you enter the host's name by itself?

Answer: Your results should be similar to the following:

```
> myserver
Server:  mynameserver.mydomain.com
Address  172.16.1.45

Name:     myserver.mydomain.com
Address:   172.16.1.13
```

h) What is the domain that was appended to the host's name when you entered just the host's name?

Answer: In the example it is `mydomain.com.` *You can see this by the line:*

```
Name:     myserver.mydomain.com
```

i) What is the IP address of the host when you entered just the host's name?

Answer: The IP address is given by the last line in the example, which is:

```
Address:   172.16.1.13
```

LAB 3.1 SELF-REVIEW QUESTIONS

In order to test your progress, you should be able to answer the following questions.

The command `nslookup` was executed and a search for a host address was requested. The network IP address of the local host is 172.16.1.45. Use the following results to answer the first three questions that follow:

```
Default Server:  localhost.0.0.127.in-addr.arpa
Address:  127.0.0.1

> tux
Server:  localhost.0.0.127.in-addr.arpa
Address:  127.0.0.1

Name:    tux.mydomain.com
Address:  172.16.1.1
```

1) The default server is at 127.0.0.1.
  a) _____True
  b) _____False

2) What is the address for `tux`?
  a) _____127.0.0.1
  b) _____172.16.1.1
  c) _____0.0.127
  d) _____1.0.0.127
  e) _____none of the above

3) The name of the nameserver is `tux.mydomain.com`.
  a) _____ True
  b) _____ False

4) If your local IP server does not find IP address information locally about a remote host, which of the following will it query next?
  a) _____root servers
  b) _____local nameserver or domain nameserver
  c) _____localhost
  d) _____destination nameserver
  e) _____destination host

5) What is the primary domain for `p1.sub11.it.mydomain.com` in Figure 3.1?
  a) _____`it.mydomain.com`
  b) _____`mydomain.com`
  c) _____`sub1.it.mydomain.com`
  d) _____`p1.sub1.it.mydomain.com`
  e) _____`com`

Quiz answers appear in Appendix A, Section 3.1.

LAB 3.2

SETTING UP A PRIMARY NAMESERVER

LAB OBJECTIVES

After this Lab, you will be able to:

Set up and understand a primary nameserver and configure the following files:

- `resolv.conf`
- `named.ca`
- `named.local`
- `named.hosts`
- `named.rev`
- `named.boot`
- `named.conf`
- Test Your Configuration

TYPES OF NAMESERVERS

There are several types of nameservers in use. You will always need at least two nameservers on your site. This is required when you register your domain. This allows people to get to your domain when one nameserver is down. They can just query the other nameserver. There are three standard types plus additional servers that combine various features. They are:

Primary nameservers—These are the nameservers you will generally be setting up. They are the most common because most domains are small enough that other types of nameservers are not needed.

Secondary nameservers—These are nameservers that are essentially the same as the primary nameserver. They can function on their own if the primary nameserver goes down. However, their data is constantly being updated from the primary nameserver. This means you only have to update the primary nameserver on your network. Any changes will filter down.

Caching nameservers—These servers do not have the standard address files used by DNS. Any information is stored in a cache. As time goes on, this cache is built up so that any queries can be resolved a lot more quickly than if you went through the process in Figure 3.1. This information is not permanently stored, however. Caching nameservers cannot function without the primary or secondary nameservers.

In this book, we will only build a `primary nameserver,` because it does not depend upon having access to other nameservers on your network. Once you understand the `primary nameserver,` it will be easier to configure the other types.

The Whole Truth

While you may have multiple nameservers listed for your system to access, DNS will only query the first available one on the list. If your first nameserver, after going through the process shown in Figure 3.2, gives an "address not found" message, it will not query the additional nameservers on your network. You may have 10 nameservers listed on your network but only the first one that responds is used. Therefore, it is important that all nameservers be kept up-to-date. You need to keep this in mind as you read further.

RECORD TYPES

Because the nameservers are really database servers, we can think of the information as being stored in records. Unlike many databases, all the files are in a character text format and are readable and editable. The record types fall into the following categories:

- *SOA*—Lists the main authority for the domain.
- *NS*—Gives the nameservers for the domain.
- *A*—Gives name to address mapping. This is the main record type you will need to be concerned with once you have set up your domain.

- *PTR*—Gives the address to name mapping, also known as the `reverse mapping` or `reverse naming`. This will take an IP address and return the name associated with it. This is often used by destination hosts to verify that you are who you say you are. Sometimes you will be refused if the destination cannot verify your name from the IP address.
- *Others*—There are other record types, but we don't need to be concerned about them now, since we want to get up to speed as quickly as possible.

LAB 3.2 EXERCISES

In these Exercises, we will build a nameserver file by file. If you are on an existing network with currently existing nameservers, you can still create your own domain and not have an impact on the rest of the network. A nameserver must be accessed directly by your program; otherwise, the rest of the network ignores it.

Note that there are several versions of DNS in use, each with subtle differences. Sometimes you may need to tweak a few items to get your DNS files to resolve names properly. Also, filenames will differ in various versions. You need to think of the file's function, not the name. We will be working with relatively standard filenames. We will also assume that all DNS host files are located in `/var/named`*, but they actually can be located anywhere that* `/etc/named.boot` *or* `/etc/name.conf` *point to.*

3.2.1 resolv.conf

This file is `/etc/resolv.conf` and was discussed in Chapter 2. This is a standard file that is in use on all systems that need to do name resolution. This time, the file must be set up in a manner similar to the following layout:

```
domain mydomain.com
search mydomain.com
nameserver 127.0.0.1
```

where `domain` is the name of the domain where you are going to resolve addresses. You should be aware that the *domain* may be unnecessary in your version. The *search* is the domain name that will be searched when given a host name. You can actually search multiple domains, one at a time, starting from left to right. The *nameserver* line tells what nameserver you are using. In this case, you are doing name resolution on your own box, so it is its own nameserver.

In these Exercises, you can use the sample domain name, create your own name, or use a currently existing one. For the purposes of this Exercise, it doesn't matter, although if you are building a permanent nameserver, you will want to use the domain name you ultimately will use and create the actual files.

Before you create the file, you should look up and document some information.

a) What is the domain that you are going to be using in your `/etc/resolv.conf` file?

____

____

b) What is the domain that you will do a search on?

____

____

There currently may be a different IP address in `/etc/resolv.conf`. You should record it so that you know the IP address of the nameserver that you will pass requests to.

c) What is the IP address for the nameserver that currently exists in `/etc/resolv.conf`?

____

____

Create your `/etc/resolv.conf` file using the information you just used to answer Questions a, b, and c.

3.2.2 named.ca

This is the cache file that lists the root nameservers as was discussed in Lab 3.1. This file is included in all versions of DNS. You never have to modify this file. You only need to get occasional updates from the Internet. You can get this file from `ftp.rs.internic.net` and retrieve the file `/domain/named.root`.

Get the file `named.root`. Copy it to your `/var/named` directory. Verify first that it doesn't exist in `/var/named`. If it does then copy the existing file to one with a different name like `/var/named.root.bak`.

a) What are the results of getting the file `/domain/named.root` from `ftp.rs.internic.net`?

Back up your current `named.ca` file in `/var/named`. Call it `named.ca.bak`. Copy `named.root` to `named.ca`.

b) Now do an `ls -l /var/named`. Do you see the files `named.ca`, `named,ca.bak`, `named.root`, along with other files?

If not, then reexamine the steps in this Exercise to be sure that you have copied everything correctly.

3.2.3 named.local

The file `/var/named/named.local` is the local nameserver configuration file. It only contains information about the local host. Let's assume my id is `myid`, my server is `myserver`, and `mydomain` is `mydomain.com`. The file for a primary nameserver looks like following:

```
@       IN SOA myserver.mydomain.com. myid.myserver.mydomain.com. (
        1989020503    ;serial
```

```
        10800       ;refresh
        3600        ;retry
        3600000      ;expire
        86400 )     ;minimum

        IN      NS      myserver.mydomain.com.
1       PTR     localhost
```


Notice that we now see three of the four record types that we discussed. The record types shown are SOA, NS, and PTR. Now we'll create or modify the `/var/named/named.local` file.

Let's take each string one at a time and determine what to put in.

`SOA myserver.mydomain.com.myid` says that the start of authority for this nameserver is `myserver.mydomain.com`, which is the computer where this file is located.

For now you can ignore any data other than what is discussed here.

a) What is the actual name that you will enter in the `/var/named/named.local` in place of `myserver.mydomain.com`?

The line `myid.myserver.mydomain.com` says the id `myid` is the e-mail id of the person who is in charge of the nameserver data. This is for someone who needs to find the contact person and is not used by any programs.

b) What is the actual name that you will enter in `/var/named/named.local` in place of `myid.myserver.mydomain.com`?

`IN NS myserver.mydomain.com` says the local computer is the nameserver to be used for address resolution.

c) What is the actual string that you will enter in /var/named/named.local in place of IN NS myserver.mydomain.com?

____

____

3.2.4 named.hosts

The file named.hosts is usually located in /var/named. It contains name-to-address translation information about hosts on your network. It uses the *A* record to resolve a name to an address.

You should note that in a DNS file, you can enter hostnames in one of two formats. One way is to just use the hostname and let the server add in the domain from the file it is in. The second way is to enter the full hostname and domain name. However, in the second case, the entries must be followed by a period. If you enter myserver.mydomain.com *without the period, then DNS will append the domain and you will actually get* myserver.mydomain.com.mydomain.com.

Let's assume your id is myid, your server is myserver, and your domain is mydomain.com. The /var/named/named.hosts file for a primary nameserver looks like the following:

```
@ IN SOA myserver.mydomain.com. root.myserver.mydomain.com. (
        1989020503    ;serial
        10800         ;refresh
        3600          ;retry
        3600000       ;expire
        86400 )       ;minimum

        NS      myserver.mydomain.com.

localhost       A       127.0.0.1
myserver        A       172.16.1.1
```

Notice that the difference between the named.local file and the named.hosts file is the last two lines in named.hosts. The first one gives a name-to-address resolution for the localhost name. The last line is the format of the line that you will use to put the addresses of the various hosts on your network. In the named.local file the last line actually does an address to name resolution.

You should go ahead replace the name `myserver` on the last line with the name of the server you are creating the nameserver on. Then replace the address in the last column of the last line with the address of this server.

LAB 3.2

a) When you created the `named.hosts` file, what is the line that you entered for your local nameserver?

____

____

3.2.5 *named.rev*

The file `named.rev` is usually located in `/var/named`. It contains information about IP addresses on your network. The file focuses on the use of the PTR, which gives the information needed to take a name and resolve it to an address.

Let's assume your id is `myid`, your server is `myserver`, and your domain is `mydomain.com`. The `/var/named/named.rev` file for a primary nameserver looks like the following:

```
@ IN SOA myserver.mydomain.com. root.myserver.mydomain.com. (
        1989020503    ;serial
        10800         ;refresh
        3600          ;retry
        3600000       ;expire
        86400 )       ;minimum


        NS      myserver.mydomain.com.


1       PTR     myserver
```

Whenever an IP address is sent to the nameserver, it will search this file for the name that is associated with it.

You can create this file; you just need to take the `named.hosts` and save it as `named.rev`. Then you can remove the localhost entry and modify the file to have addresses in the first column and names in the last, then replace the A directive with the PTR directive. Create that file now.

a) What is the new line that you created for your server in `named.rev`?

3.2.6 named.boot

Note that `/etc/named.boot` has been replaced by `/etc/named.conf` in more current versions of DNS. Your nameserver will either use one or the other. We will discuss `named.conf` in section 3.2.7.

This file is the main file that is used for pointing to further nameservice information. This file is always located at `/etc/named.boot`. However, it contains the pointer to the directory where all the nameservice files are located; in this case, it is `/var/named`.

```
;boot file for the name server
directory /var/named
;type       domain                  source host/file   backup_file

cache       .                       named.ca
primary     0.0.127.in-addr.arpa    named.local
primary     1.16.172.in-addr.arpa   named.rev
primary     mydomain.com            named.hosts
```

The file can be discussed in terms of the entries that start each line. They are:

- `directory`—The location where the nameservice files or subdirectories are located.
- `cache`—Pointing to the file in the nameservice directory, in this case `/var/named`, where the `named.root` file, which we got from `rs.internic.net` and renamed to `named.ca`, is located. This file contains the root servers for the Internet domains.

- `primary`—Means that this is a `primary nameserver` for this domain. The `primary` lines are:
  - The first `primary` line gives the information about the `localhost`, which is stored in the `named.local` file.
  - The second `primary` line refers to the reverse addressing, or address-to-name resolution provided by `named.rev`.
  - The third `primary` line refers to the forward addressing, or name-to-address resolution provided by `named.hosts`.

The only entry that you should need to change is the last line. All you need to do is replace the entry for `mydomain.com` with the domain that you are working with. Do this now.

a) What is the new line that you entered in place of the last line in `/etc/named.boot`?

____

____

3.2.7 *named.conf*

This file is used in DNS 8.1, and it replaces `/etc/named.boot` in Red Hat 5.2 and other versions of Linux. It functions the same as `named.boot`, but has the ability to add additional functionality. DNS 8.1 fixes some bugs that might have appeared in earlier versions. The Red Hat 5.2 file is shown here:

```
// generated by named-bootconf.pl

options {
 directory "/var/named";
    /*
 * If there is a firewall between you and nameservers
 you want
 * to talk to, you might need to uncomment the query-
 source
 * directive below.  Previous versions of BIND always
 asked
 * questions using port 53, but BIND 8.1 uses an
 unprivileged
 * port by default.
 */
```

```
 // query-source address * port 53;
};

zone "." {
        type hint;
        file "named.ca";
};

zone "0.0.127.in-addr.arpa" {
        type master;
        file "named.local";
};

zone "mydomain.com" {
        type master;
        file "named.hosts";
};

zone "1.16.172.in-addr.arpa" {
        type master;
        file "named.rev";
};
```

You will notice that the files `named.ca`, `named.local`, and `named.hosts` are again pointed to. In this case, a stanza or paragraph-type structure is used instead of each entry being line-based. This gives more flexibility in setting up your nameserver. In this case, you only need to change those lines that refer to `mydomain.com` and replace the values with those for your own domain.

Do the substitutions now.

a) What substitutions did you make in `/etc/named.conf` for your own domain?

3.2.8 Test Your Configuration

Once your configuration is set up, you will need to test it. In order to test it, you should repeat Lab 3.1 and be sure that the values that show up are correct. In addition, you should test for hosts that you have added to `named.hosts` and `named.rev` to be sure that the values are correct.

a) What are the results of testing your configuration?

____

____

LAB 3.2 EXERCISE ANSWERS

3.2.1 ANSWERS

a) What is the domain that you are going to be using in your `/etc/resolv.conf` file?

Answer: In these sample results, we'll use the domain name `yourdomain.com`.

You could use this name or an actual domain name that you are working in.

b) What is the domain that you will do a search on?

Answer: In these sample results, we'll use the domain name `yourdomain.com`.

You could use this name or an actual domain name that you are working in. You can actually search on more than one domain, so you might think about what other domains you want a search to be done on. When a domain is added to the searchlist, then you only need to give the hostname; the software will search for a host in the search list domains until it either finds a match or returns a "not found" message.

c) What is the IP address for the nameserver that currently exists in `/etc/resolv.conf`?

Answer: You need to examine your current `/etc/resolv.conf` *file and see what is there. For our example, we'll use the address 172.16.1.95. Replace this value with your own. Be sure to back up the original file.*

3.2.2 ANSWERS

a) What are the results of getting the file `/domain/named.root` from `ftp.rs.internic.net`?

Answer: You should have received the file without a problem. If you didn't, then you need to reexamine the commands that you used, or verify that you can access the server.

b) Now do an `ls -l /var/named`. Do you see the files `named.ca`, `named,ca.bak`, `named.root`, along with other files?

Answer: Those files should be out there. If not, then reexamine the steps above to be sure that you have copied everything correctly.

3.2.3 ANSWERS

a) What is the actual name that you will enter in the `/var/named/named.local` in place of `myserver.mydomain.com`?

Answer: In the samples here, we will use `yourdomain.com`. *Feel free to use the domain that you have chosen to use.*

b) What is the actual name that you will enter in `/var/named/named.local` in place of `myid.myserver.mydomain.com`?

Answer: Let's use `yourid.yourserver.yourdomain.com`.

c) What is the actual string that you will enter in `/var/named/named.local` in place of `IN NS myserver.mydomain.com`?

Answer: You might use the following:

```
IN  NS  yourserver.yourdomain.com
```

3.2.4 ANSWERS

a) When you created the `named.hosts` file, what is the last line that you entered for your local nameserver?

Answer: Using the sample names from above, the last line should be:

```
yourserver          A          172.16.1.95
```

3.2.5 Answers

a) What is the new line that you created for yourserver in `named.rev`?

Answer: Using the sample names from above, the last line should be:

```
1        PTR      yourserver
```

3.2.6 Answers

a) What is the new line that you entered in place of the last line in `/etc/named.boot`?

Answer: Using the sample names from above, the last line should be:

```
primary  yourdomain.com      named.hosts
```

You should note that if you are using a different network address, then you should also change the following line:

```
primary  1.16.172.in-addr.arpa  named.rev
```

You should replace the entry:

```
1.16.172
```

with the reverse address of your network minus any 0s. This network is 172.16.1.0, so the reversed number is 1.16.172. You should be sure that your network address is properly selected by looking at the `netmask`. In this case, the `netmask` is 255.255.255.0, so the numbers are correct. A netmask of 255.255.0.0 will result in you using a file called `16.172.in-addr.arpa`.

3.2.7 Answers

a) What substitutions did you make in `/etc/named.conf` for your own domain?

Answer: You should replace the following line:

```
zone "mydomain.com" {
```

with the line:

```
zone "yourdomain.com" {
```


You may also need to change the following line:

```
zone "1.16.172.in-addr.arpa" {
```

See the discussion in the answer to Question a in section 3.2.6 for a discussion of the substitution.

3.2.8 ANSWERS

a) What are the results of testing your configuration?

Answer: Your results should agree with all the data in the files. You will need to review the files to verify this.

LAB 3.2 SELF-REVIEW QUESTIONS

In order to test your progress, you should be able to answer the following questions.

1) The caching nameserver does not depend on getting information from other nameservers.

a) _____True
b) _____False

2) The *A* record type will take a name and return which of the following?

a) _____nameserver
b) _____default route
c) _____address
d) _____domain name
e) _____reverse address

3) The NS record type will have the address of which of the following?

a) _____nameserver
b) _____default route
c) _____address
d) _____domain name
e) _____reverse address

4) The file `/etc/resolv.conf` will contain the location of which of the following?

a) _____nameserver
b) _____default route
c) _____`named.hosts` file
d) _____`named.ca`
e) _____host's file

The `named.hosts` file looks like the following:

```
@ IN SOA myserver.mydomain.com. root.myserver.mydomain.com. (
            1989020503     ;serial
            10800          ;refresh
            3600           ;retry
            3600000        ;expire
            86400 )        ;minimum

            NS        myserver.mydomain.com.

localhost             A          127.0.0.1
myserver              A          172.16.1.1
```

Use this file to answer the following four questions:

5) What is the start of authority in the `named.hosts`?

a) _____`myserver.mydomain.com`
b) _____`localhost`
c) _____`myserver`
d) _____`tux`
e) _____None of the above

6) It is possible to find an IP address for a name by querying which of the following?

a) _____primary nameserver
b) _____secondary nameserver
c) _____caching nameserver
d) _____all of the above
e) _____none of the above

7) The nameserver is `myserver.mydomain.com.`

a) _____True
b) _____False

The `named.rev` file on network 172.16.1.0 looks like the following:

```
@ IN SOA myserver.mydomain.com. root.myserver.mydomain.com. (
        1989020503    ;serial
        10800         ;refresh
        3600          ;retry
        3600000       ;expire
        86400 )       ;minimum

        NS      myserver1.mydomain.com.

15       PTR       route1
19       PTR       nextone
35       PTR       bigone
```


8) Given the address 172.16.1.19, what is the actual fully qualified name of the host?

a) _____bigone
b) _____bigone.mydomain.com
c) _____nextone
d) _____nextone.mydomain.com
e) _____route1

9) What is the next domain nameserver?

a) _____route1
b) _____myserver1.mydomain.com
c) _____route1.mydomain.com
d) _____nextone.mydomain.com
e) _____bigone

Quiz answers appear in Appendix A, Section 3.2.

CHAPTER 3

TEST YOUR THINKING

1) You are to design and build a primary nameserver:

Figure out the following characteristics for your domain:

a) Use the domain name of your local domain unless you are on an insolated network, in which case you can make up any name.

b) Find a valid nameserver name and IP address in your real domain that you can use. If you are on an isolated network, then just make up an address.

c) Find a userid to be used as the contact for your domain.

d) Find the names and IP addresses of your local host and several hosts on your network. If you have no others hosts, then make up some names.

2) Create or modify the following files:

a) `/etc/resolv.conf`

b) `named.hosts`

c) `named.rev`

d) `named.ca`

e) `named.local`

f) `/etc/named.boot`

g) `/etc/named.conf` if needed.

Test the nameserver with the names in your `named.hosts` file

Test the nameserver with the IP addresses in `named.rev` by using the `nslookup` option `set querytype = A`:

3) You are to design and build a primary nameserver using the criteria in Project 1 of this section. Test it as described in Project 1.

4) You are to design and build a caching nameserver. You will not need the `named.hosts and named.rev` files. Test it as described in Project 1.

CHAPTER 4

SHARING DATA IN A WINDOWS WORLD

The gentleman gestured to the lady to dance
The Samba they'd do at every chance.
He suddenly realized few words did they know
Though languages differ, 'round the floor they would go.

—Joe

CHAPTER OBJECTIVES

In this chapter, you will learn about:

Exercises for the Masses

✔ Determine Your Current Windows Network Configuration — Page 125

Exercises for the Great and Super User

✔ Getting Samba — Page 143

✔ Getting Samba Running — Page 160

Because there are many PCs that run Microsoft Windows, it is important to be able to share data with your Linux systems. There are a number of ways of sharing data. You can buy add-on packages for the PC that include the Network Files System from Sun Microsystems. There are also packages that allow you to use the IPX protocol used by Novell servers. However, Windows has built-in networking that uses SMB (Server Message Blocks). As a result, a package called Samba has been developed to allow you to share data between Linux and UNIX systems, as well as with Microsoft-based PCs. Some of the more advanced features of sharing data and NT network administration from UNIX are being developed for Samba, so you want to keep in touch with the advances. To do all the exercises in this chapter fully, you will need a Windows 95/98/2000 or NT PC and a PC running Linux with at least Samba 2.03 installed. This chapter will focus on using a Windows 95 PC to connect to your Samba server. If you do not have at least Samba 2.03 installed, you should get it from `http://www.Samba.org`.

LAB 4.1

DETERMINE YOUR CURRENT WINDOWS NETWORK CONFIGURATION

LAB OBJECTIVES

After this Lab, you will be able to:

- Determine Your Current Windows Network Configuration
- Set up and Log into Your PC as a Windows Network User
- Verify your Windows Network Environment

Look in the man pages for the following: `Samba`, `smbd`, `smb.conf`, `smb`

THE WINDOWS REALM

The Windows SMB-based network is based on the basic premise that all systems on the network are relative equals. This allows you to set up a network at home with only two PCs with ethernet cards and perhaps an ethernet hub. This lowers the cost of network computing considerably. However, SMB network packets are not routable in the traditional sense.

They cannot be sent over the Internet without being enclosed in TCP/IP packets. This also gives a certain amount of security to your network if it is SMB-based, since the SMB packets stay on your network and don't go out to the Internet.

There are three ways to categorize an SMB-based network:

- *Peer to peer*—This is where all PCs can be either a client, server, or both at the same time.
- *Workgroups*—This extends the concept of peer-to-peer networks, whereby the network is broken up into groups that have the same group name and can share resources. Every PC on the network needs to keep track of the login ids locally and passwords for each account.
- *Domains*—A domain has a central authority called the *domain controller* that keeps track of login rights, passwords, and various user account information. There can be primary and secondary domain controllers.

There are many excellent discussions of SMB-based networking and many authors far more knowledgeable of the topic than this one. You should pick up one of these books if you are interested in delving into the depths of MS networking. This book will help you modify your computer to talk the language of SMB and to share files.

LAB 4.1 EXERCISES

4.1.1 DETERMINE YOUR CURRENT WINDOWS NETWORK CONFIGURATION

Your MS Windows-based computer should already be set up to do Windows networking and TCP/IP. You will be determining your current features and modifying them to match the Samba defaults. You should follow the standard Windows directions and setup procedures to establish your MS Windows network initially.

In this Exercise, we will determine the current SMB characteristics of your PC. This will be done in Windows 95. If you are running Windows 98, Windows 2000, or NT, you may have to make some adjustments to the steps that follow.

You need to log in to your Windows PC and get to the main screen. You should see a screen similar to the one shown in Figure 4.1.

Click on the `Start` button to view the `Start` menu options.

From here, you need to choose an appropriate menu option to find the system settings.

a) What choice did you make to find the system settings?

____

____

Now make your choice from the `Settings` menu.

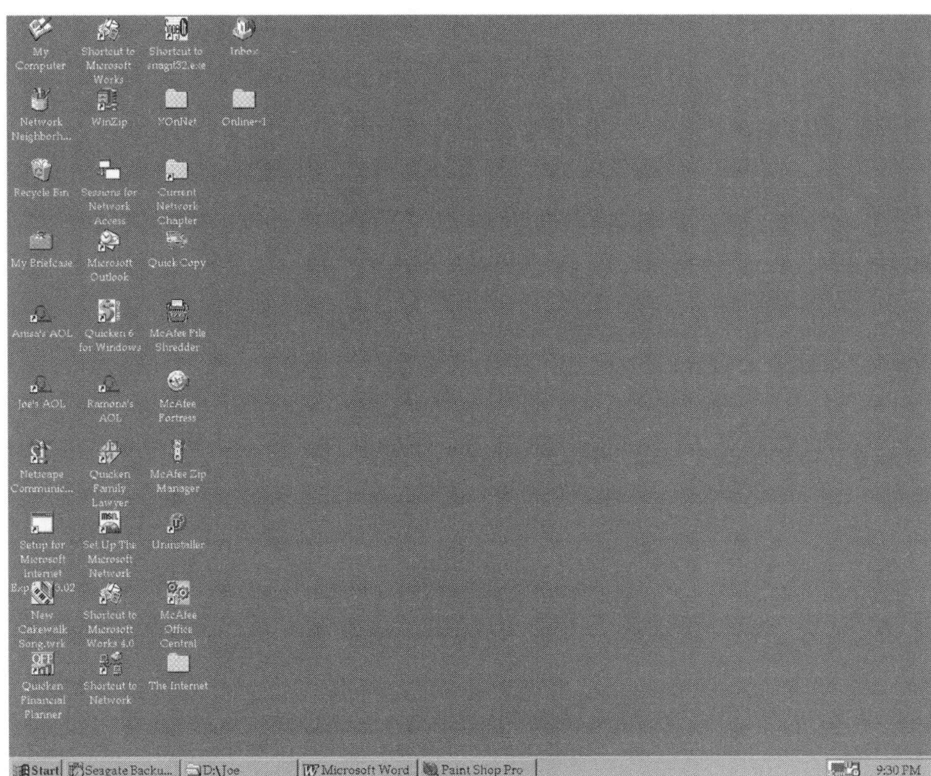

Figure 4.1 ■ A Sample Windows Main Screen

b) What choice did you make from the `Settings` menu?

Click on the `Control Panel` option.

c) What happens when you click on the `Control Panel` menu option?

At this point, you will see the `Control Panel`. This is an important window that allows you to modify most of the hardware and software settings on your system. To set up Samba, double-click on the `Network` icon to open the `Network` dialog box.

The left mouse button is generally used for selecting items and opening/closing windows. The right mouse button often offers various shortcuts associated with the selected item. Generally you are required to double-click on an item with the left mouse button, unless told otherwise.

d) When you click on the `Network` icon in the Control Panel, do you see the `Client for Microsoft Networks` enabled?

You should see the `Client for Microsoft Networks`. If you don't see it, you will need to install it. Consult your Windows documentation if you are not familiar with this. You should also see `File and printer sharing for Microsoft`.

Once `File and Printer Sharing` capability is installed, you will need to enable and verify it by clicking on the `File and Print Sharing` button.

e) When you click on the `File and Printer Sharing` button, do you see `File and Print Sharing` enabled?

If both boxes in the `File and Print Sharing` dialog box are not checked off, you should do it now. Even if you do not have a directly attached printer, you can still enable access to printing from your Windows PC.

Now click on the `OK` button. This will take you back to the `Network Identification Display`. Now you should select the middle tab labeled `Identification`.

f) What happens when you click on the `OK` button?

Next, click the middle tab, `Identification`, in the `Network` dialog box.

g) What is the *Computer Name* shown in the `Network Identification Display`?

---

h) What is the *Workgroup* shown in this panel?

---

i) What is the *Computer Description* shown in this panel?

Note that in this Exercise, you will be changing the Workgroup name. This may also affect any domain and network settings you have. Be sure that you have documented any changes you have made to your system.

In the `Network Identification Display`, you can now change the *Workgroup* setting to match the one that is used by Samba. Samba initially uses the *Workgroup* called `MYGROUP`. Once you are done with the changes, you can click on the `OK` button. Once you have succeeded at SMB networking with Linux, you can choose any workgroup name.

j) What happens when you change the *Workgroup* setting to `MYGROUP` and click on the `OK` button?

____

____

After you click on the `OK` button, you will need to return to the `Network` dialog in the Control Panel.

Next, select the tab labeled `Access Control`.

When you select the tab for the `Access Control`, you have two choices to control access to shared resources. The two choices are:

- Share-level access control
- User-level access control

For the purposes of this Exercise, choose `Share-level access control`.

k) What are the current values that your system has set for the window displayed in the `Access Control` window?

____

____

Both `Share-level access control` *and* `User-level access control` *can be used with Samba. Because* `User-level access control` *works best with a domain controller, which is usually an NT server, it will be ignored for this discussion. You should feel free to establish and test the other possibilities and see what changes need to be made to Samba. You should note that the term* user-level *is confusing*

because Samba defines user-based access as access based on userid and password where the Login ID, password and workgroup are the same between 2 or more systems in the same workgroup.

Now you should click on the `OK` button. When you do this, you may be prompted to insert your Windows 95 CD-ROM. You should have this ready to insert if necessary.

l) When you click the `OK` button, what happens? Follow the series of prompts you get.

____

____

You need to reboot your PC in order for the changes to take effect. Reboot your PC now.

m) Do you get any errors when you reboot your PC? If so, how would you explain them?

____

____

4.1.2 SET UP AND LOG INTO YOUR PC AS A WINDOWS NETWORK USER

Once you have rebooted you Windows PC, you will need to make sure that your user login environment is set up properly. Every user on a PC that has MS Windows networking installed will need to have an id created. If you already have an id that has the same name and password as on your Linux box, you can ignore this discussion except for your own learning purposes. Otherwise, you will need to create an id and password that is the same as the one on the Linux box using the following steps.

When your PC first comes back up, you should be prompted with a window that has a box with the heading `Enter Network password`. There should also be the prompts `User name` and `Password`. If you already have a user name and password, then just enter them at this time.

If you want to establish a new user name and password, then just put in any name and any password that you want. If this is a new user name, then you will be prompted for the password a second time to verify your entry.

This user name does not have to exist, nor does a password need to be assigned to it anywhere. In fact, if you don't assign a user name and password to an id on the first bootup, it can bypass the login message altogether for future reboots.

If you are running Windows NT or are in a Windows NT domain and need to use the NT verification for your logins, you may need to have an id and password setup that is recognized by the NT domain. You may also need to have a regular domain setup called `MYGROUP` *to run these exercises. You may first want to check with your NT administrator. On some sites, unauthorized domains can upset the network administrator. However, the NT administrator may even want to help you. If you show the administrator that NT networking can be more stable—and even administered remotely without a special software package—by running Samba on Linux, he may be very grateful. After all, if the NT network is unstable, the administrator may look forward to something like Samba that will keep running without needing him to spend weekends in the office.*

If everything is okay so far, you should do the exercises as they are called for here in the text. But you may need to do some NT domain cleanup later. The objective of these exercises is to be as simple as possible, but they may not be ideal in your environment. Further details about NT network administration are beyond this text, but many good books are available.

Choose an id that is the same one you will use on your Linux box. You may want to write down the password because it is important that the passwords be in sync for these exercises. If you are reluctant about doing this with your regular id, you should create a special id that you can use on both the Windows and Linux boxes.

a) What is the id that you chose to use for logging into both your Linux box and your Windows box?

---

b) What is the password that you will be using for your test account? (Note that you don't need to write this down if you are concerned about someone else using your account.)

Now enter the id and password, then log in.

c) If you get any errors, how would you handle them?

Now you should be logged into your Windows PC with the id that you will be using for testing.

4.1.3 Verify Your Windows Network Environment

Now you need to verify that your Windows network is functioning properly. To do this, you need to go to the `Network Neighborhood` icon that is on your screen, which you can see in Figure 4.1.

You will notice that the icon for `Network Neighborhood` is highlighted in the upper-left corner. If you do not see the `Network Neighborhood` icon, it means that you did not properly set up or install the Windows network software.

a) Do you see a `Network Neighborhood` icon on your screen? If not, what should you do?

Double-click on the icon. You should see a display of the hosts on your network neighborhood.

b) What are the various kinds of things that you see when you click on the `Network Neighborhood` icon?

This does not show what the real name of your Windows Workgroup really is, so you need to do one more step. You should now click on the `Entire Network` icon that is on the first line of the display.

The Whole Truth

Note that Windows takes the group you called `MYGROUP` and calls it `Mygroup`. The difference is that Windows takes all characters after the first and makes them appear as lowercase. While UNIX and Linux are case-sensitive, this change only affects the display in Windows. If you are concerned about the display, you should just revisit the earlier steps you used to create the network and be sure that everything is proper. As long as everything is consistent, you should not be concerned.

c) When you click on the `Entire Network` icon, do you see the `Mygroup` icon? What should you do if you do not see the `Mygroup` icon in the `Entire Network` Window?

____

____

If you have successfully reached this point, then you have set up your Windows network with the `MYGROUP` workgroup. Now you will learn how to set up your Linux server to run the SMB services as part of Samba.

LAB 4.1 EXERCISE ANSWERS

4.1.1 ANSWERS

a) What choice did you make to find the system settings?

Answer: You should see a pop-up menu similar to the one that you see in Figure 4.2.

If you don't see the menu in Figure 4.2, then be sure you have pressed the left button on the mouse with the pointer over the `Start` button in the lower-left corner of your screen.

b) What choice did you make from the `Settings` menu?

Answer: You should see the pop-up menu that you see in Figure 4.3.

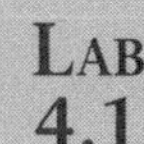

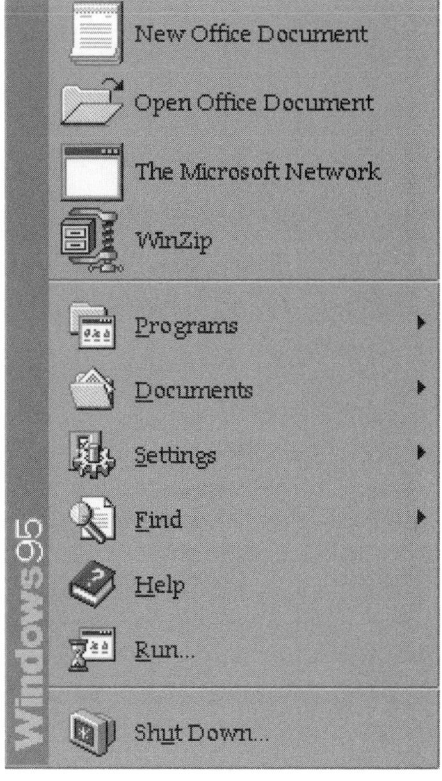

Figure 4.2 ■ Windows `Start` Menu

This is a menu that rarely changes, so if you see any differences, try to figure out why. Users do not generally have access to or have need to change this menu. Sometimes add-on software packages will add additional entries to this menu. If it is very different, you may have clicked on the wrong menu item. You may notice some difference in Windows 98, NT, or 2000.

c) What happens when you click on the Control Panel menu option?

Answer: You should see the Control Panel pop-up window that you see in Figure 4.4.

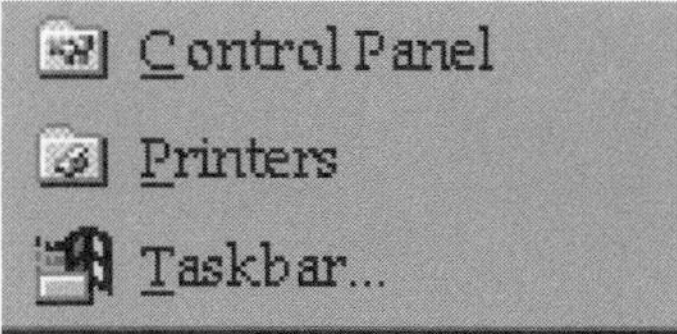

Figure 4.3 ■ Windows `Settings` Menu

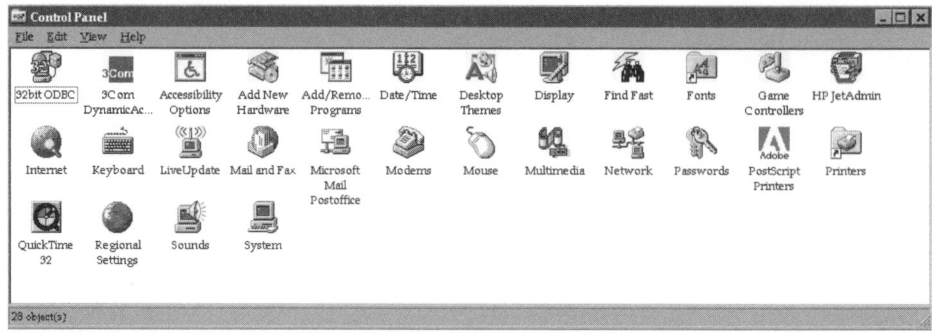

Figure 4.4 ■ Control Panel

If you don't see a similar window, then be sure you have chosen the correct menu option.

d) When you click on the `Network` icon in the Control Panel, do you see the `Client for Microsoft Networks` enabled?

Answer: You should see the windows that are displayed in Figures 4.5 and 4.6.

Since Figure 4.5 does not show the entire network configuration, you will also need to examine the display in Figure 4.6 by scrolling down in the window.

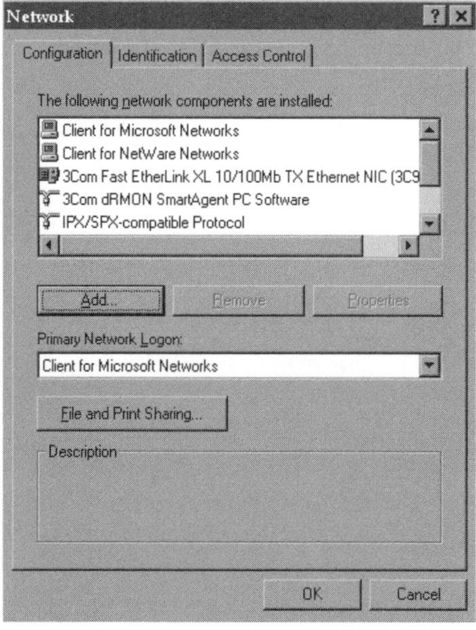

Figure 4.5 ■ `Network Configuration` Display

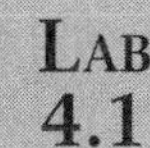

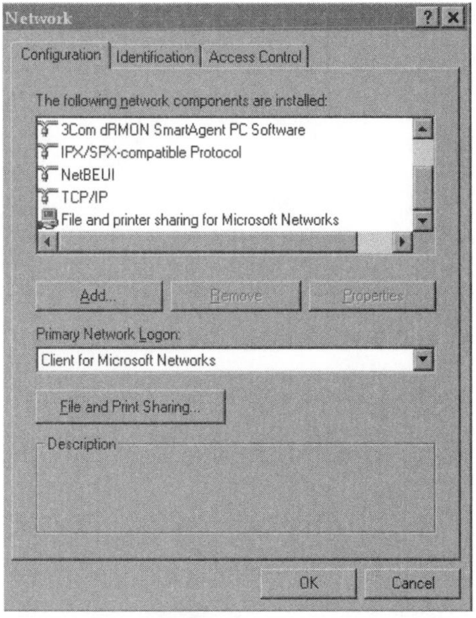

Figure 4.6 ■ More of the `Network Configuration` Display

Answer: If you do not see the Microsoft `Networking` *enabled, then you will need to consult your Windows documentation or have it installed. You also need to enable* `File and Print Sharing`.

e) When you click on the `File and Printer Sharing` button, do you see `File and Print Sharing` enabled?

Answer: You should see the window shown in Figure 4.7.

f) What happens when click on the `OK` button?

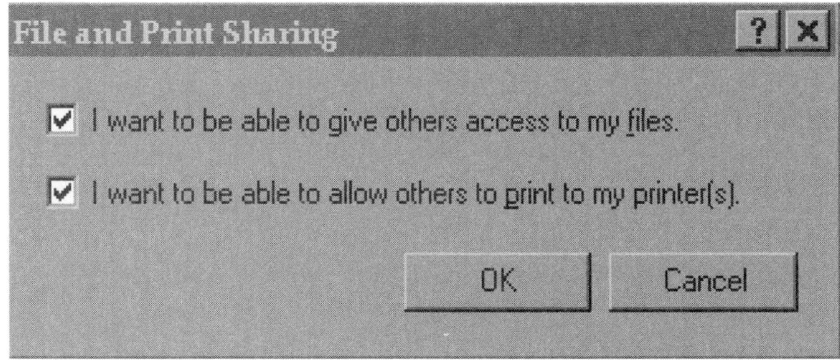

Figure 4.7 ■ `File and Print Sharing` Window

Answer: You should not see any messages or prompts. You should just return to the window shown in Figures 4.5 and 4.6. You should be returned to the `Network Identification` *display screen.*

g) What is the *Computer Name* shown in the `Identification` display?

Answer: Whatever name showed up should be okay as long as it is unique on your network or the workgroup called `MYGROUP`*. This will show up in Figure 4.8.*

You should write down the name so you can restore it later if it should get changed.

h) What is the *Workgroup* shown in this panel?

Answer: It is important that you keep track of the Workgroup *name because you will be changing it.*

i) What is the *Computer Description* shown in this panel?

Answer: The Computer Description *is not critical and only serves to identify your system on the network with a little more detail.*

j) What happens when you change the *Workgroup* setting to `MYGROUP` and click on the `OK` button?

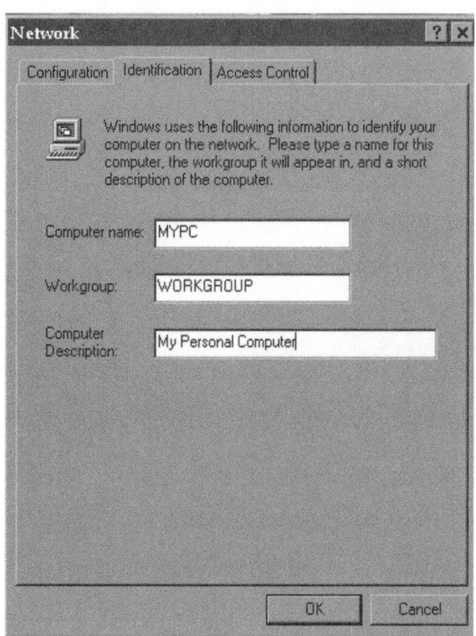

Figure 4.8 ■ `Network Identification` Display

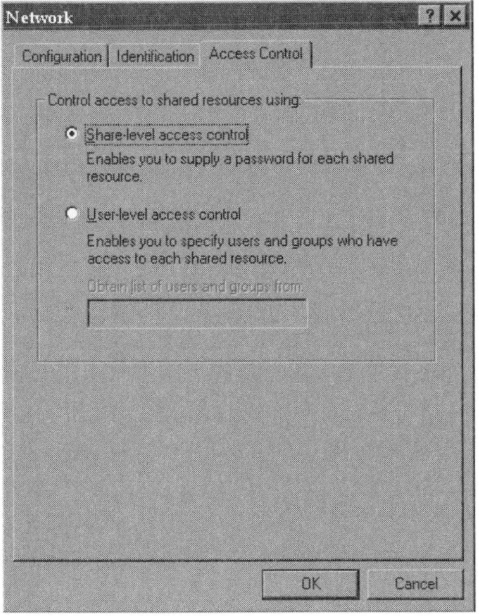

Figure 4.9 ■ `Network Access Control` Display

Answer: Just changing the name and clicking on the `OK` *button will not have any impact on the system. You will need to reboot in order for the Workgroup to take effect. The system will generally ask you if you want to reboot.*

k) What are the current values that your system has set for the window displayed in the Access Control window (Figure 4.9)?

Answer: Whatever the values are, just make the appropriate changes and keep track of what the original values were.

l) When you click on the `OK` button, what happens? Follow the series of prompts you get.

Answer: The system will prompt you with a message that you need to reboot. You should reboot your PC in order for the changes to take effect.

m) Do you get any errors when you reboot your PC? If so, how would you explain them?

Answer: You may get an error about not being able to access resources that formerly you were able to access. This may be due to using an NT server to track id information on your network for your previous Workgroup or NT domain. If you keep track of what the previous settings were, you should be able to return your PC back to its original state by resetting the values once you are finished doing these Lab Exercises.

4.1.2 Answers

a) What is the id that you chose to use for logging into both your Linux box and your Windows box?

Answer: You need to choose an id that you will be using for both Linux and Windows.

b) What is the password that you will be using for your test account? (Note that you don't need to write this down if you are concerned about someone else using your account.)

Answer: The password will be the same password that you will be using on the Linux box.

c) If you get any errors, how would you handle them?

Answer: After entering the id and password information, you should be logged into the Windows box. If you get any error messages, you will need to review them before you continue.

You should try to resolve any errors based on earlier discussions in setting up the Windows network. You should review your steps and make sure that things are set up properly. If you are still lost, you should seek your instructor, your Windows or Network Administrator, or one of the many books on Windows networking.

4.1.3 Answers

a) Do you see a `Network Neighborhood` icon on your screen? If not, what should you do?

Answer: If you do not see a `Network Neighborhood` *icon on your screen, it probably means that either your Windows software did not properly load the networking drivers or somehow the Windows software is not functioning right. If you have this problem, then you should revisit the steps you took in setting up the Windows* `Network` *software so that you are sure everything is properly loaded.*

b) What are the various kinds of things that you see when you click on the `Network Neighborhood` icon?

Answer: You should see a display similar to Figure 4.10 where the systems that are in `MYGROUP` *show up along with a display for the* `Entire Network`*. In the example here in the text, there is also information for the* `HP_Network_Printers` *on the local network. Your network may not yet show anything but the name of your PC that you are working on. If you do not see any hosts, it probably means that there are no*

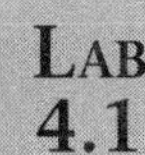

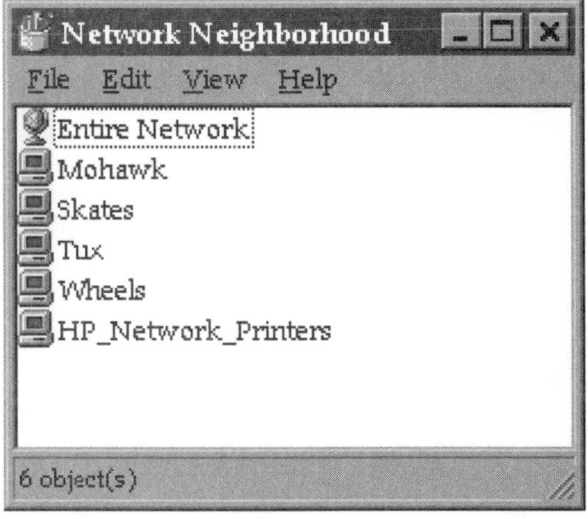

Figure 4.10 ■ The `Network Neighborhood` Window

Windows `Network` hosts on your network. You can revisit this once you set up your Linux box to do the Samba networking.

c) When you click on the `Entire Network` icon, do you see the `Mygroup` icon? What should you do if you do not see the `Mygroup` icon in the `Entire Network` Window?

Answer: You should see the `Mygroup` icon as shown in Figure 4.11. If you do not see it, then look at what you do see. If there is a name such as Workgroup, *it may mean that your Windows `Network` changes did not properly take effect. You will need to check and perhaps redo those steps. If you do not see any name, then it means that your drivers may not have loaded properly. In both cases, you will probably need to reboot. If this doesn't work, then you need to go to the Windows Control Panel and reexamine the `Network` characteristics.*

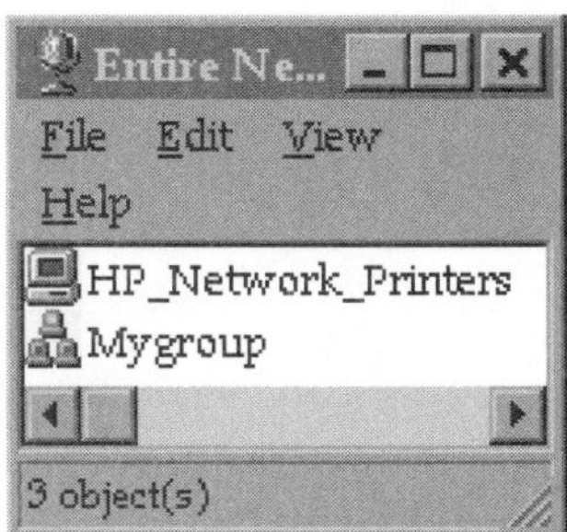

Figure 4.11 ■ The `Entire Network` Window

LAB 4.1 SELF-REVIEW QUESTIONS

In order to test your progress, you should be able to answer the following questions.

1) In Figures 4.5 and 4.6, which line entry in the `Network Configuration` display is the most important to get Samba connectivity from your MS Windows PC, assuming TCP/IP is working?

a) _____`Client for Microsoft Networks`
b) _____`Client for NetWare Networks`
c) _____`IPX/SPX-compatible Protocol`
d) _____`File and printer sharing for Microsoft Networks`
e) _____None of the above

2) An NT server is required on your network to run Samba.

a) _____True
b) _____False

3) Samba requires a unique *Workgroup* with no MS Windows PCs on it.

a) _____True
b) _____False

4) Samba requires a Windows Domain.

a) _____True
b) _____False

Quiz answers appear in Appendix A, Section 4.1.

LAB 4.2

GETTING SAMBA

LAB OBJECTIVES

After this Lab, you will be able to:

- Get the Latest Samba

GETTING SAMBA

Samba is included by default with most packaged versions of Linux today. It is a public domain software package that is free of any royalties and follows the standard GNU licensing policies for making it publicly available. GNU stands for "GNU's Not UNIX." It is a set of tools and licensing policies for public domain software. It is also available for other versions of UNIX such as AIX, HP-UX, Solaris, and others. It has been ported to other hardware architectures and operating systems.

The Whole Truth

The version of Samba that is included with Red Hat 5.2 and some other versions of Linux requires some configuration and knowledge of Windows Networking. The version number will be less than 2.0. However, Version 2.03 of Samba can be installed with a default set of values that are sufficient to get Samba running without any configuration. If you do not have version 2.03 or later, you can get it at `http://www.Samba.org`. Just download the version of Samba for your system or version of Linux. You should use the recommended installation procedures for your version of Linux, which is using the RPM for Red Hat. This Lab will help step you through getting Samba and installing software using the RPM method.

Because this book is aimed at getting you up and running, we will only talk about getting Samba with the defaults running. In addition, any network configuration will be done on the Windows PC side to match the Samba defaults. When you feel ready to tackle more detailed configuration issues, there are several excellent books on Samba, as well as much online documentation that you can use.

Lab 4.2 Exercises

4.2.1 Get the Latest Samba

It is important that we all start this discussion at the same level. Because the industry moves very quickly, the discussion is based on a particular version of Samba. When you read this discussion, you will probably have a much later version. The version we will use for discussion is version 2.03. The one you are using is probably just as compatible with this discussion. Fortunately, you can often find older versions on the Internet for compatibility and historical reasons. If you have problems with your version of Samba, you may want to go back to the version we are working with.

This discussion will show you how to download Samba. For some of you, this may be your first experience at updating your software, so this should turn out to be a great experience. We will discuss using Netscape to do your download. You may use other means of downloading the files to your PC, such as FTP or Internet Explorer, or you can install them from a CD.

In order to connect to the Samba site for purposes of this Exercise, you need to have Netscape installed. Fortunately, this is typically included with packaged versions of Linux. If you do not have Netscape with your Linux, then you will need to install it from the Netscape site, your Linux CD-ROM, or you need to purchase it from Netscape. A discussion of installing Netscape is beyond the scope of this book.

When you first log in to your Linux box, you will see a window similar to Figure 4.12. You should note that this is an actual X-windows login from a remote MS Windows 95 PC. This screen shows the standard command-line prompt for Linux.

To connect to the Samba site, you will now need to execute the `netscape` command.

a) What happens when you type the `netscape` command? If you get errors, how should you handle them?

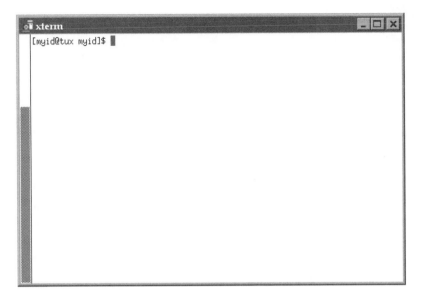

Figure 4.12 ■ Command-line Screen for Linux

You will get the default home page for Netscape. From here you should go to the location `http://www.samba.org`. This is shown in Figure 4.13.

From this screen you should choose the site to connect to.

b) What is the Samba site that you chose to connect to?

---

c) Did you have any problems connecting to the Samba site? If so, how did you get around them?

In Figure 4.14, you see a listing of various news items related to Samba. You may want to read the news items about Samba. From here, you will want to move on to the download screen. The download screen is shown in Figure 4.15.

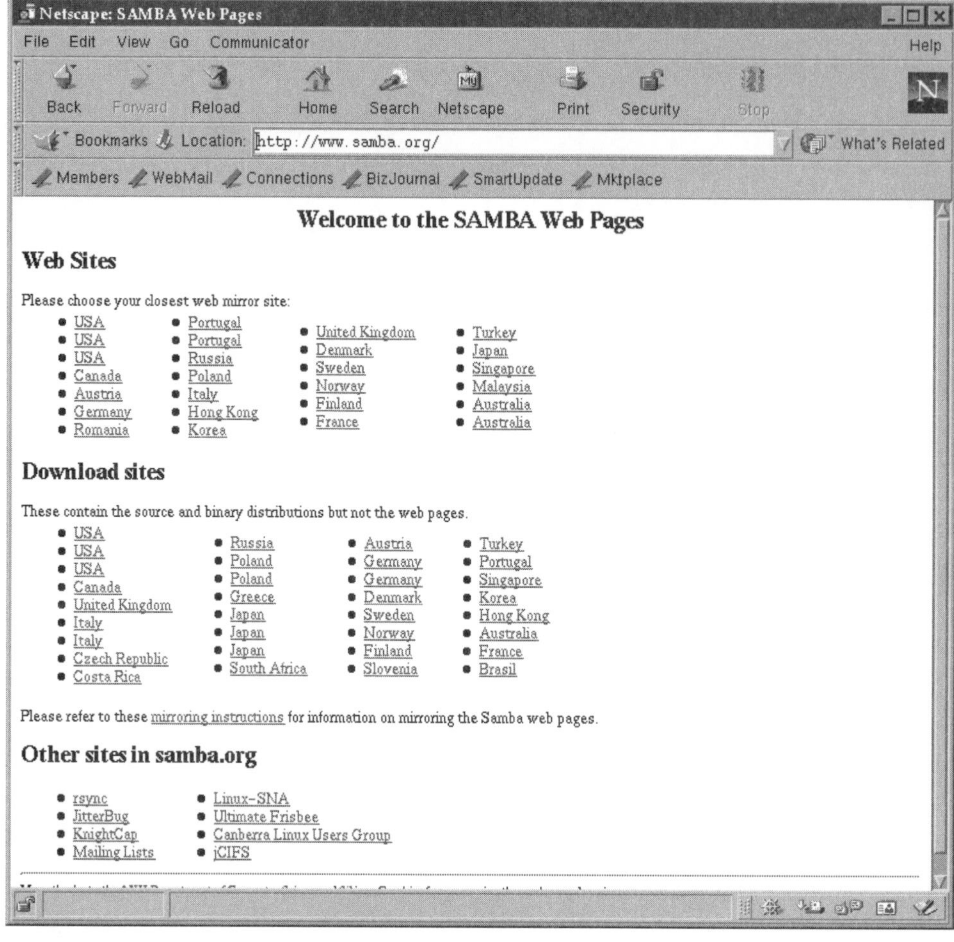

Figure 4.13 ■ The Samba Home Page

d) What choice did you make to get to the download page?

____

____

In Figure 4.15, you see that there are various choices for doing downloads. You can choose binary downloads for a number of various operating systems as well as choose source code for the versions of Samba. In this Exercise, we will choose a binary download for Linux. But if you are running other operating systems, you will want to explore and try the other versions once you get Samba running on your Linux box.

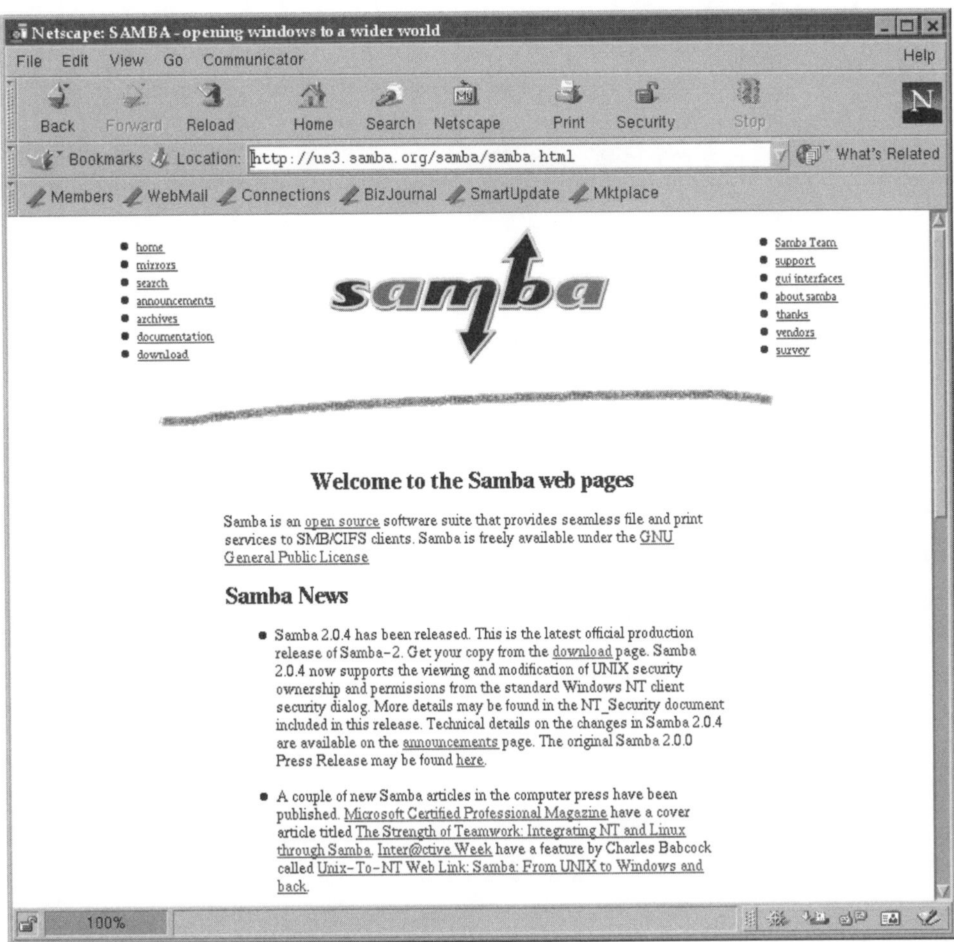

Figure 4.14 ■ Samba Web Page

You should now choose the binary download for Samba.

> **e)** What did you choose to get to the binary download page for Samba?
>
> ____
>
> ____

In Figure 4.16, you see that there are a number of binaries that are available. You will need to choose the version that is designed for your version of Linux. In this case, the example will show the download process for Red Hat Linux. There are several versions that will work with Red Hat, but this one is chosen

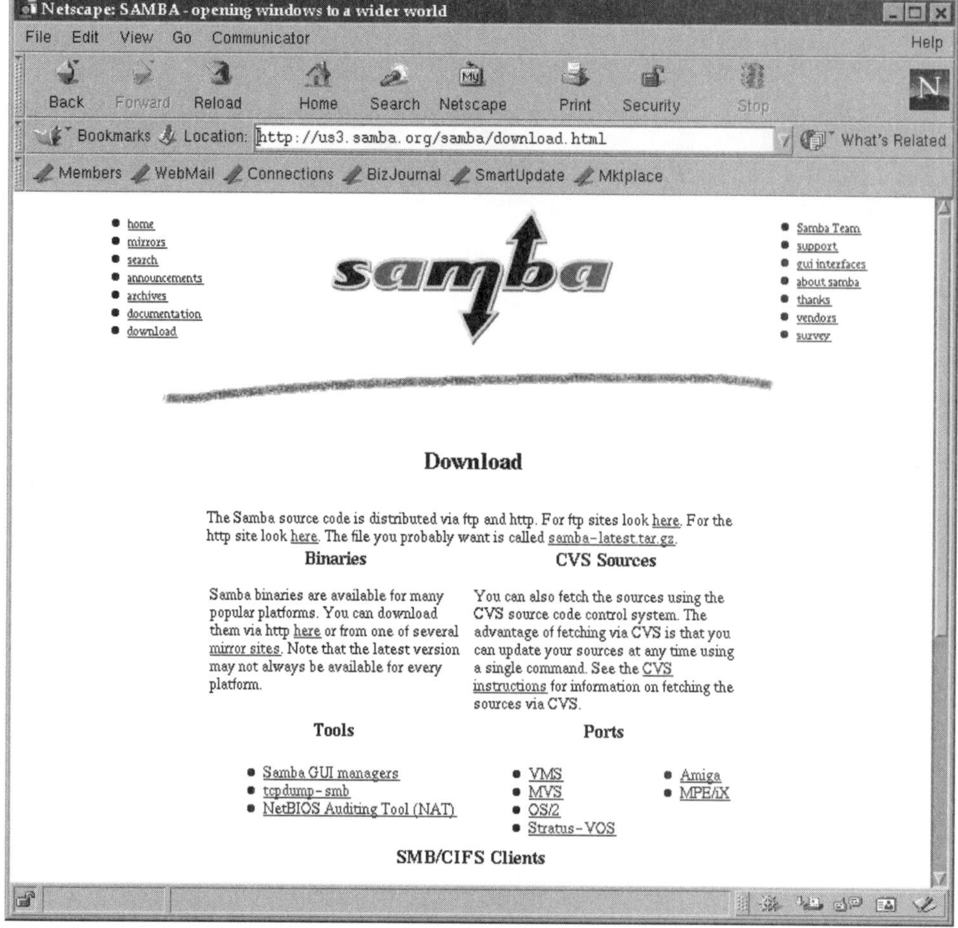

Figure 4.15 ■ Samba Download Page

because it uses the RPM method of installation. The RPM method greatly simplifies the install and update process and should be used whenever possible.

You should now choose the Samba appropriate to your version of Linux.

f) What is the operating system version that you chose?

___

___

You will see the directory for Red Hat in Figure 4.17. You will notice that there are a number of subdirectories for Red Hat. This includes files that are `README` files. These files will give you information about downloading,

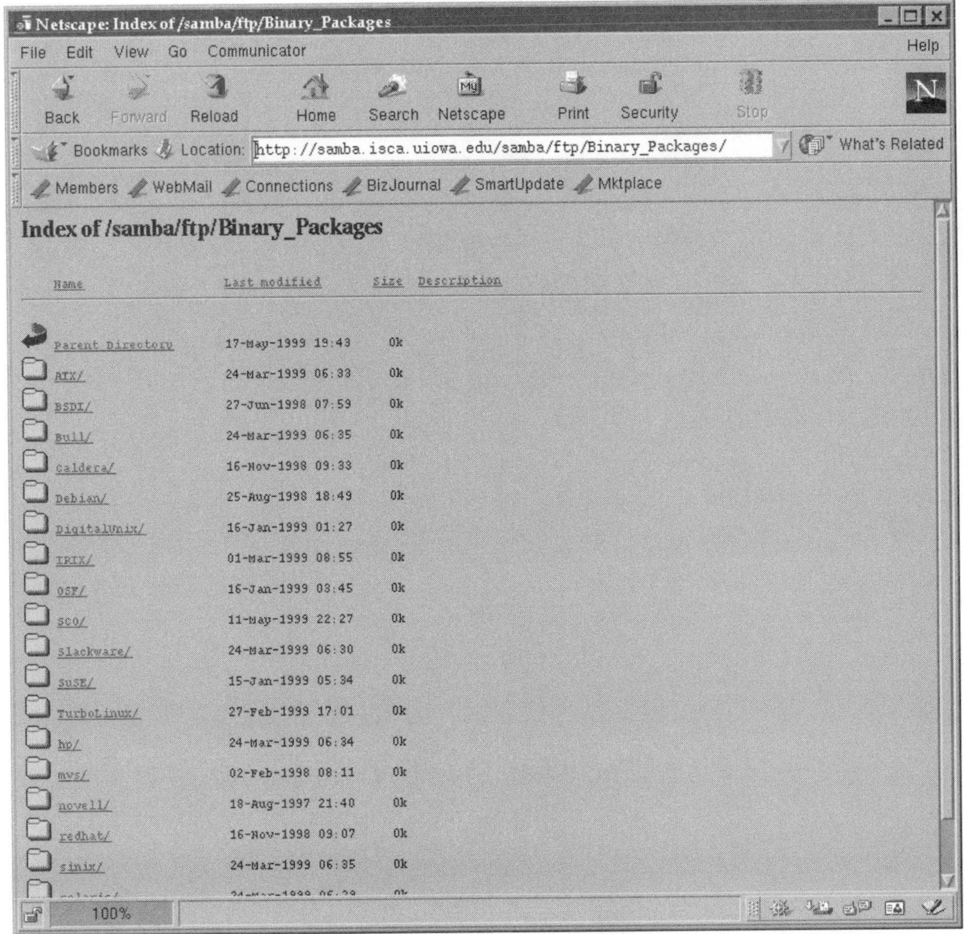

Figure 4.16 ■ FTP Screen for Selecting the Samba Version

installation, and other issues related to installing the software in this directory and possibly in subdirectories. There are two major directories here.

The SRPMS directory has files that will be useful if you want to develop installation packages for Red Hat versions of Samba, or if you have problems installing Samba and want to explore the reasons why.

The RPMS directory will have the files that you need to do a standard install or upgrade of Samba on your system.

You should now choose the RPMS directory.

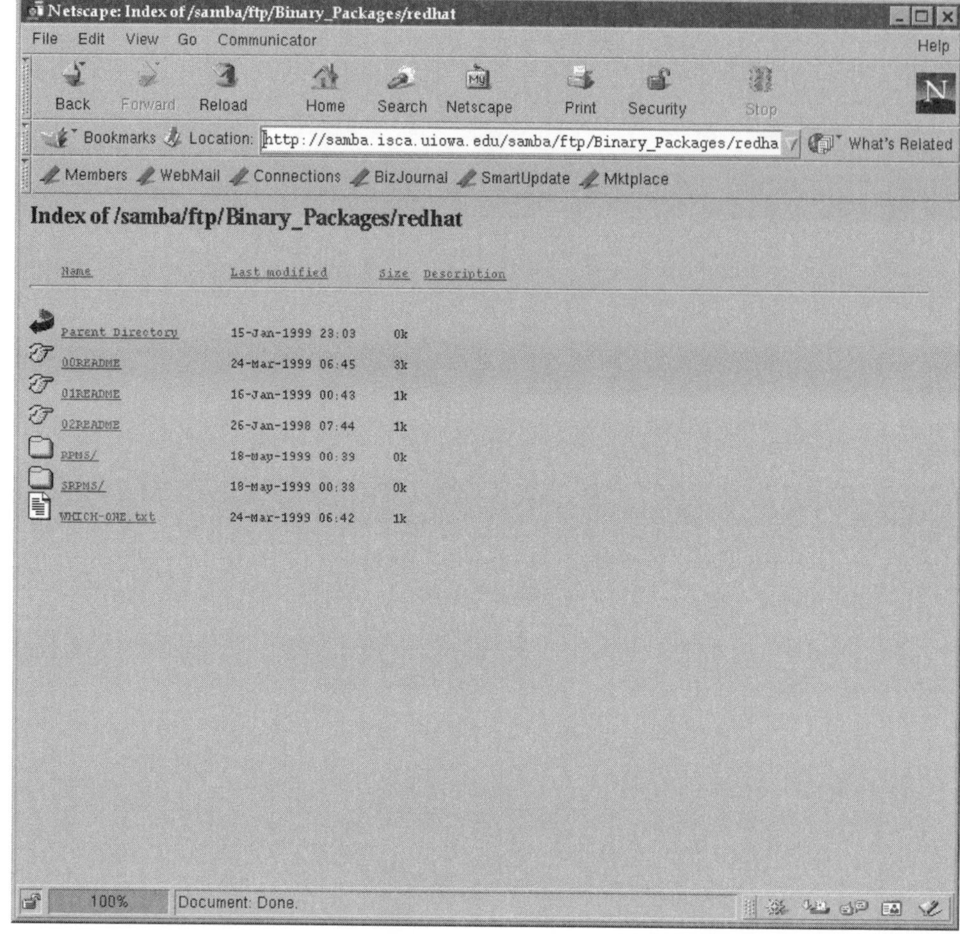

Figure 4.17 ■ Red Hat Directory for Samba Download

g) How is the RPMS directory organized?

____

____

Select the directory for your version of Red Hat or other version of Linux.

h) What screen do you see when you select the directory for your version of Linux?

____

____

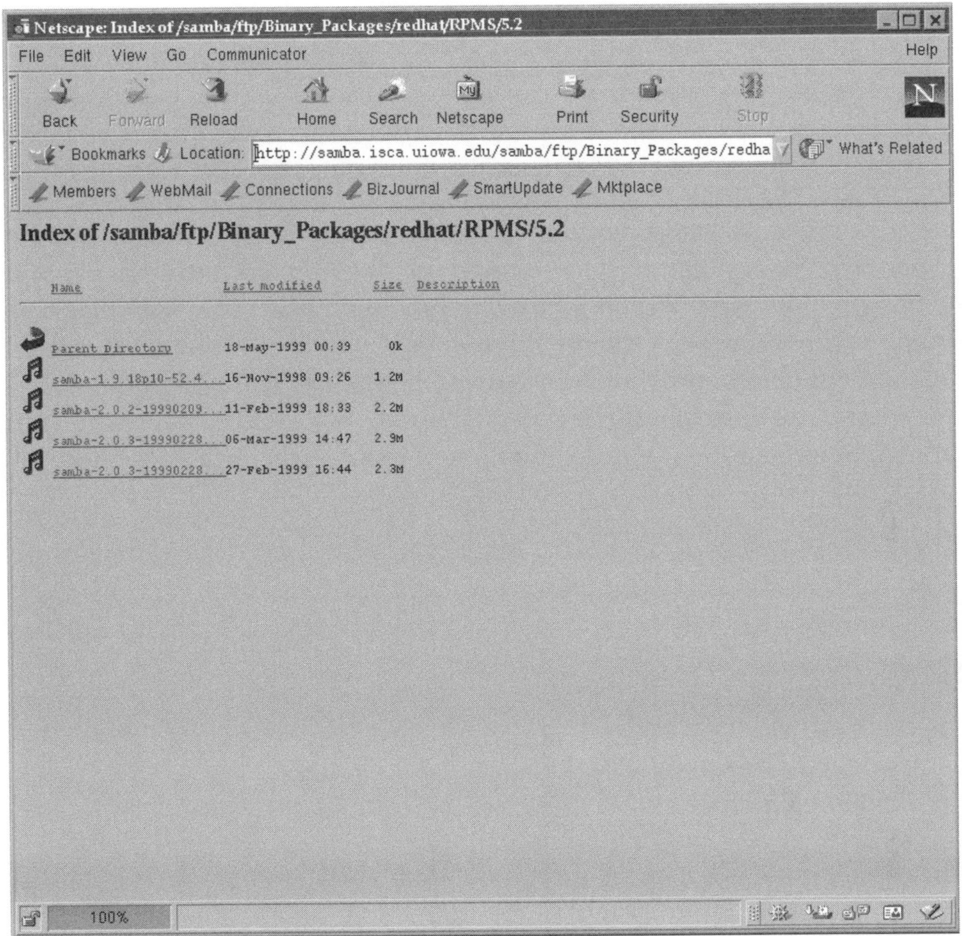

Figure 4.18 ■ Versions of Samba for Red Hat 5.2

At this point, we have reached the bottom of the directory tree. You will see in Figure 4.18 that there are four versions of Samba that you can choose. Notice that the names include Samba and a series of numbers and letters. Let's examine one of these choices.

Let's choose the name `samba-2.0.3-19990228.i386.rpm` for discussion purposes. If you examine this name, you will see that the name of the program being installed is `Samba`. The next item `2.03` is the version number. The additional numbers, `19990228`, reflect the date of the revision. There are two files with this name. If you examine this name further, you will see that one version is for the alpha processor and the other is for the Intel x86 processor. Also note that the first entry uses a slightly different numbering scheme. This is because the version numbering scheme was changed to reflect the version dates rather than a more obscure numbering scheme. All versions will have the same date if they come from the same source code. This occurs even if they are compiled for different processors. If you look at Figure 4.19, you will see that the full version name is `Samba-2.0.3-19990228.i386.rpm`.

Figure 4.19 shows what happens when you select the Samba version 2.03 for Red Hat 5.2. You will see this screen pop up. The top line shows a filter for your current directory. This filter will use `*.rpm` to just show files that have the `.rpm` extension in your current directory. The left box labeled `Directories` shows subdirectories in your current directory. The right box labeled `Files` shows the files in your current directory with the filter applied. The bottom field labeled `Selection` shows the actual file that you will be downloading.

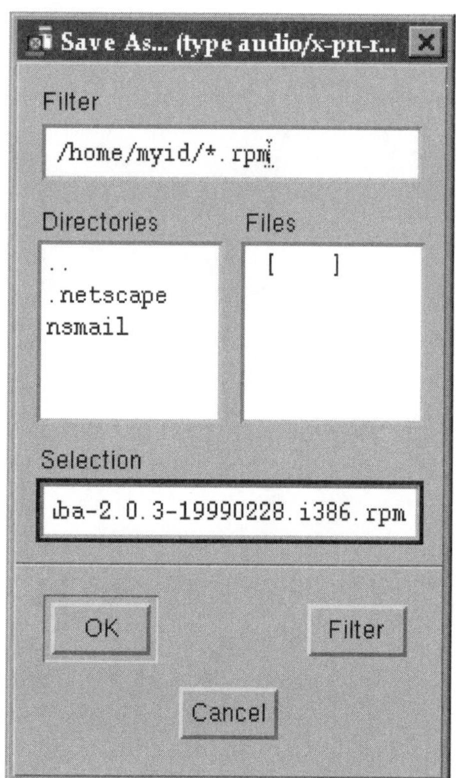

Figure 4.19 ■ Netscape Prompt to Save File

i) What is the filter that you will be using to display the directories and files similar to those in Figure 4.19?

j) What do you see in the `Directories` box on your system similar to the one in Figure 4.19?

k) What do you see on your system in the `Files` box similar to the one in Figure 4.19?

l) What is the actual selection that shows up in the `Selection` box in Figure 4.19?

You should now examine the information and make sure that the proper destination is selected. Once you are sure this is okay, then press the `OK` button.

m) What happens when you press the `OK` button?

n) What is the source address of the file you are downloading?

o) What is the destination directory for your file?

Once your file is downloaded, you will want to go back and make sure the file has been properly downloaded. You can do this by exiting Netscape and then type the `ls` command.

p) What happens when you do the `ls` command in the directory where you downloaded the Samba file?

Enter the `ls -l` command.

q) What happens when you do the `ls -l` command in the directory where you downloaded the Samba file?

r) Does the size of the file from the `ls -l` command agree with what you expect?

Lab 4.2 Exercise Answers

4.2.1 Answers

a) What happens when you type the `netscape` command? If you get errors, how should you handle them?

Answer: You will get the default home page for Netscape. If you get an error saying permission was refused, you need to properly set up your X-Windows environment. If you get an error about Netscape not being found, then you need to be sure that it is installed. If it is installed, then make sure it is in your search path. Alternatively, you can go to the Netscape directory and type `./netscape`.

b) What is the Samba site that you chose to connect to?

Answer: This is really dependent on where you are located. Just pick a site that is local to you, but in reality, you can choose any site.

c) Did you have any problems connecting to the Samba site? If so, how did you get around them?

Answer: If they are maxed out in user connections, then just try another one. There is usually a number of them that are available. If you get an error about an invalid site name, then that site could be having problems or may no longer be available. You may get an error about not being able to get to the site or a timeout. In any case, just keep trying various sites.

d) What choice did you make to get to the download page?

Answer: You should have chosen the download page that is the last item in the first column in the upper-left corner.

e) What did you choose to get to the binary download page for Samba?

Answer: In the paragraph that has the headings `Binaries`, *you should click on* `You can download them here via http` `here`.

f) What is the operating system version that you chose?

Answer: You need to choose the version of Samba appropriate to your operating system. If you are not sure about which version you need to download, you can enter the directories and subdirectories and look at the documentation.

g) How is the RPMS directory organized?

Answer: You will see various directories that are relevant to several version numbers of the operating system for which you are going to be downloading the code. In the case of Figure 4.20, you will see directories for four versions of Red Hat. Those versions are 5.0, 5.1, 5.2, and 6.0. You should choose whichever version is appropriate for you. Your display will be different.

h) What screen do you see when you select the directory for your version of Linux?

Answer: You should see several versions of Samba for your operating system. Generally, you should choose the latest version. However, in some cases, you may need to choose an older version. This happens sometimes if the current version has some

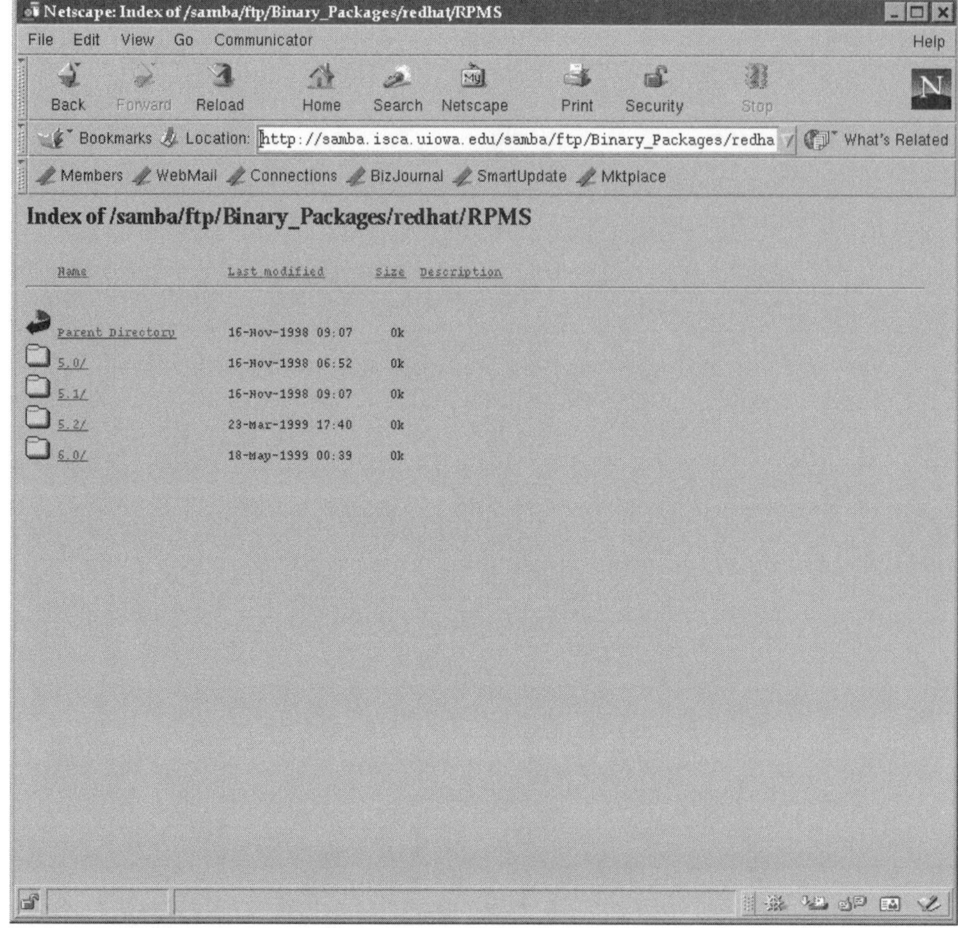

Figure 4.20 ■ Red Hat RPMS Subdirectory

problems with it, or if you want to be consistent with versions that you have already downloaded or have on your site.

i) What is the filter that you will be using to display the directories and files similar to those in Figure 4.19?

Answer: The filter should be pointing to the directory where you will be downloading the files followed by `*.rpm`.

j) What do you see in the `Directories` box on your system similar to the one in Figure 4.19?

Answer: You should see the parent directory specified by .. (double dots) and all the subdirectories under your current directory.

k) What do you see on your system in the `Files` box similar to the one in Figure 4.19?

Answer: You should see any files that match `*.rpm`. *This means any file that ends in* `.rpm`.

l) What is the actual selection that shows up in the `Selection` box in Figure 4.19?

Answer: You will see the name of the file that you will be downloading. This is the name that it will also get once it is downloaded. If you want to change the name, it is better to do it once the file is downloaded, since changing the name here may confuse Netscape.

m) What happens when you press the `OK` button?

Answer: You should notice that the bottom line will show the progress of the download, as well as the size of the file that is being downloaded and the speed of the transfer.

n) What is the source address of the file you are downloading?

Answer: The source address is displayed in the URL that is shown in Figure 4.21. Your source address will depend on where you are loading the file from.

o) What is the destination directory for your file?

Answer: The destination directory is shown in Figure 4.21 in the second line labeled `Destination`. Your actual destination will depend on where you decided to download the file.

p) What happens when you do the `ls` command in the directory where you downloaded the Samba file?

Answer: You should see the file that you have downloaded. Figure 4.22 shows a sample screen display for this. If you do not see it, then you will need to reload the file.

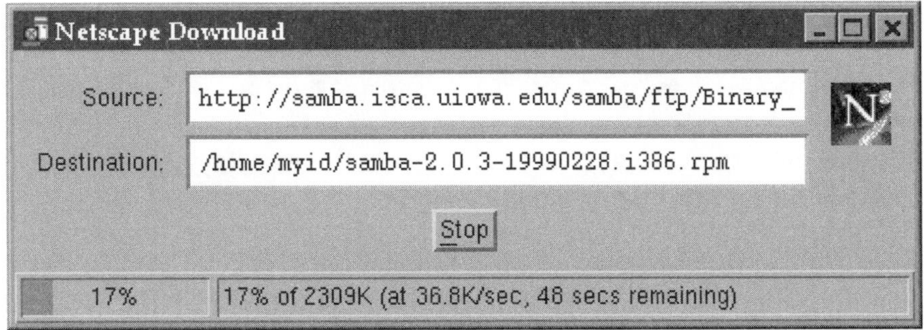

Figure 4.21 ■ Netscape Download Screen

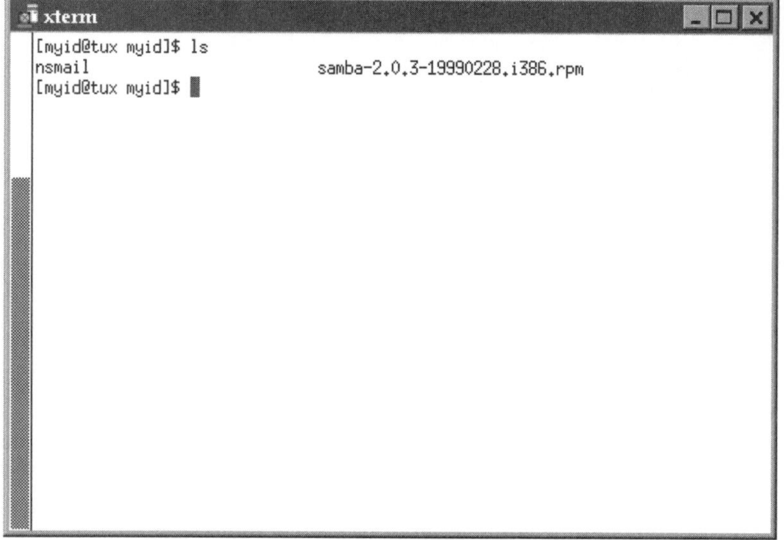

Figure 4.22 ■ Directory Listing after Downloading Samba

If the file has a size of zero, it means that the download did not complete, and you will need to redo the download.

q) What happens when you do the `ls -l` command in the directory where you downloaded the Samba file?

Answer: You should see a long listing describing the file you just downloaded. This will include file ownership characteristics, the size of the file, and the name of the file.

r) Does the size of the file from the `ls -l` command agree with what you expect?

Answer: You need to look at the file size shown in the bottom of Figure 4.21. This should agree with the size of the file in the directory that you saw in Question q. If the file you downloaded is bigger than the size shown in Figure 4.21, it is probably okay. Because of the way the files are stored, transferred, compressed, and measured, the downloaded file may be bigger. If the downloaded file is smaller, then you need to be sure that it has been totally downloaded. Oftentimes, the site you got the files from will have information about the expected file sizes.

Lab 4.2 Self-Review Questions

In order to test your progress, you should be able to answer the following questions.

1) In order to use Samba on your Linux box, from where do you need to purchase a license?
a) _____Red Hat
b) _____`www.samba.org`
c) _____Linus Torvalds
d) _____Nowhere as Samba is freeware
e) _____None of the above

2) The only way to get Samba is by using Netscape Navigator.
a) _____True
b) _____False

3) Based only on Figure 4.18, which of the following operating systems does not have a version of Samba?
a) _____IRIX
b) _____Red Hat
c) _____CP/M
d) _____MVS
e) _____Novell

4) In Figure 4.17, the file `WHICH-ONE.txt` will tell you some information that will help you decide which directories or versions to get.
a _____True
b) _____False

5) When a version of Samba is created for version 6.0 of Red Hat, which figure do you think would be most likely to change?
a) _____Fig 4.16
b) _____Fig 4.17
c) _____Fig 4.18
d) _____Fig 4.19
e) _____Fig 4.20

6) What would be the name of an RPM for Samba version 2.0.5 that is created from source code dated Nov 27, 1999?
a) _____`samba-2.0.5`
b) _____`samba-i386.rpm`
c) _____`samba -19991127.i386.rpm`
d) _____`samba-2.0.5-19991127.i386.rpm`
e) _____none of the above

Quiz answers appear in Appendix A, Section 4.2.

LAB 4.3

GETTING SAMBA RUNNING

LAB OBJECTIVES

After this Lab, you will be able to:

- Determine Your Current Version of Samba
- Remove Samba
- Install Samba
- Upgrade Samba
- Set up and Test Samba
- Connect from MS Windows to Samba
- Connect from Samba to MS Windows

THE RPM METHOD

There are several installation methods that have been developed to install software for operating systems. Some of the concerns in doing an install, upgrade, or uninstall are:

- Making sure that the proper files are installed. Oftentimes an installation package requires a number of files to be installed. These files may be versions of files that are already there, or they may be new versions of currently existing files.
- Removing any older versions of new files that are installed.
- Being sure that if the install fails, the system can be restored to its previous stage.

The Red Hat manufacturer of Linux has developed an installation method called the Red Hat Package Manager, which is RPM for short. The

RPM method is used by a number of manufacturers of Linux and is also being considered for use by at least one non-Linux vendor for software installs. The RPM method does undergo improvements over time to make it simpler, more powerful, and even more stable. We will be discussing using the RPM method in this chapter. We will discuss determining your current version of Samba, removing it, and installing an upgraded version. You may want to examine other installation methods in order to deepen your understanding of Linux.

LAB 4.3 EXERCISES

4.3.1 DETERMINE YOUR CURRENT VERSION OF SAMBA

Before you install the latest version of Samba, you need to determine what version is currently installed. Most releases of Linux now automatically include Samba, but by the time the consumer gets the software, there is usually a new version available. While it is not always smart to get the latest release until it is known to be bug-free, oftentimes the new release includes features that you will want to add your system. It may also include bug fixes and speed or reliability enhancements.

In order to determine your current version of Samba, you need to execute the `rpm` command with the appropriate option. Like many UNIX commands, `rpm` can take many options for doing various things related to installation. It is a command that you should research well if you are going to be doing many Linux installations and configurations.

The query option to `rpm` will give you information about the current version of a package that is installed. You should note that when you do an `rpm` query, you do not need to specify the version number, but when you do an installation, upgrade, or removal, you do need this information. The command you would use to do the query is the following:

```
rpm -q -i samba
```

The meaning of the options is

`-q`—Do a query
`-i`—Return all the information
`samba` —Return the information about the Samba that is installed.

Now enter the following:

```
rpm -q -i samba
```

Answer the following questions based on the results of this command.

a) What is the software name that results from the `rpm -q -i samba` command?

b) What is the distribution name that results from the `rpm` command?

c) What is the vendor name that results from the `rpm` command?

d) What is the summary description name that results from the `rpm` command?

e) Based on the `rpm` command, does your version of Samba support encrypted passwords?

4.3.2 REMOVE SAMBA

In this Exercise, you will be shown how to remove Samba. If you want, you can just do an upgrade, as you will see in Lab 4.3.4. You may also want to try an upgrade after you do an installation. Just remove the current version of Samba, install a version that is not the latest, and then upgrade to the latest.

You can remove Samba from your system by entering `rpm` with the appropriate option. The option `-e` can be used to erase Samba. You can do this by entering the command:

```
rpm -e samba-package-name
```

where `samba-package-name` is the actual name of the package with the version.


```
# rpm -e samba-2.0.3-19990228
```

However, if you only have one version of Samba on your system and have never upgraded, you can use:

```
rpm -e samba
```

This will remove the existing version of Samba.

Now remove the version of Samba that you found in Exercise 4.3.1.

a) What is the command line you used to remove Samba from your system?

___

___

b) What happens when you enter the `rpm -e` command followed by `Samba` or the samba package name?

___

___

You need to verify that there is no version of Samba left on your system.

c) What command would you use to find the version of Samba on your system?

___

___

d) What are the results from Question c?

If you still find a version of Samba on your system, you should remove that one also.

e) What is the command you used to remove the remaining version of Samba on your system?

f) What are the results from Question e?

4.3.3 INSTALL SAMBA

The process to install Samba is just as easy as the process to remove Samba or to query for Samba. Remember how we downloaded the new version of Samba in Exercise 4.2.1? Now we are going to install it. In Exercise 4.2.1, the example downloaded it to `/home/myid`. You may have downloaded it to a different directory. In addition, your version will probably be different from the one in the example.

a) Where is the new version of Samba that you downloaded to your system?

b) What is the name of the new version of Samba that you downloaded?

Now you can install Samba with the appropriate options to the `rpm` command. The only option that is necessary to reinstall is the `-i` option.

■ FOR EXAMPLE:

To install Samba from the `/home/myid` directory, you would use the following command:

```
rpm -i /home/myid/samba-2.0.3-19990228.i386.rpm
```


Do the installation of Samba now.

c) What happens when you enter the command: `rpm -i /home/myid/samba-2.0.3-19990228.i386.rpm`? (Be sure to replace the version name with the version you downloaded.)

____

____

Now you need to verify that the new version of Samba is installed.

d) What command would you execute to verify that Samba is installed?

____

____

e) What are the results of executing the command in Question d?

____

____

f) How would you explain the results if more than one version of Samba showed up?

____

____

4.3.4 Upgrade Samba

Instead of just installing Samba, you might want to just do an upgrade. Doing the upgrade assumes that you already have a version of Samba installed. If you want to try out the upgrade, then just install a version that is not the recent version and then do the upgrade. The upgrade process is very straightforward. The complete upgrade process will:

- Upgrade any files for the package on your system
- Backup any configuration files that are not consistent with the new release
- Delete any files that are no longer necessary for the new version
- Use the same `rpm` file that you used for installation.

You can give various options to the `rpm` command to keep files, delete old configuration files, and so forth.

The option `-U` will do a complete upgrade on your system of the `rpm` package. So to upgrade, just enter the command:

```
rpm -U location_of_file
```

where `location_of_file` is the location of the Samba file from which you will be installing.

FOR EXAMPLE:

To upgrade Samba from the `/home/myid` directory, you would use the following command:

```
rpm -U /home/myid/samba-2.0.3-19990228.i386.rpm
```

Now you should upgrade your version of Samba.

a) What happens when you enter the command `rpm -U /home/myid/samba-2.0.3-19990228.i386.rpm`? (Replace the version of Samba with your own version.)

____

____

Now you need to verify that Samba has been properly installed.

b) What is the command that you would enter to verify that Samba has been properly installed?

---

c) What are the results of entering the command in Question b?

---

d) If you entered the command in Question b after just a simple installation over an existing version of Samba, instead of doing an upgrade, what do you think the results would be?

4.3.5 SET UP AND TEST SAMBA

There are many configuration options available for Samba. In fact, by the time you read this chapter, the power and breadth of Samba will have grown even more because it is constantly evolving.

The Whole Truth

In order to get you started as quickly as possible, the simplest configuration choices have been made. This Exercise assumes that you have set up Windows 95 as described in Lab 4.1. In this case, there should be no changes necessary to Samba to get your Linux box working. If you are running Windows 98 or NT, you may have to make changes to your Windows network characteristics in order to match the Samba settings. I have chosen this route for simplicity's sake because Windows networking is installed by default. I could have just as easily directed you to configure Samba, but then you will probably need to make more changes to Windows to match Samba. Once you are confident about your Samba skills, you can branch out and experiment with the many options. There are also several good books on Samba, and certainly there will be more in the near future as Samba becomes essential to the enterprise.

The default configuration in Samba 2.0.3 will automatically start up the Samba daemons. This configuration is located in the file `/etc/smb.conf`. This is a very large file and has many configurable options. You want to verify the name of your *Workgroup*. This is where the `grep` command is very useful.

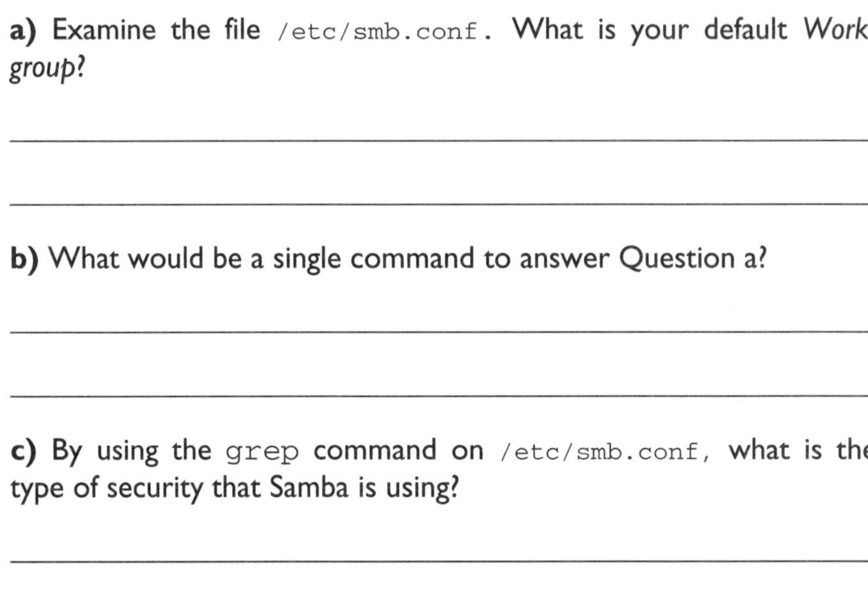

a) Examine the file `/etc/smb.conf`. What is your default *Workgroup*?

b) What would be a single command to answer Question a?

c) By using the `grep` command on `/etc/smb.conf`, what is the type of security that Samba is using?

There are two daemons that will be started up when you start Samba. Those daemons are `smbd` and `nmbd`. They listen for requests from SMB clients and give the SMB services. The `smbd` daemon is used to file and print requests. The `nmbd` daemon handles browsing. You can verify that these processes are running by using the `grep` command again. This time, use the following commands:

```
ps ax | grep smbd
```

and

```
ps ax | grep nmbd
```

d) What is the result of entering the `ps ax | grep smbd` command?

e) What is the result of entering the `ps ax | grep nmbd` command?

____

____

f) What would you do if there were no processes that showed up when you entered the commands in Questions d and e.

____

____

Once you have verified that the Samba processes are running, then you can use the following command to verify the status of Samba connections. This command is:

```
smbstatus
```

g) What happens when you enter the command `smbstatus`?

____

____

This will also tell you the status of resources that are exported.

If your Samba does not seem to have started up, then you should do the command:

```
ps ax | more
```

This will display all the processes that are running, and you can determine whether the Samba processes have started or not.

h) What kind of Samba processes do you see when you enter the `ps ax | more` command?

____

____

4.3.6 Connect from MS Windows to Samba

You can verify that your MS Windows box can connect to Samba by logging into your Windows PC. Then, you need to verify the steps that you did in Exercise 4.2.1. Your Samba default *Workgroup* is `MYGROUP`. Your MS Windows default *Workgroup* is `WORKGROUP`. You should follow the steps to get to a screen similar to what you see in Figure 4.8, but you need to make sure that the *Workgroup* field says `MYGROUP`. You can see this in Figure 4.27. If it doesn't say `MYGROUP`, then make the changes.

a) What is the default group that shows up when you go to the Windows `Network Identification` Screen on your MS Windows PC?

Be sure to save any other information that shows up so you can easily set up your PC again with whatever settings you had originally.

b) What happens when you change the Windows *Workgroup* to *MYGROUP* and exit the Windows control panel?

Follow any instructions that the screen gives you.

Now you should be at or should go back to the main Windows screen that you saw in Figure 4.1. Then you should double-click on the `Network Neighborhood` icon in the upper-left corner.

c) What do you see when you click on the `Network Neighborhood` icon?

If you do not see the server that you set up, you should click on the `Entire Network` icon.

d) What do you see when you click on the `Entire Network` display?

---

e) What do you see when you click on the `MYGROUP` entry in the `Entire Network` display?

---

f) What do you think would be the problem if the `MYGROUP` *Workgroup* does not show up in the `Entire Network` window or any of the earlier displays?

4.3.7 CONNECT FROM SAMBA TO MS WINDOWS

Now you need to verify that you can connect from Samba to your MS Windows boxes. The easiest command to use is the following:

```
smbclient
```

This command works similarly to the `FTP` command in TCP/IP and has a number of options. The purpose of this Exercise is to determine whether your Samba client can see the SMB services on your MS Windows PCs, including the drives and printers that are shared.

In order to see the drives and printers that are shared on your MS Windows PC, you will need to establish shares on each of the drives. This will be left to you as an exercise, but is relatively straightforward. You may wish to consult your documentation or someone who is familiar with SMB file sharing.

a) What happens when you just enter the smbclient command?

____

____

The option that we will now use is the -L option. This option is followed by the NETBIOS name. This is the computer name that shows up in Figure 4.27. The command line would be:


```
smbclient -L  netbios_name
```

where netbios_name is the NETBIOS name of the host.

FOR EXAMPLE:

To connect to a host called myserver, you would use the command:

```
smbclient -L mohawk
```

This will prompt you for a password on the host mohawk and will then show the NETBIOS characteristics on mohawk that Samba looks for. Run the smbclient command. The password that you will use is the same one that you would use on the PC that has the NETBIOS hostname you are using in the smbclient command.

FOR EXAMPLE:

So to connect to the PC with the NETBIOS name mohawk, you would use the id and password that you would use on mohawk.

Choose a server to connect to that has the SMB NETBIOS share setup.

b) What is the NETBIOS name of the Windows PC to which you will be connecting?

____

____

Next, enter the smbclient -L command as mentioned previously in this Exercise.

c) What happens when you enter the command `smbclient -L` followed by the `NETBIOS` name of the Windows PC to which you are connecting?

____

____

You should now be connected to the Windows PC using the SMB protocol.

d) Do you see any drives that are being shared on your MS Windows PC?

____

____

The next thing that you will see are all the servers in your current *Workgroup*.

e) What servers show up in your server listing from entering the `smbclient` command in Question c?

____

____

The last group in Figure 4.31 are all the *Workgroups* that show up.

f) What *Workgroups* show up when you enter the `smbclient` in Question c?

The Whole Truth

There are many additional features to Samba. Because of space limitations, we have only discussed those concepts necessary to get Samba running and to verify the SMB connectivity. There are many good books on Samba that you should go to for additional help. There is also much help on the Internet for Samba concepts. I would expect that Samba will gain many new features in the next few years, so stay tuned. I would also expect that it would become an essential part of any Linux administrator's toolkit.

Lab 4.3 Exercise Answers

4.3.1 Answers

a) What is the software name that results from the `rpm -q -i samba` command?

Answer: When you execute the command, you will see a display similar what your see in Figure 4.23.

The name that results from executing the command should be `samba`. *You can see this on the second line, first column of Figure 4.23.*

b) What is the distribution name that results from the `rpm` command?

Answer: You may see something like `{none}` *or the name that is assigned by the manufacturer or developer. For example, Red Hat gives the name* `Manhattan` *to the version 5.2.*

c) What is the vendor name that results from the `rpm` command?

Answer: The vendor may be `{none}` *or it could be a manufacturer's name such as* `Red Hat`.

d) What is the summary description name that results from the `rpm` command?

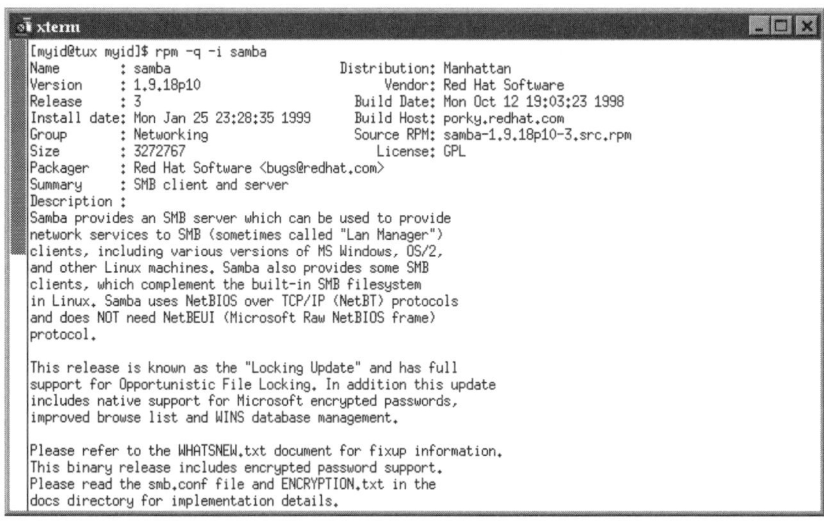

xterm
[myid@tux myid]$ rpm -q -i samba
Name : samba Distribution: Manhattan
Version : 1.9.18p10 Vendor: Red Hat Software
Release : 3 Build Date: Mon Oct 12 19:03:23 1998
Install date: Mon Jan 25 23:28:35 1999 Build Host: porky.redhat.com
Group : Networking Source RPM: samba-1.9.18p10-3.src.rpm
Size : 3272767 License: GPL
Packager : Red Hat Software <bugs@redhat.com>
Summary : SMB client and server
Description :
Samba provides an SMB server which can be used to provide
network services to SMB (sometimes called "Lan Manager")
clients, including various versions of MS Windows, OS/2,
and other Linux machines. Samba also provides some SMB
clients, which complement the built-in SMB filesystem
in Linux. Samba uses NetBIOS over TCP/IP (NetBT) protocols
and does NOT need NetBEUI (Microsoft Raw NetBIOS frame)
protocol.
This release is known as the "Locking Update" and has full
support for Opportunistic File Locking. In addition this update
includes native support for Microsoft encrypted passwords,
improved browse list and WINS database management.
Please refer to the WHATSNEW.txt document for fixup information.
This binary release includes encrypted password support.
Please read the smb.conf file and ENCRYPTION.txt in the
docs directory for implementation details.

Figure 4.23 ■ The RPM Query Command

Answer: The summary description in Figure 4.23 is `Samba SMB client and server`.

e) Based on the `rpm` command, does your version of Samba support encrypted passwords?

Answer: You may see something like the following:

```
Please refer to the WHATSNEW.txt document for fixup information.

This binary release includes encrypted password support.

Please read the smb.conf file and ENCRYPTION.txt in the

docs directory for implementation details.
```

If you do, then it tells whether encrypted passwords are supported. Versions 2.0 and greater of Samba support encrypted passwords. This is necessary if you are going to support Windows domain logins for Windows 98 using encrypted passwords.

4.3.2 Answers

a) What is the command line you used to remove Samba from your system?

Answer: You should have entered something similar to:

```
rpm -e samba-2.0.3-19990228
```

In this case, `samba-2.0.3-19990228` *is the version of Samba you are removing. You will need to replace this with the version of Samba you are using.*

b) What happens when you enter the `rpm -e` command followed by `Samba` or the Samba package name?

Answer: If there are no errors, you should just get back the command-line prompt. This is in keeping with the UNIX tradition that no news is good news.

c) What command would you use to find the version of Samba on your system?

Answer: You would use the same command that you used in Exercise 4.3.1; that is,

```
rpm -q -i samba
```

d) What are the results from Question c?

Answer: If you are running Samba version 2.0.3, you would see a display similar to that in Figure 4.26 below.

e) What is the command you used to remove the remaining version of Samba on your system?

Answer: You should use the command:

```
rpm -e samba
```


However, if you have multiple versions of Samba installed, or if you did an install without removing the previous version, you will have to specify the actual full version name. In the case of version 2.0.3 that we are using in this example, it would be:

```
rpm -e samba-2.0.3-19990228
```

f) What are the results from Question e?

Answer: If the results are successful, you should get back just the command-line prompt.

4.3.3 ANSWERS

a) Where is the new version of Samba that you downloaded to your system?

Answer: In Lab 4.2, you downloaded Samba to your `/home/myid` *directory. You can download this file anywhere because it does not affect executing the installation program, so it may be somewhere else.*

b) What is the name of the new version of Samba that you downloaded?

Answer: In Lab 4.2, you were shown the steps to download the file `samba-2.0.3-19990228.i386.rpm`. *You probably have downloaded a later version. You should use this new version as the basis of the later discussion.*

c) What happens when you enter the command: `rpm -i /home/myid/samba-2.0.3-19990228.i386.rpm`? (Be sure to replace the version name with the version you downloaded.)

Answer: If the installation was successful, you should just get back the command-line prompt.

d) What command would you execute to verify that Samba is installed?

Answer: You should execute the command to find the current installed version of Samba. That command is:

```
rpm -q -i samba
```

If you were doing an upgrade, and you saw multiple versions of Samba listed, then your installation process failed to remove some files or features. You may have entered the wrong command or option.

e) What are the results of executing the command in Question d?

Answer: You should just see the Samba package you just installed. The display is shown in Figure 4.24.

f) How would you explain the results if more than one version of Samba showed up?

Answer: If you were doing a standard installation, it means that the files from the previous versions are still there and the system thinks both are available.

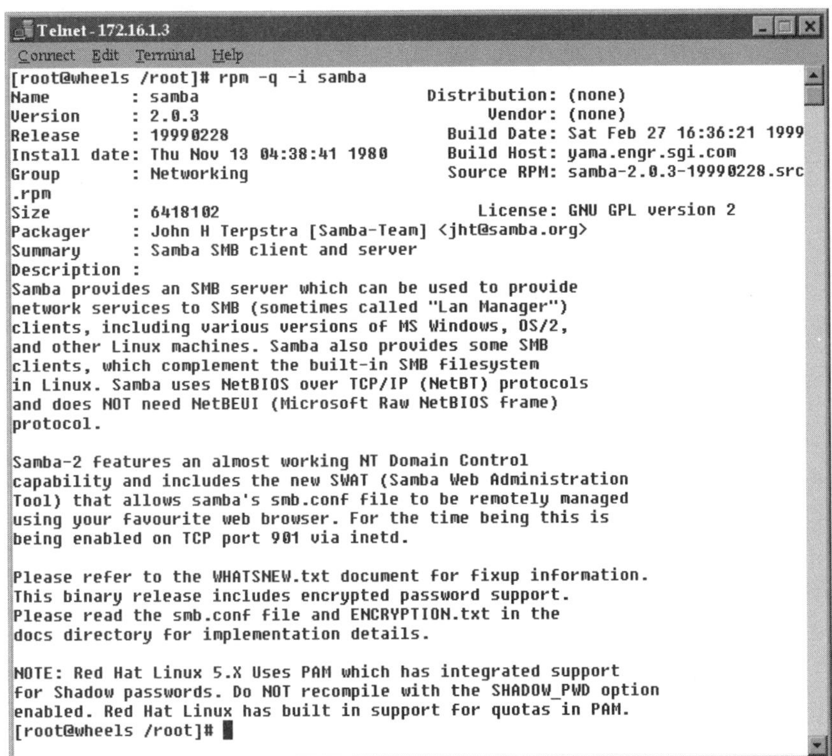

Figure 4.24 ■ Results of the RPM Query Command on Samba 2.0.3

This is not a bug, but a feature (really!!). You can run more than one version of a Linux package on the same box as long as you can either share configuration files or you can have a totally separate set of configuration files for each version.

4.3.4 Answers

a) What happens when you enter the command `rpm -U /home/myid/samba-2.0.3-19990228.i386.rpm?` (Replace the version of Samba with your own version.)

Answer: You should see the command-line prompt. There should be no messages.

b) What is the command that you would enter to verify that Samba has been properly installed?

Answer: You would use the command that shows the versions of Samba that are installed. That command would be:

```
rpm -q -i samba
```

c) What are the results of entering the command in Question b?

Answer: You should see results similar to what you see in Figure 4.26. This will show the version or versions of Samba that are installed.

d) If you entered the command in Question b after just a simple installation over an existing version of Samba, instead of doing an upgrade, what do you think the results would be?

Answer: You would see multiple versions of Samba listed. This is okay. You should refer to the answer to Question f of Exercise 4.3.3.

4.3.5 Answers

a) Examine the file `/etc/smb.conf`. What is your default *Workgroup?*

Answer: You can use `grep` *to find a particular line or lines in a file. The format is:*

```
grep string file_name
```

where `string` *is the text string that you are looking for and* `file_name` *is the name of the file you are searching in.*

FOR EXAMPLE:

Let's say you are looking for all references to a log file. Because this is more than one word, you should put it in double quotes. Quotes are not necessary for a single word. You would use the command:

```
grep "log file" /etc/smb.conf
```

If you did a standard installation of Samba, the default Workgroup *would be* MYGROUP.

b) What would be a single command to answer Question a?

Answer: By using `grep`*, you should see output similar to the following:*

```
[myid@tux myid]$ grep workgroup /etc/smb.conf
# workgroup = NT-Domain-Name or Workgroup-Name
   workgroup = MYGROUP
[myid@tux myid]$
```

c) By using the `grep` command on `/etc/smb.conf`, what is the type of security that Samba is using?

Answer: By using the `grep` *command, you would see the following results:*

```
[myid@tux myid]$ grep security /etc/smb.conf
# This option is important for security. It allows you to restrict
# Security mode. Most people will want user level security. See
# security_level.txt for details.
   security = user
# Use password server option only with security = server
[myid@tux myid]$
```

By examining these results, you would see that the security being used is given by the line:

```
security = user
```

So it is user-level security, which depends on the login name and the password. You should note that when you set up your MS Windows PC in Lab 4.1, you established share-level access control as opposed to user-level access control, although the default security setting in Samba is user. This is not necessarily conflicting or contradicting. In MS Windows, the share-level access control does not require you to have an NT domain controller and allows access by using logins and passwords on each box for each resource. In Samba, `security=user` means that the sharing is done based on login ids and passwords.

d) What is the result of entering the `ps ax | grep smbd` command?

Answer: You should see results similar to the following:

```
[myid@tux myid]$ ps ax | grep smbd
  441  ?  S     0:00 smbd -D
3412  p2 S N  0:00 grep smbd
[myid@tux myid]$
```


Here, you see that the `smbd` daemon is running with the `-D` option, which says that the `smbd` process will run as a Linux daemon.

e) What is the result of entering the `ps ax | grep nmbd` command?

Answer: The results should look similar to the following:

```
 [myid@tux myid]$ ps ax | grep nmbd
450  ?  S     0:21 nmbd -D
[myid@tux myid]$
```

Notice that the `nmbd` process also has a `-D` option, which indicates that it will run as a daemon.

f) What would you do if there were no processes that showed up when you entered the commands in Questions d and e?

Answer: The best thing to do would be to startup the daemons manually. You can do this with the commands as they appear in the result from the `ps` command. You would enter the commands:

```
smbd -D
nmbd -D
```

If you get an error about the file not being found, you can look in the directory `/usr/sbin`. You should see the commands there. Then you can execute the commands as follows:

```
/usr/sbin/smbd -D
/usr/sbin/nmbd -D
```

Now you can repeat the steps in Questions d and e above to verify that the process is running.

g) What happens when you enter the command `smbstatus`?

Answer: When you enter the `smbstatus` *command after first setting up Samba, you will probably see no connections. However, the following display does show what you might see if a connection exists:*

```
[myid@wheels myid]$ smbstatus

Samba version 2.0.3
Service    uid    gid     pid   machine
--------------------------------------
myid     myid users     783   skates   (172.16.1.14)
Tue Nov 18 00:25:25 1999
No locked files
Share mode memory usage (bytes):
   1048464(99%) free + 56(0%) used + 56(0%) overhead
= 1048576(100%) total
[myid@wheels myid]$
```

You can see here that there has been a service name called `myid` *that has been started by the user with the uid* `myid`*. The group id, or gid, is* `users`*. The machine it is connected in from is* `skates`*, which is a Windows 95 box. The address of* `skates` *is* `172.16.1.14` *and the date of the connection is Nov. 18, 1999, at 25 minutes past midnight. It also says that there are no locked files. The last item is the amount of memory usage for the share mode.*

h) What kind of Samba processes do you see when you enter the `ps ax | more` command?

Answer: You should see the `smbd` *and* `nmbd` *processes. If you don't see the Samba processes, then you can start up the Samba process manually as described in the answer to Question f. Another way you can do this is with the command:*

```
/etc/rc.d/init.d/smb start
```

This will start up the Samba processes manually. It also does more checking than the steps in Question f. You should watch this while it executes to make sure there are no errors.

4.3.6 ANSWERS

a) What is the default group that shows up when you go to the Windows `Network Identification` Screen on your MS Windows PC?

Answer: If you had previously changed your Workgroup in earlier exercises, you would see the display in Figure 4.25, which is `MYGROUP`*. In this case, you can skip Question b. By default, the Workgroup is* `WORKGROUP`*.*

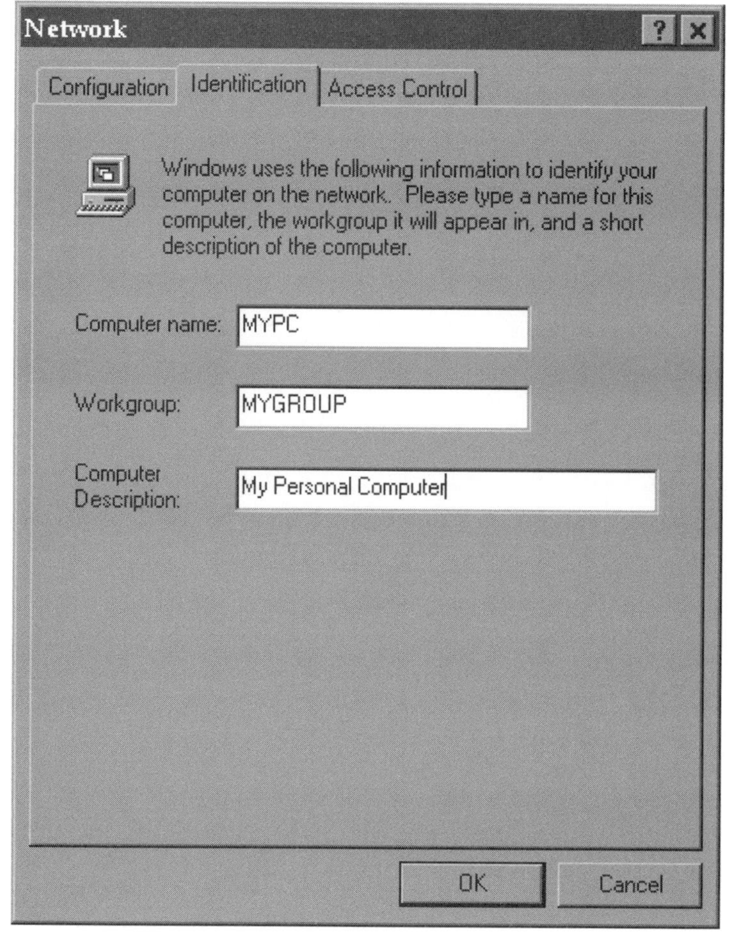

Figure 4.25 ■ Windows `Network Identification` Screen

b) What happens when you change the Windows *Workgroup* and exit the Windows control panel?

Answer: The system may ask you to install the Windows CD-ROM. If so, it will ask you to reboot when it is done.

c) What do you see when you click on the `Network Neighborhood` icon?

Answer: This will bring the screen that you see in Figure 4.26.

In this sample display, you see the listing: `Entire Network`, *5 SMB servers and* `HP_Network_Printers`.

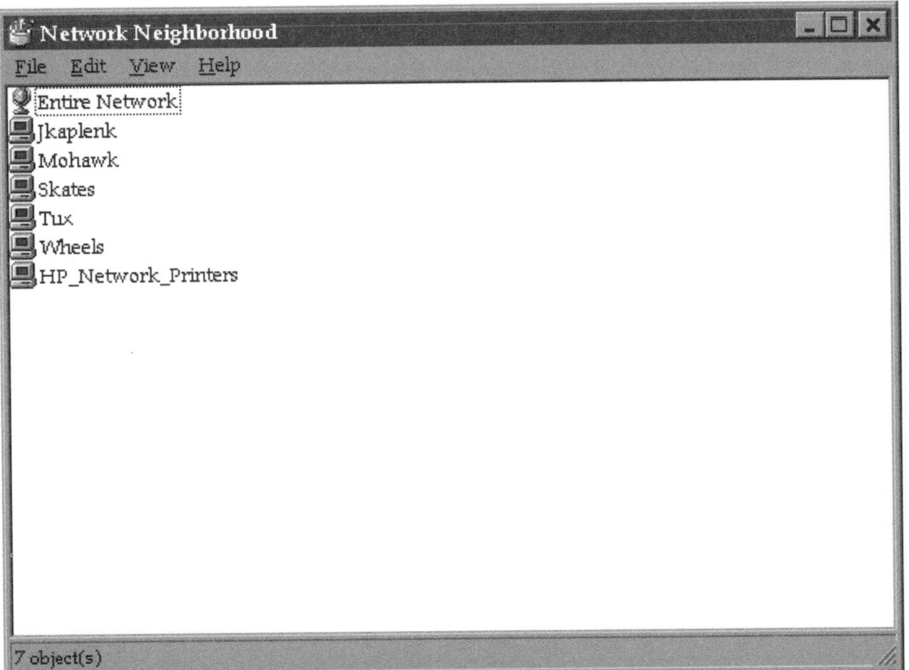

Figure 4.26 ■ MS Windows `Network Neighborhood`

d) What do you see when you click on the `Entire Network` display?

Answer: This will give you a display similar to the one that you see in Figure 4.27.

In Figure 4.27, you will see three entries. The first one is `HP_Network_Printers`. The second and third entries are the Windows *Workgroups* that show up. Double-click on the `MYGROUP` icon. The new window should look similar to the one shown in Figure 4.28.

e) What do you see when you click on the `Mygroup` entry in the `Entire Network` display?

Answer: You will see the display in Figure 4.28. This will show the hosts that belong to the `Mygroup` *Workgroup.*

f) What do you think would be the problem if the `MYGROUP` Workgroup does not show up in the `Entire Network` window or any of the earlier displays?

Answer: It would probably indicate that your Windows networking was not installed or was not configured properly. In this case, you should revisit the steps you used to set up the Windows networking.

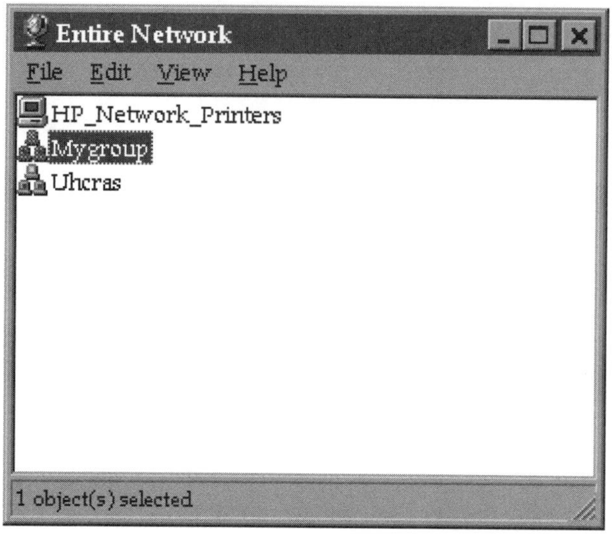

Figure 4.27 ■ MS Windows `Entire Network` Display

4.3.7 ANSWERS

a) What happens when you just enter the `smbclient` command?

Answer: You will see the display that is in Figure 4.29. This shows a number of the possible options you can use for the `smbclient` *command.*

b) What is the `NETBIOS` name of the Windows PC to which you will be connecting?

Answer: In this example, the name of the host is `mohawk`*. Your actual server name is probably different. You can see the* `NETBIOS` *name in Figure 4.25, along with the* Workgroup *name.*

c) What happens when you enter the command `smbclient -L` followed by the `NETBIOS` name of the Windows PC to which you are connecting?

Answer: You will see the display in Figure 4.30.

d) Do you see any drives that are being shared on your MS Windows PC?

Answer: You should see the drives at the beginning of the display. In Figure 4.30, you can see that the C and D drives on `mohawk` *are being shared in the column* `sharename`.

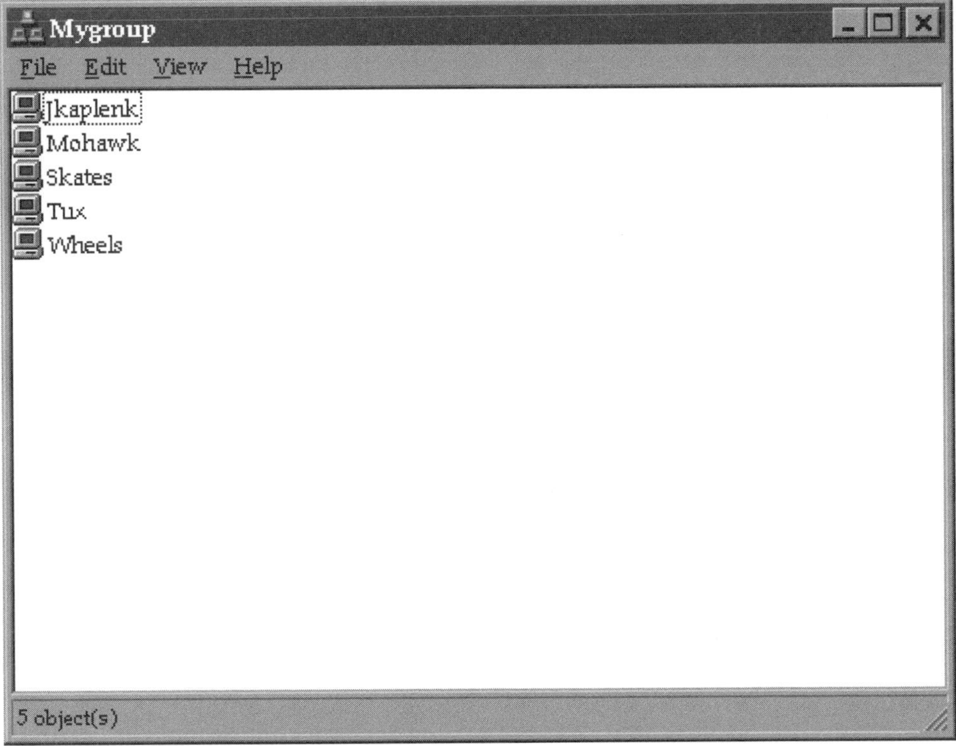

Figure 4.28 ■ An Example of an MS Windows MYGROUP Display

e) What servers show up in your server listing from entering the `smbclient` command in Question c?

Answer: In Figure 4.30, you see the SMB servers: `jkaplenk, mohawk, skates, tux, wheels`.

f) What *Workgroups* show up when you enter the `smbclient` in Question b?

Answer: In Figure 4.30, the Workgroups *displayed are:* `MYGROUP` *and* `UHCRAS`.

LAB 4.3 SELF-REVIEW QUESTIONS

In order to test your progress, you should be able to answer the following questions.

1) Based on Figure 4.23, the installation date is Monday, Oct. 12, 1998.

a) _____True
b) _____False

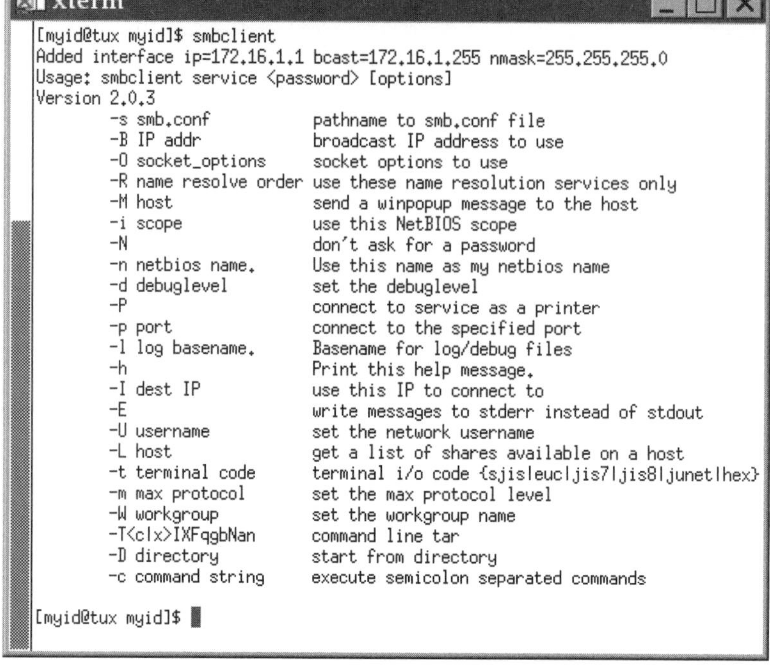

```
[myid@tux myid]$ smbclient
Added interface ip=172.16.1.1 bcast=172.16.1.255 nmask=255.255.255.0
Usage: smbclient service <password> [options]
Version 2.0.3
        -s smb.conf           pathname to smb.conf file
        -B IP addr            broadcast IP address to use
        -O socket_options     socket options to use
        -R name resolve order use these name resolution services only
        -M host               send a winpopup message to the host
        -i scope              use this NetBIOS scope
        -N                    don't ask for a password
        -n netbios name.      Use this name as my netbios name
        -d debuglevel         set the debuglevel
        -P                    connect to service as a printer
        -p port               connect to the specified port
        -l log basename.      Basename for log/debug files
        -h                    Print this help message.
        -I dest IP            use this IP to connect to
        -E                    write messages to stderr instead of stdout
        -U username           set the network username
        -L host               get a list of shares available on a host
        -t terminal code      terminal i/o code {sjis|euc|jis7|jis8|junet|hex}
        -m max protocol       set the max protocol level
        -W workgroup          set the workgroup name
        -T<c|x>IXFqgbNan      command line tar
        -D directory          start from directory
        -c command string     execute semicolon separated commands

[myid@tux myid]$
```

Figure 4.29 ■ Results of `smbclient` Command

```
Telnet - 172.16.1.1
Connect  Edit  Terminal  Help
[root@tux /root]# smbclient -L mohawk
Added interface ip=172.16.1.1 bcast=172.16.1.255 nmask=255.255.255.0
Password:

        Sharename      Type      Comment
        ---------      ----      -------
        D              Disk      D Drive
        C              Disk      C Drive
        IPC$           IPC       Remote Inter Process Communication

        Server               Comment
        ---------            -------
        JKAPLENK             Samba Server
        MOHAWK               SOLARIS/WIN95
        SKATES               Joe Kaplenk
        TUX                  Samba Server
        WHEELS               Samba Server

        Workgroup            Master
        ---------            -------
        MYGROUP              MOHAWK
        UHCRAS               RKAPLEN
[root@tux /root]#
```

Figure 4.30 ■ Results of `smbclient -L` Command

2) The only way to install Samba is to use the `rpm` command.
   a _____True
   b _____False

3) The Samba `rpm` installation method will install which of the following SMB components?
   a) _____client
   b) _____server
   c) _____client and server
   d) _____NT domain controller only
   e) _____none of the above

4) Samba requires the installation of NetBEUI.
   a) _____True
   b) _____False

5) Based on Figure 4.24, the installation date is Thursday, Nov. 13, 1980.
   a) _____True
   b) _____False

6) Based on Figure 4.24, the source file is `samba-2.0.3-19990228.src.rpm`.
   a) _____True
   b) _____False

7) Samba version 2 includes a Web-based management tool called which of the following?
   a) _____SWAT
   b) _____NetBIOS
   c) _____NetBEUI
   d) _____TCP/IP
   e) _____PAM

Quiz answers appear in Appendix A, Section 4.3.

CHAPTER 4

TEST YOUR THINKING

1) For this project, you will be doing a totally clean install of Samba.

   a) You first need to verify that there are definitely no versions or remnants of Samba on your system. If so, remove them.

   b) Get a version of Samba as described in this chapter.

   c) Install it on your system.

   d) Get it running with share-level access control on the MS Windows PC side and `security=user` on the Samba side.

   e) What differences, if any, do you find in setting up the configuration file as compared to the discussion in this text?

   f) What differences, if any, do you find in the configuration when you run the query command?

   h) Does your new version support being an NT domain controller?

   i) What other new features do you see?

2) With Samba running, you now need to make changes to your MS Windows PC setup. Change the Network Access Control screen in Figure 4.9 so that it shows user-level access control. Be sure to reboot your MS Windows PC after making the changes.

   a) What other changes did you have to do to set this up on your PC completely?

   b) What do you see in your `Network Neighborhood` display? How would you explain the differences, if any, that you might get from your original display?

   c) What happens when you run `smbclient` from your Samba client and connect to the MS Windows box?

3) With Samba running and set up as described in this chapter, you will now make changes to your Samba security setup. Change the security discussed in Exercise

4.3.5 so that /etc/smb.conf reads security=share. Restart the Samba services by entering the command:

```
/etc/rc.d/init.d/smb restart
```

You may also need to reboot the MS Windows PC for it to recognize the changes in Samba on the Linux box.

a) What other changes did you have to do to set this up completely under Linux?

b) What do you see in your Network Neighborhood display on MS Windows? You may need to refresh your MS Windows display. How would you explain the differences, if any, that you might get from your original display?

c) What happens when you run smbclient from your Samba client and connect to the MS Windows box?

4) With Samba running and set up as described in this chapter, you should now make changes to your Samba security setup. You will be changing the security level that Samba and MS Windows uses to verify users. Change the security discussed in Lab 4.3.5 so that /etc/smb.conf reads security=share. You should restart the Samba services by entering the command:

```
/etc/rc.d/init.d/smb restart
```

You should now make changes to your MS Windows PC setup. Change the Network Access Control screen in Figure 4.9 so that it shows user-level access control. Be sure to reboot your MS Windows PC after making the changes.

a) What other changes did you have to do to set this up completely on your MS Windows PC?

b) What other changes did you have to do to set this up completely in Samba on your Linux box?

c) What do you see in your Network Neighborhood display? You may need to refresh the MS Windows display. How would you explain the differences, if any, that you might get from your original display?

d) What happens when you run smbclient from your Samba client and connect to the MS Windows box?

5) There are additional network options and setups that you can explore. These generally require an NT box set up as an NT domain controller, as well as having an MS Windows PC and your Linux PC. These choices will not be discussed here, but you should examine the various choices and experiment with how they perform in your network.

CHAPTER 5

SHARING DATA IN AN NFS WORLD

It doesn't matter what side of the road you drive on as long as the driver coming toward you shares the same philosophy about which side to drive on.

—*Joe*

CHAPTER OBJECTIVES

In this chapter, you will learn about:

Exercises for the Great and Super User

 Setting Up NFS Page 192

One of the earliest methods of sharing files in a UNIX system was by using the Network File System (NFS). This was developed by Sun Microsystems in the 1980s to share files and use other systems on the network for data storage. NFS is found on all versions of UNIX today and is included by default. There are versions available for all major computer operating systems. You can use NFS to make your Linux PC into a fileserver. NFS is available for your Windows PC, but this is something you would need to buy or possibly find in the public domain.

LAB 5.1

SETTING UP NFS

LAB OBJECTIVES

After this Lab, you will be able to:

- Set up Your `/etc/exports` File to Allow Mounting
- Do a Remote NFS Mount

In this Lab, you will learn how to share files using NFS. You will need two PCs or systems running NFS. While they both should be running Linux, NFS is pretty much the same on all UNIX systems, so one of them can be a UNIX system or PC running NFS.

In these Exercises, you will be:

- creating a mount point
- creating or modifying the `/etc/exports` file to include the mount point
- testing the mount on your local system

This will be followed by Exercises to mount the drive from a remote system.

LAB 5.1 EXERCISES

5.1.1 SET UP YOUR /ETC/EXPORTS FILE TO ALLOW MOUNTING

Look in the man pages for the following:
`nfs /etc/exports mount rpc.mountd rpd.nfsd fstab`

Before someone can access the data on your system, you need to give them access and control how they access the information. Some of the things you need to be concerned about when you give others access to your data include:

- read access
- write access
- root versus regular user-access rights
- verifying the user and server that will be accessing your data
- whether encryption is necessary
- whether there are any issues with large files since some versions of UNIX have a maximum file size of 2 gigs
- the version of NFS that is being used
- whether there are any issues with timeouts and how the system deals with lost connections or slow connections

Many of these issues can be addressed once you learn how to use NFS. For now, we will just be concerned about getting your system to share files. Then you can fine-tune the access rights and other features.

Your `/etc/exports` file controls what kind of access rights other systems have to mount your filesystems.

■ *FOR EXAMPLE:*

Figure 5.1 shows a sample `/etc/exports` file:

```
# Sample /etc/exports file
/usr *(ro)
/home *(rw)     # Home Directories
/usr/local      *.mydomain.com (rw) titanic.sunk.com (ro)
```

Figure 5.1 ■ A Sample `/etc/exports` File

The first column in Figure 5.1 is the name of the directory that you are exporting. In the first line, `/usr` is being exported. The second column is the grouping of servers and their appropriate access rights. On the second line, the `*` means that `/home` can be mounted by any system. The `(rw)` says that this is mounted with read/write access. You can grant access to multiple systems by grouping them with a pattern that matches the host and domain. So, as you see on the third line, any server that matches the pattern `*. mydomain.com` has read/write access because of the `(rw)` . This is followed by the system that has the name `titanic.sunk.com`, which is read-only because of the `(ro)`.

The Whole Truth

You cannot mount a directory if a directory below it in the directory tree is currently mounted. So you cannot mount `/usr/local/exportdir` if you already exported `/usr/local`. This prevents you from having multiple mount points and probably prevents some circular routes. This is true of the reverse situation where you cannot mount a directory that is above a currently mounted directory. Therefore you cannot mount `/usr/local` if `/usr/local/exportdir` is exported.

With some versions of UNIX you can, however, mount a directory in this situation if the new mount point is on a separate filesystem or partition. So if you have separate partitions or filesystems for `/usr/local` and `/usr`, then you can export each one separately.

Login with the root id or become super user.

You first need to check to see if you have a `/usr/local/exportdir` directory. To do this, you can enter the command:

```
ls -ld /usr/local/exportdir
```

a) What are the results of the `ls -ld /usr/local/exportdir` command?

If you do not find the `/usr/local/exportdir` directory, you will need to create it.

b) What command and format would you use to create the directory?

c) What are the results now of the `ls -ld /usr/local/exportdir` command?

You now are going to add a file to the `/usr/local/exportdir` directory. You can create an empty file with the `touch` command. You should now enter the command:

```
touch /usr/local/exportdir/export_file
```

d) What happens when you create the `/usr/local/exportdir/export_file` with the `touch` command?

Now you need to check out the file you just created. You can do this with the command:

```
ls -l /usr/local/exportdir/export_file
```

e) What happens when you run the `ls -l /usr/local/exportdir/export_file` command?

LAB 5.1

Go ahead and unmount the mounted directory. You are now going to add /usr/local/exportdir to your /etc/exports file. You will need to add the following line to the /etc/exports file:

```
/usr/local/exportdir  *(rw)
```

f) What is in your /etc/exports file now?

5.1.2 Do a Remote NFS Mount

You will now use NFS to mount the directory you created in Exercise 4.1.1. You will mount this on a second system on the same network. Figure 5.2 shows a picture of what is happening when you export a directory on the first box you worked with in Exercise 4.1.1 and then mount it remotely on the second box.

Figure 5.2 shows the view of the shared directory area that is created by an NFS mount. As you can see from the picture, the mount is totally transparent to the user. The directories that are mounted remotely look just like directories that are on the local box.

In order to mount a remote directory, you need to create a mount point. Then you need to use the mount command. To mount a drive remotely in NFS, you use the following format:

```
system_name:directory_name
```

■ FOR EXAMPLE:

The directory /usr/local/exportdir on the host tux would be designated as:

```
tux:/usr/local/exportdir
```

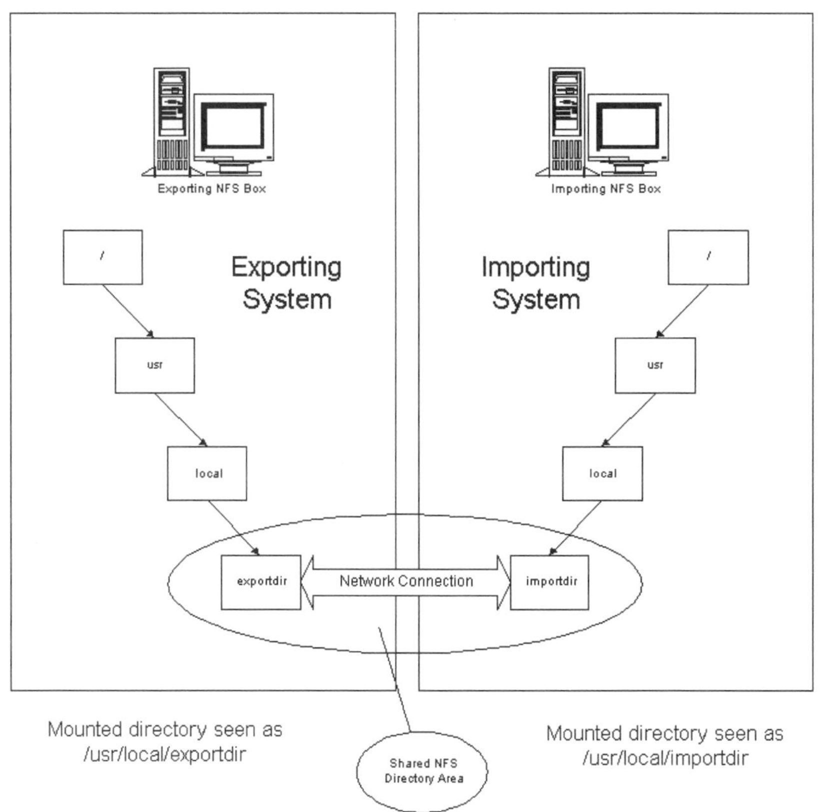

Figure 5.2 ■ The Sample NFS Local and Remote Directory Structure Used in this Chapter

Now to do the `mount` command, you use the format:

```
mount various_options system_name:directory_name local_mount_point
```

where

> `various_options`—Are options to NFS. There are various formats that these options take, so these will be show later in the examples.
>
> `system_name`—Is the name of the remote or exporting system.
>
> `directory_name`—Is the absolute pathname of the directory on the remote or exporting system.
>
> `local_mount_point`—Is where you are going to make the remote directory visible on your local system.

■ *FOR EXAMPLE:*

To mount the directory `/usr/local/exportdir` on the host `tux` on the local system using the `/usr/local/importdir` directory, you would use the command:

```
mount -t nfs tux:/usr/local/exportdir /usr/local/
importdir
```

You will now create the mount point and do the remote mount. You will make the directory `/usr/local/importdir`. But first, you will need to verify that it does not exist.

a) What did you find out when you checked to see if the `/usr/local/importdir` exists?

____

____

b) What command did you use in Question a?

____

____

If the directory `/usr/local/importdir` does not exist, then you need to create the mount point directory. Do this now.

c) What command did you use to create the `/usr/local/importdir` mount point directory?

____

____

Now you will mount the remote directory on your newly created mount point. Use the command shown earlier:

```
mount  various_options system_name:directory_name
local_mount_point
```

Now mount the remote directory you created in Exercise 5.1.1. Use the `-t nfs` option to do the mounting.

d) What is the complete command that you used to mount the remote drive on your local mount point?

---

e) What kind of results did you get when you did the remote mount?

Now you should leave off the `-t nfs` option to do the mounting.

f) What is the complete command that you used to mount the remote drive on your local mount point without the `-t nfs` option?

---

g) What kind of results did you get when you did the remote mount without the `-t nfs` option?

Now you should look at the contents of the directory you just mounted.

h) What are the contents of `/usr/local/importdir`, the directory you just mounted?

You can tell what directories are mounted by using the `mount` command.

i) What kind of results do you get from the `mount` command?

Now you can create a file on the newly mounted directory by just using the `touch` command. Use the command:

```
touch /usr/local/importdir/import_file
```

j) What kind of results do you get from the `touch` command?

There are several kinds of errors you can get. You need to resolve them before going on.

k) If you got any error messages, what were they and how did you resolve them?

Now you can go to the system that you used in Exercise 5.1.1. From there you should look at the contents of the directory `/usr/local/exportdir`.

l) What are the contents of `/usr/local/exportdir`?

LAB 5.1 EXERCISE ANSWERS

5.1.1 ANSWERS

a) What are the results of the `ls -ld /usr/local/exportdir` command?

Answer: Your results will depend on your individual system. If your directory doesn't exist, you would see results similar to what you see in Figure 5.3.

If you already have such a directory, you might see something similar to what you see in Figure 5.4.

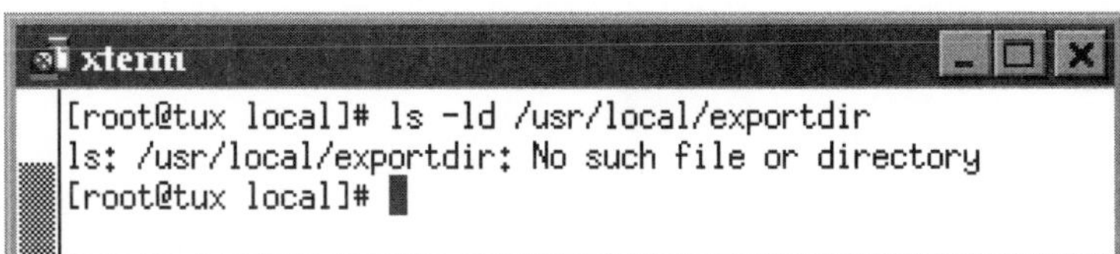

Figure 5.3 ■ Results from the `ls` Command for a Missing Directory

In this case, you might want to use a different directory name. Just replace `/usr/local/exportdir` with whatever name you want to use in the Lab discussion.

b) What command and format would you use to create the directory?

Answer: You can use the following command:

```
mkdir /usr/local/exportdir
```

This would result in the display:

```
[root@tux local]# mkdir /usr/local/exportdir
[root@tux local]#
```

Even better, you can use the following:

```
mkdir -p /usr/local/exportdir
```

You would then see these results:

```
[root@tux local]# mkdir -p /usr/local/exportdir
[root@tux local]#
```

This will create all of the parent directories, if they don't already exist.

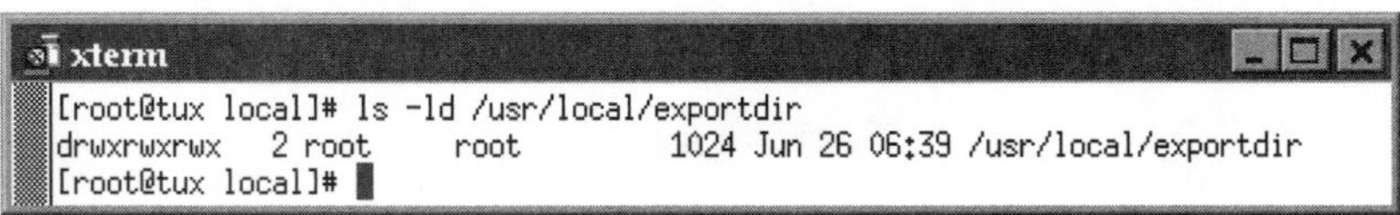

Figure 5.4 ■ Results from the `ls` Command for an Existing Directory

c) What are the results now of the `ls -ld /usr/local/exportdir` command?

Answer: You should see the results that you see in Figure 5.4.

d) What happens when your create the `/usr/local/exportdir/export_file` with the `touch` command?

Answer: Your results will be similar to the following:

```
[root@tux local]# touch /usr/local/exportdir/
export_file
[root@tux local]#
```

e) What happens when you run the `ls -l /usr/local/exportdir/export_file` command?

Answer: You will see the results shown in Figure 5.5.

If your display is different, you will want to figure out why. Some of the things you might see are:

- File not found—The file may not exist, so you need to retrace your steps. You might also want to make sure that you entered the proper path when the file was created. In addition, be sure that there were no mounts on the filesystem that might have changed. You may have a remote or local mount that was added or removed.
- Different path—Be sure that you specify the proper path as shown in Figure 5.2. You might be tempted to do your own thing, which is okay, but be sure everything is consistent.
- The ownership access rights are different—If you do not see:

  ```
  - rw - r - - r - -
  ```

  you might need to change the access rights. You could leave it alone for now, but if you get any access errors in the future, you can just run the command:

  ```
  chmod 644 export_file
  ```

```
xterm
[root@tux local]# ls -l /usr/local/exportdir/export_file
-rw-r--r--   1 root     root            0 Jun 26 06:39 /usr/local/exportdir/export_file
[root@tux local]#
```

Figure 5.5 ■ Using the `ls` Command to Display a File

This will change the access rights to the file. You will then need to set your `umask` on the system where it is being created to `644`. Do this with the command:

`umask 644`

This will set the proper bits for any future files you create.

- Improper ownership or group—This may not be a problem. The sample shows the file created by `root`, but since the mounting is done by `root`, then it will override any rights of the owner. However, if you do get some ownership errors later on, you should return here and reset the ownership of the file. You can do this with the command, `Chown root:root export_file`, from `root` (only `root` can give ownership to `root`).

f) What is in your `/etc/exports` file now?

Answer: When you look at your `/etc/exports` file, you will see a display similar to what you see in Figure 5.6.

You will see the line that you added at the bottom of the file.

```
[root@tux local]# cat /etc/exports
# Red Hat /etc/exports file
/usr *(ro)
/home *(rw,no_root_squash,link_relative)  # Home Directories
/mnt/cdrom *(ro)
/mnt/cdrom/RedHat *(ro)
/mnt/cdrom/RedHat/images *(ro)
/home/myid *(rw)
/usr/local/exportdir  *(ro) localhost(ro)
[root@tux local]#
```

Figure 5.6 ■ Looking at the Modified `/etc/exports` File

5.1.2 Answers

a) What did you find out when you checked to see if the `/usr/local/importdir` exists?

Answer: Your results will depend on your individual system. If your directory doesn't exist, you would see something similar to what's shown in Figure 5.7.

If you already have such a directory, you might see something similar to what's shown in Figure 5.8.

In this case, you might want to use a different directory name. Just replace `/usr/local/importdir` with whatever name you want to use in the Lab discussion.

b) What command did you use in Question a?

Answer: The best command to use is:

```
ls -ld /usr/local/importdir
```

There are other commands that can list the attributes, such as the following:

```
ls -d /usr/local/importdir
ls -l /usr/local
ls /usr/local
```

c) What command did you use to create the `/usr/local/importdir` mount point directory?

Answer: You can use the command:

```
mkdir /usr/local/importdir
```

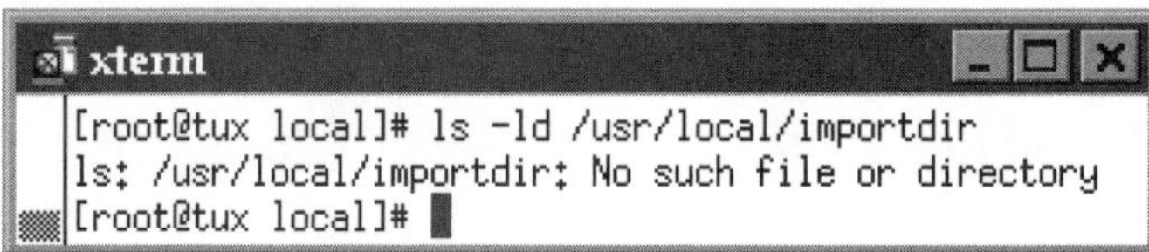

Figure 5.7 ■ Results of Looking for a Non-existent `importdir` Directory

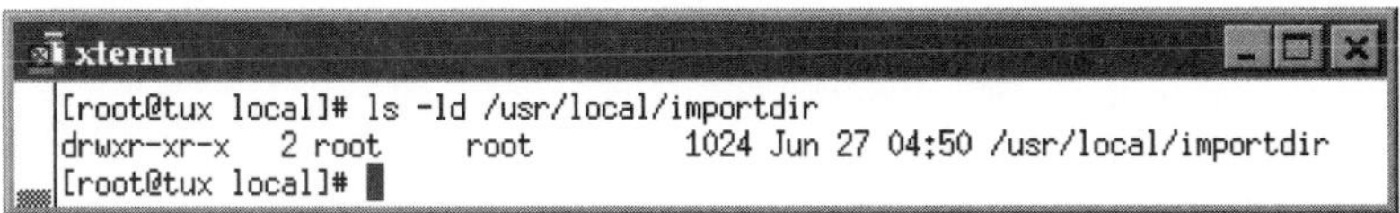
```
[root@tux local]# ls -ld /usr/local/importdir
drwxr-xr-x   2 root     root        1024 Jun 27 04:50 /usr/local/importdir
[root@tux local]#
```

Figure 5.8 ■ Results of Finding an Existing `importdir` Directory

This would result in the following display:

```
[root@tux local]# mkdir /usr/local/ importdir
[root@tux local]#
```

Even better, you can use the following:

```
mkdir -p /usr/local/ importdir
```

You would then see these results:

```
[root@tux local]# mkdir -p /usr/local/ importdir
[root@tux local]#
```

This will create all of the parent directories, if they don't already exist.

d) What is the complete command that you used to mount the remote drive on your local mount point?

Answer: You can use the following command:

```
mount -t nfs tux:/usr/local/exportdir /usr/local/
importdir
```

You just need to replace the name `tux` with the name of the remote system where the original directory that you are mounting is located.

e) What kind of results did you get when you did the remote mount?

Answer: You will see a display similar to the following:

```
[root@tux local]# mount -t nfs tux:/usr/local/exportdir
/usr/local/importdir
[root@tux local]#
```

f) What is the complete command that you used to mount the remote drive on your local mount point without the `-t nfs` option?

Answer: You would use the following:

```
mount tux:/usr/local/exportdir /usr/local/importdir
```

This will mount your remote directory with NFS, which is the default for a remote mount.

g) What kind of results did you get when you did the remote mount without the `-t nfs` option?

Answer: You will see a display similar to the following:

```
[root@tux local]# mount tux:/usr/local/exportdir/
usr/local/importdir
[root@tux local]#
```

Just replace `tux` with the name of your remote system where the directory to be mounted is located. If you get an error here, but did not get an error in Question d, then be sure that you typed everything correctly. The two commands should be the same. However, in some versions of Linux, you may find that any NFS mounting is not supported and needs to be added. But, in this case, both commands should fail.

h) What are the contents of `/usr/local/importdir`, the directory you just mounted?

Answer: You can use the command:

```
ls -l /usr/local/importdir
```

This will show the contents of the mounted directory with the results in Figure 5.9.

Note that this is the file that you created with the `touch` command on the remote system before you did the NFS mount. So, now both the local and remote systems can share files and directories.

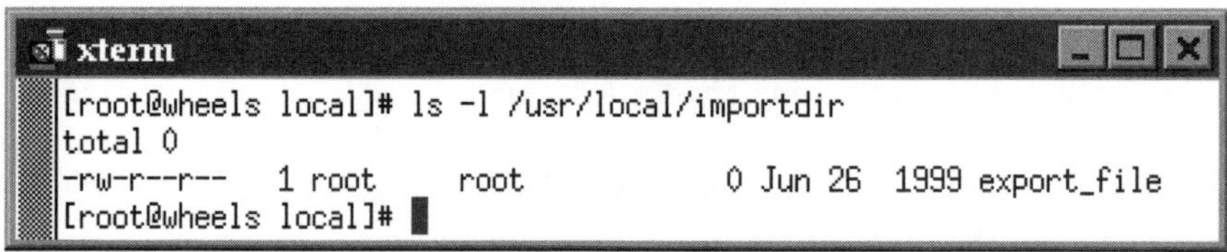

xterm
[root@wheels local]# ls -l /usr/local/importdir
total 0
-rw-r--r--   1 root   root   0 Jun 26 1999 export_file
[root@wheels local]#

Figure 5.9 ■ The Contents of the `importdir` Directory

i) What kind of results do you get from the `mount` command?

Answer: The `mount` command will give you results in Figure 5.10.

The last line that results from the `mount` command shows the remote mount. This line is:

```
tux:/usr/local/exportdir on /usr/local/importdir type nfs
(rw,addr=172.16.1.1)
```

This line can be broken down as follows:

- `tux:/usr/local/exportdir`—Shows the name of the host, which is `tux` in this case. That is followed by the colon, which is an indicator that the previous word or string is the name of the host. The colon is followed by the name of the remote directory.
- `/usr/local/importdir`—Is the name of the local directory where the mount occurs.
- `type nfs`—Shows that the mount is an NFS mount.
- `(rw,addr=172.16.1.1)`—Says that the mount type is read/write and the remote address is `172.16.1.1`.

j) What kind of results do you get from the `touch` command?

Answer: You should get an error message like the one you see in Figure 5.11.

Permission is denied because the remote directory has the following attributes on the remote server:

```
[root@tux local]# ls -ld exportdir
drwxr-xr-x   2 root     root          1024 Jun 26 06:10 exportdir
[root@tux local]#
```

This prevents a remote user, or any user other than `root` on the remote system, from writing to the directory.

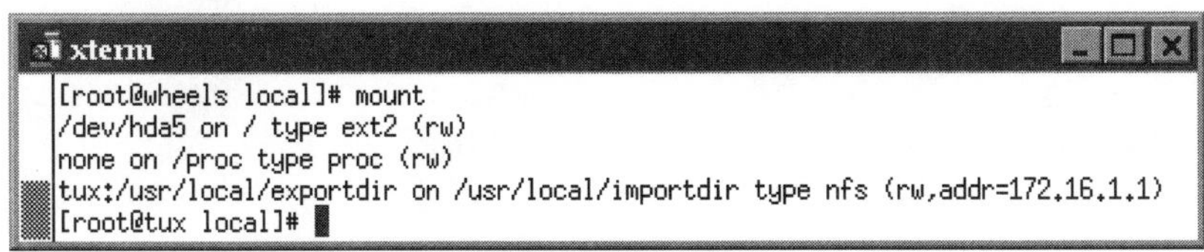

Figure 5.10 ■ The Results of the mount Command

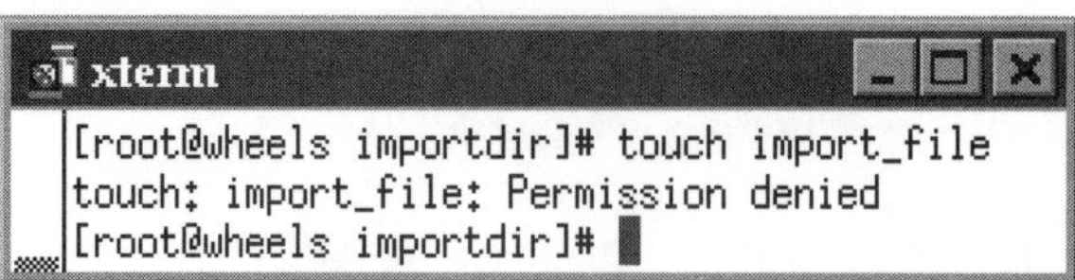

Figure 5.11 ■ `Permission Denied` Error Message

k) If you got any error messages, what were they and how did you resolve them?

Answer: You should have seen the results that you saw in Figure 5.11.

What you now need to do is unmount the remote directory on your local box. You can use the command:

```
umount tux:/usr/local/exportdir
```

or

```
umount /usr/local/importdir
```

It is necessary to unmount the remote directory, because any changes you make in the file or directory attributes may not take effect until you remount the directory again.

Now you should go to the remote system and run the following command:

```
chmod 777 /usr/local/exportdir
```

Now do the command:

```
ls -ld /usr/local/exportdir
```

This should give you the following results:

```
drwxrwxrwx  2 root     root          1024 Jun 26 06:10 exportdir
```

Now you should go back to your local box and redo the steps starting with Question d and enter the following command:

```
mount -t nfs tux:/usr/local/exportdir /usr/local/importdir
```

Then you can do the `touch` command:

```
touch /usr/local/importdir/import_file
```

This should give the following results:

```
[root@wheels importdir]# touch/usr/local/importdir/import_file
[root@wheels importdir]#
```

You should not have gotten any errors from these steps. If you do get an error, then you need to revisit the previous steps. In particular, if you are denied access, you need to be sure that you have allowed read/write access on the the remote server so that your local system can mount the filesystem and make it writeable. If you do the `mount` command, one of the characteristics should be `rw` which means read/writeable. If not, you did not set up the proper permissions on the remote box. You should go back to the remote system and compare the `/etc/exports` file with the results in Figure 5.10.

l) What are the contents of `/usr/local/exportdir`?

Answer: You should use the `ls` *command to determine the contents of the directory (see Figure 5.12).*

In the directory, the file `export_file` was created before the NFS mount existed. The file is owned by `root` and the group ownership is `root`. The new file `import_file` was created after the NFS mount was created. In this case, the owner is `nobody` and the group is `nobody`. This is because we gave total access to the directory, and NFS uses the id `nobody` as the default owner and group for files and directories that are created. Because the directory was originally created in Question c with rights of `rwxr-xr-x`, only `root` on the remote system could write to it until the access rights were changed to `rwx`.

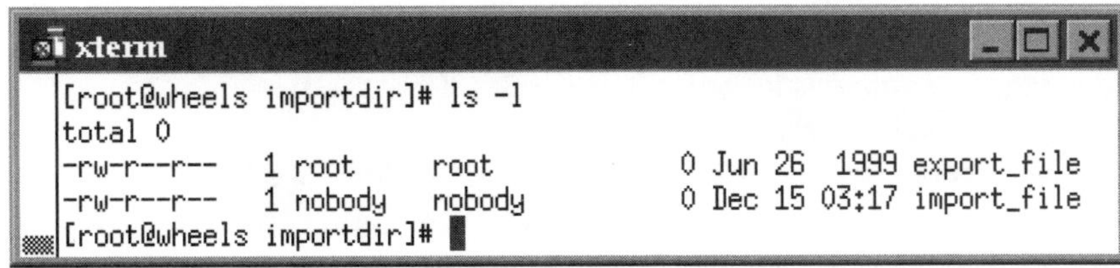

Figure 5.12 ■ Contents of the Mounted `/usr/local/importdir`

You should now unmount the directory you mounted remotely, then go back to the remote host and change the access rights of the directory with the following command:

```
chmod 755 /usr/local/exportdir
```

This is because the directory is a security hole if it has the rights of `rwxrwxrwx`.

LAB 5.1 SELF-REVIEW QUESTIONS

In order to test your progress, you should be able to answer the following questions.

1) Based on Figure 5.1, the number of directories that are exported is which of the following?

a) _____0
b) _____1
c) _____2
d) _____3
e) _____4

2) Based on Figure 5.1, the number of hosts that can access the `/usr/local` directory is which of the following?

a) _____0
b) _____1
c) _____2
d) _____3
e) _____indeterminate

3) Based on Figure 5.2, the contents of the directory `/usr/local/exportdir` on the exporting box and `/usr/local/importdir` on the importing box are identical to any user with full access rights to the directories.

a) _____True
b) _____False

4) What is the format used for the imported directory location when importing the directory `/usr/local/yourdir` from the system named `ghost` and mounting it on the system named `virtuoso` on the mount point `/usr/local/your_sys`? (Hint: In Figure 5.2, `ghost` is on the left and `virtuoso` is on the right. Just replace all the names with the new names.)

a) _____/usr/local/yourdir:ghost
b) _____virtuoso:/usr/local/yourdir
c) _____ghost:/usr/local/yourdir
d) _____virtuoso:/usr/local/your_sys
e) _____/usr/local/your_sys

5) Using the system described in Question 4,what is the format used to describe the mount point on the local box?

a) _____/usr/local/yourdir:ghost
b) _____virtuoso:/usr/local/yourdir
c) _____ghost:/usr/local/yourdir
d) _____virtuoso:/usr/local/your_sys
e) _____/usr/local/your_sys

6) If you are on the box named helix, the command:

```
mount -t nfs topdog:/usr/local/hair /usr/local/shed
```

will do which of the following mounts?

a) _____shed on topdog
b) _____hair on helix where the contents of hair on topdog and shed on helix are the same
c) _____hair on helix where the contents of /usr/local is the same on both boxes
d) _____shed on helix
e) _____none of the above

Quiz answers appear in Appendix A, Section 5.1.

CHAPTER 5

TEST YOUR THINKING

1) There are a number of options that you can use when you allow an NFS mount. The best way to learn about these options is to set up your test environment and see what the effects are. Some of the options you can add to the `/etc/exports` file on your exporting system that can be tested are as follows:

   `insecure`
   `unix-rpc`–(default behavior)
   `root_squash`
   `no_root_squash`–(default behavior)
   `ro`–(default behavior)
   `rw`

   There are a number of other options, but these are ones that you will want to test. You should set up two networked systems so that you can test these characteristics. You should attempt to recreate the NFS mounts in this chapter.

   a) Test the `insecure` option. What happens when you try to do the NFS mount? What are the results of using the `touch` command to create a file?

   b) Test the `unix-rpc` option. What happens when you try to do the NFS mount? What are the results of using the `touch` command to create a file?

   c) Test the `root_squash` option. What happens when you try to do the NFS mount? What are the results of using the `touch` command to create a file?

   d) Test the `no-root_squash` option. What happens when you try to do the NFS mount? What are the results of using the `touch` command to create a file?

   e) Test the `ro` option. What happens when you try to do the NFS mount? What are the results of using the `touch` command to create a file?

   f) Test the `rw` option. What happens when you try to do the NFS mount? What are the results of using the `touch` command to create a file?

2) When you do a mount on a remote system on your local system, you can give several options to the `mount` command. The `mount` command can be displayed as follows:

```
mount  various_options system_name:directory_name
local_mount_point
```

This is the format of the command you have been using in this chapter.

You have already used `nfs` as an option. Some of the options that can be tested are:

`hard`
`soft`
`timeo=n`, where `n` is tenths of a second

a) Test the `hard` option. What happens when you try to do the NFS mounts with an existing host that you have previously mounted successfully? Repeat the command with a host that doesn't exist.

b) Test the `soft` option. What happens when you try to do the NFS mounts with an existing host that you have previously mounted successfully? Repeat the command with a host that doesn't exist.

c) Test the `timeo=n` option. Use the values of 1 second, 10 seconds and a minute. (Don't forget about converting the value of `n` to seconds.) What happens when you try to do the NFS mounts with an existing host that you have previously mounted successfully? Repeat the command with a host that doesn't exist.

APPENDIX A

ANSWERS TO SELF-REVIEW QUESTIONS

Lab 1.1 Self-Review Answers

Question	Answer	Comments
1)	a	
2)	b	
3)	b	
4)	c	
5)	d	
6)	c	
7)	a	
8)	a	
9)	b	
10)	a	

Lab 1.2 Self-Review Answers

Question	Answer	Comments
1)	b	
2)	b	
3)	b	
4)	c	
5)	a	
6)	d	
7)	d	
8)	b	

Question	Answer	Comments
9)	a	
10)	c	
11)	b	
12)	c	
13)	d	
14)	a	

Lab 2.1 Self-Review Answers

Question	Answer	Comments
1)	c	
2)	a	
3)	b	
4)	b	
5)	e	
6)	a	
7)	b	
8)	a	
9)	d	
10)	a	

Lab 3.1 Self-Review Answers

Question	Answer	Comments
1)	a	
2)	b	
3)	b	
4)	b	
5)	b	

Lab 3.2 Self-Review Answers

Question	Answer	Comments
1)	b	
2)	c	

Question	Answer	Comments
3)	a	
4)	a	
5)	a	
6)	d	
7)	a	
8)	d	
9)	b	

Lab 4.1 Self-Review Answers

Question	Answer	Comments
1)	a	
2)	b	
3)	b	
4)	b	

Lab 4.2 Self-Review Answers

Question	Answer	Comments
1)	d	
2)	b	
3)	c	
4)	a	
5)	c	
6)	d	

Lab 4.3 Self-Review Answers

Question	Answer	Comments
1)	b	
2)	b	
3)	c	
4)	b	See Figure 4.25

Question	Answer	Comments
5)	a	No Samba did not exist then. Did this wake you up?
6)	a	
7)	a	

Lab 5.1 Self-Review Answers

Question	Answer	Comments
1)	d	
2)	e	
3)	a	
4)	c	
5)	e	
6)	b	

APPENDIX B

USING MINIMAL LINUX

The tools we use do not need to be complicated or expensive if all we want to do is hammer a nail.

—*Joe*

LINUX

There are a number of versions of Linux that can run on minimal resources. These are called Minimal Linux or Tiny Linux. These versions can run on systems from a simple 8086 PC and a Palm Pilot to a system containing hundreds of processors. This makes it ideal to do prototyping of software and for a student to be `root` without having to work from a permanent installation.

The accompanying CD-ROM includes Stampede Linux as well as several Minimal Linux versions. These versions of Linux can give you many of the features of a full-blow version of Linux. In addition, there are features such as:

- The operating system and the programs you need are loaded into RAM disks, which act like real disks, but are actually memory. You can make any changes you want to the files in memory without making any permanent changes to your system. You can use this environment to test features before implementing them permanently.
- You can run programs much faster than they would run off disk. Since the access time of information in memory is much faster than the access time of a disk, you can use it for critical

situations where speed is of the essence and the applications are not very memory-intensive.

- They are usually tarred and gzipped files that are expanded when the system boots up. Typically, you will get 10 megs of filesystem space from two diskettes. It is easy to expand the filesystem space available if you have more memory.
- Some versions of Linux, such as Trinux, allow you to load in diskettes of software continually up to the limits of the space you have set aside.
- Once your networking is in place, some versions will allow you to do NFS mounts, thus giving you even more power.
- You can embed Linux on a ROM, EEPROM, or into firmware and have it load into memory everytime it boots up. This is very useful for devices such as TV controllers, cell phones, routers, bridges, game machines, etc. Since they typically can run in 10 megs of ramdisk, the cost of producing such equipment can be greatly reduced. Since it is a full-blown operating system, any features can be prototyped on larger systems and then minimized to run in the space available.
- They often include a full range of security and system diagnostic tools so that you can take a couple of diskettes to a workstation, boot from the diskettes, and look for networking or system problems from those workstations. Once you are done, you can just reboot the PC without the diskettes, and the original PC software is unaffected. This can be done by MS-DOS, but then you are more limited in running your programs from one diskette.
- PC diskette formats are either standard or recognized in several versions, so that you can either edit from Windows PCs or save them on a Novell or NT network disk for general consumption.

Some of the drawbacks of Minimal Linuxes are:

- You need to feed the system diskettes continually if you are using more than one diskette.
- The software and kernels that are used are typically stripped-down versions of the generally available versions. This is done by removing features from the kernel. So you may not find the features you want, or you may need to compile them in. Fortunately, you do have access to the source code.
- Some of the commands and tools that you are used to will not be on the diskettes. What is missing depends on who assembled the distribution. You will then need to add the commands you want.

- Support for these versions is more limited than the standard packages, since they can have much of the functionality removed.
- In some cases, the diskette format is a non-standard format, so you have to go through several additional steps to add files to the diskette. At least one version uses a diskette of 1.7 megs, which is non-standard and sometimes causes some system confusion when you are doing mounts and file manipulation.

Trinux

I am going to discuss a version of Minimal Linux called Trinux. This is available at `http://www.trinux.org`. When you are installing a Minimal Linux, you should investigate the versions that are available on the Internet. Remember that just because a version is the latest doesn't mean it is workable for you. Trinux 0.49 supports a number of ethernet cards that are not currently supported by versions 0.51 and 0.61. This is because the later versions changed libraries and it just takes time to recompile the drivers.

I am providing an analysis of Trinux that you might use to analyze any version of minimal Linux that you are interested in using. The features of Trinux that I found useful are:

- The disk is DOS formatted, which allows me to move back-and-forth between Linux and DOS. In an academic environment, this is very useful because the Internet access is typically via Windows-based PCs. When the software is downloaded off the Internet, the process becomes a lot easier. On UNIX or Linux boxes in academic environments, the diskette drive is either not available or limited to `root` only—not a good situation for the beginning Linux user.
- The number of diskettes that can be loaded in the boot process is limited only by the amount of RAM that is available, unused by the system, and configured in the boot files.
- You can load the software that you want in modular format. You can boot from a diskette. Then you can use a diskette that will run:
  - Apache Web server
  - a name server
  - X-Windows

- network analysis tools
- several other kinds of software

  This is very useful for an academic or research environment in which you want to focus on a particular feature of a piece of software without permanently affecting the software on the diskette that you have loaded.

- There are very few files that need to be configured to modify the boot process. There are two main files: `pre.rc` and `post.rc`. These are executed at different stages of the bootup process to execute any modifications you want.

Some of the features that I would have found useful, but were not available at the time of this writing are:

- NFS support, which is useful when additional mounting across the network is needed to make more files available.
- Samba support, which would allow me to access MS Windows files across the network.
- Support for `ext2` filesystem diskettes, which is very useful, especially in a learning environment and is standard in Linux.

Some disadvantages of Trinux include:

- More ethernet drivers should be available, or clearer pointers to where the drivers are available should be evident. Trinux is based on standard Linux, so the drivers are available in many places, but having the source information clearer would be useful.
- Other versions of Linux can be run totally from one diskette and do support some of these features.

What you need to do is to research the various versions of Linux that are available to you and find one that gives you what you need to accomplish your goals.

APPENDIX C

BUILDING YOUR LINUX HOME NETWORK

When you can control your own system and network, you can test out your ideas and learn quicker than otherwise would be the case. It also allows you to be more reckless, which would again help you test out your ideas and learn more quickly. The home network can give you more freedom to pursue your ideas. You are only limited by your dreams and resources.

—Joe

This appendix will discuss:

- The Budget
- Family Impact
- The Work Space
- Electrical Needs
- Network Cabling
- Networking Equipment
- Cable and Broadband Network
- Local and Internet Access
- Computer Software

In many work environments, it is impossible to test out your ideas or to spend time delving into some of the more obscure aspects of your operating system. There are concerns about network security, integrity, and impact on production environments. In this Appendix, the basic concept and the necessary components that it takes to build a network will be discussed. This sections will discuss some of the things you need to consider when you create a network. The ideal environment will be presented. Your setup will be different and your mileage may vary.

The Budget

The number-one constraint we all have is the amount of money we can put toward building the network. It is possible to spend thousands of dollars before you even realize how much you have spent. It can even become an obsession. But that is a topic for another book. You need to find a way to balance the money you spend with benefits you will derive from it.

If your goal is to develop new skills for your career, you can be certain that any new Linux and UNIX skills you develop can have a financial return, either in your current or future positions. If you are doing software development on some public-domain project, you will be furthering your skills and gaining some admiration in the programming community. If you are writing a book, as I am, you find that you need to have the proper resources to test out your ideas before you put them into print. But here there is a direct financial return also.

Whatever your goals are, you should also consider what kind of investment you can make. You should expect that, over time, you will spend several times whatever your original goal was. This is because it is difficult to anticipate the needs that you would have. That old 486 may be perfect for doing command-line work in Linux and for use as a file and print server. It will do okay for the basic X-windows stuff. But once you start loading up the software on your screen, you'll be happier with a faster box.

Once someone buys a new computer, its value immediately plummets. This is like the proverbial $1,000 that you lose by driving the car out of the dealer's lot. You can take advantage of this, since a Linux box will run a lot better on older computers than MS Windows products. Many companies now totally write-off the value of a new computer in three years. This means that it has no value after this time. But if you look back at the kinds of computers we were buying three years ago, they were generally Pentiums with speeds of approximately 150 MHz. These boxes work well as Linux boxes and can often be purchased for $100 at computer swaps, or for less if you are willing to do some dumpster diving. Your employer may be glad to give you a system or two just to get them off the books. PCs sometimes present a disposal problem due to chemicals that are used in making the computer boards. Some countries now even require an environmental fee to be paid for each computer to cover disposal costs.

In any case, Linux computers can be acquired for a minimal expense if you are patient. In fact, if you are just learning Linux, you are better off working with older equipment because it is more likely to have drivers written for them than the latest video card would. You don't need to have the added frustration of hardware that doesn't work with Linux or that needs to have special drivers loaded or compiled into the kernel. This is where you need to have a Linux hardware compatibility list available.

Most ethernet equipment lasts for years. An ethernet cable does not deteriorate in a normal networking environment. Fortunately, the equipment for ethernet gets cheaper, so here it pays to just check around for the best deals on new equipment. Prices for the same ethernet cable can vary from $5.00 to $15.00. The same is true of ethernet hubs and ethernet cards. Even 100 MHz networking for the home can be set up for a very small price increase over a 10 MHz network.

Fortunately, you can load Linux on a Windows PC that you already have. The only thing you might need is a larger hard drive. This will allow you to run both operating systems and boot up one or the other.

Family Impact

What is the impact of having extra equipment around the house? What will the time or money you spend do to the family relationships? If you are single, how will it affect your dating life? Of course, you might be able to make this a family project. Remember the phrase "The family that plays together, stays together." Is this a family project?

The Work Space

The work space can determine a lot about what kind of network you can have. If you just have a corner or a wall in a room, you cannot do a very extensive network, and you may be limited to two PCs. You should consider running multiple operating systems on the same box and use a boot manager to control which PC you will be working with. You can also purchase a switch box that can allow you to switch your monitor to several

PCs. This can save a lot of space and money and can allow you to use a bigger monitor than you might otherwise use.

If you have a spare room, you can put together a more extensive network or spread things out more and have individual monitors for each PC.

Electrical Needs

You need to be sure that you have adequate electric power to cover your new systems. It is possible to overload your circuits and cause your electric breaker to trip and disconnect the power to your PCs. This might cause damage to the hardware because of the sudden shutting down of the power. There are electrical devices such as transformers and capacitors that can feed back electric to the circuit once the breaker flips off. An even worse scenario would be where the breaker does not trip and the main breaker will get tripped, thus turnung off power to your whole house.

If you are going to add more than a few PCs, you will want to have an electrician examine your electrical needs. You may want to increase the number of circuits to handle the increase in your power needs. To keep your costs down, you might want to put your PCs in several rooms that are on separate electrical circuits. This will keep the electrical impact lower and will help protect your PCs in case one circuit should get overloaded and trip the breaker. You will also want to put your systems close to the main breaker, so that the electrician can easily and cheaply run new circuits.

You should also examine whether the power coming into the home needs to be increased. This is measured by the amount of Amps in your electrical service. Many homes have a 100 Amp service. Newer homes will typically run a 200 Amp service. By examining your breaker box and looking at the main breaker, you can determine if you have 100 or 200 Amp service. Increasing your electric service may also require running new lines from the electric companies' power transformer or digging and running new lines underground. However, many homes are already able to handle an increase to a 200 Amp service from 100 Amp service because the cabling that was installed is a lot heavier than needed. You will need to consult your electrician or call your electric company to determine whether your cables will handle the new power load.

Speaking from personal experience, fixing the power problems at one point can push the problem closer to the power source. This then becomes a fire hazard. Also, when you use numerous power strips that are plugged into other power strips, and so on, you run power cords across the floor, creating a hazardous situation. So the electrician will need to put enough outlets in so that you do not need to run many power strips. Many municipalities consider power strips as temporary power taps and may fine you for creating a fire hazard if your electric power is overtaxed.

If you are not sure how much power you need, you can contact one of the websites for the companies that make Universal Power Supplies (UPS). These are basically battery backup systems that can run your PCs for a short time when there is no power. Several of them have calculators that can allow you to calculate how much power you are going to need. One of the sites is `http://www.apcc.com`.

Network Cabling

There are several kinds of cabling that you may be using in your home for connecting your computer to other computers. Based on the type of connectors they use, they are:

- **RJ11**—This is the common type of cabling used to connect your modem to your phone connection. The type of cable that is usually used is called a Category 3, or a Cat 3, cable. This cabling is not very good for connecting a computer to a network, but works well enough for your modem. However, Intel and several manufacturers have announced networks that can run on Cat 3 cable. In any case, you can only run a max of 10 MBPS on this type of wiring, if you are lucky.
- **RJ45**—This is used for cabling commonly referred to as UTP. This is short for Unshielded Twisted Pair, which is also known as 10BaseT. The actual cabling type can be Cat 3 or Cat 5, though Cat 3 is used typically for phones and is very poor for networking. The connector looks very much like the connector and cable that you would use for your phone, but it is specially designed for networks. This requires that you purchase an ethernet hub. In the ethernet hub, every PC has a separate socket to plug its ethernet cable into. It is more reliable than thin ethernet.
- **Thin ethernet**—This looks like the same type of round cabling that you would use for your TV connection. Only the electrical characteristics and the connectors are different. This is also known as 10Base2. This type of cabling is losing popularity, but is the cheapest and easiest way to set up a network. It does not require a hub to plug into. Each PC talks to every other PC on the network by using this one cable. However, if

you have a bad cable or a bad connection on a thin ethernet network, you can bring down the whole network.

- **Other types**—Another type of ethernet connection is called thick ethernet or 10Base5. This is not very common anymore and requires that the cable actually has a hole punched into it, or tapped, to connect a transceiver. This uses an AUI cable to connect between the system and the network.

Ethernet cabling does not require an electrician in most communities to run the cables because the power it carries is insignificant. There are many electricians and electrical companies that specialize in running data cables for networking. You might want to consider one of these electricians if you are going to be doing extensive wiring, building a new house, or if you just want to make sure everything is done right and neatly.

Networking Equipment

When you create your home network, you will need several pieces of networking hardware. The hardware will depend on the type of cabling you have chosen. Once you have decided on a cabling method, you can choose the remainder of the equipment.

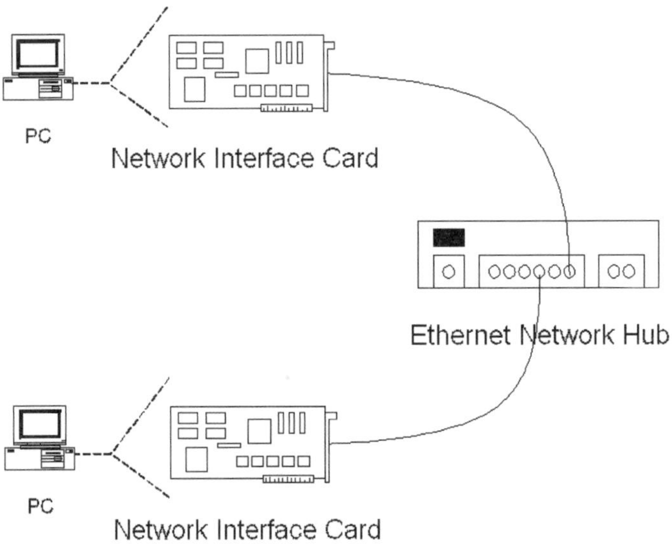

Figure C.1 ■ A Simple Network Connecting Two PCs

THE NETWORK INTERFACE CARD

The *Network Interface Card,* commonly known as the NIC, goes into the PC and is how the PC connects to the network. The term *NIC* is a generic term for any card that connects a device to a network. You can see the NIC in Figure C.1. The NIC card for the PC is typically 10 MBPS (megabytes per second), 100 MBPS or 10/100 MBPS ethernet. The 10/100 MBPS cards have dropped drastically in price, and you can usually get 10/100 MBPS card for about $20.00 more than an 10 MBPS card. In general, 10 MBPS cards use RJ45 connectors. The 100 MBPS and 10/100 MBPS cards are all RJ45. Ethernet combo cards that have both RJ45 and thin ethernet connectors are still relatively easy to find.

The 10/100 MBPS cards are more recent devices, so you need to be sure that any card that you buy is fully supported by Linux. You can access the hardware compatibility lists at the various websites for vendors such as Red Hat and Caldera to determine if your NIC card is supported. The website for Red Hat is at `http://www.redhat.com` and the website for Caldera is at `http://www.caldera.com`.

THE NETWORK HUB

The network hub allows you to connect together several systems. You see a hub displayed in Figure C.1. This is generally used for RJ45 or UTP ethernet cabling, although they can also have a thin ethernet or a specialized connector called an AUI connector. The only other type of hub that you might find is a token ring hub, which is rarely used in the home and is usually twice the price for all the hardware. Then you need to decide on a speed. In a home environment, you will rarely hit the maximum transfer rate or 100 MBPS, unless you are doing a lot of graphics or file transfers back and forth.

It is possible to connect or cascade two or more hubs together as shown in Figure C.2. If you do this, it is better to connect together two or more hubs that are identical. While it is possible to connect together 10 MBPS and 10/100 MBPS hubs, this can sometimes cause instabilities due to the different network characteristics. If you do this, you should be sure to test connectivity from all devices on the network. You should also be sure to get quality network components—in this case, to ensure a stable network. The old adage about getting what you pay for is true here also. You should read the documentation that comes with your hubs to be sure that there are no special limitations, such as the number of hubs that can be cascaded together.

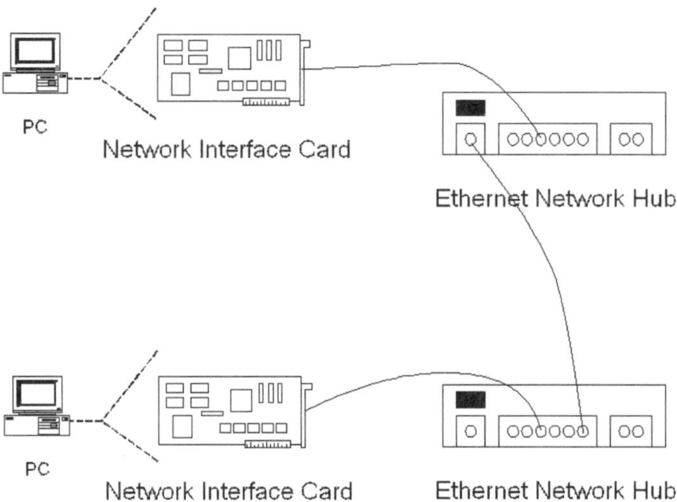

Figure C.2 ■ Adding a Second Hub to the Network

Cable and Broadband Network

A version of networking that is gaining in popularity very quickly is *broadband* for the home. Broadband has been around for years in highly specialized, high-speed commercial networks to carry television signals as well as networking signals. It has now come home to the consumer. Broadband provides the basis for Internet access to the home from cable companies. The cable-to-home network includes the TV signal and the network signal. This requires a specialized cable modem which will convert the broadband signal to an ethernet signal. The modem also controls access to the user's home network and provides a number of features needed by the cable company, such as filtering of packets, access control, and information gathering.

Figure C.3 shows a typical network configuration for a home connection to a broadband network.

In one version of broadband used by Mediaone, the cable network has a 10 MBPS fiber optic cable connected to a hub in your neighborhood. This is split into a maximum of twenty 3 MBPS copper cable connections to cable modems in the homes. The cable modem then provides a 1.5 MBPS ethernet connection to the home network or individual PC. The upload speed from the home to the Internet is 300 KBPS. This is the speed that you can send information out to the Internet. The cable modem can be either connected directly to your PC or to an ethernet hub. Both connec-

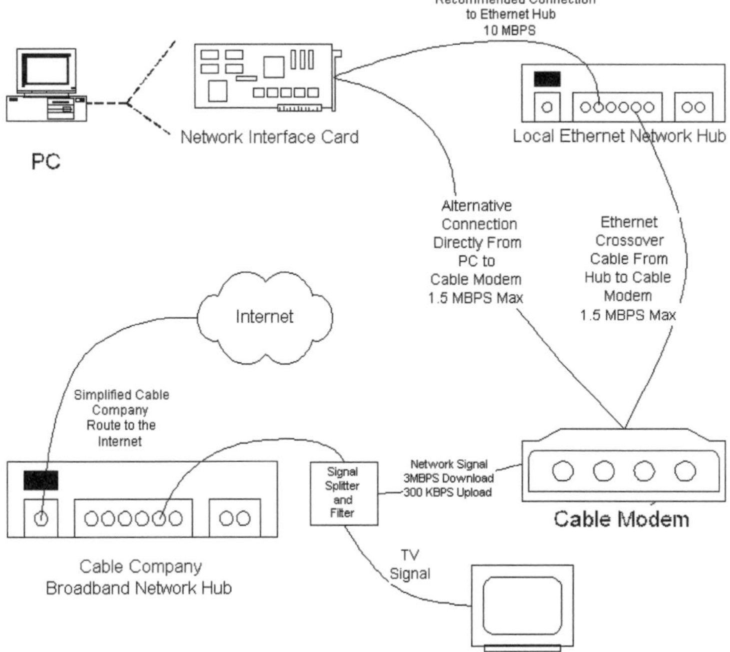

Figure C.3 ■ A Typical Broadband Network Configuration for the Home

tion types are shown in Figure C.3. The IP addresses are assigned dynamically by a process known as DHCP (Dynamic Host Control Protocol) which stores the unique information about a system and organizes it by the ethernet hardware address.

If you use a hub, then you can then connect multiple PCs to the Internet. However, if you are only limited to one IP address at a time for connection to the Internet, you will need to bring down the first PC and then, after a length of time, bring up the second PC. This time period depends on how long it takes the Broadband network to reset its DHCP tables. The only way you can determine this is to try it and see how long it takes to get your Internet access from the second PC. Once the PC has established an Internet connection, you can bring up the one you shut down, although it will not have Internet access. If you have four IP addresses and want to bring in a fifth PC, you will need to bring down one of the four that are currently connected and then bring up the fifth one. Once this connects to the Internet, you can bring back the one that you shut down. The IP addresses are assigned dynamically by DHCP, which stores the unique information about a system and organizes it by the ethernet hardware address.

A fee for cable internet access in some localities is $39.95 per month for one IP address. Some locations allow for up to four IP addresses for $59.95 a month. The speed compares with commercial T1 connections that are 1.5 MBPS and can run from $600.00 per month and up.

Unfortunately, cable modem access is available in only a limited number of locations in this country and depends on your local cable company. However, it is expected that, as many of the telephone companies get involved in cable access, the number of users will grow even more rapidly than the current pace.

Local and Internet Access

In Figure C.4 you see an example of a network configuration that utilizes the single IP address that is provided either by a cable modem network, a dialup network, T1, or other network configuration for accessing the Internet. This is the most common way of connecting a home network to the Internet. The most popular way of doing this is using a software package called PPP (Point-to-Point Protocol) which sets up a dial-up IP network between your PC and the destination network. Any Internet access that you have will go through the dial-up network and then through the

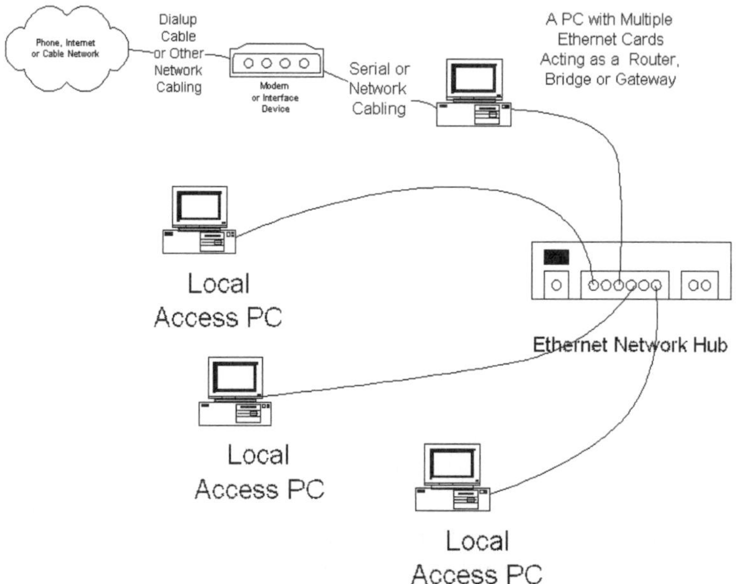

Figure C.4 ■ A Sample Home Network Configuration with One IP Address Acting as a Router

network of your Internet Service Provider. Another, less common method, is the use of SLIP (Serial Line Interface Protocol). PPP is the standard used by practically all dial-up Internet Service Providers. This includes AOL and MSN, as well as many others.

You can set up a local network that can prevent access to the Internet from some PCs by using certain reserved IP Addresses. You can also keep your private packets of information on your local network and prevent them from going out on the Internet. When you set up the local home network, you would use the Private or General-Purpose IP Addresses show in Table C.1.

The addresses in Table C.1 are not routable to the Internet. They can be safely used on your local IP network without worrying about conflicting with IP addresses that are already in use.

If you are fortunate and can have more than one IP address directly on the Internet, you should use a configuration similar to the one in Figure C.5.

The network configuration shown in Figure C.5 allows your network of four PCs to have access directly to the Internet. Some of these PCs have two ethernet NIC cards. The second card will be for access to a local network. Each PC with two NIC cards can also act as a router or gateway to the Internet for local systems that do not have the Internet access. In the home IP local network with four IP addresses, you will still use the private or general-purpose IP addresses shown in Table C.1. The PCs with local access can access the Internet by sending packets of information to one of the PCs with two NIC cards, if that PC is set up to route packets to the Internet.

Computer Software

The software that can be used to access the Internet is already included in Linux. The complete set of TCP/IP software is included in Linux. In addi-

Table C.1 ■ Private or General Purpose IP Addresses

Network Class	Start Address	End Address	Standard Subnet Mask
A	10.0.0.0	10.255.255.255	255.0.0.0
B	172.16.0.0	172.31.255.255	255.255.0.0
C	192.168.1.0	192.168.255.255	255.255.255.0

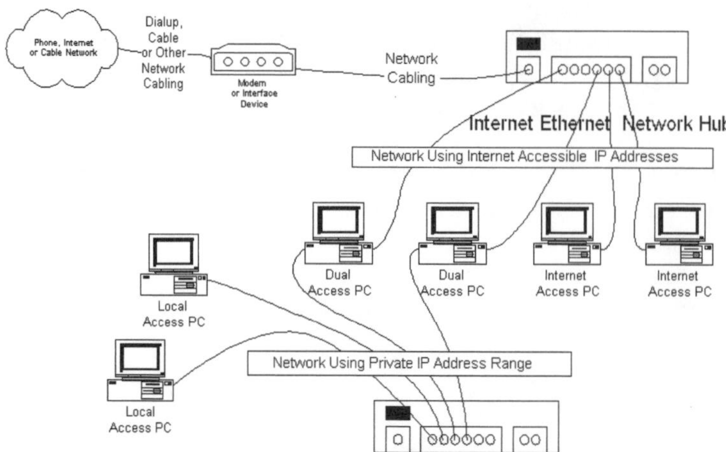

Figure C.5 ■ A Recommended Home Network Configuration with Four IP Addresses

tion, there is usually a menu that allows you to configure the TCP/IP software if you are not very familiar with networking. Also, the dial-up software and configuration for PPP needed for dial-up remote IP address is included.

A basic TCP/IP software package is included in MS Windows software. However, the X-windows software is not included. In many cases, X-windows is not accessible via the Internet because the ethernet ports used are sometimes blocked at routers or at firewalls.

APPENDIX D

SAMBA DOCUMENTATION

Documentation is one of those things that you think you'll never need, is always in the way, and you can never get when you need it.

—Joe

Appendix Objectives

- ✔ GNU License
- ✔ The Samba FAQ
- ✔ Just What is SMB?

This appendix contains some documentation that you might find useful in learning Samba.

Appendix D.1 The GNU License

Software that is in the public domain can follow several license formats. Some allow you to resell the software, but must pay a royalty. Others allow you only to sell and make money on the costs of the duplication. The GNU license is shown here and is something that you will commonly encounter in the Linux and UNIX World.

GNU GENERAL PUBLIC LICENSE
Version 2, June 1991
Copyright (C) 1989, 1991 Free Software Foundation, Inc.
675 Mass Ave, Cambridge, MA 02139, USA

Everyone is permitted to copy and distribute verbatim copies
of this license document, but changing it is not allowed.

Preamble

The licenses for most software are designed to take away your freedom to share and change it. By contrast, the GNU General Public License is intended to guarantee your freedom to share and change free software—to make sure the software is free for all its users. This General Public License applies to most of the Free Software Foundation's software and to any other program whose authors commit to using it. (Some other Free Software Foundation software is covered bythe GNU Library General Public License instead.) You can apply it to your programs, too.

When we speak of free software, we are referring to freedom, not price. Our General Public Licenses are designed to make sure that you have the freedom to distribute copies of free software (and charge for this service if you wish), that you receive source code or can get it if you want it, that you can change the software or use pieces of it in new free programs; and that you know you can do these things.

To protect your rights, we need to make restrictions that forbid anyone to deny you these rights or to ask you to surrender the rights. These restrictions translate to certain responsibilities for you if you distribute copies of the software, or if you modify it.

For example, if you distribute copies of such a program, whether gratis or for a fee, you must give the recipients all the rights that you have. You must make sure that they, too, receive or can get the source code. And you must show them these terms so they know their rights.

We protect your rights with two steps: (1) copyright the software, and (2) offer you this license which gives you legal permission to copy, distribute and/or modify the software.

Also, for each author's protection and ours, we want to make certain that everyone understands that there is no warranty for this free software. If the software is modified by someone else and passed on, we want its recipients to know that what they have is not the original, so that any problems introduced by others will not reflect on the original authors' reputations.

Finally, any free program is threatened constantly by software patents. We wish to avoid the danger that redistributors of a free program will individually obtain patent licenses, in effect making the program proprietary. To prevent this, we have made it clear that any patent must be licensed for everyone's free use or not licensed at all. The precise terms and conditions for copying, distribution and modification follow.

GNU GENERAL PUBLIC LICENSE
TERMS AND CONDITIONS FOR COPYING, DISTRIBUTION
AND MODIFICATION

0. This License applies to any program or other work which contains a notice placed by the copyright holder saying it may be distributed under the terms of this General Public License. The "Program", below, refers to any such program or work, and a "work based on the Program" means either the Program or any derivative work under copyright law: that is to say, a work containing the Program or a portion of it, either verbatim or with modifications and/or translated into another language. (Hereinafter, translation is included without limitation in the term "modification".) Each licensee is addressed as "you".

Activities other than copying, distribution and modification are not covered by this License; they are outside its scope. The act of running the Program is not restricted, and the output from the Program is covered only if its contents constitute a work based on the Program (independent of having been made by running the Program). Whether that is true depends on what the Program does.

1. You may copy and distribute verbatim copies of the Program's source code as you receive it, in any medium, provided that you conspicuously and appropriately publish on each copy an appropriate copyright notice and disclaimer of warranty; keep intact all the notices that refer to this License and to the absence of any warranty; and give any other recipients of the Program a copy of this License along with the Program.

You may charge a fee for the physical act of transferring a copy, and you may at your option offer warranty protection in exchange for a fee.

2. You may modify your copy or copies of the Program or any portion of it, thus forming a work based on the Program, and copy and distribute such modifications or work under the terms of Section 1 above, provided that you also meet all of these conditions:

a) You must cause the modified files to carry prominent notices stating that you changed the files and the date of any change.

b) You must cause any work that you distribute or publish, that in whole or in part contains or is derived from the Program or any part thereof, to be licensed as a whole at no charge to all third parties under the terms of this License.

c) If the modified program normally reads commands interactively when run, you must cause it, when started running for such interactive use in the most ordinary way, to print or display an announcement including an appropriate copyright notice and a notice that there is no warranty (or else, saying that you provide a warranty) and that users may redistribute the program under these conditions, and telling the user how to view a copy of this License. (Exception: if the Program itself is interactive but does not normally print such an announcement, your work based on The Program is not required to print an announcement.)

These requirements apply to the modified work as a whole. If identifiable sections of that work are not derived from the Program, and can be reasonably considered independent and separate works in themselves, then this License, and its terms, do not apply to those sections when you distribute them as separate works. But when you distribute the same sections as part of a whole which is a work based on the Program, the distribution of the whole must be on the terms of this License, whose permissions for other licensees extend to the entire whole, and thus to each and every part regardless of who wrote it.

Thus, it is not the intent of this section to claim rights or contest your rights to work written entirely by you; rather, the intent is to exercise the right to control the distribution of derivative or collective works based on the Program.

In addition, mere aggregation of another work not based on the Program with the Program (or with a work based on the Program) on a volume of a storage or distribution medium does not bring the other work under the scope of this License.

3. You may copy and distribute the Program (or a work based on it, under Section 2) in object code or executable form under the terms of Sections 1 and 2 above provided that you also do one of the following:

a) Accompany it with the complete corresponding machine-readable source code, which must be distributed under the terms of Sections 1 and 2 above on a medium customarily used for software interchange; or,

b) Accompany it with a written offer, valid for at least three years, to give any third party, for a charge no more than your cost of physically performing source distribution, a complete machine-readable copy of the corresponding source code, to be distributed under the terms of Sections 1 and 2 above on a medium customarily used for software interchange; or,

c) Accompany it with the information you received as to the offer to distribute corresponding source code. (This alternative is allowed only for noncommercial distribution and only if you received the program in object code or executable form with such an offer, in accord with Subsection b above.)

The source code for a work means the preferred form of the work for making modifications to it. For an executable work, complete source code means all the source code for all modules it contains, plus any associated interface definition files, plus the scripts used to control compilation and installation of the executable. However, as a special exception, the source code distributed need not include anything that is normally distributed (in either source or binary form) with the major components (compiler, kernel, and so on) of the operating system on which the executable runs, unless that component itself accompanies the executable.

If distribution of executable or object code is made by offering access to copy from a designated place, then offering equivalent access to copy the source code from the same place counts as distribution of the source code, even though third parties are not compelled to copy the source along with the object code.

4. You may not copy, modify, sublicense, or distribute the Program except as expressly provided under this License. Any attempt otherwise to copy, modify, sublicense or distribute the Program is void, and will automatically terminate your rights under this License. However, parties who have received copies, or rights, from you under this License will not have their licenses terminated so long as such parties remain in full compliance.

5. You are not required to accept this License, since you have not signed it. However, nothing else grants you permission to modify or distribute the Program or its derivative works. These actions are prohibited by law if you do not accept this License. Therefore, by modifying or distributing the Program (or any work based on the Program), you indicate your acceptance of this License to do so, and all its terms and conditions for copying, distributing or modifying the Program or works based on it.

6. Each time you redistribute the Program (or any work based on the Program), the recipient automatically receives a license from the original licensor to copy, distribute or modify the Program subject to these terms and conditions. You may not impose any further restrictions on the recipients' exercise of the rights granted herein. You are not responsible for enforcing compliance by third parties to his License.

7. If, as a consequence of a court judgment or allegation of patent infringement or for any other reason (not limited to patent issues), conditions are imposed on you (whether by court order, agreement or otherwise) that contradict the conditions of this License, they do not excuse you from the conditions of this License. If you cannot distribute so as to satisfy simultaneously your obligations under this License and any other pertinent obligations, then as a consequence you may not distribute the Program at all. For example, if a patent license would not permit royalty-free redistribution of the Program by all those who receive copies directly or indirectly through you, then the only way you could satisfy both it and this License would be to refrain entirely from distribution of the Program.

If any portion of this section is held invalid or unenforceable under any particular circumstance, the balance of the section is intended to apply and the section as a whole is intended to apply in other circumstances.

It is not the purpose of this section to induce you to infringe any patents or other property right claims or to contest validity of any such claims; this section has the sole purpose of protecting the integrity of the free software distribution system, which is implemented by public license practices. Many people have made generous contributions to the wide range of software distributed through that system in reliance on consistent application of that system; it is up to the author/donor to decide if he or she is willing to distribute software through any other system and a licensee cannot impose that choice.

This section is intended to make thoroughly clear what is believed to be a consequence of the rest of this License.

8. If the distribution and/or use of the Program is restricted in certain countries either by patents or by copyrighted interfaces, the original copyright holder who places the Program under this License may add an explicit geographical distribution limitation excluding those countries, so that distribution is permitted only in or among countries not thus excluded. In such case, this License incorporates the limitation as if written in the body of this License.

9. The Free Software Foundation may publish revised and/or new versions of the General Public License from time to time. Such new versions will be similar in spirit to the present version, but may differ in detail to address new problems or concerns.

Each version is given a distinguishing version number. If the Program specifies a version number of this License which applies to it and "any later version", you have the option of following the terms and conditions either of that version or of any later version published by the Free Software Foundation. If the Program does not specify a version number of this License, you may choose any version ever published by the Free Software Foundation.

10. If you wish to incorporate parts of the Program into other free programs whose distribution conditions are different, write to the author to ask for permission. For software which is copyrighted by the Free Software Foundation, write to the Free Software Foundation; we sometimes make exceptions for this. Our decision will be guided by the two goals of preserving the free status of all derivatives of our free software and of promoting the sharing and reuse of software generally.

NO WARRANTY

11. BECAUSE THE PROGRAM IS LICENSED FREE OF CHARGE, THERE IS NO WARRANTY FOR THE PROGRAM, TO THE EXTENT PERMITTED BY APPLICABLE LAW. EXCEPT WHEN OTHERWISE STATED IN WRITING THE COPYRIGHT HOLDERS AND/OR OTHER PARTIES PROVIDE THE PROGRAM "AS IS" WITHOUT WARRANTY OF ANY KIND, EITHER EXPRESSED OR IMPLIED, INCLUDING, BUT NOT LIMITED TO, THE IMPLIED WARRANTIES OF MERCHANTABILITY AND FITNESS FOR A PARTICULAR PURPOSE. THE ENTIRE RISK AS TO THE QUALITY AND PERFORMANCE OF THE PROGRAM IS WITH YOU. SHOULD THE PROGRAM PROVE DEFECTIVE, YOU ASSUME THE COST OF ALL NECESSARY SERVICING, REPAIR OR CORRECTION.

12. IN NO EVENT UNLESS REQUIRED BY APPLICABLE LAW OR AGREED TO IN WRITING WILL ANY COPYRIGHT HOLDER, OR ANY OTHER PARTY WHO MAY MODIFY AND/OR REDISTRIBUTE THE PROGRAM AS PERMITTED ABOVE, BE LIABLE TO YOU FOR DAMAGES, INCLUDING ANY GENERAL, SPECIAL, INCIDENTAL OR CONSEQUENTIAL DAMAGES ARISING OUT OF THE USE OR INABILITY TO USE THE PROGRAM (INCLUDING BUT NOT LIMITED TO LOSS OF DATA OR DATA BEING RENDERED INACCURATE OR LOSSES SUSTAINED BY YOU OR THIRD PARTIES OR A FAILURE OF THE PROGRAM TO OPERATE WITH ANY OTHER PROGRAMS), EVEN IF SUCH HOLDER OR OTHER PARTY HAS BEEN ADVISED OF THE POSSIBILITY OF SUCH DAMAGES.

END OF TERMS AND CONDITIONS

APPENDIX: HOW TO APPLY THESE TERMS TO YOUR NEW PROGRAMS

If you develop a new program, and you want it to be of the greatest possible use to the public, the best way to achieve this is to make it free software which everyone can redistribute and change under these terms.

To do so, attach the following notices to the program. It is safest to attach them to the start of each source file to most effectively convey the exclusion of warranty; and each file should have at least the "copyright" line and a pointer to where the full notice is found.

```
    <one line to give the program's name and a brief
idea of what it does.>

    Copyright (C) 19yy  <name of author>
```

This program is free software; you can redistribute it and/or modify it under the terms of the GNU General Public License as published by the Free Software Foundation; either version 2 of the License, or (at your option) any later version.

This program is distributed in the hope that it will be useful, but WITHOUT ANY WARRANTY; without even the implied warranty of MERCHANTABILITY or FITNESS FOR A PARTICULAR PURPOSE. See the GNU General Public License for more details.

You should have received a copy of the GNU General Public License along with this program; if not, write to the Free Software Foundation, Inc., 675 Mass Ave, Cambridge, MA 02139, USA.

Also add information on how to contact you by electronic and paper mail.

If the program is interactive, make it output a short notice like this when it starts in an interactive mode:

Gnomovision version 69, Copyright © 19yy name of author
Gnomovision comes with ABSOLUTELY NO WARRANTY; for details type 'show w'.
This is free software, and you are welcome to redistribute it
under certain conditions; type 'show c' for details.

The hypothetical commands 'show w' and 'show c' should show the appropriate parts of the General Public License. Of course, the commands you use may be called something other than `show w' and `show c'; they could even be mouse-clicks or menu items—whatever suits your program.

You should also get your employer (if you work as a programmer) or your school, if any, to sign a "copyright disclaimer" for the program, if necessary. Here is a sample; alter the names:

Yoyodyne, Inc., hereby disclaims all copyright interest in the program

'Gnomovision' (which makes passes at compilers) written by James Hacker.

<signature of Ty Coon>, 1 April 1989

Ty Coon, President of Vice

This General Public License does not permit incorporating your program into proprietary programs. If your program is a subroutine library, you may consider it more useful to permit linking proprietary applications with the library. If this is what you want to do, use the GNU Library General Public License instead of this License.

Appendix D.2 The Samba FAQ

Author's Comments: The following FAQ is copied from the online documentation for SAMBA at http://www.samba.com. It is copied under the GNU License listed above.

SAMBA FAQ

This FAQ is automatically generated from the Samba bug tracking system As such it contains answers that we frequently send to users who report problems to samba-bugs@samba.org.Please report inaccuracies or out of date information so it can be fixed

INDEX

CRLF-LF Conversions
Closed Off 1.9.18
Couldn't open status file STATUS..LCK
Domain Controller
Get NTDOM Code
IP Address Change
Linux & mmap()

Logon errors in NT Event Viewer
Macintosh Clients
NT Guest Access
NT SP3 and Encryption
NTDOMAIN code
NetWkstaUserLogon
Not listening for calling name
OpLock Break Errors
PLEASE Start by Reading Docs!
PWL Files
Password Cracking
Pizza Vouchers
SMBFS not Part of Samba
SWAT on Red Hat Linux
Samba 2.x and PAM (especially FreeBSD)
System Error 1240
This is not a helpdesk
Time off by 1 hour
Trapdoor UID
Unix Permissions control Access
User Access Control
Using NT to Browse Samba Shares
Win95 or 98 and Encryption
Win9X in User Level Access mode
Windows98 Passwords
XXX isn't in user level security mode
Y2K
Case sensitive
Comp.protocols.smb
Dont descend & security
File caching
Generic icons displayed
Linux 2.0.x and smbmount
Linux compile problem
Setting times when not owner
Setup.exe and 16 bit programs
Smbclient -N
Smbfs for other Unixes
Smbpasswd: rejected session request
Smbsh and glibc-2.1
Smbtar blocksize
Unsubscribe
Win98 slowdown
Your server software is being unfriendly

CRLF-LF CONVERSIONS

We get many requests for CRLF/LF format conversion handling by samba. The problem is that there is no clean way to determine which files should / could be converted and which MUST not be.

Since Unix and DOS/Windows uses alike will use .txt to represent a file containing ASCII text we can not reliably use the file extension. The same applies to the .doc extension.

Samba operates around the premise that we should leave all files unchanged. By not implementing CRLF/LF conversions we can not be guilty of damaging anyone's files.

When someone comes along with a sound implementation that guarantees file integrity we will jump at the opportunity to implement this feature. Until such time there is no prospect for action on this topic.

CLOSED OFF 1.9.18

Thank you for reporting your difficulties with samba-1.9.18 series code. We regret to advise however that all work on the 1.9.18 code tree has been closed off with the release of samba-1.9.18p10.

All development efforts are now being focussed on stabilizing samba-2.0.0 so it can go into release to stable code as soon as possible.

If you could download the most recent beta release and report back any difficulties you may have we will do our best to close them out before the stable release.

We will still fix major bugs and security holes in 1.9.18p10, but minor bugs will be fixed if the problem still exists in the 2.0 tree.

For information about accessing the latest CVS source code please refer to http://samba.org/cvs.html

COULDN'T OPEN STATUS FILE STATUS..LCK

If you run smbstatus before anyone has ever connected to your new Samba installation then you may get the error:

```
   Couldn't open status file
/var/lock/samba/STATUS..LCK
```

or possibly the error:

```
 ERROR smb_shm_open : open failed with code No such
file or directory
 ERROR: Failed to initialize share modes!
 Can't initialize shared memory - exiting
```

both of these errors are harmless. The appropriate files and memory segments get automatically created the first time you connect to Samba. Try connecting with smbclient and you should find that smbstatus is happy after your first connection.

DOMAIN CONTROLLER

```
> Unknown parameter encountered: "domain controller"
> Ignoring unknown parameter "domain controller"
```

As of 1.9.18 the "domain controller" parameter has changed. You should not need it, but in it's place may need "networkstation user logon = yes". Please check the smb.conf man page BEFORE using this option so you understand it's significance.

GET NTDOM CODE

The domain controller code is now integrated into the main Samba source code.

Please see http://samba.org/cvs.html for information on how to download the latest version. You may also wish to join the samba-ntdom mailing list. See http://lists.samba.org/ for details.

There is also a separate Samba NTDOM FAQ available in the documentation section of the samba web site at http://samba.org/samba/

IP ADDRESS CHANGE

The following is an example of a problem we see from time to time:

"Samba was working fine. We had to change the IP address of the Samba server. Following the change Samba does not work. We have tried EVERYTHING—it still does not work!"

What to check:

1) Follow all instructions in DIAGNOSIS.txt from the samba docs directory.

2) Locate you browse.dat and wins.dat files. They may be found in the following

typical locations:

/usr/local/samba/var/locks

/var/locks/samba

/opt/samba/var/locks

If you can not locate where samba stores these files you can always run:

testparm | grep lock

3) Shut down samba.

4) Delete the browse.dat and wins.dat files

5) Restart samba.

6) Check that any files you deleted have been recreated.

7) Now follow DIAGNOSIS.txt again.

Cause:

———

Samba will place into these files entries for itself with your old IP address. When you restart Samba it preloads it's name cache with this information and expects to be able to resolve it's own address to the same address as it has just read from these files.

Deleting the files means samba takes a little longer to stabilize on startup but otherwise will now operate correctly.

In Samba 2.0 this problem has been fixed properly by storing signature information in the relevant files.

LINUX & MMAP()

Early versions of Linux did not support shared writeable mmap(). I believe it was introduced in kernel version 2.0.

There are 3 possible fixes:

1) upgrade to a newer version of the Linux kernel

2) don't compile Samba with FAST_SHARE_MODES defined

3) use Samba 1.9.18 which provides FAST_SHARE_MODES via SysV IPC

shared memory. I believe Linux 1.2 supported this.

In Samba 2.0 configure script will auto-detect the OS capabilities and will enable shared memory only if available.

LOGON ERRORS IN NT EVENT VIEWER

The logon errors in the NT event viewer are caused by Samba trying to detect broken NT password servers.

Some NT servers will accept any username/password for session setup requests and always validate it, returning a positive session setup response without the guest bit set. Samba checks for this by deliberately sending an incorrect password when calling the password server in server level security. If the incorrect password succeeds then Samba logs an error and refuses to use the password server.

You can remove this check from the code if you want, but as we have not yet worked out what causes a NT server to show this behavior there is a risk that your NT server will start behaving incorrectly and thus make your Samba server insecure.

Future versions Samba will have a new security option "security = domain" which will use the same protocols that NT uses for domain authentication (currently Samba uses the method that MS documents, rather than that which Microsoft actually use). Once that in place this problem should be solved.

MACINTOSH CLIENTS

```
> Are there any Macintosh clients for Samba?
```

Yes. Thursby now have a CIFS Client/Server called DAVE—see http://www.thursby.com/

They test it against Windows 95, Windows NT and samba for compatibility issues. At the time of writing, DAVE was at version 1.0.1. The 1.0.0 to 1.0.1 update is available as a free download from the Thursby web site (the speed of finder copies has been greatly enhanced, and there are bug-fixes included).

Alternatives—There are two free implementations of AppleTalk for several kinds of UNIX machines, and several more commercial ones. These products allow you to run file services and print services natively to Macintosh users, with no additional support required on the Macintosh. The two free implementations are Netatalk, http://www.umich.edu/~rsug/netatalk/, and CAP, http://www.cs.mu.oz.au/appletalk/atalk.html. What Samba offers MS Windows users, these packages offer to Macs. For more info on these packages, Samba, and Linux (and other UNIX-based systems) see http://www.eats.com/linux_mac_win.html

NT GUEST ACCESS

What you are seeing is normal and deliberate.

MS Windows NT can be configured with the guest account enabled. When this is the case no logon attempt will ever fail. Instead NT will allow the user access as the guest account IF the username and/or password are incorrect. In a situation where Samba is using and NT system to validate user passwords, if the NT server guest account is enabled then a user logging on as "root" will always be validated even if the password was incorrect. There is NO way that samba can tell from the reply packet from NT whether the password was correct and normal user privilege has been granted, or whether the password was incorrect and the user has been given only "guest" privileges.

In short, if we were NOT to do what we do, then there would be no way of telling whether or not the password server allows guest only logons. Were we to just accept the validation response from such a server the a user could easily gain "root" level access to a Samba server.

Now you would not really want us to change the current behavior, would you?

```
> Hi folks ... I don't know if you have seen this,
have corrected this yet
> or it is my configuration.
```

```
> I am using our company PDC for passwd
authentication and it works OK
> except for one snag.
> The authentication process between the our Samba
server & the PDC always
> includes one unsuccessful pass thru attempt.
>     This initial pass thru validation has an
incorrect user password
> (1F1F1F1F......). A SMB reject from the PDC forces
the Samba Svr to
> immediately send a second validation with the
correct
> encrypted Bell Master Domain user password.
>     It would be nice to get rid of the first bad
validation attempt.
```

NT SP3 AND ENCRYPTION

Microsoft changed WinNT in service pack 3 to refuse to connect to servers that do not support SMB password encryption.

There are two main solutions:

1) enable SMB password encryption in Samba. See ENCRYPTION.txt in the Samba docs (this is best done with samba versions more recent than 1.9.18)

2) disable this new behavior in NT. See WinNT.txt in the Samba docs

Note that Samba-1.9.18 and later support encrypted passwords without need to recompile and link with the libdes (DES) library. Refer to the man page for smb.conf and to ENCRYPTION.txt for information about use of encrypted passwords.

Please refer to the following URL for more information on this subject:

http://support.microsoft.com/support/kb/articles/q166/7/30.asp

NTDOMAIN CODE

If you are trying the NTDOMAIN version of Samba then please join the samba-technical list and listen there for a while. I also suggest you read the list archives. See http://lists.samba.org/ for more info.

Samba support for NT domain control is still very experimental. Only try it if you are a programmer willing to experiment.

All bug reports regarding this experimental code should be directed ONLY at the samba-technical or samba-ntdom mailing lists.

In response to concerns over profile handling: Profile handling will be looked at seriously once we get the domain code to stabilize. Until then, what we document in Samba and what works can be in conflict. We stress again the highly experimental nature of all the NTDOMAIN code.

In response to concerns over compilation problems: Code updates to the head branch code tree are to samba-2.1.0 NOT samba-2.0.0. The Samba-2.1.0 code may not compile and may not work at any time. Please use this at your own risk.

Samba-2.0.0 is being readied for release within a few days. It is the release candidate stable code but does not have fully functional PDC support. This is precursor code to the samba-2.1.0 branch.

NETWKSTAUSERLOGON

The password server behavior changed because we discovered that bugs in some NT servers allowed anyone to login with no password if they chose an account name that did not exist on the password server. The NT password server was saying "yes, it's OK to login" even when the account didn't exist at all! Adding the NetWkstaUserLogon call fixed the problem, and follows the "recommended" method that MS have recently documented for pass through authentication.

The problem now is that some NT servers (in particular NT workstation?) don't support the NetWkstaUserLogon call. The call also doesn't work for accounts in trust relationships.

The eventual solution for this will be to replace the password server code in Samba with NT domain code as that is developed. For now you have the choice of compiling Samba either with or without the NetWkstaUser-Logon call in the password server code.

In 1.9.18p3 and later you can disable the NetWkstaUserLogon call with an option in your smb.conf using the "networkstation user login" option.

NOT LISTENING FOR CALLING NAME

```
> Session request failed (131,129) with myname=HOBBES
destname=CALVIN
> Not listening for calling name
```

If you get this when talking to a Samba box then it means that your global "hosts allow" or "hosts deny" settings are causing the Samba server to refuse the connection.

Look carefully at your "hosts allow" and "hosts deny" lines in the global section of smb.conf.

It can also be a problem with reverse DNS lookups not functioning correctly, leading to the remote host identity not being able to be confirmed, but that is less likely.

OPLOCK BREAK ERRORS

```
>  I'm receiving the same error from the following
versions of samba:
>
>   smbd version 1.9.18p10 started
>   smbd version 2.0.0beta2 started.
>
> The following error message appears multiple times
in the log files with
> either version, and eventually locks up the entire
samba server:
>
> [1998/12/11 22:29:07, 0]
smbd/oplock.c:request_oplock_break(909)
>   request_oplock_break: no response received to
oplock break request to pid
> 19883 on port 2328 for dev = 810000a, inode =
332533
>
> I'm running this on Digital UNIX V4.0B on an
AlphaStation 255.  We've also
> seen this same error message on DU V3.2C running
various flavors of samba.
>
```

The advisory message means that you have either a defective network card on one of your clients, or else an MS Windows application is refusing to respond to an oplock break request from another MS Windows client that wishes to access an already locked file.

PLEASE START BY READING DOCS!

We are glad you are interested in Samba, but please read the documentation!

English: http://samba.anu.edu.au/samba

German: http://samba.sernet.de

Japanese: http://samba.bento.ad.jp

French: http://www.bde.espci.fr/homepage/Patrick.Mevzek/samba

From the README file:

DOCUMENTATION

There is quite a bit of documentation included with the package, including man pages, and lots of .txt files with hints and useful info. This is also available from the web pages. There is a growing collection of information under docs/faq; by the next release expect this to be the default starting point.

FTP SITE

Please use a mirror site! The list of mirrors is in docs/MIRRORS.txt.

The master ftp site is samba.anu.edu.au in the directory pub/samba.

MAILING LIST

There is a mailing list for discussion of Samba. To subscribe send mail to listproc@samba.anu.edu.au with a body of "subscribe samba Your Name" Please do NOT send this request to the list alias instead.

To send mail to everyone on the list mail to samba@listproc.anu.edu.au

There is also an announcement mailing list where new versions are announced. To subscribe send mail to listproc@samba.anu.edu.au with a body of "subscribe samba-announce Your Name". All announcements also go to the samba list.

NEWS GROUP

You might also like to look at the usenet news group comp.protocols.smb as it often contains lots of useful info and is frequented by lots of Samba users. The newsgroup was initially setup by people on the Samba mailing list. It is not, however, exclusive to Samba, it is a forum for discussing the SMB protocol (which Samba implements). The samba list is gatewayed to this newsgroup.

PWL FILES

If you are worried about the security of PWL files then I suggest you look at http://samba.org/pub/samba/docs/security.html

PASSWORD CRACKING

```
> Could you please send me Frank Stevensons program
for cracking .pwl
> files.
>
> If you have any other programs for cracking windows
95 pwl files, could
> you send them to me or tell me where I can find
them.
>
```

No. These are not part of samba—we will provide only samba components. For obvious reasons we can not offer any other software like password cracking tools. These are available from sites like BugTraq.

```
Pizza Vouchers
```

FAQ Answer about pizza vouchers:

The note about pizza vouchers in the Samba documentation started out as a bit of a joke. Since then I've been amazed at the number of people who have managed to send a pizza voucher in one way or another! I've had many happy evenings eating pizza thanks to these generous folks!

Some people also write to us wondering how to get a pizza voucher to Australia. Here are the techniques that have worked for others:

1) a few people have successfully talked their local Pizza Hut shop into sending vouchers to Australia. Apparently the staff look at you a bit strangely at first but at least 2 people have succeeded!

2) Others have rung up a local pizza outlet in Canberra (where I live) and have offered their credit card numbers over the phone. They then emailed me telling me which shop to ring up to order pizza. This has worked with two different shops here in Canberra—Pizza Hut and Dominos Pizza.

3) I've received several pizza vouchers that are valid in various places around the world and have started a small collection. Some day I hope to eat my way through them when I visit some of these places.

4) I've received several .gif files of pizzas and even some nice pictures and cardboard pizzas!

Please remember that the "pizza voucher for Samba" thing started as a joke. It's a lot of fun but you certainly are not required to send anything. I won't starve without them and maybe I'll put on a bit less weight :-)

Also remember all the other people who help with Samba. If someone helps you particularly then maybe just send them a thank you email? This sort of thing really is appreciated!

Anyway, if you still want to send a pizza my address is:

3 Ballow Crescent
Macgregor A.C.T
2615 Australia
Phone: +61 2 6254 8209

and the nearest pizza outlet is "Kippax Pizza Hut"

Thanks!

```
SMBFS not Part of Samba
```

We regret to advise that including smbmount and smbumount in the Samba tarball has been a mistake. These programs are part of the smbfs package and are NOT maintained by the Samba-Team. We are currently contemplating the removal of these programs from the samba tarball since they are a constant cause of complaint and we do NOT have spare capacity to handle additional load.

SMBFS is available only for Linux. In Samba 2.0 we are introducing a tool called smbsh that offers similar functionality but is portable to a large number of Unixes.

SWAT ON RED HAT LINUX

```
> I hope this is not something stupid I overlooked
somehow. I browsed the
> mailingarchive and I noticed I wasn't the only one
with this problem.
> This is what happend:
```

Now please excuse my revised version of what you did: You followed the Sinatra method of software installation—the "I did it my way!" And you found it does not work because something was over looked. Maybe?

Here is how my Sinatra method works:

1) Unpack the samba tarball

2) rename the directory "samba-2.0.0beta5" to "samba-2.0.0".

3) cd samba-2.0.0/packaging/redHat

4) sh makerpms.sh

5) cd /usr/src/redhat/RPMS/i386

6) rpm -Uvh samba-2.0.0-1.i386.rpm

NOTE: This installation does a "kill -HUP" on the PID for inetd, so SWAT is available.

7) launch a web browser from a client (any client)

8) Go to the URL http://"samba_host":901

9) User = root, enter root's password.

Now you are ready to configure samba.

```
>
> First I used the Redhat section of the install
procedure witch uses an rpm
> statement to buils a rpm package. I installed the
package and tried to use
> SWAT, the grafical web interface.
```

If you built the Red Hat RPMs, then all you had to do was install the binary RPM and all should work. If it does not work then you most likely have a TCP/IP configuration problem, not a samba problem.

```
> This failed because it assumes the
> samba directory tree in /usr/local/samba and the
redhat rpm file installs stuff
> in /usr/share or similar.
```

Please explain this statement. Nowhere in the samba2.spec file do we show any dependency on /usr/local/samba, and if you built the packages using the shell script provided, then all paths will have been changed to reflect the standard Linux path layouts.

```
> Eventually, after making a some
> simlinks I thought it would be better to compile
and install the
> distrubution-independed way (just make and make
install that is)
> Fine, now SWAT seems to work. However I have to put
it in demo mode because
> When it asks me to login I can't use my root login
with root-password
> anymore. It's not valid anymore to SWAT.
```

But the Samba installer is meant for people who REALLY know what they are doing and therefore does not attempt to install SWAT. Oh, yes, it installs the binary files but it does not modify /etc/inetd.conf and /etc/services.

```
>
> The question is: what is beiing validaded here: my
Linux passwd word for root
```

```
> or is somthing involved here with the samba
passwords? Or is this authentication
> handled by SWAT itself?
```

Red Hat Linux uses PAM (Pluggable Authentication Modules) and the authentication method is specified in the /etc/pam.d files. SWAT uses the /etc/pam.d/{samba,login} control files.

```
>
>
> I have RedHat 5.2 which I believe uses the egcs
compiler (not sure though..) I
> run it on an i386 pentium 166 MMX, so this is
pretty standard I think. I used
> beta 4 of the Samba release
>
> Hope this helps...
```

SAMBA 2.X AND PAM (ESPECIALLY FREEBSD)

Samba 2.x detects whether your OS has PAM (Pluggable Authentication Module) support at compile time and uses it if it is available. This leads to a problem on systems that have PAM support in the libraries but where PAM is not configured. These "sleeping" PAM implementations cause all unix password authentication attempts to fail.

We have fixed this for the next release of Samba (version 2.0.4) by adding a—with-pam configure option. If you don't use that option then PAM won't be used.

SYSTEM ERROR 1240

System error 1240 means that the client is refusing to talk to a non-encrypting server. Microsoft changed WinNT in service pack 3 to refuse to connect to servers that do not support SMB password encryption.

There are two main solutions:

1) enable SMB password encryption in Samba. See ENCRYPTION.txt in the Samba docs

2) disable this new behaviour in NT. See WinNT.txt in the Samba docs

THIS IS NOT A HELPDESK

The address samba-bugs@samba.org is meant for reporting bugs or for obtaining help where you suspect that a Samba bug is involved. It is not meant as a general helpdesk service. It's not that we don't want to help (we do!) but we get thousands of emails and have only a few people to deal with them. Trying to help with each Samba install personally is way beyond our abilities.

Instead I suggest that you try one of the following resources:

1) The Samba web site at http://samba.org/samba/

2) The mailing list samba@samba.org.

Read http://lists.samba.org/ for more info on that.

3) The newsgroup comp.protocols.smb

4) a newsgroup specific to your OS, such as comp.os.linux.*

If you can afford it you could also contact one of the many companies that provide commercial Samba support. See http://samba.org/samba/ and follow the links.

TIME OFF BY 1 HOUR

It sounds like either your PCs or your server don't have their timezones set up correctly for daylight savings time or just disagree on the time zone your are in.

Without knowing what sort of system you are running Samba on it is difficult to know what to change. If you want to use a "quick fix" then maybe the "time offset" command in smb.conf will be useful.

TRAPDOOR UID

```
> Log message "you appear to have a trapdoor uid
system"
```

This can have several causes. It might be because you are using a uid or gid of 65535 or -1. This is a VERY bad idea, and is a big security hole. Check carefully in your /etc/passwd file and make sure that no user has uid 65535 or -1. Especially check the "nobody" user, as many broken systems are shipped with nobody setup with a uid of 65535.

It might also mean that your OS has a trapdoor uid/gid system

This means that once a process changes effective uid from root to another user it can't go back to root. Unfortunately Samba relies on being able to change effective uid from root to non-root and back again to implement its security policy. If your OS has a trapdoor uid system this won't work, and several things in Samba may break. Less things will break if you use user or server level security instead of the default share level security, but you may still strike problems.

The problems don't give rise to any security holes, so don't panic, but it does mean some of Samba's capabilities will be unavailable. In particular you will not be able to connect to the Samba server as two different uids at once. This may happen if you try to print as a guest" while accessing a share as a normal user. It may also affect your ability to list the available shares as this is normally done as the guest user.

Complain to your OS vendor and ask them to fix their system.

Note: the reason why 65535 is a VERY bad choice of uid and gid is that it casts to -1 as a uid, and the setreuid() system call ignores (with no error) uid changes to -1. This means any daemon attempting to run as uid 65535 will actually run as root. This is not good!

UNIX PERMISSIONS CONTROL ACCESS

Typical question:

```
> So here's the problem (and I apologise if this is
just a configuration
> issue). On any of our NT Workstation clients (with
the reg edit to allow plain
> passwords), once a drive is mapped using userid and
password with \\host\anyuser,
> that user can subsequently issue \\host\root and
mount the unix box at the root
> directory without any authentication required ..
they have access to the whole
> machine.
```

Samba does NOT second guess the security policy you wish to impose upon your site. You, as a system administrator for your Unix system, have the responsibility to determine by means of setting correct user, group and other permissions who can access what on your Unix system.

If you really want to restrict users so they can not connect to any other users' home directory then you will need to set the Unix permissions on your users home directory to drwx——— (Octal 0x700).

USER ACCESS CONTROL

```
> In windows when i set up a share in "user mode" i
get the message:
>  "You cannot view the list of users at this time.
Please try again later."
>
> I know you have lists of users for access and
aliasing purposes, but i
> have read nothing to support the idea that these
lists control the Domain
> Users List...
```

Samba does NOT at this time support user mode access control for Window 9x although we hope to support it in an upcoming release.

USING NT TO BROWSE SAMBA SHARES

```
> WIN-NT workstations (nt4.0, service pack 3)
> samba with
>   security = user
>   encrypt passwords = yes
>   guest account = guest
>
> start the explorer on a win-nt workstation and
select network. I find
> my unix server running samba, but I can not see the
list of shares
> unless I am  a user, who is known in the smbpasswd
of the unix machine.
> The guest account "guest" exists on my unix
machine. For testing I even
> made him a regular user with a password.
>
> With my network monitor I can see, that the win-nt
workstation uses the
> current login, to connect to IPC$ on the samba
server
> (for example "administrator"), not the guest
account.
```

This is exactly how Windows NT works. You MUST have a valid account on the Windows NT box you are trying to see the resource list on. If your currently logged in account details do NOT match an account on the NT machine you are trying to access then you will be presented with a logon box for that machine. When you enter the name of an account on that machine / domain, together with a valid password then the resource list is made available. If the account details are not correct then no resource list is shown.

Samba follows the behaviour of Windows NT exactly.

Samba can be compiled with the GUEST_SESSION_SETUP option at 0,1 or 2. The default is 0. If this is set to 1 or 2 then Windows NT machines that DO NOT have an account on the Samba server will see the resource list. Unfortunately Windows client bugs mean that using this option will probably cause more problems than it will solve. We do not suggest that you use it.

WIN95 OR 98 AND ENCRYPTION

FAQ answer about Win95 (with TCP/IP update or OSR2 version) and Win98 and Samba:

Microsoft changed Win95 upon release of their OSR2 version to refuse to connect to servers that do not support SMB password encryption. This change was also released in a TCP/IP update for Win95 and is included in all versions of Win98 that we've seen so far.

There are two main solutions:

1) enable SMB password encryption in Samba. See ENCRYPTION.txt in the Samba docs

2) disable this new behavior in Win95/98. See Win95.txt in the Samba docs

The Samba docs directory is included with any recent Samba distribution or available at ftp://samba.anu.edu.au/pub/samba/docs/

NOTE: You must reboot your machine for these registry changes to take effect.

WIN9X IN USER LEVEL ACCESS MODE

```
> I've Samba running as a NT-Server, but there is a
problem:
>
> When i want to share something on the win95-client,
this client wants a
> userlist from the NT-Server (Samba).
> How can I make Samba providing a userlist?
```

Sorry. This is not yet supported. Some time after we release samba-2.0.0 we will commence the long task of implementing this functionality. For now you can should not put your Win95 or Win98 system into User Level Access mode.

```
Windows98 Passwords
```

Please refer to the following URL:
http://support.microsoft.com/support/kb/articles/q187/2/28.asp

*** NOTE ***

After making the registry changes referred to in this document you MUST reboot your Windows 98 PC for the changes to take effect.

^^^
^^^^^^^

Note—the best way to solve this problem is to enable encrypted passwords on your Samba server. Windows 98 works well with Samba when Samba is running in encrypted password mode. Samba versions 1.9.18 and later support encrypted passwords providing it is correctly configured in smb.conf and an smbpasswd file has been created.

To enable encrypted passwords on Samba, read the file docs/ENCRYPTION.txt in the Samba distribution.

If you wish to change Windows 98 to send plaintext passwords again, look on the Win98 CD in the directory '/tools/mtsutil/' you should find the files: 'ptxt_on.inf' and 'ptxt_off.inf' here is a clip from the mtsutil.txt file in that directory:

```
==========================================================================
====
```

PTXT_ON.INF - SENDS PLAIN-TEXT PASSWORDS TO YOUR NETWORK SERVER

==
====

For security reasons, Windows 98 will not allow you to send plain-text passwords. The password is encrypted by default. However, Samba servers can be configured to require plain-text passwords, so you will not be able to connect to Samba servers configured in this mode unless you change a Registry entry to enable plain-text passwords.

Caution: Enabling plain-text passwords could compromise security.

To enable plain-text passwords, add the Registry entry for EnablePlainTextPassword (as a Dword) and set the value to 1 in the following Registry location:

HKEY_LOCAL_MACHINE\System

\CurrentControlSet\Services\VxD\Vnetsup

To set the value for EnablePlainTextPassword to 1:

---

1. Select PTXT_ON.INF found in the \Tools\MTSutil folder on the Windows 98 CD.

2. Right-Click PTXT_ON.INF.

-or-

Hold down the SHIFT key and press the function key, F10.

3. Choose INSTALL to add the EnablePlainTextPassword entry and set its value to 1.

==
====

PTXT_OFF.INF - SENDS ENCRYPTED PASSWORDS TO YOUR NETWORK SERVER

===

====

To re-enable the sending of encrypted passwords to your network server, add the Registry entry EnablePlainTextPassword (as a Dword) and set the value to 0 in the following Registry location:

HKEY_LOCAL_MACHINE\System

\CurrentControlSet\Services\VxD\Vnetsup

To set the value for EnablePlainTextPassword to 0:

---

1. Select PTXT_OFF.INF found in the \Tools\MTSutil folder on the Windows 98 CD.

2. Right-Click PTXT_OFF.INF.

-or-

Hold down the SHIFT key and press the function key, F10.

3. Choose INSTALL to add the EnablePlainTextPassword entry and set its value to 0.

XXX ISN'T IN USER LEVEL SECURITY MODE

This error message means you are using server level security with a password server that isn't in user level security mode. The password server code relies on being able to send username/password pairs and getting back a yes/no response. This isnt possible unless the server is in user level security mode.

The most common reasons for this problem are:

1) you are trying to use a Win95 box as the password server. That won't work.

2) you are using a Samba server as the password server and that server is configured in share level security.

Y2K

Samba is year 2000 complient so long as the underlying operating system that Samba is running upon are year 2000 compliant (Linux is, as are most modern UNIX systems, along with VMS, MVS and many others that Samba runs on.)

For a much more detailed discussion and the latest information see http://samba.anu.edu.au/samba/y2k.html

CASE SENSITIVE

Many Microsoft clients and applications cannot handle case sensitive servers. They often change the case of a filename before sending it over the wire.

In Samba, Just use "short preserve case = yes" and "preserve case = yes". Never use "case sensitive = yes"

COMP.PROTOCOLS.SMB

FAQ about comp.protocols.smb:

The newsgroup comp.protocols.smb is quite separate from the samba mailing list. Someone from outside the Samba team ways gatewaying messages from the Samba mailing list to comp.protocols.smb for a while but hopefully this has stopped now.

comp.protocols.smb does contain a lot of discussion about Samba so it is often a useful resource for Samba users.

For info on accessing usenet newsgroups like comp.protocols.smb please ask a local internet guru. The Samba Team has no way of knowing how your local news system is setup so we can't help you.

DONT DESCEND & SECURITY

Dont descend is not meant to be a security feature, it's an administrative convenience. It can be easily bypassed.

It is meant for things like /proc to prevent utilities like file manager from recursing themselves to death in a filesystem that has links back into itself.

Please use the underlying unix security of file permissions to give you real security.

FILE CACHING

Some people report problems with "caching" of data. Generally the bug report goes like this:

- create a file on a Unix box

- view the file on a PC via Samba

- change the file on the Unix box

- look at the file again on the PC via Samba and the changes are not visible

The first thing to realize is that this is the expected behavior! The SMB protocol uses a thing called "opportunistic locking". This allows the client to "safely" do client side caching of file data. The problem is that this caching is only safe if all programs access the files via SMB. As soon as you access the data via a non-SMB client then you will get data inconsistencies.

The solution is simple! Disable oplocks in smb.conf for those shares that need to be accessed simultaneously from Unix and windows. See the "oplocks" and "veto oplock files" options in smb.conf(5)

Samba-1.9.18 and the samba-2.x series support oplocks.

Samba-1.9.17 series does NOT.

In addition, you may care to explore the effect of making the following registry entries under MS Windows NT4:

```
=============================================================
=========================

[HKEY_LOCAL_MACHINE\SYSTEM\CurrentControlSet\Services\
LanmanWorkstation\Paramete

rs]

"BufFilesDenyWrite"=dword:00000000

"BufNamedPipes"=dword:00000000

"UseOpportunisticLocking"=dword:00000000
```

"DormantFileLimit"=dword:00000000

[HKEY_LOCAL_MACHINE\SYSTEM\CurrentControlSet\Services\LanmanWorkstation\Parameters\Linkage]

"UtilizeNtCaching"=dword:00000000

[HKEY_LOCAL_MACHINE\SYSTEM\CurrentControlSet\Control\Filesystem]

"Win95TruncateExtensions"=dword:00000000

[HKEY_LOCAL_MACHINE\SYSTEM\CurrentControlSet\Services\LanManServer\Parameters]

"EnableOpLockForceClose"=dword:00000001

"EnableOpLocks"=dword:00000000

==

The following registry entry may help under Windows 9X also:

[HKEY_LOCAL_MACHINE\System\CurrentControlSet\Services\VxD\VREDIR]

"DiscardCacheOnOpen"=string:00000001

GENERIC ICONS DISPLAYED

Some Samba users have reported a problem where the icons for programs stored on the server are not displayed, with generic "exe" icons being displayed instead. This problem seems to be caused by the client detecting the connection to the server as "slow". When this happens the client tries to make things a bit faster by not reading icon information from the remote .exe files.

The problem happens particularly when running Samba with "security=server". In server level security Samba delays the negprot and session setup replies while talking to the password server (this is necessary). To make matters worse Samba initially sends a deliberately bad password to the password server in order to detect a known bug in some NT servers where they say "yes" to all passwords. The NT server replies to this bad password very slowly (probably in an attempt to stop passwor cracking over the network). All this introduces a approximately 3 second delay in making the connection which is sufficient to trigger the Win95 "don't display icons" code.

We don't have a solution to this problem, but we can say that (apart from cosmetics) it is harmless.

LINUX 2.0.X AND SMBMOUNT

If you had read the following (cut and pasted from the 1.9.18p1 Makefile) you will have noticed the first sentence specifically says that pre-2.1.70 Linux kernels cannot use the version of smbmount included with Samba. As it states you should use the smbfs utilities available via anon ftp from the site below.

```
# If you are using Linux kernel version 2.1.70 and
later, you should
# uncomment the following line to compile the
smbmount utilities
# together with Samba. If you are using Linux kernel
version 2.0.x
# you must use the smbfs utilities from
# ftp://ftp.gwdg.de/pub/linux/misc/smbfs
```

LINUX COMPILE PROBLEM

```
 [snip]
> Machine OS:  Linux: Slackware 3.4
[snip]
> What Happened:
[snip]
> Compiling smbpass.c
> gcc:  Internal compiler error: program cc1 got
fatal signal 6
> make:  *** [smbpass.o] Error 1
```

There appears to be a problem with the GCC binaries supplied with Slackware 3.4 (and possibly a few other systems). For some reason they fall over when trying to compile the encrypted passwords code in Samba. There are 2 solutions, the first is a short term fix which doesn't always work, and as far as I can work out the second should always work:

1. Remove the -O from FLAGS1 in your Makefile.

2. Download a new set of GCC binaries (there is one somewhere under

ftp://sunsite.unc.edu/pub/Linux) or rebuild it from the source.

SETTING TIMES WHEN NOT OWNER

```
> If I open a Microsoft Office's file like Word for
instance from my workstation,
> and I'm not the owner of that file but I have the
right to write on it,
> Microsoft Office will change the file's date to the
current date even if I did
> not make any modification to the file. This doesn't
appear if I'm the owner of
> the file. The result of this matter is that the
date of the files on the network
> doesn't mean nothing because the date change of a
file as soon as somebody else
> than the owner open it .
```

This is the expected behaviour and is a result of POSIX semantics. You can ask Samba to override this, however.

Please see the "dos filetimes" option in the smb.conf man page.

SETUP.EXE AND 16 BIT PROGRAMS

Running 16 bit programs from Windows NT on a Samba mapped drive

---

The Windows NT redirector has a bug when running against a Samba or Windows 95 mapped drive and attempting to run a 16 bit executable.

The problem occurs when the pathname to a 16 bit executable contains a non 8.3 filename complient directory component, Windows NT will fail to load the program and complain it cannot find the path to the program.

It can be verified that this is a bug in Windows NT and not Samba as the same problem can be reproduced exactly when attempting to run the same program with the same pathname from a Windows 95 server (ie. the problem still exists even with no Samba server involved).

Microsoft have been made aware of this problem, it is unknown if they regard it as serious enough to provide a fix for this.

One of the reasons this problem is reported frequently is that InstallShield setup.exe executables are frequently written as 16 bit programs, and so hit this problem.

As a workaround, you may create (on a Samba server at least) a symbolic link with an 8.3 complient name to the non 8.3 complient directory name, and then the 16 bit program will run. Alternatively, use the 8.3 complient mangled name to specify the path to run the binary.

This will be fixed when Samba adds the NT-specific SMB calls in Samba 2.0 as once the NT SMB calls are used this problem no longer occurs (which is why the problem doesn't occur when running against a drive mapped to a Windows NT server).

SMBCLIENT -N

```
> When getting the list of shares available on a host
using the command
>    smbclient -N -L <server>
> the program always prompts for the password if the
server is a Samba server.
> It also ignores the "-N" argument when querying
some (but not all) of our
> NT servers.
```

No, it does not ignore -N, it is just that your server rejected the null password in the connection, so smbclient prompts for a password to try again.

To get the behaviour that you probably want use

```
smbclient -L host -U%
```

this will set both the username and password to null, which is an anonymous login for SMB. Using -N would only set the password to null, and this is not accepted as an anonymous login for most SMB servers.

SMBFS FOR OTHER UNIXES

```
> mount -ufs \\NTSERVER\MOUNT_DIR /sun_mount_point
```

smbfs is only available for Linux.

I\In Samba 2.0 we are introducing a utility called smbsh that will provide similar functionality but is portable to a wide range of Unixes.

SMBPASSWD: REJECTED SESSION REQUEST

```
> I have installed samba everything seems to be
working fine except the
> smbpasswd executable file i can change a users
password as root with
> no problem but if a users tries to change his own
password.. it would
> give this error:
>
>  smbpasswd: machine 127.0.0.1 rejected the session
request.
>    Error was : code 131
>
> im not sure what i have to add for it to allow this
users to change
> their own password..  it seems to be defaulting to
the local ip
> address.. ???
>
> please help  .. thanks for your time.
>
```

Firstly, make sure that you do NOT have "bind interfaces only = yes" in your smb.conf file.

Secondly, if you have specified "hosts allow = xxx.xxx.xxx.xxx/yy" please add to it "localhost". ie: hosts allow = 123.45.67.0/24 127.

smbpasswd needs to be able to connect to smbd on the local machine, hence it is trying to connect to the 127.0.0.1 address.

SMBSH AND GLIBC-2.1

smbsh doesn't work with glibc-2.1 on Linux systems. That includes RedHat 6.0 and many other recent Linux distributions. It is very hard to fix this as the glibc maintainers have deliberately removed the necessary hooks for smbsh to work. They don't like the idea of user space filesystems.

The only thing we can suggest right now is to use smbfs instead.

SMBTAR BLOCKSIZE

There was a slight error in early versions of smbtar which prevents the blocksize parameter from working correctly. This was fixed in Samba version 1.9.18.

UNSUBSCRIBE

For information on unsubscribing or changing your subscribed address please see the instructions at http://lists.samba.org/

WIN98 SLOWDOWN

```
> Further to my previous post, I have made an
interesting discovery.  This
> particular slowdown only occurs from clients that
are running
> Windows 98.
```

The Windows98 explorer (and possibly other programs) incorrectly set the "sync" bit in write requests to network shares. This causes an enormous slowdown as Samba (quite correctly) does a fsync() on the file after each write. Combine this with the fact that Windows98 explorer uses very small write sizes (around 1.5k) and you get really terrible results.

In Samba 1.9.18p10 and later we modified Samba to by default ignore these incorrect sync requests. This results in an enormous performance increase when using Windows98 explorer.

You can get the old (slow) behavior back using the "strict sync" option.

YOUR SERVER SOFTWARE IS BEING UNFRIENDLY

If you get "your server software is being unfriendly" when you try to connect to a server using smbclient then it means that smbclient established a TCP connection to the server but got garbage (or nothing) back when it tried to do a NBT "session request" on the open socket. The "unfriendly" bit comes from the fact that the client is expecting one of a number of possible error codes as defined in the spec (see RFC1001/1002) but instead it got something totally different.

This usually means that you aren't successfully talking to a SMB server at all, and that the socket is connected to something else. A common cause if Samba is the server is that smbd failed to startup correctly and exited before it got to the point of answering the session request. Faulty/missing config files can do this or if you are launching via inetd then maybe your inetd.conf or /etc/services is setup incorrectly.

Appendix D.3 Just what is SMB?

Author's Note: I have added web addresses for items that were just links. Otherwise the document is the same as the one that is available from http://www.samba.org

Just what is SMB?

V1.1
Richard Sharpe
24-Apr-1999

Copying

Please see the section on Copying this document for details of my policy on use of this document.

Disclaimer

This document attempts to provide a service to people involved with the SMB (soon to be CIFS) protocol in some way. Every attempt has been made to ensure that the information is correct, but no warranties are implied. Richard Sharpe can not be held liable for any loss or consequences resulting from your use or misuse of this information.

If you have any comments, please send me mail at sharpe@ns.aus.com.

Acknowledgments

I would like to thank Andrew Tridgell for getting me started in this area by suggesting that I might like to start on smblib, Dan Shearer for much encouragement and information, Paul Blackman for helping with this page, and a number of other people who have not given me approval to name them.

I would also like to thank the many people who have sent me positive comments and constructive feedback.

Trademarks

Microsoft, MS, Windows, Windows 95, and Windows NT are either registered trademarks or trademarks of Microsoft Corporation. Microsoft Corporation in no way endorses this document, nor is the author in any way affiliated with Microsoft Corporation.

All other trademarks are the sole property of their respective owners.

Table of Contents

Introduction

What's New?

What is SMB?

SMB Clients and Servers Currently Available

SMB Servers

SMB Clients

Further resources on the web

Copying this document

Introduction

This document explains what the SMB protocol is and discusses the many client and server implementations of SMB that are available. The document grew out of my interest in implementing SMBlib, a portable library of SMB client routines.

SMB is an important protocol because of the large number of PCs out there that already have client and server implementations running on them. All Windows for Workgroups, Windows 95 and Windows NT systems are (or are capable of) running SMB as either a client, a server, or both.

What's New

While there are many things out there that are new, perhaps the thing of greatest interest as far as the SMB protocol is concerned is CIFS, the Common Internet File System.

What is SMB?

SMB, which stands for Server Message Block, is a protocol for sharing files, printers, serial ports, and communications abstractions such as named pipes and mail slots between computers.

The earliest document I have on the SMB protocol is an IBM document from 1985. It is a copy of an IBM Personal Computer Seminar Proceedings from May 1985. It contains the **IBM PC Network SMB Protocol**. The next document I have access to is a Microsoft/Intel document called **Microsoft Networks/OpenNET-FILE SHARING PROTOCOL** from 1987. The protocol was subsequently developed further by Microsoft and others. Many of the documents that define the SMB protocol(s) are available at ftp.microsoft.com in the SMB documentation area.

SMB is a client server, request-response protocol. The diagram to the left illustrates the way in which SMB works. The only exception to the request-response nature of SMB (that is, where the client makes requests and the server sends back responses) is when the client has requested opportunistic locks (oplocks) and the server subsequently has to break an already granted oplock because another client has requested a file open with a mode that is incompatible with the granted oplock. In this case, the server sends an unsolicited message to the client signalling the oplock break.

Servers make file systems and other resources (printers, mailslots, named pipes, APIs) available to clients on the network. Client computers may have their own hard disks, but they also want access to the shared file systems and printers on the servers.

Clients connect to servers using TCP/IP (actually NetBIOS over TCP/IP as specified in RFC1001 and RFC1002), NetBEUI or IPX/SPX. Once they have established a connection, clients can then send commands (SMBs) to the server that allow them to access shares, open files, read and write files, and generally do all the sort of things that you want to do with a file system. However, in the case of SMB, these things are done over the network.

As mentioned, SMB can run over multiple protocols. The following diagram shows this:

SMB can be used over TCP/IP, NetBEUI and IPX/SPX. If TCP/IP or NetBEUI are in use, the NetBIOS API is being used.

NetBIOS over TCP/IP seems to be referred to by many names. Microsoft refers to it as NBT in some places and NetBT in others (specifically in their Windows NT documentation and in the Windows NT registry). Others refer to it as RFCNB. NetBEUI is sometimes refered to as NBF (NetBIOS Frame Format?) by Microsoft.

NetBIOS Names

If SMB is used over TCP/IP or NetBEUI, then NetBIOS names must be used in a number of cases. NetBIOS names are up to 15 characers long, and are usually the name of the computer that is running NetBIOS. Microsoft, and some other implementors, insist that NetBIOS names be in upper case, especially when presented to servers as the CALLED NAME.

SMB Protocol Variants

Since the inception of SMB, many protocol variants have been developed to handle the increasing complexity of the environments that it has been employed in.

The actual protocol variant client and server will use is negotiated using the *negprot* SMB which must be the first SMB sent on a connection.

The first protocol variant was the Core Protocol, known to SMB implementations as PC NETWORK PROGRAM 1.0. It could handle a fairly basic set of operations that included:

connecting to and disconnecting from file and print shares

opening and closing files

opening and closing print files

reading and writing files

creating and deleting files and direcories

searching directories

getting and setting file attributes

locking and unlocking byte ranges in files

Subsequent variants were introduced as more functionality was needed. Some of these variants and the related version of LAN Manager are:

SMB Protocol Variant	Protocol Name	Comments
PC NETWORK PROGRAM 1.0	Core Protocol	The original version of SMB as defined in IBM's PC Network Program. Some versions were called PCLAN1.0
MICROSOFT NETWORKS 1.03	Core Plus Protocol	Included Lock&Read and Write&Unlock SMBs with different versions of raw read and raw write SMBs
MICROSOFT NETWORKS 3.0	DOS LAN Manager 1.0	The same as LANMAN1.0, but OS/2 errors must be translated to DOS errors.
LANMAN1.0	LAN Manager 1.0	The full LANMAN1.0 protocol.
DOS LM1.2X002	LAN Manager 2.0	The same as LM1.2X002, but errors must be translated to DOS errors.
LM1.2X002	LAN Manager 2.0	The full LANMAN2.0 protocol.
DOS LANMAN2.1	LAN Manager 2.1	The same as LANMAN2.1, but errors must be translated to DOS errors.
LANMAN2.1	LAN Manager 2.1	The full LANMAN2.1 protocol.
Windows for Workgroups 3.1a	LAN Manager 2.1?	Windows for Workgroups 1.0?
NT LM 0.12	NT LAN Manager 1.0?	Contains special SMBs for NT

Samba	NT LAN Manager 1.0?	Samba's version of NT LM 0.12?
CIFS 1.0	NT LAN Manager 1.0	Really NT LM 0.12 plus a bit?

Some variants introduced new SMBs, some simply changed the format of existing SMBs or responses, and some variants did both.

Security The SMB model defines two levels of security:

Share level. Protection is applied at the share level on a server. Each share can have a password, and a client only needs that password to access all files under that share. This was the first security model that SMB had and is the only security model available in the Core and CorePlus protocols. Windows for Workgroups' vserver.exe implements share level security by default, as does Windows 95.

User Level.Protection is applied to individual files in each share and is based on user access rights. Each user (client) must log in to the server and be authenticated by the server. When it is authenticated, the client is given a UID which it must present on all subsequent accesses to the server. This model has been available since LAN Manager 1.0.

Browsing the network Having lots of servers out in the network is not much good if users cannot find them. Of course, clients can simply be configured to know about the servers in their environment, but this does not help when new servers are to be introduced or old ones removed.

To solve this problem, browsing has been introduced. Each server broadcasts information about its presence. Clients listen for these broadcasts and build up browse lists. In a NetBEUI environment, this is satisfactory, but in a TCP/IP environment, problems arise. The problems exist because TCP/IP broadcasts are not usually sent outside the subnet in which they originate (although some routers can selectively transport broadcasts to other subnets).

Microsoft have introduced browse servers and the Windows Internet Name Service (WINS) to help overcome these problems.

CIFS: The latest incarnation? Microsoft and a group of other vendors (Digital Equipment, Data General, SCO, Network Appliance Corp, etc) are engaged in developing a public version of the SMB protocol. It is expected that CIFS 1.0 will be essentially NT LM 0.12 with some modifications for easier use over the Internet.

An Example SMB Exchange The protocol elements (requests and responses) that clients and servers exchange are called SMBs. They have a specific format that is very similar for both requests and responses. Each consists of a fixed size header portion, followed by a variable sized parameter and data portion.

After connecting at the NetBIOS level, either via NBF, NetBT, etc, the client is ready to request services from the server. However, the client and server must first identify which protocol variant they each understand.

The client sends a *negprot* SMB to the server, listing the protocol dialects that it understands. The server responds with the index of the dialect that it wants to use, or 0xFFFF if none of the dialects was acceptable.

Dialects more recent than the Core and CorePlus protocols supply information in the negprot response to indicate their capabilities (max buffer size, canonical file names, etc).

Once a protocol has been established. The client can proceed to logon to the server, if required. They do this with a *sesssetupX* SMB. The response indicates whether or not they have supplied a valid username password pair and if so, can provide additional information. One of the most important aspects of the response is the UID of the logged on user. This UID must be submitted with all subsequent SMBs on that connection to the server.

Once the client has logged on (and in older protocols-Core and CorePlus-you cannot logon), the client can proceed to connect to a tree.

The client sends a *tcon* or *tconX* SMB specifying the network name of the share that they wish to connect to, and if all is kosher, the server responds with a TID that the client will use in all future SMBs relating to that share.

Having connected to a tree, the client can now open a file with an open SMB, followed by reading it with read SMBs, writing it with write SMBs, and closing it with close SMBs.

SMB Clients and Servers Currently Available

There are a few SMB clients available today and a relatively large number of servers available from a range of vendors.

The main clients are from Microsoft, and are included in Windows for WorkGroups 3.x, Windows 95, and Windows NT. They are most evident when you use the File Manager or the Windows 95 Explorer, as these allow you to connect to servers across the network. However they are also used when you open files using a UNC (universal naming convention).

Some other clients that I am aware of are:

smbclient from Samba

smbfs for Linux

SMBlib (an SMB client library that is in development)

Server implementations are available from many sources. Some that I am aware of are:

Samba

Microsoft Windows for Workgroups 3.x

Microsoft Windows 95

Microsoft Windows NT

The PATHWORKS family of servers from Digital

LAN Manager for OS/2, SCO, etc

VisionFS from SCO

TotalNET Advanced Server from Syntax

Advanced Server for UNIX from AT&T (NCR?)

LAN Server for OS/2 from IBM

The next two sections will discuss each of the above in turn.

SMB Servers

Before discussing SMB servers, it is useful to discuss the difference between Workgroups and Domains.

Workgroups A workgroup is a collection of computers that each maintain their own security information. With Windows for Workgroups, each server is pretty much in share level security. Windows 95 can pass user authentication off to an NT or LAN Manager server.

However, the point of a workgroup is that security is distributed, not centralized.

Domain A domain is a collection of computers where security is handled centrally. Each domain has one or more domain controllers. There is usually a primary domain controller and several backup domain controllers. The domain controllers maintain account style information related to users (clients), like account names, encrypted passwords, authorized hours of use, groups the user belongs to, etc.

Samba Samba is a freely available SMB server for UNIX, OpenVMS (recently ported and maybe not very stable) developed by Andrew Tridgell and maintained by a loosely knit group of people all over the world. Samba runs on a great many UNIX variants (Linux, Solaris, SunOS, HP-UX, ULTRIX, DEC OSF/1, Digital UNIX, Dynix (Sequent), IRIX (SGI), SCO Open Server, DG-UX, UNIXWARE, AIX, BSDI, NetBSD, NEXTSTEP, A/UX, etc).

Samba implements the NT LM 0.12 protocol dialect. Samba can now participate in a domain (both as a PDC and a Member of a domain), and it can participate in browsing and can be a browse master. Samba can also process logon requests for Windows 95 systems

Samba implements user level security, but shares can be public where access is mapped to the owner etc of the share.

Microsoft Windows Servers Microsoft has a number of SMB server implementations for the Windows range of operating systems. These are not separate products, rather, they are integral to the appropriate version of the Windows operating system. However, they can be switched off either though the Control Panel or at the command line (**net stop server** at DOS prompt).

It is clear from the fact that the Windows 95 and Windows NT SMB servers react differently to certain sequences of SMBs, that Microsoft do not use the same code for each of these servers (although the Windows for Workgroups and Windows 95 implementations may be derived from the same code).

Windows for Workgroups 3.11 implements the Windows for Workgroups 3.0a protocol variant, and implements share level security.

Windows 95 implements the NT LM 0.12 protocol level and implements both share and user level security.

Windows NT implements the NT LM 0.12 protocol level and implements both share and user level security.

LAN Manager and LAN Manager for UNIX (LM/X) Microsoft and AT&T GIS ported various LAN Manager versions to the UNIX operating system. This code formed the basis of many SMB servers available for UNIX operating systems from many vendors.

Some examples are: LM/X for SCO, LM Server for HP-UX (Advanced Server/9000), etc.

The most recent version of this software seems to be LAN Manager for UNIX Version 2.2, which implements the LANMAN2.1 protocol variant.

VisionFS VisionFS is a written-from-scratch SMB server from SCO. It is available for Solaris 2.x, HP-UX and SCO (both SCO OpenServer and UNIXware).

TotalNET Advanced Server This product is from Syntax. It is a completely independently written SMB server, that was perhaps the first SMB server for UNIX. These days, it comes with additional modules providing AppleShare and NetWare serving all in the one product.

Advanced Server for UNIX After LM/X, NCR (which used to be ATT GIS) (perhaps with help from Microsoft) ported the Windows NT SMB server code to UNIX to provide the same level of functionality as Windows NT.

PATHWORKS PATHWORKS is the name of a product family from Digital equipment corporation. It included both servers and clients, with the servers running on:

VAX and Alpha VMS

VAX and MIPS ULTRIX

DEC OSF/1 for AXP and Digital UNIX (DEC OSF/1 renamed)

OS/2

The clients ran on DOS, Windows, Windows for Workgroups, Windows NT and Windows 95 and are explained below.

Digital's clients and server implement SMB over DECnet as well as TCP/IP and more recently, NetBEUI. The SMB over DECnet specification has never been released.

Digital's original PATHWORKS servers were for VAX/VMS and implemented the CorePlus protocol (MICROSOFT NETWORKS 1.03 dialect). This product went through several versions and culminated in version 4.2. After a time, a version was done for ULTRIX and called PATHWORKS for ULTRIX V1, the highest version of which was 1.3. Both of these product streams were internally developed.

Subsequently, Digital used the AT&T and Microsoft LAN Manager for UNIX (LM/X) code. This was released as PATHWORKS V5.0 for OpenVMS (LAN Manager) and PATHWORKS V5.0 for Digital UNIX (LAN Manager). This product implements LAN Manager for UNIX V2.2 and the highest SMB dialect that it recognizes is LANMAN2.1 (and DOS LANMAN2.1). The reason for the LAN Manager in brackets at the end of each product name is that the products also support NetWare functionality.

PATHWORKS V5 is able to participate in a Windows NT based domain, albeit only as a Backup Domain Controller or a member server.

Recently, Digital has announced PATHWORKS V6.0 for UNIX (Advanced Server), which is based on AT&T's ASU (Advanced Server for UNIX) product.

LAN Server for OS/2 This is an IBM product that seems to be derived in some way from Microsoft's LAN Manager code.

SMB Clients

There are several SMB clients out there:

Microsoft Clients

Windows NT

Windows 95

Windows for Workgroups 3.11

Digital's PATHWORKS clients

Samba's smbclient

Linux's smbfs

SMBlib

Further Resources On The Web

The following are some other web pages that you can visit that are relevant to the SMB protocol:

Samba http://samba.anu.edu.au/samba

SMBlib http://samba.anu.edu.au/samba/smblib

SCO's VisionFS http://www.sco.com/products/visionfs

Syntax's TotalNET Advanced Server http://www.syntax.com/totalnet/tasbody2.htm

Digital's PATHWORKS products http://www.digital.com/info/pathworks

Microsoft's Windows NT products http://www.microsoft.com/NTServer

IBM's LAN Server products
http://www.austin.ibm.com/pspinfo/lsinfo.html

IBM's PC Integration with AIX
HTTP://www.austin.ibm.com/resource/technology/aixpcint.html

Data General's Support of Advanced Server for UNIX
http://www.dg.com/products/html/dg_ux.html

smbfs http://www.boutell.com/lsm/lsmbyid.cgi/000948 LSM entry (and smbfs ftp ftp://ftp.gwdg.de/pub/linux/misc/smbfs location)

CIFS Home page http://www.microsoft.com/intdev/cifs

Network Appliance's Support for CIFS
http://www.netapp.com/news/level3b/news_rel_960613.html

HP Ships NT Server Network Operating System on Enterprise-Class HP-UX Platform http://www.hp.com/pressrel/apr96/08apr96d.htm

AT&T GIS announces Advanced Server for UNIX Systems

http://www.att.com/press/0894/940822.nca.html

Thursby's Dave, Macintosh Client Software for Microsoft Networking http://www.thursby.com

Solstice LM Server http://www.sun.com/sunsoft/solstice/Networking-products/lmserver.html

Triteal's TEDfs, an SMB server for CDE (Unix) machines.
http://www.triteal.com/WinTEX/evalguide/index.html

Copying this document

I have had a number of requests for permission to use this document in other material. In one case, I was asked if someone could include this document as an appendix in a book. In another case, I was asked if the document could be handed to customers and potential customers. In both cases I felt that the request was reasonable.

My view on these matters is that this document was written to be read.

However, I would ask that you send me email stating your intended use and requesting my permission.

FeedBack

This document will be updated from time to time. If you have any comments, please feel free to send me email at *sharpe@ns.aus.com*

Visit me at NS Computer Software and Services P/L for more info on where I currently work.

Last updated 24-Apr-1999.

APPENDIX E

SAMBA MAN PAGES

When in doubt, check it out.

—Origin unknown

Appendix Objectives

- ✔ Lmhosts(5)
- ✔ Nmbd
- ✔ Samba(7)
- ✔ Samba.conf
- ✔ Smbclient(1)
- ✔ Smbd(8)
- ✔ Smbpasswd(5)
- ✔ Smbpasswd(8)
- ✔ Smbstatus(1)

Author's Note: In this Appendix, I have chosen those manual pages that I feel will be most useful to you in working with Samba. There are other commands that you will find useful as you progress in learning Samba.

APPENDIX E.1 LMHOSTS(5)

LMHOSTS (5)

SAMBA

23 OCT 1998

NAME

lmhosts—The Samba NetBIOS hosts file

SYNOPSIS

lmhosts is the **Samba** NetBIOS name to IP address mapping file.

DESCRIPTION

This file is part of the **Samba** suite.

lmhosts is the **Samba** NetBIOS name to IP address mapping file. It is very similar to the **/etc/hosts** file format, except that the hostname component must correspond to the NetBIOS naming format.

FILE FORMAT

It is an ASCII file containing one line for NetBIOS name. The two fields on each line are separated from each other by white space. Any entry beginning with # is ignored. Each line in the lmhosts file contains the following information :

- **IP Address**—in dotted decimal format.
- **NetBIOS Name**—This name format is a maximum fifteen character host name, with an optional trailing `'#'` character followed by the NetBIOS name type as two hexadecimal digits.

If the trailing `'#'` is omitted then the given IP address will be returned for all names that match the given name, whatever the NetBIOS name type in the lookup.

An example follows :

#

Sample Samba lmhosts file.

#

192.9.200.1 TESTPC

192.9.200.20 NTSERVER#20

192.9.200.21 SAMBASERVER

Contains three IP to NetBIOS name mappings. The first and third will be returned for any queries for the names `"TESTPC"` and `"SAMBASERVER"` respectively, whatever the type component of the NetBIOS name requested.

The second mapping will be returned only when the `"0x20"` name type for a name `"NTSERVER"` is queried. Any other name type will not be resolved.

The default location of the **lmhosts** file is in the same directory as the **smb.conf** file.

VERSION

This man page is correct for version 2.0 of the Samba suite.

SEE ALSO

SMB.CONF (5), SMBCLIENT (1), SMBPASSWD (8), SAMBA (7).

AUTHOR

The original Samba software and related utilities were created by Andrew Tridgell *samba-bugs@samba.org*. Samba is now developed by the Samba Team as an Open Source project similar to the way the Linux kernel is developed.

The original Samba man pages were written by Karl Auer. The man page sources were converted to YODL format (another excellent piece of Open Source software, available at **ftp://ftp.icce.rug.nl/pub/unix/**) and updated for the Samba2.0 release by Jeremy Allison. *samba-bugs@samba.org*.

See **samba (7)** to find out how to get a full list of contributors and details on how to submit bug reports, comments etc.

Appendix E.2 NMBD

NMBD

SAMBA

23 OCT 1998

NAME

nmbd—NetBIOS name server to provide NetBIOS over IP naming services to clients

SYNOPSIS

nmbd [-D] [-o] [-a] [-H lmhosts file] [-d debuglevel] [-l log file basename] [-n primary NetBIOS name] [-p port number] [-s configuration file] [-i NetBIOS scope] [-h]

DESCRIPTION

This program is part of the **Samba** suite.

nmbd is a server that understands and can reply to NetBIOS over IP name service requests, like those produced by SMBD/CIFS clients such as Windows 95/98, Windows NT and LanManager clients. It also participates in the browsing protocols which make up the Windows "Network Neighborhood" view.

SMB/CIFS clients, when they start up, may wish to locate an SMB/CIFS server. That is, they wish to know what IP number a specified host is using.

Amongst other services, **nmbd** will listen for such requests, and if its own NetBIOS name is specified it will respond with the IP number of the host it is running on. Its "own NetBIOS name" is by default the primary DNS name of the host it is running on, but this can be overridden with the **-n** option (see OPTIONS below). Thus **nmbd** will reply to broadcast queries for its own name(s). Additional names for **nmbd** to respond on can be set via parameters in the **smb.conf(5)** configuration file.

nmbd can also be used as a WINS (Windows Internet Name Server) server. What this basically means is that it will act as a WINS database server, creating a database from name registration requests that it receives and replying to queries from clients for these names.

In addition, **nmbd** can act as a WINS proxy, relaying broadcast queries from clients that do not understand how to talk the WINS protocol to a WIN server.

OPTIONS

- **D** If specified, this parameter causes **nmbd** to operate as a daemon. That is, it detaches itself and runs in the background, fielding requests on the appropriate port. By default, **nmbd** will NOT operate as a daemon. nmbd can also be operated from the inetd meta-daemon, although this is not recommended.
- **-a** If this parameter is specified, each new connection will append log messages to the log file. This is the default.
- **-o** If this parameter is specified, the log files will be overwritten when opened. By default, the log files will be appended to.
- **-H filename** NetBIOS lmhosts file.

  The lmhosts file is a list of NetBIOS names to IP addresses that is loaded by the nmbd server and used via the name resolution mechanism **name resolve order** described in **smb.conf (5)** to resolve any NetBIOS name queries needed by the server. Note that the contents of this file are *NOT* used by **nmbd** to answer any name queries. Adding a line to this file affects name NetBIOS resolution from this host *ONLY*.

  The default path to this file is compiled into Samba as part of the build process. Common defaults are */usr/local/samba/lib/lmhosts*, */usr/samba/lib/lmhosts* or */etc/lmhosts*. See the **lmhosts (5)** man page for details on the contents of this file.
- **-d debuglevel** debuglevel is an integer from 0 to 10.

The default value if this parameter is not specified is zero.

The higher this value, the more detail will be logged to the log files about the activities of the server. At level 0, only critical errors and serious warnings will be logged. Level 1 is a reasonable level for day to day running—it generates a small amount of information about operations carried out.

Levels above 1 will generate considerable amounts of log data, and should only be used when investigating a problem. Levels above 3 are designed for use only by developers and generate HUGE amounts of log data, most of which is extremely cryptic.

Note that specifying this parameter here will override the **log level** parameter in the **smb.conf (5)** file.

- **-l logfile** The **-l** parameter specifies a path and base filename into which operational data from the running nmbd server will be logged. The actual log file name is generated by appending the extension ".nmb" to the specified base name. For example, if the name specified was "log" then the file log.nmb would contain the debugging data.

  The default log file path is compiled into Samba as part of the build process. Common defaults are */usr/local/samba/var/log .nmb*, */usr/samba/var/log.nmb* or */var/log/log.nmb*.
- **-n primary NetBIOS name** This option allows you to override the NetBIOS name that Samba uses for itself. This is identical to setting the **NetBIOS name** parameter in the **smb.conf** file but will override the setting in the **smb.conf** file.
- **-p UDP port number** UDP port number is a positive integer value.

  This option changes the default UDP port number (normally 137) that **nmbd** responds to name queries on. Don't use this option unless you are an expert, in which case you won't need help!
- **-s configuration file** The default configuration file name is set at build time, typically as */usr/local/samba/lib/smb.conf*, but this may be changed when Samba is autoconfigured.

  The file specified contains the configuration details required by the server. See **smb.conf (5)** for more information.
- **-i scope** This specifies a NetBIOS scope that **nmbd** will use to communicate with when generating NetBIOS names. For details on the use of NetBIOS scopes, see rfc1001.txt and rfc1002.txt. NetBIOS scopes are *very* rarely used, only set this parameter if you are the system administrator in charge of all the NetBIOS systems you communicate with.
- **-h** Prints the help information (usage) for **nmbd**.

FILES

/ETC/INETD.CONF

If the server is to be run by the inetd meta-daemon, this file must contain suitable startup information for the meta-daemon.

/ETC/RC

(or whatever initialization script your system uses).

If running the server as a daemon at startup, this file will need to contain an appropriate startup sequence for the server.

/USR/LOCAL/SAMBA/LIB/SMB.CONF

This is the default location of the **smb.conf** server configuration file. Other common places that systems install this file are */usr/samba/lib/smb.conf* and */etc/smb.conf*.

When run as a **WINS** server (see the **wins support** parameter in the **smb.conf (5)** man page), **nmbd** will store the WINS database in the file `wins.dat` in the `var/locks` directory configured under wherever Samba was configured to install itself.

If **nmbd** is acting as a **browse master** (see the **local master** parameter in the **smb.conf (5)** man page), **nmbd** will store the browsing database in the file `browse.dat` in the `var/locks` directory configured under wherever Samba was configured to install itself.

SIGNALS

To shut down an **nmbd** process it is recommended that SIGKILL (-9) *NOT* be used, except as a last resort, as this may leave the name database in an inconsistent state. The correct way to terminate **nmbd** is to send it a SIGTERM (-15) signal and wait for it to die on its own.

nmbd will accept SIGHUP, which will cause it to dump out it's namelists into the file `namelist.debug` in the */usr/local/samba/var/locks* directory (or the *var/locks* directory configured under wherever Samba was configured to install itself). This will also cause **nmbd** to dump out it's server database in the log.nmb file. In addition, the debug log level of nmbd may be raised by sending it a SIGUSR1 (`kill -USR1 <nmbd-pid>`) and lowered by sending it a SIGUSR2 (`kill -USR2 <nmbd-pid>`). This is to allow transient problems to be diagnosed, whilst still running at a normally low log level.

VERSION

This man page is correct for version 2.0 of the Samba suite.

SEE ALSO

inetd (8), **smbd (8)**, **smb.conf (5)**, **smbclient (1)**, **testparm (1)**, **testprns (1)**, and the Internet RFC's **rfc1001.txt**, **rfc1002.txt**. In addition the CIFS (formerly SMB) specification is available as a link from the Web page: http://samba.org/cifs/.

AUTHOR

The original Samba software and related utilities were created by Andrew Tridgell *samba-bugs@samba.org*. Samba is now developed by the Samba Team as an Open Source project similar to the way the Linux kernel is developed.

The original Samba man pages were written by Karl Auer. The man page sources were converted to YODL format (another excellent piece of Open Source software, available at **ftp://ftp.icce.rug.nl/pub/unix/**) and updated for the Samba2.0 release by Jeremy Allison. *samba-bugs@samba.org*.

See **samba (7)** to find out how to get a full list of contributors and details on how to submit bug reports, comments etc.

APPENDIX E.3 SAMBA(7)

SAMBA (7)

SAMBA

23 OCT 1998

NAME

Samba—A Windows SMB/CIFS fileserver for UNIX

SYNOPSIS

SAMBA

DESCRIPTION

The Samba software suite is a collection of programs that implements the Server Message Block(commonly abbreviated as SMB) protocol for UNIX systems. This protocol is sometimes also referred to as the Common Internet File System (CIFS), LanManager or NetBIOS protocol.

COMPONENTS

The Samba suite is made up of several components. Each component is described in a separate manual page. It is strongly recommended that you read the documentation that comes with Samba and the manual pages of those components that you use. If the manual pages aren't clear enough then please send a patch or bug report to *samba-bugs@samba.org*.

- **smbd**
- The **smbd** (8) daemon provides the file and print services to SMB clients, such as Windows 95/98, Windows NT, Windows for Workgroups or LanManager. The configuration file for this daemon is described in **smb.conf (5)**.
- **nmbd**
- The **nmbd** (8) daemon provides NetBIOS nameserving and browsing support. The configuration file for this daemon is described in **smb.conf (5)**.
- **smbclient**
- The **smbclient** (1) program implements a simple ftp-like client. This is useful for accessing SMB shares on other compatible servers (such as Windows NT), and can also be used to allow a UNIX box to print to a printer attached to any SMB server (such as a PC running Windows NT).
- **testparm**
- The **testparm (1)** utility allows you to test your **smb.conf (5)** configuration file.
- **testprns**
- the **testprns (1)** utility allows you to test the printers defined in your printcap file.
- **smbstatus**
- The **smbstatus** (1) utility allows you list current connections to the **smbd (8)** server.
- **nmblookup**
- the **nmblookup (1)** utility allows NetBIOS name queries to be made from the UNIX machine.

- **make_smbcodepage**
- The **make_smbcodepage (1)** utility allows you to create SMB code page definition files for your **smbd (8)** server.
- **smbpasswd**
- The **smbpasswd (8)** utility allows you to change SMB encrypted passwords on Samba and Windows NT(tm) servers.

AVAILABILITY

The Samba software suite is licensed under the GNU Public License (GPL). A copy of that license should have come with the package in the file COPYING. You are encouraged to distribute copies of the Samba suite, but please obey the terms of this license.

The latest version of the Samba suite can be obtained via anonymous ftp from samba.org in the directory pub/samba/. It is also available on several mirror sites worldwide.

You may also find useful information about Samba on the newsgroup comp.protocols.smb and the Samba mailing list. Details on how to join the mailing list are given in the README file that comes with Samba.

If you have access to a WWW viewer (such as Netscape or Mosaic) then you will also find lots of useful information, including back issues of the Samba mailing list, at http://samba.org/samba/.

VERSION

This man page is correct for version 2.0 of the Samba suite.

CONTRIBUTIONS

If you wish to contribute to the Samba project, then I suggest you join the Samba mailing list at *samba@samba.org*. See the Web page at http://samba.org/listproc for details on how to do this.

If you have patches to submit or bugs to report then you may mail them directly to *samba-bugs@samba.org*. Note, however, that due to the enormous popularity of this package the Samba Team may take some time to respond to mail. We prefer patches in *diff -u* format.

CREDITS

Contributors to the project are now too numerous to mention here but all deserve the thanks of all Samba users. To see a full list, look at ftp://samba.org/pub/samba/alpha/change-log for the pre-CVS changes and at ftp://samba.org/pub/samba/alpha/cvs.log for the contributors to Samba post-CVS. CVS is the Open Source source code control system used by the Samba Team to develop Samba. The project would have been unmanageable without it.

In addition, several commercial organizations now help fund the Samba Team with money and equipment. For details see the Samba Web pages at http://samba.org/samba/samba-thanks.html.

AUTHOR

The original Samba software and related utilities were created by Andrew Tridgell *samba-bugs@samba.org*. Samba is now developed by the Samba Team as an Open Source project similar to the way the Linux kernel is developed.

The original Samba man pages were written by Karl Auer. The man page sources were converted to YODL format (another excellent piece of Open Source software, available at **ftp://ftp.icce.rug.nl/pub/unix/**) and updated for the Samba2.0 release by Jeremy Allison. *samba-bugs@samba.org*.

APPENDIX E.4 SMB.CONF

SMB.CONF (5)

SAMBA

23 OCT 1998

NAME

smb.conf—The configuration file for the Samba suite

SYNOPSIS

smb.conf The **smb.conf** file is a configuration file for the Samba suite. **smb.conf** contains runtime configuration information for the Samba programs. The **smb.conf** file is designed to be configured and administered by the **swat (8)** program. The complete description of the file format and possible parameters held within are here for reference purposes.

FILE FORMAT

The file consists of sections and parameters. A section begins with the name of the section in square brackets and continues until the next section begins. Sections contain parameters of the form

```
'name = value'
```

The file is line-based—that is, each newline-terminated line represents either a comment, a section name or a parameter.

Section and parameter names are not case sensitive.

Only the first equals sign in a parameter is significant. Whitespace before or after the first equals sign is discarded. Leading, trailing and internal whitespace in section and parameter names is irrelevant. Leading and trailing whitespace in a parameter value is discarded. Internal whitespace within a parameter value is retained verbatim.

Any line beginning with a semicolon (';') or a hash ('#') character is ignored, as are lines containing only whitespace.

Any line ending in a `'\'` is "continued" on the next line in the customary UNIX fashion.

The values following the equals sign in parameters are all either a string (no quotes needed) or a boolean, which may be given as yes/no, 0/1 or true/false. Case is not significant in boolean values, but is preserved in string values. Some items such as create modes are numeric.

SECTION DESCRIPTIONS

Each section in the configuration file (except for the **[global]** section) describes a shared resource (known as a *"share"*). The section name is the name of the shared resource and the parameters within the section define the shares attributes.

There are three special sections, **[global]**, **[homes]** and **[printers]**, which are described under **'special sections'**. The following notes apply to ordinary section descriptions.

A share consists of a directory to which access is being given plus a description of the access rights which are granted to the user of the service. Some housekeeping options are also specifiable.

Sections are either filespace services (used by the client as an extension of their native file systems) or printable services (used by the client to access print services on the host running the server).

Sections may be designated **guest** services, in which case no password is required to access them. A specified UNIX **guest account** is used to define access privileges in this case.

Sections other than guest services will require a password to access them. The client provides the username. As older clients only provide passwords and not usernames, you may specify a list of usernames to check against the password using the **"user="** option in the share definition. For modern clients such as Windows 95/98 and Windows NT, this should not be necessary.

Note that the access rights granted by the server are masked by the access rights granted to the specified or guest UNIX user by the host system. The server does not grant more access than the host system grants.

The following sample section defines a file space share. The user has write access to the path `/home/bar`. The share is accessed via the share name "foo":

```
[foo]
 path = /home/bar
 writeable = true
```

The following sample section defines a printable share. The share is read-only, but printable. That is, the only write access permitted is via calls to open, write to and close a spool file. The `'guest ok'` parameter means access will be permitted as the default guest user (specified elsewhere):

```
[aprinter]
 path = /usr/spool/public
 read only = true
 printable = true
 guest ok = true
```

SPECIAL SECTIONS

- **The [global] section**
- Parameters in this section apply to the server as a whole, or are defaults for sections which do not specifically define certain items. See the notes under **'PARAMETERS'** for more information.

- **The [homes] section**
- If a section called `'homes'` is included in the configuration file, services connecting clients to their home directories can be created on the fly by the server.

When the connection request is made, the existing sections are scanned. If a match is found, it is used. If no match is found, the requested section name is treated as a user name and looked up in the local password file. If the name exists and the correct password has been given, a share is created by cloning the [homes] section.

Some modifications are then made to the newly created share:

- The share name is changed from `'homes'` to the located username
- If no path was given, the path is set to the user's home directory.

If you decide to use a **path=** line in your [homes] section then you may find it useful to use the **%S** macro. For example :

```
path=/data/pchome/%S
```

would be useful if you have different home directories for your PCs than for UNIX access.

This is a fast and simple way to give a large number of clients access to their home directories with a minimum of fuss.

A similar process occurs if the requested section name is `"homes"`, except that the share name is not changed to that of the requesting user. This method of using the [homes] section works well if different users share a client PC.

The [homes] section can specify all the parameters a normal service section can specify, though some make more sense than others. The following is a typical and suitable [homes] section:

```
[homes]
 writeable = yes
```

An important point is that if guest access is specified in the [homes] section, all home directories will be visible to all clients **without a password**. In the very unlikely event that this is actually desirable, it would be wise to also specify **read only access**.

Note that the **browseable** flag for auto home directories will be inherited from the global browseable flag, not the [homes] browseable flag. This is useful as it means setting browseable=no in the [homes] section will hide the [homes] share but make any auto home directories visible.

- **The [printers] section**

This section works like **[homes]**, but for printers.

If a [printers] section occurs in the configuration file, users are able to connect to any printer specified in the local host's printcap file.

When a connection request is made, the existing sections are scanned. If a match is found, it is used. If no match is found, but a **[homes]** section exists, it is used as described above. Otherwise, the requested section name is treated as a printer name and the appropriate printcap file is scanned to see if the requested section name is a valid printer share name. If a match is found, a new printer share is created by cloning the [printers] section.

A few modifications are then made to the newly created share:

- The share name is set to the located printer name
- If no printer name was given, the printer name is set to the located printer name
- If the share does not permit guest access and no username was given, the username is set to the located printer name.

Note that the [printers] service MUST be printable—if you specify otherwise, the server will refuse to load the configuration file.

Typically the path specified would be that of a world-writeable spool directory with the sticky bit set on it. A typical [printers] entry would look like this:

```
[printers]
 path = /usr/spool/public
 writeable = no
 guest ok = yes
 printable = yes
```

All aliases given for a printer in the printcap file are legitimate printer names as far as the server is concerned. If your printing subsystem doesn't work like that, you will have to set up a pseudo-printcap. This is a file consisting of one or more lines like this:

```
alias|alias|alias|alias...
```

Each alias should be an acceptable printer name for your printing subsystem. In the **[global]** section, specify the new file as your printcap. The server will then only recognize names found in your pseudo-printcap, which of course can contain whatever aliases you like. The same technique could be used simply to limit access to a subset of your local printers.

An alias, by the way, is defined as any component of the first entry of a printcap record. Records are separated by newlines, components (if there are more than one) are separated by vertical bar symbols ("|").

NOTE: On SYSV systems which use lpstat to determine what printers are defined on the system you may be able to use **"printcap name = lpstat"** to automatically obtain a list of printers. See the **"printcap name"** option for more details.

PARAMETERS

Parameters define the specific attributes of sections.

Some parameters are specific to the **[global]** section (e.g., **security**). Some parameters are usable in all sections (e.g., **create mode**). All others are permissible only in normal sections. For the purposes of the following descriptions the **[homes]** and **[printers]** sections will be considered normal. The letter `'G'` in parentheses indicates that a parameter is specific to the **[global]** section. The letter `'S'` indicates that a parameter can be specified in a service specific section. Note that all `'S'` parameters can also be specified in the **[global]** section—in which case they will define the default behavior for all services.

Parameters are arranged here in alphabetical order—this may not create best bedfellows, but at least you can find them! Where there are synonyms, the preferred synonym is described, others refer to the preferred synonym.

VARIABLE SUBSTITUTIONS

Many of the strings that are settable in the config file can take substitutions. For example the option `"path = /tmp/%u"` would be interpreted as `"path = /tmp/john"` if the user connected with the username john.

These substitutions are mostly noted in the descriptions below, but there are some general substitutions which apply whenever they might be relevant. These are:

- **%S** = the name of the current service, if any.
- **%P** = the root directory of the current service, if any.
- **%u** = user name of the current service, if any.
- **%g** = primary group name of **%u**.
- **%U** = session user name (the user name that the client wanted, not necessarily the same as the one they got).
- **%G** = primary group name of **%U**.
- **%H** = the home directory of the user given by **%u**.
- **%v** = the Samba version.
- **%h** = the internet hostname that Samba is running on.
- **%m** = the NetBIOS name of the client machine (very useful).
- **%L** = the NetBIOS name of the server. This allows you to change your config based on what the client calls you. Your server can have a "dual personality".
- **%M** = the internet name of the client machine.
- **%N** = the name of your NIS home directory server. This is obtained from your NIS auto.map entry. If you have not compiled Samba with the **—with-automount** option then this value will be the same as **%L**.
- **%p** = the path of the service's home directory, obtained from your NIS auto.map entry. The NIS auto.map entry is split up as "%N:%p".
- **%R** = the selected protocol level after protocol negotiation. It can be one of CORE, COREPLUS, LANMAN1, LANMAN2 or NT1.
- **%d** = The process id of the current server process.
- **%a** = the architecture of the remote machine. Only some are recognized, and those may not be 100% reliable. It currently recognizes Samba, WfWg, WinNT and Win95. Anything else will be known as "UNKNOWN". If it gets it wrong then sending a level 3 log to *samba-bugs@samba.org* should allow it to be fixed.
- **%I** = The IP address of the client machine.
- **%T** = the current date and time.

There are some quite creative things that can be done with these substitutions and other smb.conf options.

NAME MANGLING

Samba supports *"name mangling"* so that DOS and Windows clients can use files that don't conform to the 8.3 format. It can also be set to adjust the case of 8.3 format filenames.

There are several options that control the way mangling is performed, and they are grouped here rather than listed separately. For the defaults look at the output of the testparm program.

All of these options can be set separately for each service (or globally, of course).

The options are:

"mangle case = yes/no" controls if names that have characters that aren't of the "default" case are mangled. For example, if this is yes then a name like `"Mail"` would be mangled. Default *no*.

"case sensitive = yes/no" controls whether filenames are case sensitive. If they aren't then Samba must do a filename search and match on passed names. Default *no*.

"default case = upper/lower" controls what the default case is for new filenames. Default *lower*.

"preserve case = yes/no" controls if new files are created with the case that the client passes, or if they are forced to be the `"default"` case. Default *Yes*.

"short preserve case = yes/no" controls if new files which conform to 8.3 syntax, that is all in upper case and of suitable length, are created upper case, or if they are forced to be the `"default"` case. This option can be use with **"preserve case = yes"** to permit long filenames to retain their case, while short names are lowered. Default *Yes*.

By default, Samba 2.0 has the same semantics as a Windows NT server, in that it is case insensitive but case preserving.

NOTE ABOUT USERNAME/PASSWORD VALIDATION

There are a number of ways in which a user can connect to a service. The server follows the following steps in determining if it will allow a connection to a specified service. If all the steps fail then the connection request is rejected. If one of the steps pass then the following steps are not checked.

If the service is marked **"guest only = yes"** then steps 1 to 5 are skipped.

Step 1: If the client has passed a username/password pair and that username/password pair is validated by the UNIX system's password programs then the connection is made as that username. Note that this includes the `\\server\service%username` method of passing a username.

Step 2: If the client has previously registered a username with the system and now supplies a correct password for that username then the connection is allowed.

Step 3: The client's netbios name and any previously used user names are checked against the supplied password, if they match then the connection is allowed as the corresponding user.

Step 4: If the client has previously validated a username/password pair with the server and the client has passed the validation token then that username is used. This step is skipped if **"revalidate = yes"** for this service.

Step 5: If a **"user = "** field is given in the smb.conf file for the service and the client has supplied a password, and that password matches (according to the UNIX system's password checking) with one of the usernames from the **user=** field then the connection is made as the username in the **"user="** line. If one of the username in the **user=** list begins with a `'@'` then that name expands to a list of names in the group of the same name.

Step 6: If the service is a guest service then a connection is made as the username given in the **"guest account ="** for the service, irrespective of the supplied password.

COMPLETE LIST OF GLOBAL PARAMETERS

Here is a list of all global parameters. See the section of each parameter for details. Note that some are synonyms.

announce as
announce version
auto services
bind interfaces only
browse list
change notify timeout
character set
client code page
coding system
config file
deadtime
debug timestamp
debuglevel
default
default service
dfree command
dns proxy
domain admin group
domain admin users
domain controller
domain group map
domain groups
domain guest group
domain guest users
domain logons
domain master
domain user map
encrypt passwords
getwd cache
homedir map
hosts equiv
interfaces
keepalive
kernel oplocks
ldap bind as
ldap passwd file
ldap port
ldap server
ldap suffix
lm announce
lm interval
load printers
local group map
local master
lock dir
lock directory
log file
log level
logon drive
logon home
logon path
logon script
lpq cache time
machine password timeout
mangled stack
max disk size
max log size
max mux
max open files
max packet
max ttl
max wins ttl
max xmit
message command
min wins ttl
name resolve order
netbios aliases
netbios name
nis homedir
nt pipe support
nt smb support
null passwords
ole locking compatibility
os level
packet size
panic action
passwd chat
passwd chat debug
passwd program
password level
password server
prefered master
preferred master
preload
printcap
printcap name
printer driver file
protocol
read bmpx
read prediction
read raw
read size
remote announce
remote browse sync
root
root dir
root directory
security
server string
shared mem size
smb passwd file
smbrun
socket address
socket options
ssl
ssl CA certDir
ssl CA certFile
ssl ciphers
ssl client cert
ssl client key
ssl compatibility
ssl hosts
ssl hosts resign
ssl require clientcert
ssl require servercert
ssl server cert
ssl server key
ssl version
stat cache
stat cache size
strip dot
syslog
syslog only
time offset
time server
timestamp logs
unix password sync
unix realname
update encrypted
use rhosts
username level
username map
valid chars
wins proxy
wins server
wins support
workgroup
write raw

COMPLETE LIST OF SERVICE PARAMETERS

Here is a list of all service parameters. See the section of each parameter for details. Note that some are synonyms.

admin users
allow hosts
alternate permissions
available
blocking locks
browsable
browseable
case sensitive
casesignames
comment
copy
create mask
create mode
default case
delete readonly
delete veto files
deny hosts
directory
directory mask
directory mode
dont descend
dos filetime resolution
dos filetimes
exec
fake directory create times
fake oplocks
follow symlinks
force create mode
force directory mode
force group
force user
fstype
group
guest account
guest ok
guest only
hide dot files
hide files
hosts allow
hosts deny
include
invalid users
locking
lppause command
lpq command
lpresume command
lprm command
magic output
magic script
mangle case
mangled map
mangled names
mangling char
map archive
map hidden
map system
map to guest
max connections
min print space
only guest
only user
oplocks
path
postexec
postscript
preexec
preserve case
print command
print ok
printable
printer
printer driver
printer driver location
printer name
printing
public
queuepause command
queueresume command
read list
read only
revalidate
root postexec
root preexec
set directory
share modes
short preserve case
status
strict locking
strict sync
sync always
user
username
users
valid users
veto files
veto oplock files
volume
wide links
writable
write list
write ok
writeable

EXPLANATION OF EACH PARAMETER

- **admin users (S)**
- This is a list of users who will be granted administrative privileges on the share. This means that they will do all file operations as the super-user (root).
- You should use this option very carefully, as any user in this list will be able to do anything they like on the share, irrespective of file permissions.

- **Default:**
  `no admin users`
- **Example:**
  `admin users = jason`
- **allow hosts (S)**
- A synonym for this parameter is '**hosts allow**'

This parameter is a comma, space, or tab delimited set of hosts which are permitted to access a service.

If specified in the **[global]** section then it will apply to all services, regardless of whether the individual service has a different setting.

You can specify the hosts by name or IP number. For example, you could restrict access to only the hosts on a Class C subnet with something like `"allow hosts = 150.203.5."`. The full syntax of the list is described in the man page **hosts_access (5)**. Note that this man page may not be present on your system, so a brief description will be given here also.

NOTE: IF you wish to allow the **smbpasswd (8)** program to be run by local users to change their Samba passwords using the local **smbd (8)** daemon, then you *MUST* ensure that the localhost is listed in your **allow hosts** list, as **smbpasswd (8)** runs in client-server mode and is seen by the local **smbd** process as just another client.

You can also specify hosts by network/netmask pairs and by netgroup names if your system supports netgroups. The *EXCEPT* keyword can also be used to limit a wildcard list. The following examples may provide some help:

Example 1: allow localhost and all IPs in 150.203.*.* except one

```
hosts allow = localhost, 150.203. EXCEPT 150.203.6.66
```

Example 2: allow localhost and hosts that match the given network/netmask

```
hosts allow = localhost, 150.203.15.0/255.255.255.0
```

Example 3: allow a localhost plus a couple of hosts

```
hosts allow = localhost, lapland, arvidsjaur
```

Example 4: allow only hosts in NIS netgroup "foonet" or localhost, but deny access from one particular host

`hosts allow = @foonet, localhost hosts deny = pirate`

Note that access still requires suitable user-level passwords.

See **testparm (1)** for a way of testing your host access to see if it does what you expect.

Default: `none (i.e., all hosts permitted access)`

Example: `allow hosts = 150.203.5. localhost myhost.mynet.edu.au`

- **alternate permissions (S)**

This is a deprecated parameter. It no longer has any effect in Samba2.0. In previous versions of Samba it affected the way the DOS "read only" attribute was mapped for a file. In Samba2.0 a file is marked "read only" if the UNIX file does not have the 'w' bit set for the owner of the file, regardless if the owner of the file is the currently logged on user or not.

- **announce as (G)**

This specifies what type of server **nmbd** will announce itself as, to a network neighborhood browse list. By default this is set to Windows NT. The valid options are : "NT", "Win95" or "WfW" meaning Windows NT, Windows 95 and Windows for Workgroups respectively. Do not change this parameter unless you have a specific need to stop Samba appearing as an NT server as this may prevent Samba servers from participating as browser servers correctly.

Default: `announce as = NT`

Example `announce as = Win95`

- **announce version (G)**

This specifies the major and minor version numbers that nmbd will use when announcing itself as a server. The default is 4.2. Do not change this parameter unless you have a specific need to set a Samba server to be a downlevel server.

Default: `announce version = 4.2`

Example: `announce version = 2.0`

- **auto services (G)**

This is a list of services that you want to be automatically added to the browse lists. This is most useful for homes and printers services that would otherwise not be visible.

Note that if you just want all printers in your printcap file loaded then the **"load printers"** option is easier.

Default: `no auto services`

Example: `auto services = fred lp colorlp`

- **available (S)**

This parameter lets you *'turn off'* a service. If `'available = no'`, then *ALL* attempts to connect to the service will fail. Such failures are logged.

Default: `available = yes`

Example: `available = no`

- **bind interfaces only (G)**

This global parameter allows the Samba admin to limit what interfaces on a machine will serve smb requests. If affects file service **smbd** and name service **nmbd** in slightly different ways.

For name service it causes **nmbd** to bind to ports 137 and 138 on the interfaces listed in the **'interfaces'** parameter. **nmbd** also binds to the 'all addresses' interface (0.0.0.0) on ports 137 and 138 for the purposes of reading broadcast messages. If this option is not set then **nmbd** will service name requests on all of these sockets. If **"bind interfaces only"** is set then **nmbd** will check the source address of any packets coming in on the broadcast sockets and discard any that don't match the broadcast addresses of the interfaces in the **'interfaces'** parameter list. As unicast packets are received on the other sockets it allows **nmbd** to refuse to serve names to machines that send packets that arrive through any interfaces not listed in the **"interfaces"** list. IP Source address spoofing does defeat this simple check, however so it must not be used seriously as a security feature for **nmbd**.

For file service it causes **smbd** to bind only to the interface list given in the **'interfaces'** parameter. This restricts the networks that **smbd** will serve to packets coming in those interfaces. Note that you should not use this parameter for machines that are serving PPP or other intermittent or non-broadcast network interfaces as it will not cope with non-permanent interfaces.

In addition, to change a users SMB password, the **smbpasswd** by default connects to the *"localhost"—127.0.0.1* address as an SMB client to issue the password change request. If **"bind interfaces only"** is set then unless the network address *127.0.0.1* is added to the **'interfaces'** parameter list then **smbpasswd** will fail to connect in it's default mode. **smbpasswd** can be forced to use the primary IP interface of the local host by using its **"-r remote machine"** parameter, with **"remote machine"** set to the IP name of the primary interface of the local host.

Default: `bind interfaces only = False`

Example: `bind interfaces only = True`

- **blocking locks (S)**

This parameter controls the behavior of **smbd** when given a request by a client to obtain a byte range lock on a region of an open file, and the request has a time limit associated with it.

If this parameter is set and the lock range requested cannot be immediately satisfied, Samba 2.0 will internally queue the lock request, and periodically attempt to obtain the lock until the timeout period expires.

If this parameter is set to "False", then Samba 2.0 will behave as previous versions of Samba would and will fail the lock request immediately if the lock range cannot be obtained.

This parameter can be set per share.

Default: `blocking locks = True`

Example: `blocking locks = False`

- **browsable (S)**

Synonym for **browseable**.

- **browse list(G)**

This controls whether **smbd** will serve a browse list to a client doing a NetServerEnum call. Normally set to true. You should never need to change this.

Default: `browse list = Yes`

- **browseable**

This controls whether this share is seen in the list of available shares in a net view and in the browse list.

Default: `browseable = Yes`

Example: `browseable = No`

- **case sensitive (G)**

See the discussion in the section **NAME MANGLING**.

- **casesignames (G)**

Synonym for "**case sensitive**".

- **change notify timeout (G)**

One of the new NT SMB requests that Samba 2.0 supports is the "ChangeNotify" requests. This SMB allows a client to tell a server to *"watch"* a particular directory for any changes and only reply to the SMB request when a change has occurred. Such constant scanning of a directory is expensive under UNIX, hence an **smbd** daemon only performs such a scan on each requested directory once every **change notify timeout** seconds.

change notify timeout is specified in units of seconds.

Default: `change notify timeout = 60`

Example: `change notify timeout = 300`

Would change the scan time to every 5 minutes.

- **character set (G)**

This allows a smbd to map incoming filenames from a DOS Code page (see the **client code page** parameter) to several built in UNIX character sets. The built in code page translations are:

- **ISO8859-1** Western European UNIX character set. The parameter **client code page** *MUST* be set to code page 850 if the **character set** parameter is set to iso8859-1 in order for the conversion to the UNIX character set to be done correctly.
- **ISO8859-2** Eastern European UNIX character set. The parameter **client code page** *MUST* be set to code page 852 if the **character set** parameter is set to ISO8859-2 in order for the conversion to the UNIX character set to be done correctly.
- **ISO8859-5** Russian Cyrillic UNIX character set. The parameter **client code page** *MUST* be set to code page 866 if the **character set** parameter is set to ISO8859-2 in order for the conversion to the UNIX character set to be done correctly.
- **KOI8-R** Alternate mapping for Russian Cyrillic UNIX character set. The parameter **client code page** *MUST* be set to code page 866 if the **character set** parameter is set to KOI8-R in order for the conversion to the UNIX character set to be done correctly.

BUG. These MSDOS code page to UNIX character set mappings should be dynamic, like the loading of MS DOS code pages, not static.

See also **client code page**. Normally this parameter is not set, meaning no filename translation is done.

Default: `character set = <empty string>`

Example: `character set = ISO8859-1`

- **client code page (G)**

This parameter specifies the DOS code page that the clients accessing Samba are using. To determine what code page a Windows or DOS client is using, open a DOS command prompt and type the command "chcp". This will output the code page. The default for USA MS-DOS, Windows 95, and Windows NT releases is code page 437. The default for western european releases of the above operating systems is code page 850.

This parameter tells **smbd** which of the `codepage.XXX` files to dynamically load on startup. These files, described more fully in the manual page **make_smbcodepage (1)**, tell **smbd** how to map lower to upper case characters to provide the case insensitivity of filenames that Windows clients expect.

Samba currently ships with the following code page files :

- **Code Page 437—MS-DOS Latin US**
- **Code Page 737—Windows '95 Greek**
- **Code Page 850—MS-DOS Latin 1**
- **Code Page 852—MS-DOS Latin 2**
- **Code Page 861—MS-DOS Icelandic**
- **Code Page 866—MS-DOS Cyrillic**
- **Code Page 932—MS-DOS Japanese SJIS**
- **Code Page 936—MS-DOS Simplified Chinese**
- **Code Page 949—MS-DOS Korean Hangul**
- **Code Page 950—MS-DOS Traditional Chinese**

Thus this parameter may have any of the values 437, 737, 850, 852, 861, 932, 936, 949, or 950. If you don't find the codepage you need, read the comments in one of the other codepage files and the **make_smbcodepage (1)** man page and write one. Please remember to donate it back to the Samba user community.

This parameter co-operates with the **"valid chars"** parameter in determining what characters are valid in filenames and how capitalization is done. If you set both this parameter and the **"valid chars"** parameter the **"client code page"** parameter *MUST* be set before the **"valid chars"** parameter in the **smb.conf** file. The **"valid chars"** string will then augment the character settings in the "client code page" parameter.

If not set, **"client code page"** defaults to 850.

See also : **"valid chars"**

Default: `client code page = 850`

Example: `client code page = 936`

- **codingsystem (G)**

This parameter is used to determine how incoming Shift-JIS Japanese characters are mapped from the incoming **"client code page"** used by the client, into file names in the UNIX filesystem. Only useful if **"client code page"** is set to 932 (Japanese Shift-JIS).

The options are :

- **SJIS** Shift-JIS. Does no conversion of the incoming filename.
- **JIS8, J8BB, J8BH, J8@B, J8@J, J8@H** Convert from incoming Shift-JIS to eight bit JIS code with different shift-in, shift out codes.
- **JIS7, J7BB, J7BH, J7@B, J7@J, J7@H** Convert from incoming Shift-JIS to seven bit JIS code with different shift-in, shift out codes.
- **JUNET, JUBB, JUBH, JU@B, JU@J, JU@H** Convert from incoming Shift-JIS to JUNET code with different shift-in, shift out codes.
- **EUC** Convert an incoming Shift-JIS character to EUC code.
- **HEX** Convert an incoming Shift-JIS character to a 3 byte hex representation, i.e. `:AB`.
- **CAP** Convert an incoming Shift-JIS character to the 3 byte hex representation used by the Columbia AppleTalk Program (CAP), i.e. `:AB`. This is used for compatibility between Samba and CAP.

- **comment (S)**

This is a text field that is seen next to a share when a client does a queries the server, either via the network neighborhood or via "net view" to list what shares are available.

If you want to set the string that is displayed next to the machine name then see the server string command.

Default: `No comment string`

Example: `comment = Fred's Files`

- **config file (G)**

This allows you to override the config file to use, instead of the default (usually **smb.conf**). There is a chicken and egg problem here as this option is set in the config file!

For this reason, if the name of the config file has changed when the parameters are loaded then it will reload them from the new config file.

This option takes the usual substitutions, which can be very useful.

If the config file doesn't exist then it won't be loaded (allowing you to special case the config files of just a few clients).

Example: `config file = /usr/local/samba/lib/smb.conf.%m`

- **copy (S)**

This parameter allows you to *'clone'* service entries. The specified service is simply duplicated under the current service's name. Any parameters specified in the current section will override those in the section being copied.

This feature lets you set up a 'template' service and create similar services easily. Note that the service being copied must occur earlier in the configuration file than the service doing the copying.

Default: `none`

Example: `copy = otherservice`

- **create mask (S)**

A synonym for this parameter is **'create mode'**.

When a file is created, the necessary permissions are calculated according to the mapping from DOS modes to UNIX permissions, and the resulting UNIX mode is then bit-wise 'AND'ed with this parameter. This parameter may be thought of as a bit-wise MASK for the UNIX modes of a file. Any bit **not** set here will be removed from the modes set on a file when it is created.

The default value of this parameter removes the 'group' and 'other' write and execute bits from the UNIX modes.

Following this Samba will bit-wise 'OR' the UNIX mode created from this parameter with the value of the "force create mode" parameter which is set to 000 by default.

This parameter does not affect directory modes. See the parameter **'directory mode'** for details.

See also the **"force create mode"** parameter for forcing particular mode bits to be set on created files. See also the **"directory mode"** parameter for masking mode bits on created directories.

Default: `create mask = 0744`

Example: `create mask = 0775`

- **create mode (S)**

This is a synonym for **create mask**.

- **deadtime (G)**

The value of the parameter (a decimal integer) represents the number of minutes of inactivity before a connection is considered dead, and it is disconnected. The deadtime only takes effect if the number of open files is zero.

This is useful to stop a server's resources being exhausted by a large number of inactive connections.

Most clients have an auto-reconnect feature when a connection is broken so in most cases this parameter should be transparent to users.

Using this parameter with a timeout of a few minutes is recommended for most systems.

A deadtime of zero indicates that no auto-disconnection should be performed.

Default: `deadtime = 0`

Example: `deadtime = 15`

- **debug timestamp (G)**

Samba2.0 debug log messages are timestamped by default. If you are running at a high **"debug level"** these timestamps can be distracting. This boolean parameter allows them to be turned off.

Default: `debug timestamp = Yes`

Example: `debug timestamp = No`

- **debug level (G)**

The value of the parameter (an integer) allows the debug level (logging level) to be specified in the **smb.conf** file. This is to give greater flexibility in the configuration of the system.

The default will be the debug level specified on the command line or level zero if none was specified.

Example: `debug level = 3`

- **default (G)**

A synonym for default service.

- **default case (S)**

See the section on **"NAME MANGLING"**. Also note the **"short preserve case"** parameter.

- **default service (G)**

This parameter specifies the name of a service which will be connected to if the service actually requested cannot be found. Note that the square brackets are *NOT* given in the parameter value (see example below).

There is no default value for this parameter. If this parameter is not given, attempting to connect to a nonexistent service results in an error.

Typically the default service would be a **guest ok**, **read-only** service.

Also note that the apparent service name will be changed to equal that of the requested service, this is very useful as it allows you to use macros like **%S** to make a wildcard service.

Note also that any '_' characters in the name of the service used in the default service will get mapped to a '/'. This allows for interesting things.

Example:

```
default service = pub

[pub]
        path = /%S
```

- **delete readonly (S)**

This parameter allows readonly files to be deleted. This is not normal DOS semantics, but is allowed by UNIX.

This option may be useful for running applications such as rcs, where UNIX file ownership prevents changing file permissions, and DOS semantics prevent deletion of a read only file.

Default: `delete readonly = No`

Example: `delete readonly = Yes`

- **delete veto files (S)**

This option is used when Samba is attempting to delete a directory that contains one or more vetoed directories (see the **'veto files'** option). If this option is set to False (the default) then if a vetoed directory contains any non-vetoed files or directories then the directory delete will fail. This is usually what you want.

If this option is set to True, then Samba will attempt to recursively delete any files and directories within the vetoed directory. This can be useful for integration with file serving systems such as **NetAtalk**, which create meta-files within directories you might normally veto DOS/Windows users from seeing (e.g. `.AppleDouble`)

Setting `'delete veto files = True'` allows these directories to be transparently deleted when the parent directory is deleted (so long as the user has permissions to do so).

See also the **veto files** parameter.

Default: `delete veto files = False`

Example: `delete veto files = True`

- **deny hosts (S)**

The opposite of **'allow hosts'**—hosts listed here are *NOT* permitted access to services unless the specific services have their own lists to override this one. Where the lists conflict, the **'allow'** list takes precedence.

Default: `none (i.e., no hosts specifically excluded)`

Example: `deny hosts = 150.203.4. badhost.mynet.edu.au`

- **dfree command (G)**

The dfree command setting should only be used on systems where a problem occurs with the internal disk space calculations. This has been known to happen with Ultrix, but may occur with other operating systems. The symptom that was seen was an error of "Abort Retry Ignore" at the end of each directory listing.

This setting allows the replacement of the internal routines to calculate the total disk space and amount available with an external routine. The example below gives a possible script that might fulfill this function.

The external program will be passed a single parameter indicating a directory in the filesystem being queried. This will typically consist of the string `"./"`. The script should return two integers in ascii. The first should be the total disk space in blocks, and the second should be the number of available blocks. An optional third return value can give the block size in bytes. The default blocksize is 1024 bytes.

Note: Your script should *NOT* be setuid or setgid and should be owned by (and writeable only by) root!

Default: `By default internal routines for determining the disk capacity and remaining space will be used.`

Example: `dfree command = /usr/local/samba/bin/dfree`

Where the script dfree (which must be made executable) could be:

```
#!/bin/sh
df $1 | tail -1 | awk '{print $2" "$4}'
```

or perhaps (on Sys V based systems):

```
#!/bin/sh
/usr/bin/df -k $1 | tail -1 | awk '{print $3" "$5}'
```

Note that you may have to replace the command names with full path names on some systems.

- **directory (S)**

Synonym for **path**.

- **directory mask (S)**

This parameter is the octal modes which are used when converting DOS modes to UNIX modes when creating UNIX directories.

When a directory is created, the necessary permissions are calculated according to the mapping from DOS modes to UNIX permissions, and the resulting UNIX mode is then bit-wise 'AND'ed with this parameter. This parameter may be thought of as a bit-wise MASK for the UNIX modes of a directory. Any bit **not** set here will be removed from the modes set on a directory when it is created.

The default value of this parameter removes the 'group' and 'other' write bits from the UNIX mode, allowing only the user who owns the directory to modify it.

Following this Samba will bit-wise 'OR' the UNIX mode created from this parameter with the value of the "force directory mode" parameter. This parameter is set to 000 by default (i.e. no extra mode bits are added).

See the **"force directory mode"** parameter to cause particular mode bits to always be set on created directories.

See also the **"create mode"** parameter for masking mode bits on created files.

Default: `directory mask = 0755`

Example: `directory mask = 0775`

- **directory mode (S)**

Synonym for **directory mask**.

- **dns proxy (G)**

Specifies that **nmbd** when acting as a WINS server and finding that a NetBIOS name has not been registered, should treat the NetBIOS name word-for-word as a DNS name and do a lookup with the DNS server for that name on behalf of the name-querying client.

Note that the maximum length for a NetBIOS name is 15 characters, so the DNS name (or DNS alias) can likewise only be 15 characters, maximum.

nmbd spawns a second copy of itself to do the DNS name lookup requests, as doing a name lookup is a blocking action.

See also the parameter **wins support**.

Default: `dns proxy = yes`

domain admin group (G)

This is an **EXPERIMENTAL** parameter that is part of the unfinished Samba NT Domain Controller Code. It has been removed as of November 98. To work with the latest code builds that may have more support for Samba NT Domain Controller functionality please subscribe to the mailing list **Samba-ntdom** available by sending email to *listproc@samba.org*

- **domain admin users (G)**

This is an **EXPERIMENTAL** parameter that is part of the unfinished Samba NT Domain Controller Code. It has been removed as of November 98. To work with the latest code builds that may have more support for Samba NT Domain Controller functionality please subscribe to the mailing list **Samba-ntdom** available by sending email to *listproc@samba.org*

- **domain controller (G)**

This is a **DEPRECATED** parameter. It is currently not used within the Samba source and should be removed from all current smb.conf files. It is left behind for compatibility reasons.

- **domain group map (G)**

This option allows you to specify a file containing unique mappings of individual NT Domain Group names (in any domain) to UNIX group names. This allows NT domain groups to be presented correctly to NT users, despite the lack of native support for the NT Security model (based on VAX/VMS) in UNIX. The reader is advised to become familiar with the NT Domain system and its administration.

This option is used in conjunction with **'local group map'** and **'domain user map'**. The use of these three options is trivial and often unnecessary in the case where Samba is not expected to interact with any other SAM databases (whether local workstations or Domain Controllers).

The map file is parsed line by line. If any line begins with a `'#'` or a `';'` then it is ignored. Each line should contain a single UNIX group name on the left then a single NT Domain Group name on the right, separated by a tabstop or `'='`. If either name contains spaces then it should be enclosed in quotes. The line can be either of the form:

```
UNIXgroupname \\DOMAIN_NAME\\DomainGroupName
```

or:

```
UNIXgroupname DomainGroupName
```

In the case where Samba is either an **EXPERIMENTAL** Domain Controller or it is a member of a domain using **"security = domain"**, the latter format can be used: the default Domain name is the Samba Server's Domain name, specified by **"workgroup = MYGROUP"**.

Any UNIX groups that are *NOT* specified in this map file are assumed to be either Local or Domain Groups, depending on the role of the Samba Server.

In the case when Samba is an **EXPERIMENTAL** Domain Controller, Samba will present *ALL* such unspecified UNIX groups as its own NT Domain Groups, with the same name.

In the case where Samba is member of a domain using **"security = domain"**, Samba will check the UNIX name with its Domain Controller (see **"password server"**) as if it was an NT Domain Group. If the Domain Controller says that it is not, such unspecified (unmapped) UNIX groups which also are not NT Domain Groups are treated as Local Groups in the Samba Server's local SAM database. NT Administrators will recognise these as Workstation Local Groups, which are managed by running **USRMGR.EXE** and selecting a remote Domain named "\\WORKSTATION_NAME", or by running **MUSRMGR.EXE** on a local Workstation.

This may sound complicated, but it means that a Samba Server as either a member of a domain or as an **EXPERIMENTAL** Domain Controller will act like an NT Workstation (with a local SAM database) or an NT PDC (with a Domain SAM database) respectively, without the need for any of the map files at all. If you **want** to get fancy, however, you can.

Note that adding an entry to map an arbitrary NT group in an arbitrary Domain to an arbitrary UNIX group *REQUIRES* the following:

- that the UNIX group exists on the UNIX server.
- that the NT Domain Group exists in the specified NT Domain
- that the UNIX Server knows about the specified Domain;
- that all the UNIX users (who are expecting to access the Samba Server as the correct NT user and with the correct NT group permissions) in the UNIX group be mapped to the correct NT Domain users in the specified NT Domain using **'domain user map'**.

Failure to meet any of these requirements may result in either (or both) errors reported in the log files or (and) incorrect or missing access rights granted to users.

- **domain groups (G)**

This is an **EXPERIMENTAL** parameter that is part of the unfinished Samba NT Domain Controller Code. It has been removed as of November 98. To work with the latest code builds that may have more support for Samba NT Domain Controller functionality please subscribe to the mailing list **Samba-ntdom** available by sending email to *listproc@samba.org*

- **domain guest group (G)**

This is an **EXPERIMENTAL** parameter that is part of the unfinished Samba NT Domain Controller Code. It has been removed as of November 98. To work with the latest code builds that may have more support for Samba NT Domain Controller functionality please subscribe to the mailing list **Samba-ntdom** available by sending email to *listproc@samba.org*

- **domain guest users (G)**

This is an **EXPERIMENTAL** parameter that is part of the unfinished Samba NT Domain Controller Code. It has been removed as of November 98. To work with the latest code builds that may have more support for

Samba NT Domain Controller functionality please subscribe to the mailing list **Samba-ntdom** available by sending email to *listproc@samba.org*

- **domain logons (G)**

If set to true, the Samba server will serve Windows 95/98 Domain logons for the **workgroup** it is in. For more details on setting up this feature see the file DOMAINS.txt in the Samba documentation directory `docs/` shipped with the source code.

Note that Win95/98 Domain logons are *NOT* the same as Windows NT Domain logons. NT Domain logons require a Primary Domain Controller (PDC) for the Domain. It is intended that in a future release Samba will be able to provide this functionality for Windows NT clients also.

Default: `domain logons = no`

- **domain master (G)**

Tell **nmbd** to enable WAN-wide browse list collation. Setting this option causes **nmbd** to claim a special domain specific NetBIOS name that identifies it as a domain master browser for its given **workgroup**. Local master browsers in the same **workgroup** on broadcast-isolated subnets will give this **nmbd** their local browse lists, and then ask **smbd** for a complete copy of the browse list for the whole wide area network. Browser clients will then contact their local master browser, and will receive the domain-wide browse list, instead of just the list for their broadcast-isolated subnet.

Note that Windows NT Primary Domain Controllers expect to be able to claim this **workgroup** specific special NetBIOS name that identifies them as domain master browsers for that **workgroup** by default (i.e. there is no way to prevent a Windows NT PDC from attempting to do this). This means that if this parameter is set and **nmbd** claims the special name for a **workgroup** before a Windows NT PDC is able to do so then cross subnet browsing will behave strangely and may fail.

By default ("auto") Samba will attempt to become the domain master browser only if it is the Primary Domain Controller.

Default: `domain master = auto`

Example: `domain master = no`

- **domain user map (G)**

This option allows you to specify a file containing unique mappings of individual NT Domain User names (in any domain) to UNIX user names. This allows NT domain users to be presented correctly to NT systems, despite the lack of native support for the NT Security model (based on VAX/VMS) in UNIX. The reader is advised to become familiar with the NT Domain system and its administration.

This option is used in conjunction with **'local group map'** and **'domain group map'**. The use of these three options is trivial and often unnecessary in the case where Samba is not expected to interact with any other SAM databases (whether local workstations or Domain Controllers).

This option, which provides (and maintains) a one-to-one link between UNIX and NT users, is *DIFFERENT* from **'username map'**, which does *NOT* maintain a distinction between the name(s) it can map to and the name it maps.

The map file is parsed line by line. If any line begins with a `'#'` or a `';'` then the line is ignored. Each line should contain a single UNIX user name on the left then a single NT Domain User name on the right, separated by a tabstop or `'='`. If either name contains spaces then it should be enclosed in quotes. The line can be either of the form:

```
UNIXusername \\DOMAIN_NAME\\DomainUserName
```

or:

```
UNIXusername DomainUserName
```

In the case where Samba is either an **EXPERIMENTAL** Domain Controller or it is a member of a domain using **"security = domain"**, the latter format can be used: the default Domain name is the Samba Server's Domain name, specified by **"workgroup = MYGROUP"**.

Any UNIX users that are *NOT* specified in this map file are assumed to be either Domain or Workstation Users, depending on the role of the Samba Server.

In the case when Samba is an **EXPERIMENTAL** Domain Controller, Samba will present *ALL* such unspecified UNIX users as its own NT Domain Users, with the same name.

In the case where Samba is a member of a domain using **"security = domain"**, Samba will check the UNIX name with its Domain Controller (see **"password server"**) as if it was an NT Domain User. If the Domain Controller says that it is not, such unspecified (unmapped) UNIX users which also are not NT Domain Users are treated as Local Users in the Samba Server's local SAM database. NT Administrators will recognise these as Workstation Users, which are managed by running **USRMGR.EXE** and selecting a remote Domain named"\\WORKSTATION_NAME", or by running **MUSRMGR.EXE** on a local Workstation.

This may sound complicated, but it means that a Samba Server as either a member of a domain or as an **EXPERIMENTAL** Domain Controller will act like an NT Workstation (with a local SAM database) or an NT PDC (with a Domain SAM database) respectively, without the need for any of the map files at all. If you **want** to get fancy, however, you can.

Note that adding an entry to map an arbitrary NT User in an arbitrary Domain to an arbitrary UNIX user *REQUIRES* the following:

- that the UNIX user exists on the UNIX server.
- that the NT Domain User exists in the specified NT Domain.
- that the UNIX Server knows about the specified Domain.

Failure to meet any of these requirements may result in either (or both) errors reported in the log files or (and) incorrect or missing access rights granted to users.

- **dont descend (S)**

There are certain directories on some systems (e.g., the `/proc` tree under Linux) that are either not of interest to clients or are infinitely deep (recursive). This parameter allows you to specify a comma-delimited list of directories that the server should always show as empty.

Note that Samba can be very fussy about the exact format of the "dont descend" entries. For example you may need `"./proc"` instead of just `"/proc"`. Experimentation is the best policy :-)

Default: `none (i.e., all directories are OK to descend)`

Example: `dont descend = /proc,/dev`

- **dos filetime resolution (S)**

Under the DOS and Windows FAT filesystem, the finest granularity on time resolution is two seconds. Setting this parameter for a share causes Samba to round the reported time down to the nearest two second boundary when a query call that requires one second resolution is made to **smbd**.

This option is mainly used as a compatibility option for Visual C++ when used against Samba shares. If oplocks are enabled on a share, Visual C++ uses two different time reading calls to check if a file has changed since it was last read. One of these calls uses a one-second granularity, the other uses a two second granularity. As the two second call rounds any odd second down, then if the file has a timestamp of an odd number of seconds then the two timestamps will not match and Visual C++ will keep reporting the file has changed. Setting this option causes the two timestamps to match, and Visual C++ is happy.

Default: `dos filetime resolution = False`

Example: `dos filetime resolution = True`

- **dos filetimes (S)**

Under DOS and Windows, if a user can write to a file they can change the timestamp on it. Under POSIX semantics, only the owner of the file or root may change the timestamp. By default, Samba runs with POSIX semantics and refuses to change the timestamp on a file if the user smbd is acting on behalf of is not the file owner. Setting this option to True allows DOS semantics and smbd will change the file timestamp as DOS requires.

Default: `dos filetimes = False`

Example: `dos filetimes = True`

- **encrypt passwords (G)**

This boolean controls whether encrypted passwords will be negotiated with the client. Note that Windows NT 4.0 SP3 and above and also Windows 98 will by default expect encrypted passwords unless a registry entry is changed. To use encrypted passwords in Samba see the file ENCRYPTION.txt in the Samba documentation directory `docs/` shipped with the source code.

In order for encrypted passwords to work correctly **smbd** must either have access to a local **smbpasswd (5)** file (see the **smbpasswd (8)** program for information on how to set up and maintain this file), or set the **security=** parameter to either "**server**" or "**domain**" which causes **smbd** to authenticate against another server.

- **exec (S)**

This is a synonym for **preexec**.

- **fake directory create times (S)**

NTFS and Windows VFAT file systems keep a create time for all files and directories. This is not the same as the ctime—status change time—that Unix keeps, so Samba by default reports the earliest of the various times Unix does keep. Setting this parameter for a share causes Samba to always report midnight 1-1-1980 as the create time for directories.

This option is mainly used as a compatibility option for Visual C++ when used against Samba shares. Visual C++ generated makefiles have the object directory as a dependency for each object file, and a make rule to create the directory. Also, when NMAKE compares timestamps it uses the creation time when examining a directory. Thus the object directory will be created if it does not exist, but once it does exist it will always have an earlier timestamp than the object files it contains.

However, Unix time semantics mean that the create time reported by Samba will be updated whenever a file is created or deleted in the directory. NMAKE therefore finds all object files in the object directory bar the last one built are out of date compared to the directory and rebuilds them. Enabling this option ensures directories always predate their contents and an NMAKE build will proceed as expected.

Default: `fake directory create times = False`

Example: `fake directory create times = True`

- **fake oplocks (S)**

Oplocks are the way that SMB clients get permission from a server to locally cache file operations. If a server grants an oplock (opportunistic lock) then the client is free to assume that it is the only one accessing the file and it will aggressively cache file data. With some oplock types the client may even cache file open/close operations. This can give enormous performance benefits.

When you set `"fake oplocks = yes"` **smbd** will always grant oplock requests no matter how many clients are using the file.

It is generally much better to use the real **oplocks** support rather than this parameter.

If you enable this option on all read-only shares or shares that you know will only be accessed from one client at a time such as physically read-only media like CDROMs, you will see a big performance improvement on many operations. If you enable this option on shares where multiple clients may be accessing the files read-write at the same time you can get data corruption. Use this option carefully!

This option is disabled by default.

- **follow symlinks (S)**

This parameter allows the Samba administrator to stop **smbd** from following symbolic links in a particular share. Setting this parameter to *"No"* prevents any file or directory that is a symbolic link from being followed (the user will get an error). This option is very useful to stop users from adding a symbolic link to `/etc/passwd` in their home directory for instance. However it will slow filename lookups down slightly.

This option is enabled (i.e. **smbd** will follow symbolic links) by default.

- **force create mode (S)**

This parameter specifies a set of UNIX mode bit permissions that will **always* be set on a file created by Samba. This is done by bitwise 'OR'ing these bits onto the mode bits of a file that is being created. The default for this parameter is (in octal) 000. The modes in this parameter are bitwise 'OR'ed onto the file mode after the mask set in the **"create mask"** parameter is applied.

See also the parameter **"create mask"** for details on masking mode bits on created files.

Default: `force create mode = 000`

Example: `force create mode = 0755`

would force all created files to have read and execute permissions set for 'group' and 'other' as well as the read/write/execute bits set for the 'user'.

- **force directory mode (S)**

This parameter specifies a set of UNIX mode bit permissions that will **always* be set on a directory created by Samba. This is done by bitwise 'OR'ing these bits onto the mode bits of a directory that is being created. The default for this parameter is (in octal) 0000 which will not add any extra permission bits to a created directory. This operation is done after the mode mask in the parameter **"directory mask"** is applied.

See also the parameter **"directory mask"** for details on masking mode bits on created directories.

Default: `force directory mode = 000`

Example: `force directory mode = 0755`

would force all created directories to have read and execute permissions set for 'group' and 'other' as well as the read/write/execute bits set for the 'user'.

- **force group (S)**

This specifies a UNIX group name that will be assigned as the default primary group for all users connecting to this service. This is useful for sharing files by ensuring that all access to files on service will use the named group for their permissions checking. Thus, by assigning permissions for this group to the files and directories within this service the Samba administrator can restrict or allow sharing of these files.

Default: `no forced group`

Example: `force group = agroup`

- **force user (S)**

This specifies a UNIX user name that will be assigned as the default user for all users connecting to this service. This is useful for sharing files. You should also use it carefully as using it incorrectly can cause security problems.

This user name only gets used once a connection is established. Thus clients still need to connect as a valid user and supply a valid password. Once connected, all file operations will be performed as the `"forced user"`, no matter what username the client connected as.

This can be very useful.

Default: `no forced user`

Example: `force user = auser`

- **fstype (S)**

This parameter allows the administrator to configure the string that specifies the type of filesystem a share is using that is reported by **smbd** when a client queries the filesystem type for a share. The default type is **"NTFS"** for compatibility with Windows NT but this can be changed to other strings such as "Samba" or "FAT" if required.

Default: `fstype = NTFS`

Example: `fstype = Samba`

- **getwd cache (G)**

This is a tuning option. When this is enabled a caching algorithm will be used to reduce the time taken for getwd() calls. This can have a significant impact on performance, especially when the **widelinks** parameter is set to False.

Default: `getwd cache = No`

Example: `getwd cache = Yes`

- **group (S)**

Synonym for **"force group"**.

- **guest account (S)**

This is a username which will be used for access to services which are specified as **'guest ok'** (see below). Whatever privileges this user has will be available to any client connecting to the guest service. Typically this user will exist in the password file, but will not have a valid login. The user account **"ftp"** is often a good choice for this parameter. If a username is specified in a given service, the specified username overrides this one.

One some systems the default guest account "nobody" may not be able to print. Use another account in this case. You should test this by trying to log in as your guest user (perhaps by using the `"su -"` command) and trying to print using the system print command such as **lpr (1)** or **lp (1)**.

Default: `specified at compile time, usually "nobody"`

Example: `guest account = ftp`

- **guest ok (S)**

If this parameter is *'yes'* for a service, then no password is required to connect to the service. Privileges will be those of the **guest account**.

See the section below on **security** for more information about this option.

Default: `guest ok = no`

Example: `guest ok = yes`

- **guest only (S)**

If this parameter is *'yes'* for a service, then only guest connections to the service are permitted. This parameter will have no affect if **"guest ok"** or **"public"** is not set for the service.

See the section below on **security** for more information about this option.

Default: `guest only = no`

Example: `guest only = yes`

- **hide dot files (S)**

This is a boolean parameter that controls whether files starting with a dot appear as hidden files.

Default: `hide dot files = yes`

Example: `hide dot files = no`

- **hide files(S)**

This is a list of files or directories that are not visible but are accessible. The DOS 'hidden' attribute is applied to any files or directories that match.

Each entry in the list must be separated by a '/', which allows spaces to be included in the entry. '*' and '?' can be used to specify multiple files or directories as in DOS wildcards.

Each entry must be a Unix path, not a DOS path and must not include the Unix directory separator '/'.

Note that the case sensitivity option is applicable in hiding files.

Setting this parameter will affect the performance of Samba, as it will be forced to check all files and directories for a match as they are scanned.

See also **"hide dot files"**, **"veto files"** and **"case sensitive"**.

Default

```
No files or directories are hidden by this option
(dot files are
hidden by default because of the "hide dot files" op-
tion).
```

Example `hide files = /.*/DesktopFolderDB/TrashFor%m/resource.frk/`

The above example is based on files that the Macintosh SMB client (DAVE) available from **Thursby** creates for internal use, and also still hides all files beginning with a dot.

- **homedir map (G)**

If **"nis homedir"** is true, and **smbd** is also acting as a Win95/98 **logon server** then this parameter specifies the NIS (or YP) map from which the server for the user's home directory should be extracted. At present, only the Sun auto.home map format is understood. The form of the map is:

```
username server:/some/file/system
```

and the program will extract the servername from before the first ':'. There should probably be a better parsing system that copes with different map formats and also Amd (another automounter) maps.

NB: A working NIS is required on the system for this option to work.

See also **"nis homedir"**, **domain logons**.

Default: `homedir map = auto.home`

Example: `homedir map = amd.homedir`

- **hosts allow (S)**

Synonym for **allow hosts**.

- **hosts deny (S)**

Synonym for **denyhosts**.

- **hosts equiv (G)**

If this global parameter is a non-null string, it specifies the name of a file to read for the names of hosts and users who will be allowed access without specifying a password.

This is not be confused with **allow hosts** which is about hosts access to services and is more useful for guest services. **hosts equiv** may be useful for NT clients which will not supply passwords to samba.

NOTE: The use of **hosts equiv** can be a major security hole. This is because you are trusting the PC to supply the correct username. It is very easy to get a PC to supply a false username. I recommend that the **hosts equiv** option be only used if you really know what you are doing, or perhaps on a home network where you trust your spouse and kids. And only if you *really* trust them :-).

Default `No host equivalences`

Example `hosts equiv = /etc/hosts.equiv`

- **include (G)**

This allows you to include one config file inside another. The file is included literally, as though typed in place.

It takes the standard substitutions, except **%u**, **%P** and **%S**.

- **interfaces (G)**

This option allows you to setup multiple network interfaces, so that Samba can properly handle browsing on all interfaces.

The option takes a list of ip/netmask pairs. The netmask may either be a bitmask, or a bitlength.

For example, the following line:

```
interfaces = 192.168.2.10/24 192.168.3.10/24
```

would configure two network interfaces with IP addresses 192.168.2.10 and 192.168.3.10. The netmasks of both interfaces would be set to 255.255.255.0.

You could produce an equivalent result by using:

```
interfaces = 192.168.2.10/255.255.255.0 192.168.3.10/
255.255.255.0
```

if you prefer that format.

If this option is not set then Samba will attempt to find a primary interface, but won't attempt to configure more than one interface.

See also **"bind interfaces only"**.

- **invalid users (S)**

This is a list of users that should not be allowed to login to this service. This is really a *"paranoid"* check to absolutely ensure an improper setting does not breach your security.

A name starting with a `'@'` is interpreted as an NIS netgroup first (if your system supports NIS), and then as a UNIX group if the name was not found in the NIS netgroup database.

A name starting with `'+'` is interpreted only by looking in the UNIX group database. A name starting with `'&'` is interpreted only by looking in the NIS netgroup database (this requires NIS to be working on your system). The characters `'+'` and `'&'` may be used at the start of the name in either order so the value `"+&group"` means check the UNIX group database, followed by the NIS netgroup database, and the value `"&+group"` means check the NIS netgroup database, followed by the UNIX group database (the same as the `'@'` prefix).

The current servicename is substituted for **%S**. This is useful in the **[homes]** section.

See also "**valid users**".

Default: `No invalid users`

Example: `invalid users = root fred admin @wheel`

- **keepalive (G)**

The value of the parameter (an integer) represents the number of seconds between '**keepalive**' packets. If this parameter is zero, no keepalive packets will be sent. Keepalive packets, if sent, allow the server to tell whether a client is still present and responding.

Keepalives should, in general, not be needed if the socket being used has the SO_KEEPALIVE attribute set on it (see "**socket options**"). Basically you should only use this option if you strike difficulties.

Default: `keep alive = 0`

Example: `keep alive = 60`

- **kernel oplocks (G)**

For UNIXs that support kernel based **oplocks** (currently only IRIX but hopefully also Linux and FreeBSD soon) this parameter allows the use of them to be turned on or off.

Kernel oplocks support allows Samba **oplocks** to be broken whenever a local UNIX process or NFS operation accesses a file that **smbd** has oplocked. This allows complete data consistency between SMB/CIFS, NFS and local file access (and is a *very* cool feature :-).

This parameter defaults to *"On"* on systems that have the support, and *"off"* on systems that don't. You should never need to touch this parameter.

- **ldap bind as (G)**

This parameter is part of the *EXPERIMENTAL* Samba support for a password database stored on an LDAP server. These options are only available if your version of Samba was configured with the **—with-ldap** option.

This parameter specifies the entity to bind to an LDAP directory as. Usually it should be safe to use the LDAP root account; for larger installations it may be preferable to restrict Samba's access. See also **ldap passwd file**.

Default: `none (bind anonymously)`

Example: `ldap bind as = "uid=root, dc=mydomain, dc=org"`

- **ldap passwd file (G)**

This parameter is part of the *EXPERIMENTAL* Samba support for a password database stored on an LDAP server. These options are only available if your version of Samba was configured with the **—with-ldap** option.

This parameter specifies a file containing the password with which Samba should bind to an LDAP server. For obvious security reasons this file must be set to mode 700 or less.

Default: `none (bind anonymously)`

Example: `ldap passwd file = /usr/local/samba/private/ldappasswd`

- **ldap port (G)**

This parameter is part of the *EXPERIMENTAL* Samba support for a password database stored on an LDAP server. These options are only available if your version of Samba was configured with the **—with-ldap** option.

This parameter specifies the TCP port number of the LDAP server.

Default: `ldap port = 389.`

- **ldap server (G)**

This parameter is part of the *EXPERIMENTAL* Samba support for a password database stored on an LDAP server back-end. These options are only available if your version of Samba was configured with the **—with-ldap** option.

This parameter specifies the DNS name of the LDAP server to use when storing and retrieving information about Samba users and groups.

Default: `ldap server = localhost`

- **ldap suffix (G)**

This parameter is part of the *EXPERIMENTAL* Samba support for a password database stored on an LDAP server back-end. These options are only available if your version of Samba was configured with the **—with-ldap** option.

This parameter specifies the node of the LDAP tree beneath which Samba should store its information. This parameter MUST be provided when using LDAP with Samba.

Default: `none`

Example: `ldap suffix = "dc=mydomain, dc=org"`

- **lm announce (G)**

This parameter determines if **nmbd** will produce Lanman announce broadcasts that are needed by **OS/2** clients in order for them to see the Samba server in their browse list. This parameter can have three values, `"true"`, `"false"`, or `"auto"`. The default is `"auto"`. If set to `"false"` Samba will never produce these broadcasts. If set to `"true"` Samba will produce Lanman announce broadcasts at a frequency set by the parameter **"lm interval"**. If set to `"auto"` Samba will not send Lanman announce broadcasts by default but will listen for them. If it hears such a broadcast on the wire it will then start sending them at a frequency set by the parameter **"lm interval"**.

See also **"lm interval"**.

Default: `lm announce = auto`

Example: `lm announce = true`

- **lm interval (G)**

If Samba is set to produce Lanman announce broadcasts needed by **OS/2** clients (see the **"lm announce"** parameter) then this parameter defines the frequency in seconds with which they will be made. If this is set to zero then no Lanman announcements will be made despite the setting of the **"lm announce"** parameter.

See also **"lm announce"**.

Default: `lm interval = 60`

Example: `lm interval = 120`

- **load printers (G)**

A boolean variable that controls whether all printers in the printcap will be loaded for browsing by default. See the **"printers"** section for more details.

Default: `load printers = yes`

Example: `load printers = no`

- **local group map (G)**

This option allows you to specify a file containing unique mappings of individual NT Local Group names (in any domain) to UNIX group names. This allows NT Local groups (aliases) to be presented correctly to NT users, despite the lack of native support for the NT Security model (based on VAX/VMS) in UNIX. The reader is advised to become familiar with the NT Domain system and its administration.

This option is used in conjunction with **'domain group map'** and **'domain name map'**. The use of these three options is trivial and often unnecessary in the case where Samba is not expected to interact with any other SAM databases (whether local workstations or Domain Controllers).

The map file is parsed line by line. If any line begins with a `'#'` or a `';'` then it is ignored. Each line should contain a single UNIX group name on the left then a single NT Local Group name on the right, separated by a tabstop or `'='`. If either name contains spaces then it should be enclosed in quotes. The line can be either of the form:

```
UNIXgroupname \\DOMAIN_NAME\\LocalGroupName
```

or:

```
UNIXgroupname LocalGroupName
```

In the case where Samba is either an **EXPERIMENTAL** Domain Controller or it is a member of a domain using **"security = domain"**, the latter format can be used: the default Domain name is the Samba Server's Domain name, specified by **"workgroup = MYGROUP"**.

Any UNIX groups that are *NOT* specified in this map file are treated as either Local or Domain Groups depending on the role of the Samba Server.

In the case when Samba is an **EXPERIMENTAL** Domain Controller, Samba will present *ALL* unspecified UNIX groups as its own NT Domain Groups, with the same name, and *NOT* as Local Groups.

In the case where Samba is member of a domain using **"security = domain"**, Samba will check the UNIX name with its Domain Controller (see **"password server"**) as if it was an NT Domain Group. If the Domain Controller says that it is not, such unspecified (unmapped) UNIX groups which also are not NT Domain Groups are treated as Local Groups in the Samba Server's local SAM database. NT Administrators will recognise these as Workstation Local Groups, which are managed by running **USRMGR.EXE** and selecting a remote Domain named "\\WORKSTATION_NAME", or by running **MUSRMGR.EXE** on a local Workstation.

This may sound complicated, but it means that a Samba Server as either a member of a domain or as an **EXPERIMENTAL** Domain Controller will act like an NT Workstation (with a local SAM database) or an NT PDC (with a Domain SAM database) respectively, without the need for any of the map files at all. If you **want** to get fancy, however, you can.

Note that adding an entry to map an arbitrary NT group in an arbitrary Domain to an arbitrary UNIX group *REQUIRES* the following:

- that the UNIX group exists on the UNIX server.
- that the NT Domain Group exists in the specified NT Domain
- that the UNIX Server knows about the specified Domain;
- that all the UNIX users (who are expecting to access the Samba Server as the correct NT user and with the correct NT group permissions) in the UNIX group be mapped to the correct NT Domain users in the specified NT Domain using **'domain user map'**.

Failure to meet any of these requirements may result in either (or both) errors reported in the log files or (and) incorrect or missing access rights granted to users.

- **local master (G)**

This option allows **nmbd** to try and become a local master browser on a subnet. If set to False then **nmbd** will not attempt to become a local master browser on a subnet and will also lose in all browsing elections. By default this value is set to true. Setting this value to true doesn't mean that Samba will *become* the local master browser on a subnet, just that **nmbd** will *participate* in elections for local master browser.

Setting this value to False will cause **nmbd** *never* to become a local master browser.

Default: `local master = yes`

- **lock dir (G)**

Synonym for **"lock directory"**.

- **lock directory (G)**

This option specifies the directory where lock files will be placed. The lock files are used to implement the **"max connections"** option.

Default: `lock directory = /tmp/samba`

Example: `lock directory = /usr/local/samba/var/locks`

- **locking (S)**

This controls whether or not locking will be performed by the server in response to lock requests from the client.

If `"locking = no"`, all lock and unlock requests will appear to succeed and all lock queries will indicate that the queried lock is clear.

If `"locking = yes"`, real locking will be performed by the server.

This option *may* be useful for read-only filesystems which *may* not need locking (such as cdrom drives), although setting this parameter of `"no"` is not really recommended even in this case.

Be careful about disabling locking either globally or in a specific service, as lack of locking may result in data corruption. You should never need to set this parameter.

Default: `locking = yes`

Example: `locking = no`

- **log file (G)**

This options allows you to override the name of the Samba log file (also known as the debug file).

This option takes the standard substitutions, allowing you to have separate log files for each user or machine.

Example: `log file = /usr/local/samba/var/log.%m`

- **log level (G)**

Synonym for "**debug level**".

- **logon drive (G)**

This parameter specifies the local path to which the home directory will be connected (see "**logon home**") and is only used by NT Workstations.

Note that this option is only useful if Samba is set up as a **logon server**.

Example: `logon drive = h:`

- **logon home (G)**

This parameter specifies the home directory location when a Win95/98 or NT Workstation logs into a Samba PDC. It allows you to do

```
"NET USE H: /HOME"
```

from a command prompt, for example.

This option takes the standard substitutions, allowing you to have separate logon scripts for each user or machine.

Note that this option is only useful if Samba is set up as a **logon server**.

Example: `logon home = "\\remote_smb_server\%U"`

Default: `logon home = "\\%N\%U"`

- **logon path (G)**

This parameter specifies the home directory where roaming profiles (USER.DAT / USER.MAN files for Windows 95/98) are stored.

This option takes the standard substitutions, allowing you to have separate logon scripts for each user or machine. It also specifies the directory from which the `"desktop"`, `"start menu"`, `"network neighborhood"` and "programs" folders, and their contents, are loaded and displayed on your Windows 95/98 client.

The share and the path must be readable by the user for the preferences and directories to be loaded onto the Windows 95/98 client. The share must be writeable when the logs in for the first time, in order that the Windows 95/98 client can create the user.dat and other directories.

Thereafter, the directories and any of the contents can, if required, be made read-only. It is not advisable that the USER.DAT file be made read-only—rename it to USER.MAN to achieve the desired effect (a *MAN*datory profile).

Windows clients can sometimes maintain a connection to the [homes] share, even though there is no user logged in. Therefore, it is vital that the logon path does not include a reference to the homes share (i.e. setting this parameter to `\\%N\HOMES\profile_path` will cause problems).

This option takes the standard substitutions, allowing you to have separate logon scripts for each user or machine.

Note that this option is only useful if Samba is set up as a **logon server**.

Default: `logon path = \\%N\%U\profile`

Example: `logon path = \\PROFILESERVER\HOME_DIR\%U\PROFILE`

- **logon script (G)**

This parameter specifies the batch file (.bat) or NT command file (.cmd) to be downloaded and run on a machine when a user successfully logs in. The file must contain the DOS style cr/lf line endings. Using a DOS-style editor to create the file is recommended.

The script must be a relative path to the `[netlogon]` service. If the `[netlogon]` service specifies a **path** of /usr/local/samba/netlogon, and logon script = STARTUP.BAT, then the file that will be downloaded is:

`/usr/local/samba/netlogon/STARTUP.BAT`

The contents of the batch file is entirely your choice. A suggested command would be to add `NET TIME \\SERVER /SET /YES`, to force every machine to synchronize clocks with the same time server. Another use would be to add `NET USE U: \\SERVER\UTILS` for commonly used utilities, or `NET USE Q: \\SERVER\ISO9001_QA` for example.

Note that it is particularly important not to allow write access to the `[netlogon]` share, or to grant users write permission on the batch files in a secure environment, as this would allow the batch files to be arbitrarily modified and security to be breached.

This option takes the standard substitutions, allowing you to have separate logon scripts for each user or machine.

Note that this option is only useful if Samba is set up as a **logon server**.

Example: `logon script = scripts\%U.bat`

- **lppause command (S)**

This parameter specifies the command to be executed on the server host in order to stop printing or spooling a specific print job.

This command should be a program or script which takes a printer name and job number to pause the print job. One way of implementing this is by using job priorities, where jobs having a too low priority won't be sent to the printer.

If a `"%p"` is given then the printername is put in its place. A `"%j"` is replaced with the job number (an integer). On HPUX (see **printing=hpux**), if the `"-p%p"` option is added to the lpq command, the job will show up with the correct status, i.e. if the job priority is lower than the set fence priority it will have the PAUSED status, whereas if the priority is equal or higher it will have the SPOOLED or PRINTING status.

Note that it is good practice to include the absolute path in the lppause command as the PATH may not be available to the server.

See also the **"printing"** parameter.

Default: Currently no default value is given to this string, unless the value of the **"printing"** parameter is `SYSV`, in which case the default is:

```
lp -i %p-%j -H hold
```

or if the value of the **"printing"** parameter is `softq`, then the default is:

```
qstat -s -j%j -h
```

Example for HPUX: lppause command = /usr/bin/lpalt %p-%j -p0

- **lpq cache time (G)**

This controls how long lpq info will be cached for to prevent the **lpq** command being called too often. A separate cache is kept for each variation of the **lpq** command used by the system, so if you use different **lpq** commands for different users then they won't share cache information.

The cache files are stored in `/tmp/lpq.xxxx` where xxxx is a hash of the **lpq** command in use.

The default is 10 seconds, meaning that the cached results of a previous identical **lpq** command will be used if the cached data is less than 10 seconds old. A large value may be advisable if your **lpq** command is very slow.

A value of 0 will disable caching completely.

See also the "**printing**" parameter.

Default: `lpq cache time = 10`

Example: `lpq cache time = 30`

- **lpq command (S)**

This parameter specifies the command to be executed on the server host in order to obtain `"lpq"`-style printer status information.

This command should be a program or script which takes a printer name as its only parameter and outputs printer status information.

Currently eight styles of printer status information are supported; BSD, AIX, LPRNG, PLP, SYSV, HPUX, QNX and SOFTQ. This covers most UNIX systems. You control which type is expected using the "**printing =**" option.

Some clients (notably Windows for Workgroups) may not correctly send the connection number for the printer they are requesting status information about. To get around this, the server reports on the first printer service connected to by the client. This only happens if the connection number sent is invalid.

If a `%p` is given then the printername is put in its place. Otherwise it is placed at the end of the command.

Note that it is good practice to include the absolute path in the **lpq command** as the PATH may not be available to the server.

See also the "**printing**" parameter.

Default: `depends on the setting of printing =`

Example: `lpq command = /usr/bin/lpq %p`

- **lpresume command (S)**

This parameter specifies the command to be executed on the server host in order to restart or continue printing or spooling a specific print job.

This command should be a program or script which takes a printer name and job number to resume the print job. See also the "**lppause command**" parameter.

If a `%p` is given then the printername is put in its place. A `%j` is replaced with the job number (an integer).

Note that it is good practice to include the absolute path in the **lpresume command** as the PATH may not be available to the server.

See also the "**printing**" parameter.

Default:

Currently no default value is given to this string, unless the value of the "**printing**" parameter is `SYSV`, in which case the default is :

```
lp -i %p-%j -H resume
```

or if the value of the "**printing**" parameter is `softq`, then the default is:

```
qstat -s -j%j -r
```

Example for HPUX: `lpresume command = /usr/bin/lpalt %p-%j -p2`

- **lprm command (S)**

This parameter specifies the command to be executed on the server host in order to delete a print job.

This command should be a program or script which takes a printer name and job number, and deletes the print job.

If a `%p` is given then the printername is put in its place. A `%j` is replaced with the job number (an integer).

Note that it is good practice to include the absolute path in the **lprm command** as the PATH may not be available to the server.

See also the **"printing"** parameter.

Default: `depends on the setting of "printing ="`

Example 1: `lprm command = /usr/bin/lprm -P%p %j`

Example 2: `lprm command = /usr/bin/cancel %p-%j`

- **machine password timeout (G)**

If a Samba server is a member of an Windows NT Domain (see the **"security=domain"**) parameter) then periodically a running **smbd** process will try and change the **MACHINE ACCOUNT PASWORD** stored in the file called `<Domain>.<Machine>.mac` where `<Domain>` is the name of the Domain we are a member of and `<Machine>` is the primary **"NetBIOS name"** of the machine **smbd** is running on. This parameter specifies how often this password will be changed, in seconds. The default is one week (expressed in seconds), the same as a Windows NT Domain member server.

See also **smbpasswd (8)**, and the **"security=domain"**) parameter.

Default: `machine password timeout = 604800`

- **magic output (S)**

This parameter specifies the name of a file which will contain output created by a magic script (see the **"magic script"** parameter below).

Warning: If two clients use the same **"magic script"** in the same directory the output file content is undefined.

Default: `magic output = <magic script name>.out`

Example: `magic output = myfile.txt`

- **magic script (S)**

This parameter specifies the name of a file which, if opened, will be executed by the server when the file is closed. This allows a UNIX script to be sent to the Samba host and executed on behalf of the connected user.

Scripts executed in this way will be deleted upon completion, permissions permitting.

If the script generates output, output will be sent to the file specified by the **"magic output"** parameter (see above).

Note that some shells are unable to interpret scripts containing carriage-return-linefeed instead of linefeed as the end-of-line marker. Magic scripts must be executable *"as is"* on the host, which for some hosts and some shells will require filtering at the DOS end.

Magic scripts are *EXPERIMENTAL* and should *NOT* be relied upon.

Default: `None. Magic scripts disabled.`

Example: `magic script = user.csh`

- **mangle case (S)**

See the section on **"NAME MANGLING"**.

- **mangled map (S)**

This is for those who want to directly map UNIX file names which can not be represented on Windows/DOS. The mangling of names is not always what is needed. In particular you may have documents with file extensions that differ between DOS and UNIX. For example, under UNIX it is common to use `".html"` for HTML files, whereas under Windows/DOS `".htm"` is more commonly used.

So to map `"html"` to `"htm"` you would use:

```
mangled map = (*.html *.htm)
```

One very useful case is to remove the annoying `";1"` off the ends of filenames on some CDROMS (only visible under some UNIXs). To do this use a map of (*;1 *).

Default: `no mangled map`

Example: `mangled map = (*;1 *)`

- **mangled names (S)**

This controls whether non-DOS names under UNIX should be mapped to DOS-compatible names ("mangled") and made visible, or whether non-DOS names should simply be ignored.

See the section on **"NAME MANGLING"** for details on how to control the mangling process.

If mangling is used then the mangling algorithm is as follows:

- The first (up to) five alphanumeric characters before the rightmost dot of the filename are preserved, forced to upper case, and appear as the first (up to) five characters of the mangled name.
- A tilde `"~"` is appended to the first part of the mangled name, followed by a two-character unique sequence, based on the original root name (i.e., the original filename minus its final extension). The final extension is included in the hash calculation only if it contains any upper case characters or is longer than three characters.

  Note that the character to use may be specified using the **"mangling char"** option, if you don't like `'~'`.
- The first three alphanumeric characters of the final extension are preserved, forced to upper case and appear as the extension of the mangled name. The final extension is defined as that part of the original filename after the rightmost dot. If there are no dots in the filename, the mangled name will have no extension (except in the case of **"hidden files"**—see below).
- Files whose UNIX name begins with a dot will be presented as DOS hidden files. The mangled name will be created as for other filenames, but with the leading dot removed and `"___"` as its extension regardless of actual original extension (that's three underscores).

The two-digit hash value consists of upper case alphanumeric characters.

This algorithm can cause name collisions only if files in a directory share the same first five alphanumeric characters. The probability of such a clash is 1/1300.

The name mangling (if enabled) allows a file to be copied between UNIX directories from Windows/DOS while retaining the long UNIX filename. UNIX files can be renamed to a new extension from Windows/DOS and will retain the same basename. Mangled names do not change between sessions.

Default: `mangled names = yes`

Example: `mangled names = no`

- **mangling char (S)**

This controls what character is used as the *"magic"* character in **name mangling**. The default is a `'~'` but this may interfere with some software. Use this option to set it to whatever you prefer.

Default: `mangling char = ~`

Example: `mangling char = ^`

- **mangled stack (G)**

This parameter controls the number of mangled names that should be cached in the Samba server **smbd**.

This stack is a list of recently mangled base names (extensions are only maintained if they are longer than 3 characters or contains upper case characters).

The larger this value, the more likely it is that mangled names can be successfully converted to correct long UNIX names. However, large stack sizes will slow most directory access. Smaller stacks save memory in the server (each stack element costs 256 bytes).

It is not possible to absolutely guarantee correct long file names, so be prepared for some surprises!

Default: `mangled stack = 50`

Example: `mangled stack = 100`

- **map archive (S)**

This controls whether the DOS archive attribute should be mapped to the UNIX owner execute bit. The DOS archive bit is set when a file has been modified since its last backup. One motivation for this option it to keep Samba/your PC from making any file it touches from becoming executable under UNIX. This can be quite annoying for shared source code, documents, etc...

Note that this requires the **"create mask"** parameter to be set such that owner execute bit is not masked out (i.e. it must include 100). See the parameter **"create mask"** for details.

Default: `map archive = yes`

Example: `map archive = no`

- **map hidden (S)**

This controls whether DOS style hidden files should be mapped to the UNIX world execute bit.

Note that this requires the **"create mask"** to be set such that the world execute bit is not masked out (i.e. it must include 001). See the parameter **"create mask"** for details.

Default: `map hidden = no`

Example: `map hidden = yes`

- **map system (S)**

This controls whether DOS style system files should be mapped to the UNIX group execute bit.

Note that this requires the **"create mask"** to be set such that the group execute bit is not masked out (i.e. it must include 010). See the parameter **"create mask"** for details.

Default: `map system = no`

Example: `map system = yes`

- **map to guest (G)**

This parameter is only useful in **security** modes other than **"security=share"**—i.e. user, server, and domain.

This parameter can take three different values, which tell **smbd** what to do with user login requests that don't match a valid UNIX user in some way.

The three settings are :

- "**Never**"—Means user login requests with an invalid password are rejected. This is the default.
- "**Bad User**" —Means user logins with an invalid password are rejected, unless the username does not exist, in which case it is treated as a guest login and mapped into the "**guest account**".
- "**Bad Password**"—Means user logins with an invalid password are treated as a guest login and mapped into the "**guest account**". Note that this can cause problems as it means that any user incorrectly typing their password will be silently logged on a "**guest**"—and will not kn—there will have been no message given to them that they got their password wrong. Helpdesk services will **hate** you if you set the "**map to guest**" parameter this way :-).

Note that this parameter is needed to set up "**Guest**" share services when using **security** modes other than share. This is because in these modes the name of the resource being requested is **not** sent to the server until after the server has successfully authenticated the client so the server cannot make authentication decisions at the correct time (connection to the share) for "**Guest**" shares.

For people familiar with the older Samba releases, this parameter maps to the old compile-time setting of the GUEST_SESSSETUP value in local.h.

Default: `map to guest = Never` **Example:** `map to guest = Bad User`

- **max connections (S)**

This option allows the number of simultaneous connections to a service to be limited. If "**max connections**" is greater than 0 then connections will be refused if this number of connections to the service are already open. A value of zero mean an unlimited number of connections may be made.

Record lock files are used to implement this feature. The lock files will be stored in the directory specified by the "**lock directory**" option.

Default: `max connections = 0`

Example: `max connections = 10`

- **max disk size (G)**

This option allows you to put an upper limit on the apparent size of disks. If you set this option to 100 then all shares will appear to be not larger than 100 MB in size.

Note that this option does not limit the amount of data you can put on the disk. In the above case you could still store much more than 100 MB on the disk, but if a client ever asks for the amount of free disk space or the total disk size then the result will be bounded by the amount specified in **"max disk size"**.

This option is primarily useful to work around bugs in some pieces of software that can't handle very large disks, particularly disks over 1GB in size.

A **"max disk size"** of 0 means no limit.

Default: `max disk size = 0`

Example: `max disk size = 1000`

- **max log size (G)**

This option (an integer in kilobytes) specifies the max size the log file should grow to. Samba periodically checks the size and if it is exceeded it will rename the file, adding a `".old"` extension.

A size of 0 means no limit.

Default: `max log size = 5000`

Example: `max log size = 1000`

- **max mux (G)**

This option controls the maximum number of outstanding simultaneous SMB operations that samba tells the client it will allow. You should never need to set this parameter.

Default: `max mux = 50`

- **maxopenfiles (G)**

This parameter limits the maximum number of open files that one **smbd** file serving process may have open for a client at any one time. The default for this parameter is set very high (10,000) as Samba uses only one bit per unopened file.

The limit of the number of open files is usually set by the UNIX per-process file descriptor limit rather than this parameter so you should never need to touch this parameter.

Default: `max open files = 10000`

- **max packet (G)**

Synonym for "packetsize""(packetsize).

- **max ttl (G)**

This option tells **nmbd** what the default 'time to live' of NetBIOS names should be (in seconds) when **nmbd** is requesting a name using either a broadcast packet or from a WINS server. You should never need to change this parameter. The default is 3 days.

Default: `max ttl = 259200`

- **max wins ttl (G)**

This option tells **nmbd** when acting as a WINS server **(wins support =true)** what the maximum 'time to live' of NetBIOS names that **nmbd** will grant will be (in seconds). You should never need to change this parameter. The default is 6 days (518400 seconds).

See also the **"min wins ttl"** parameter.

Default: `max wins ttl = 518400`

- **max xmit (G)**

This option controls the maximum packet size that will be negotiated by Samba. The default is 65535, which is the maximum. In some cases you may find you get better performance with a smaller value. A value below 2048 is likely to cause problems.

Default: `max xmit = 65535`

Example: `max xmit = 8192`

- **message command (G)**

This specifies what command to run when the server receives a WinPopup style message.

This would normally be a command that would deliver the message somehow. How this is to be done is up to your imagination.

An example is:

```
message command = csh -c 'xedit %s;rm %s' &
```

This delivers the message using **xedit**, then removes it afterwards. *NOTE THAT IT IS VERY IMPORTANT THAT THIS COMMAND RETURN IMMEDIATELY*. That's why I have the `'&'` on the end. If it doesn't return immediately then your PCs may freeze when sending messages (they should recover after 30secs, hopefully).

All messages are delivered as the global guest user. The command takes the standard substitutions, although **%u** won't work (**%U** may be better in this case).

Apart from the standard substitutions, some additional ones apply. In particular:

- `"%s"` = the filename containing the message.
- `"%t"` = the destination that the message was sent to (probably the server name).
- `"%f"` = who the message is from.

You could make this command send mail, or whatever else takes your fancy. Please let us know of any really interesting ideas you have.

Here's a way of sending the messages as mail to root:

```
message command = /bin/mail -s 'message from %f on %m'
root < %s; rm %s
```

If you don't have a message command then the message won't be delivered and Samba will tell the sender there was an error. Unfortunately

WfWg totally ignores the error code and carries on regardless, saying that the message was delivered.

If you want to silently delete it then try:

```
"message command = rm %s".
```

Default: `no message command`

Example: `message command = csh -c 'xedit %s;rm %s' &`

- **min print space (S)**

This sets the minimum amount of free disk space that must be available before a user will be able to spool a print job. It is specified in kilobytes. The default is 0, which means a user can always spool a print job.

See also the **printing** parameter.

Default: `min print space = 0`

Example: `min print space = 2000`

- **min wins ttl (G)**

This option tells **nmbd** when acting as a WINS server **(wins support = true)** what the minimum 'time to live' of NetBIOS names that **nmbd** will grant will be (in seconds). You should never need to change this parameter. The default is 6 hours (21600 seconds).

Default: `min wins ttl = 21600`

- **name resolve order (G)**

This option is used by the programs in the Samba suite to determine what naming services and in what order to resolve host names to IP addresses. The option takes a space separated string of different name resolution options.

The options are :"lmhosts", "host", "wins" and "bcast". They cause names to be resolved as follows:

- **lmhosts** : Lookup an IP address in the Samba lmhosts file.
- **host** : Do a standard host name to IP address resolution, using the system /etc/hosts, NIS, or DNS lookups. This method of name resolution is operating system depended for instance on IRIX or Solaris this may be controlled by the */etc/nsswitch.conf* file).
- **wins** : Query a name with the IP address listed in the **wins server** parameter. If no WINS server has been specified this method will be ignored.
- **bcast** : Do a broadcast on each of the known local interfaces listed in the **interfaces** parameter. This is the least reliable of the name resolution methods as it depends on the target host being on a locally connected subnet.

Default: `name resolve order = lmhosts host wins bcast`

Example: `name resolve order = lmhosts bcast host`

This will cause the local lmhosts file to be examined first, followed by a broadcast attempt, followed by a normal system hostname lookup.

- **netbios aliases (G)**

This is a list of NetBIOS names that **nmbd** will advertise as additional names by which the Samba server is known. This allows one machine to appear in browse lists under multiple names. If a machine is acting as a **browse server** or **logon server** none of these names will be advertised as either browse server or logon servers, only the primary name of the machine will be advertised with these capabilities.

See also **"netbios name"**.

Default: `empty string (no additional names)`

Example: `netbios aliases = TEST TEST1 TEST2`

- **netbios name (G)**

This sets the NetBIOS name by which a Samba server is known. By default it is the same as the first component of the host's DNS name. If a machine is a **browse server** or **logon server** this name (or the first component of the hosts DNS name) will be the name that these services are advertised under.

See also **"netbios aliases"**.

Default: `Machine DNS name.`

Example: `netbios name = MYNAME`

- **nis homedir (G)**

Get the home share server from a NIS map. For UNIX systems that use an automounter, the user's home directory will often be mounted on a workstation on demand from a remote server.

When the Samba logon server is not the actual home directory server, but is mounting the home directories via NFS then two network hops would be required to access the users home directory if the logon server told the client to use itself as the SMB server for home directories (one over SMB and one over NFS). This can be very slow.

This option allows Samba to return the home share as being on a different server to the logon server and as long as a Samba daemon is running on the home directory server, it will be mounted on the Samba client directly from the directory server. When Samba is returning the home share to the client, it will consult the NIS map specified in **"homedir map"** and return the server listed there.

Note that for this option to work there must be a working NIS system and the Samba server with this option must also be a **logon server**.

Default: `nis homedir = false`

Example: `nis homedir = true`

- **nt pipe support (G)**

This boolean parameter controls whether **smbd** will allow Windows NT clients to connect to the NT SMB specific `IPC$` pipes. This is a developer debugging option and can be left alone.

Default: `nt pipe support = yes`

- **nt smb support (G)**

This boolean parameter controls whether **smbd** will negotiate NT specific SMB support with Windows NT clients. Although this is a developer debugging option and should be left alone, benchmarking has discovered that Windows NT clients give faster performance with this option set to "no". This is still being investigated. If this option is set to "no" then Samba offers exactly the same SMB calls that versions prior to Samba2.0 offered. This information may be of use if any users are having problems with NT SMB support.

Default: `nt support = yes`

- **null passwords (G)**

Allow or disallow client access to accounts that have null passwords.

See also **smbpasswd (5)**.

Default: `null passwords = no`

Example: `null passwords = yes`

- **ole locking compatibility (G)**

This parameter allows an administrator to turn off the byte range lock manipulation that is done within Samba to give compatibility for OLE applications. Windows OLE applications use byte range locking as a form of inter-process communication, by locking ranges of bytes around the 2^32 region of a file range. This can cause certain UNIX lock managers to crash or otherwise cause problems. Setting this parameter to "no" means you trust your UNIX lock manager to handle such cases correctly.

Default: `ole locking compatibility = yes`

Example: `ole locking compatibility = no`

- **only guest (S)**

A synonym for "**guest only**".

- **only user (S)**

This is a boolean option that controls whether connections with usernames not in the **user=** list will be allowed. By default this option is disabled so a client can supply a username to be used by the server.

Note that this also means Samba won't try to deduce usernames from the service name. This can be annoying for the **[homes]** section. To get around this you could use "**user = %S**" which means your "**user**" list will be just the service name, which for home directories is the name of the user.

See also the **user** parameter.

Default: `only user = False`

Example: `only user = True`

- **oplocks (S)**

This boolean option tells smbd whether to issue oplocks (opportunistic locks) to file open requests on this share. The oplock code can dramatically (approx. 30% or more) improve the speed of access to files on Samba servers. It allows the clients to aggressively cache files locally and you may want to disable this option for unreliable network environments (it is turned on by default in Windows NT Servers). For more information see the file Speed.txt in the Samba docs/ directory.

Oplocks may be selectively turned off on certain files on a per share basis. See the 'veto oplock files' parameter. On some systems oplocks are recognized by the underlying operating system. This allows data synchronization between all access to oplocked files, whether it be via Samba or NFS or a local UNIX process. See the **kernel oplocks** parameter for details.

Default: `oplocks = True`

Example: `oplocks = False`

- **os level (G)**

This integer value controls what level Samba advertises itself as for browse elections. The value of this parameter determines whether **nmbd** has a chance of becoming a local master browser for the **WORKGROUP** in the local broadcast area. Setting this to zero will cause **nmbd** to always lose elections to Windows machines. See BROWSING.txt in the Samba docs/ directory for details.

Default: `os level = 32`

Example: `os level = 65 ; This will win against any NT Server`

- **packet size (G)**

This is a deprecated parameter that how no effect on the current Samba code. It is left in the parameter list to prevent breaking old **smb.conf** files.

- **panic action (G)**

This is a Samba developer option that allows a system command to be called when either **smbd** or **nmbd** crashes. This is usually used to draw attention to the fact that a problem occurred.

Default: `panic action = <empty string>`

- **passwd chat (G)**

This string controls the *"chat"* conversation that takes places between **smbd** and the local password changing program to change the users password. The string describes a sequence of response-receive pairs that **smbd** uses to determine what to send to the **passwd** program and what to expect back. If the expected output is not received then the password is not changed.

This chat sequence is often quite site specific, depending on what local methods are used for password control (such as NIS etc).

The string can contain the macros `"%o"` and `"%n"` which are substituted for the old and new passwords respectively. It can also contain the standard macros `"\n"`, `"\r"`, `"\t"` and `"\s"` to give line-feed, carriage-return, tab and space.

The string can also contain a `'*'` which matches any sequence of characters.

Double quotes can be used to collect strings with spaces in them into a single string.

If the send string in any part of the chat sequence is a fullstop `"."` then no string is sent. Similarly, is the expect string is a fullstop then no string is expected.

Note that if the **"unix password sync"** parameter is set to true, then this sequence is called **AS ROOT** when the SMB password in the smbpasswd file is being changed, without access to the old password cleartext. In this case the old password cleartext is set to `""` (the empty string).

See also **"unix password sync"**, **"passwd program"** and **"passwd chat debug"**.

Example:

```
passwd chat = "*Enter OLD password*" %o\n "*Enter NEW
password*" %n\n "*Reenter NEW password*" %n\n "*Password
changed*"
```

Default:

```
passwd chat = *old*password* %o\n *new*password* %n\n
*new*password* %n\n *changed*
```

- **passwd chat debug (G)**

This boolean specifies if the passwd chat script parameter is run in "`debug`" mode. In this mode the strings passed to and received from the passwd chat are printed in the **smbd** log with a **"debug level"** of 100. This is a dangerous option as it will allow plaintext passwords to be seen in the **smbd** log. It is available to help Samba admins debug their **"passwd chat"** scripts when calling the **"passwd program"** and should be turned off after this has been done. This parameter is off by default.

See also **"passwd chat"**, **"passwd program"**.

Example: `passwd chat debug = True`

Default: `passwd chat debug = False`

- **passwd program (G)**

The name of a program that can be used to set UNIX user passwords. Any occurrences of **%u** will be replaced with the user name. The user name is checked for existence before calling the password changing program.

Also note that many passwd programs insist in *"reasonable"* passwords, such as a minimum length, or the inclusion of mixed case chars and digits. This can pose a problem as some clients (such as Windows for Workgroups) uppercase the password before sending it.

Note that if the **"unix password sync"** parameter is set to "`True`" then this program is called **AS ROOT** before the SMB password in the **smb-**

passwd file is changed. If this UNIX password change fails, then **smbd** will fail to change the SMB password also (this is by design).

If the **"unix password sync"** parameter is set this parameter *MUST USE ABSOLUTE PATHS* for *ALL* programs called, and must be examined for security implications. Note that by default **"unix password sync"** is set to `"False"`.

See also **"unix password sync"**.

Default: `passwd program = /bin/passwd`

Example: `passwd program = /sbin/passwd %u`

- **password level (G)**

Some client/server combinations have difficulty with mixed-case passwords. One offending client is Windows for Workgroups, which for some reason forces passwords to upper case when using the LANMAN1 protocol, but leaves them alone when using COREPLUS!

This parameter defines the maximum number of characters that may be upper case in passwords.

For example, say the password given was `"FRED"`. If **password level** is set to 1, the following combinations would be tried if `"FRED"` failed:

```
"Fred", "fred", "fRed", "frEd", "freD"
```

If **password level** was set to 2, the following combinations would also be tried:

```
"FRed", "FrEd", "FreD", "fREd", "fReD", "frED", ..
```

And so on.

The higher value this parameter is set to the more likely it is that a mixed case password will be matched against a single case password. However, you should be aware that use of this parameter reduces security and increases the time taken to process a new connection.

A value of zero will cause only two attempts to be made—the password as is and the password in all-lower case.

Default: `password level = 0`

Example: `password level = 4`

- **password server (G)**

By specifying the name of another SMB server (such as a WinNT box) with this option, and using **"security = domain"** or **"security = server"** you can get Samba to do all its username/password validation via a remote server.

This options sets the name of the password server to use. It must be a NetBIOS name, so if the machine's NetBIOS name is different from its internet name then you may have to add its NetBIOS name to the lmhosts file which is stored in the same directory as the **smb.conf** file.

The name of the password server is looked up using the parameter **"name resolve order="** and so may resolved by any method and order described in that parameter.

The password server much be a machine capable of using the "LM1.2X002" or the "LM NT 0.12" protocol, and it must be in user level security mode.

NOTE: Using a password server means your UNIX box (running Samba) is only as secure as your password server. *DO NOT CHOOSE A PASSWORD SERVER THAT YOU DON'T COMPLETELY TRUST.*

Never point a Samba server at itself for password serving. This will cause a loop and could lock up your Samba server!

The name of the password server takes the standard substitutions, but probably the only useful one is **%m**, which means the Samba server will use the incoming client as the password server. If you use this then you better trust your clients, and you better restrict them with hosts allow!

If the **"security"** parameter is set to **"domain"**, then the list of machines in this option must be a list of Primary or Backup Domain controllers for the **Domain**, as the Samba server is cryptographicly in that domain, and will use cryptographicly authenticated RPC calls to authenticate the user logging on. The advantage of using **"security=domain"** is that if you list several hosts in the **"password server"** option then **smbd** will try each in turn till it finds one that responds. This is useful in case your primary server goes down.

If the **"security"** parameter is set to **"server"**, then there are different restrictions that **"security=domain"** doesn't suffer from:

- You may list several password servers in the **"password server"** parameter, however if an **smbd** makes a connection to a password server, and then the password server fails, no more users will be able to be authenticated from this **smbd**. This is a restriction of the SMB/CIFS protocol when in **"security=server"** mode and cannot be fixed in Samba.
- If you are using a Windows NT server as your password server then you will have to ensure that your users are able to login from the Samba server, as when in **"security=server"** mode the network logon will appear to come from there rather than from the users workstation.

See also the **"security"** parameter.

Default: `password server = <empty string>`

Example: `password server = NT-PDC, NT-BDC1, NT-BDC2`

- **path (S)**

This parameter specifies a directory to which the user of the service is to be given access. In the case of printable services, this is where print data will spool prior to being submitted to the host for printing.

For a printable service offering guest access, the service should be read-only and the path should be world-writeable and have the sticky bit set. This is not mandatory of course, but you probably won't get the results you expect if you do otherwise.

Any occurrences of **%u** in the path will be replaced with the UNIX username that the client is using on this connection. Any occurrences of **%m** will be replaced by the NetBIOS name of the machine they are connecting from. These replacements are very useful for setting up pseudo home directories for users.

Note that this path will be based on **"root dir"** if one was specified.

Default: `none`

Example: `path = /home/fred`

- **postexec (S)**

This option specifies a command to be run whenever the service is disconnected. It takes the usual substitutions. The command may be run as the root on some systems.

An interesting example may be do unmount server resources:

```
postexec = /etc/umount /cdrom
```

See also **preexec**.

Default: `none (no command executed)`

Example: `postexec = echo "%u disconnected from %S from %m (%I)" >> /tmp/log`

- **postscript (S)**

This parameter forces a printer to interpret the print files as postscript. This is done by adding a `%!` to the start of print output.

This is most useful when you have lots of PCs that persist in putting a control-D at the start of print jobs, which then confuses your printer.

Default: `postscript = False`

Example: `postscript = True`

- **preexec (S)**

This option specifies a command to be run whenever the service is connected to. It takes the usual substitutions.

An interesting example is to send the users a welcome message every time they log in. Maybe a message of the day? Here is an example:

```
preexec = csh -c 'echo \"Welcome to %S!\" | /usr/local/samba/bin/smbclient -M %m -I %I' &
```

Of course, this could get annoying after a while :-)

See also **postexec**.

Default: `none (no command executed)`

Example: `preexec = echo \"%u connected to %S from %m (%I)\" >> /tmp/log`

- **preferred master (G)**

This boolean parameter controls if **nmbd** is a preferred master browser for its workgroup.

If this is set to true, on startup, **nmbd** will force an election, and it will have a slight advantage in winning the election. It is recommended that this parameter is used in conjunction with **"domain master = yes"**, so that **nmbd** can guarantee becoming a domain master. Indeed the default ("auto") enables "preferred master" if Samba is configured as the domain master browser.

Use this option with caution, because if there are several hosts (whether Samba servers, Windows 95 or NT) that are preferred master browsers on the same subnet, they will each periodically and continuously attempt to become the local master browser. This will result in unnecessary broadcast traffic and reduced browsing capabilities.

See also **os level**.

Default: `preferred master = auto`

Example: `preferred master = yes`

- **prefered master (G)**

Synonym for **"preferred master"** for people who cannot spell :-).

- **preload** Synonym for **"auto services"**.
- **preserve case (S)**

This controls if new filenames are created with the case that the client passes, or if they are forced to be the `"default"` case.

Default: `preserve case = yes`

See the section on **"NAME MANGLING"** for a fuller discussion.

- **print command (S)**

After a print job has finished spooling to a service, this command will be used via a `system()` call to process the spool file. Typically the command specified will submit the spool file to the host's printing subsystem, but there is no requirement that this be the case. The server will not remove the spool file, so whatever command you specify should remove the spool file when it has been processed, otherwise you will need to manually remove old spool files.

The print command is simply a text string. It will be used verbatim, with two exceptions: All occurrences of `"%s"` will be replaced by the appropriate spool file name, and all occurrences of `"%p"` will be replaced by the appropriate printer name. The spool file name is generated automatically by the server, the printer name is discussed below.

The full path name will be used for the filename if `"%s"` is not preceded by a `'/'`. If you don't like this (it can stuff up some lpq output) then use `"%f"` instead. Any occurrences of `"%f"` get replaced by the spool filename without the full path at the front.

The print command *MUST* contain at least one occurrence of `"%s"` or `"%f"`—the `"%p"` is optional. At the time a job is submitted, if no printer name is supplied the `"%p"` will be silently removed from the printer command.

If specified in the **"[global]"** section, the print command given will be used for any printable service that does not have its own print command specified.

If there is neither a specified print command for a printable service nor a global print command, spool files will be created but not processed and (most importantly) not removed.

Note that printing may fail on some UNIXs from the `"nobody"` account. If this happens then create an alternative guest account that can print and set the **"guest account"** in the **"[global]"** section.

You can form quite complex print commands by realizing that they are just passed to a shell. For example the following will log a print job, print the file, then remove it. Note that `';'` is the usual separator for command in shell scripts.

```
print command = echo Printing %s >> /tmp/print.log; lpr
-P %p %s; rm %s
```

You may have to vary this command considerably depending on how you normally print files on your system. The default for the parameter varies depending on the setting of the **"printing="** parameter.

Default: For **"printing="** BSD, AIX, QNX, LPRNG or PLP : `print command = lpr -r -P%p %s`

For **"printing="** SYS or HPUX : `print command = lp -c -d%p %s; rm %s`

For **"printing="** SOFTQ : `print command = lp -d%p -s %s; rm %s`

Example: `print command = /usr/local/samba/bin/myprint-script %p %s`

- **print ok (S)**

Synonym for **printable**.

- **printable (S)**

If this parameter is `"yes"`, then clients may open, write to and submit spool files on the directory specified for the service.

Note that a printable service will ALWAYS allow writing to the service path (user privileges permitting) via the spooling of print data. The **"read only"** parameter controls only non-printing access to the resource.

Default: `printable = no`

Example: `printable = yes`

- **printcap (G)**

Synonym for **printcapname**.

- **printcap name (G)**

This parameter may be used to override the compiled-in default printcap name used by the server (usually /etc/printcap). See the discussion of the **[printers]** section above for reasons why you might want to do this.

On System V systems that use **lpstat** to list available printers you can use `"printcap name = lpstat"` to automatically obtain lists of available printers. This is the default for systems that define SYSV at configure time in Samba (this includes most System V based systems). If **"printcap name"** is set to **lpstat** on these systems then Samba will launch `"lpstat -v"` and attempt to parse the output to obtain a printer list.

A minimal printcap file would look something like this:

```
print1|My Printer 1

print2|My Printer 2

print3|My Printer 3

print4|My Printer 4

print5|My Printer 5
```

where the `'|'` separates aliases of a printer. The fact that the second alias has a space in it gives a hint to Samba that it's a comment.

NOTE: Under AIX the default printcap name is `"/etc/qconfig"`. Samba will assume the file is in AIX `"qconfig"` format if the string `"/qconfig"` appears in the printcap filename.

Default: `printcap name = /etc/printcap`

Example: `printcap name = /etc/myprintcap`

- **printer (S)**

This parameter specifies the name of the printer to which print jobs spooled through a printable service will be sent.

If specified in the **[global]** section, the printer name given will be used for any printable service that does not have its own printer name specified.

Default: none (but may be `"lp"` on many systems)

Example: printer name = laserwriter

- **printer driver (S)**

This option allows you to control the string that clients receive when they ask the server for the printer driver associated with a printer. If you are using Windows95 or WindowsNT then you can use this to automate the setup of printers on your system.

You need to set this parameter to the exact string (case sensitive) that describes the appropriate printer driver for your system. If you don't know the exact string to use then you should first try with no **"printer driver"** option set and the client will give you a list of printer drivers. The appropriate strings are shown in a scrollbox after you have chosen the printer manufacturer.

See also **"printer driver file"**.

Example: printer driver = HP LaserJet 4L

- **printer driver file (G)**

This parameter tells Samba where the printer driver definition file, used when serving drivers to Windows 95 clients, is to be found. If this is not set, the default is :

```
SAMBA_INSTALL_DIRECTORY/lib/printers.def
```

This file is created from Windows 95 `"msprint.def"` files found on the Windows 95 client system. For more details on setting up serving of printer drivers to Windows 95 clients, see the documentation file in the docs/ directory, PRINTER_DRIVER.txt.

Default: `None (set in compile).`

Example: `printer driver file = /usr/local/samba/printers/drivers.def`

See also **"printer driver location"**.

- **printer driver location (S)**

This parameter tells clients of a particular printer share where to find the printer driver files for the automatic installation of drivers for Windows 95 machines. If Samba is set up to serve printer drivers to Windows 95 machines, this should be set to

```
\\MACHINE\aPRINTER$
```

Where MACHINE is the NetBIOS name of your Samba server, and PRINTER$ is a share you set up for serving printer driver files. For more details on setting this up see the documentation file in the docs/ directory, PRINTER_DRIVER.txt.

Default: `None`

Example: `printer driver location = \\MACHINE\PRINTER$`

See also **"printer driver file"**.

- **printer name (S)**

Synonym for **printer**.

- **printing (S)**

This parameters controls how printer status information is interpreted on your system, and also affects the default values for the **"print command"**, **"lpq command"** **"lppause command"**, **"lpresume command"**, and **"lprm command"**.

Currently eight printing styles are supported. They are **"print-ing=BSD"**, **"printing=AIX"**, **"printing=LPRNG"**, **"printing=PLP"**, **"printing=SYSV"**,**"printing="HPUX"**,**"printing=QNX"** and **"printing=SOFTQ"**.

To see what the defaults are for the other print commands when using these three options use the **"testparm"** program.

This option can be set on a per printer basis

See also the discussion in the **[printers]** section.

- **protocol (G)**

The value of the parameter (a string) is the highest protocol level that will be supported by the server.

Possible values are :

- CORE: Earliest version. No concept of user names.
- COREPLUS: Slight improvements on CORE for efficiency.
- LANMAN1: First *"modern"* version of the protocol. Long filename support.
- LANMAN2: Updates to Lanman1 protocol.

- NT1: Current up to date version of the protocol. Used by Windows NT. Known as CIFS.

Normally this option should not be set as the automatic negotiation phase in the SMB protocol takes care of choosing the appropriate protocol.

Default: `protocol = NT1`

Example: `protocol = LANMAN1`

- **public (S)**

Synonym for "**guest ok**".

- **queuepause command (S)**

This parameter specifies the command to be executed on the server host in order to pause the printerqueue.

This command should be a program or script which takes a printer name as its only parameter and stops the printerqueue, such that no longer jobs are submitted to the printer.

This command is not supported by Windows for Workgroups, but can be issued from the Printer's window under Windows 95 & NT.

If a `"%p"` is given then the printername is put in its place. Otherwise it is placed at the end of the command.

Note that it is good practice to include the absolute path in the command as the PATH may not be available to the server.

Default: `depends on the setting of "printing ="`

Example: `queuepause command = disable %p`

- **queueresume command (S)**

This parameter specifies the command to be executed on the server host in order to resume the printerqueue. It is the command to undo the behavior that is caused by the previous parameter ("**queuepause command**).

This command should be a program or script which takes a printer name as its only parameter and resumes the printerqueue, such that queued jobs are resubmitted to the printer.

This command is not supported by Windows for Workgroups, but can be issued from the Printer's window under Windows 95 & NT.

If a `"%p"` is given then the printername is put in its place. Otherwise it is placed at the end of the command.

Note that it is good practice to include the absolute path in the command as the PATH may not be available to the server.

Default: `depends on the setting of "printing ="`

Example: `queuepause command = enable %p`

- **read bmpx (G)**

This boolean parameter controls whether **smbd** will support the "Read Block Multiplex" SMB. This is now rarely used and defaults to off. You should never need to set this parameter.

Default: read bmpx = No

- **read list (S)**

This is a list of users that are given read-only access to a service. If the connecting user is in this list then they will not be given write access, no matter what the **"read only"** option is set to. The list can include group names using the syntax described in the **"invalid users"** parameter.

See also the **"write list"** parameter and the **"invalid users"** parameter.

Default: `read list = <empty string>`

Example: `read list = mary, @students`

- **read only (S)**

Note that this is an inverted synonym for **"writeable"** and **"write ok"**.

See also **"writeable"** and **"write ok"**.

- **read prediction (G)**

NOTE: This code is currently disabled in Samba2.0 and may be removed at a later date. Hence this parameter has no effect.

This options enables or disables the read prediction code used to speed up reads from the server. When enabled the server will try to pre-read data from the last accessed file that was opened read-only while waiting for packets.

Default: `read prediction = False`

- **read raw (G)**

This parameter controls whether or not the server will support the raw read SMB requests when transferring data to clients.

If enabled, raw reads allow reads of 65535 bytes in one packet. This typically provides a major performance benefit.

However, some clients either negotiate the allowable block size incorrectly or are incapable of supporting larger block sizes, and for these clients you may need to disable raw reads.

In general this parameter should be viewed as a system tuning tool and left severely alone. See also "**write raw**".

Default: `read raw = yes`

- **read size (G)**

The option "**read size**" affects the overlap of disk reads/writes with network reads/writes. If the amount of data being transferred in several of the SMB commands (currently SMBwrite, SMBwriteX and SMBreadbraw) is larger than this value then the server begins writing the data before it has received the whole packet from the network, or in the case of SMBreadbraw, it begins writing to the network before all the data has been read from disk.

This overlapping works best when the speeds of disk and network access are similar, having very little effect when the speed of one is much greater than the other.

The default value is 2048, but very little experimentation has been done yet to determine the optimal value, and it is likely that the best value will vary greatly between systems anyway. A value over 65536 is pointless and will cause you to allocate memory unnecessarily.

Default: `read size = 2048`

Example: `read size = 8192`

- **remote announce (G)**

This option allows you to setup **nmbd** to periodically announce itself to arbitrary IP addresses with an arbitrary workgroup name.

This is useful if you want your Samba server to appear in a remote workgroup for which the normal browse propagation rules don't work. The remote workgroup can be anywhere that you can send IP packets to.

For example:

```
remote announce = 192.168.2.255/SERVERS 192.168.4.255/
STAFF
```

the above line would cause nmbd to announce itself to the two given IP addresses using the given workgroup names. If you leave out the workgroup name then the one given in the "**workgroup**" parameter is used instead.

The IP addresses you choose would normally be the broadcast addresses of the remote networks, but can also be the IP addresses of known browse masters if your network config is that stable.

See the documentation file BROWSING.txt in the docs/ directory.

Default: `remote announce = <empty string>`

Example: `remote announce = 192.168.2.255/SERVERS 192.168.4.255/ STAFF`

- **remote browse sync (G)**

This option allows you to setup **nmbd** to periodically request synchronization of browse lists with the master browser of a samba server that is on a remote segment. This option will allow you to gain browse lists for multiple workgroups across routed networks. This is done in a manner that does not work with any non-samba servers.

This is useful if you want your Samba server and all local clients to appear in a remote workgroup for which the normal browse propagation rules don't work. The remote workgroup can be anywhere that you can send IP packets to.

For example:

```
remote browse sync = 192.168.2.255 192.168.4.255
```

the above line would cause **nmbd** to request the master browser on the specified subnets or addresses to synchronize their browse lists with the local server.

The IP addresses you choose would normally be the broadcast addresses of the remote networks, but can also be the IP addresses of known browse masters if your network config is that stable. If a machine IP address is given Samba makes NO attempt to validate that the remote machine is available, is listening, nor that it is in fact the browse master on it's segment.

Default: `remote browse sync = <empty string>`

Example: `remote browse sync = 192.168.2.255 192.168.4.255`

- **revalidate (S)**

Note that this option only works with "**security=share**" and will be ignored if this is not the case.

This option controls whether Samba will allow a previously validated username/password pair to be used to attach to a share. Thus if you connect to `\\server\share1` then to `\\server\share2` it won't automatically allow the client to request connection to the second share as the same username as the first without a password.

If "**revalidate**" is `"True"` then the client will be denied automatic access as the same username.

Default: `revalidate = False`

Example: `revalidate = True`

- **root (G)**

Synonym for "**root directory**".

- **root dir (G)**

Synonym for **"root directory"**.

- **root directory (G)**

The server will `"chroot()"` (i.e. Change it's root directory) to this directory on startup. This is not strictly necessary for secure operation. Even without it the server will deny access to files not in one of the service entries. It may also check for, and deny access to, soft links to other parts of the filesystem, or attempts to use `".."` in file names to access other directories (depending on the setting of the **"wide links"** parameter).

Adding a **"root directory"** entry other than `"/"` adds an extra level of security, but at a price. It absolutely ensures that no access is given to files not in the sub-tree specified in the **"root directory"** option, **including** some files needed for complete operation of the server. To maintain full operability of the server you will need to mirror some system files into the **"root directory"** tree. In particular you will need to mirror /etc/passwd (or a subset of it), and any binaries or configuration files needed for printing (if required). The set of files that must be mirrored is operating system dependent.

Default: `root directory = /`

Example: `root directory = /homes/smb`

- **root postexec (S)**

This is the same as the **"postexec"** parameter except that the command is run as root. This is useful for unmounting filesystems (such as cdroms) after a connection is closed.

See also **"postexec"**.

- **root preexec (S)**

This is the same as the **"preexec"** parameter except that the command is run as root. This is useful for mounting filesystems (such as cdroms) before a connection is finalized.

See also **"preexec"**.

- **security (G)**

This option affects how clients respond to Samba and is one of the most important settings in the **smb.conf** file.

The option sets the `"security mode bit"` in replies to protocol negotiations with **smbd** to turn share level security on or off. Clients decide based on this bit whether (and how) to transfer user and password information to the server.

The default is "security=user", as this is the most common setting needed when talking to Windows 98 and Windows NT.

The alternatives are **"security = share"**, **"security = server"** or **"security=domain"**.

******NOTE THAT THIS DEFAULT IS DIFFERENT IN SAMBA2.0 THAN FOR PREVIOUS VERSIONS OF SAMBA ********.

In previous versions of Samba the default was **"security=share"** mainly because that was the only option at one stage.

There is a bug in WfWg that has relevance to this setting. When in user or server level security a WfWg client will totally ignore the password you type in the "connect drive" dialog box. This makes it very difficult (if not impossible) to connect to a Samba service as anyone except the user that you are logged into WfWg as.

If your PCs use usernames that are the same as their usernames on the UNIX machine then you will want to use **"security = user"**. If you mostly use usernames that don't exist on the UNIX box then use **"security = share"**.

You should also use **security=share** if you want to mainly setup shares without a password (guest shares). This is commonly used for a shared printer server. It is more difficult to setup guest shares with **security=user**, see the **"map to guest"**parameter for details.

It is possible to use **smbd** in a *"hybrid mode"* where it is offers both user and share level security under different **NetBIOS aliases**. See the **NetBIOS aliases** and the **include** parameters for more information.

The different settings will now be explained.

- *"***security=share***"* When clients connect to a share level security server then need not log onto the server with a valid username and password before attempting to connect to a shared resource (although modern clients such as Windows 95/98 and Windows NT will send a logon request with a username but no password when talking to a **security=share** server). Instead, the clients send authentication information (passwords) on a per-share basis, at the time they attempt to connect to that share.

  Note that **smbd** **ALWAYS** uses a valid UNIX user to act on behalf of the client, even in "**security=share**" level security.

  As clients are not required to send a username to the server in share level security, **smbd** uses several techniques to determine the correct UNIX user to use on behalf of the client.

  A list of possible UNIX usernames to match with the given client password is constructed using the following methods :

- If the "**guest only**" parameter is set, then all the other stages are missed and only the "**guest account**" username is checked.
- Is a username is sent with the share connection request, then this username (after mapping—see "**username map**"), is added as a potential username.
- If the client did a previous *"logon"* request (the SessionSetup SMB call) then the username sent in this SMB will be added as a potential username.
- The name of the service the client requested is added as a potential username.
- The NetBIOS name of the client is added to the list as a potential username.
- Any users on the "**user**" list are added as potential usernames.

  If the "**guest only**" parameter is not set, then this list is then tried with the supplied password. The first user for whom the password matches will be used as the UNIX user.

  If the "**guest only**" parameter is set, or no username can be determined then if the share is marked as available to the "**guest account**", then this guest user will be used, otherwise access is denied.

Note that it can be **very** confusing in share-level security as to which UNIX username will eventually be used in granting access.

See also the section **"NOTE ABOUT USERNAME/PASSWORD VALIDATION"**.

- **"security=user"**

  This is the default security setting in Samba2.0. With user-level security a client must first `"log-on"` with a valid username and password (which can be mapped using the **"username map"** parameter). Encrypted passwords (see the **"encrypted passwords"** parameter) can also be used in this security mode. Parameters such as **"user"** and **"guest only"**, if set are then applied and may change the UNIX user to use on this connection, but only after the user has been successfully authenticated.

  Note that the name of the resource being requested is **not** sent to the server until after the server has successfully authenticated the client. This is why guest shares don't work in user level security without allowing the server to automatically map unknown users into the **"guest account"**. See the **"map to guest"** parameter for details on doing this.

  See also the section **"NOTE ABOUT USERNAME/PASSWORD VALIDATION"**.

- **"security=server"**

  In this mode Samba will try to validate the username/password by passing it to another SMB server, such as an NT box. If this fails it will revert to **"security = user"**, but note that if encrypted passwords have been negotiated then Samba cannot revert back to checking the UNIX password file, it must have a valid smbpasswd file to check users against. See the documentation file in the docs/ directory ENCRYPTION.txt for details on how to set this up.

  Note that from the clients point of view **"security=server"** is the same as **"security=user"**. It only affects how the server deals with the authentication, it does not in any way affect what the client sees.

Note that the name of the resource being requested is **not** sent to the server until after the server has successfully authenticated the client. This is why guest shares don't work in server level security without allowing the server to automatically map unknown users into the **"guest account"**. See the **"map to guest"** parameter for details on doing this.

See also the section **"NOTE ABOUT USERNAME/PASSWORD VALIDATION"**.

See also the **"password server"** parameter. and the **"encrypted passwords"** parameter.

- **"security=domain"**

  This mode will only work correctly if **smbpasswd** has been used to add this machine into a Windows NT Domain. It expects the **"encrypted passwords"** parameter to be set to `"true"`. In this mode Samba will try to validate the username/password by passing it to a Windows NT Primary or Backup Domain Controller, in exactly the same way that a Windows NT Server would do.

  Note that a valid UNIX user must still exist as well as the account on the Domain Controller to allow Samba to have a valid UNIX account to map file access to.

  Note that from the clients point of view **"security=domain"** is the same as **"security=user"**. It only affects how the server deals with the authentication, it does not in any way affect what the client sees.

  Note that the name of the resource being requested is **not** sent to the server until after the server has successfully authenticated the client. This is why guest shares don't work in domain level security without allowing the server to automatically map unknown users into the **"guest account"**. See the **"map to guest"** parameter for details on doing this.

  e,(BUG:) There is currently a bug in the implementation of **"security=domain** with respect to multi-byte character set usernames. The communication with a Domain Controller must be done in UNICODE and Samba currently does not widen multi-byte user names to UNICODE correctly, thus a multi-byte username will not be recognized correctly at the Domain Controller. This issue will be addressed in a future release.

See also the section **"NOTE ABOUT USERNAME/PASSWORD VALIDATION"**.

See also the **"password server"** parameter. and the **"encrypted passwords"** parameter.

Default: `security = USER`

Example: `security = DOMAIN`

- **server string (G)**

This controls what string will show up in the printer comment box in print manager and next to the IPC connection in `"net view"`. It can be any string that you wish to show to your users.

It also sets what will appear in browse lists next to the machine name.

A `"%v"` will be replaced with the Samba version number.

A `"%h"` will be replaced with the hostname.

Default: `server string = Samba %v`

Example: `server string = University of GNUs Samba Server`

- **set directory (S)**

If `"set directory = no"`, then users of the service may not use the setdir command to change directory.

The setdir command is only implemented in the Digital Pathworks client. See the Pathworks documentation for details.

Default: `set directory = no`

Example: `set directory = yes`

- **share modes (S)**

This enables or disables the honoring of the `"share modes"` during a file open. These modes are used by clients to gain exclusive read or write access to a file.

These open modes are not directly supported by UNIX, so they are simulated using shared memory, or lock files if your UNIX doesn't support shared memory (almost all do).

The share modes that are enabled by this option are DENY_DOS, DENY_ALL, DENY_READ, DENY_WRITE, DENY_NONE and DENY_FCB.

This option gives full share compatibility and enabled by default.

You should **NEVER** turn this parameter off as many Windows applications will break if you do so.

Default: `share modes = yes`

- **shared mem size (G)**

It specifies the size of the shared memory (in bytes) to use between **smbd** processes. This parameter defaults to one megabyte of shared memory. It is possible that if you have a large server with many files open simultaneously that you may need to increase this parameter. Signs that this parameter is set too low are users reporting strange problems trying to save files (locking errors) and error messages in the smbd log looking like `"ERROR smb_shm_alloc : alloc of XX bytes failed"`.

Default: `shared mem size = 1048576`

Example: `shared mem size = 5242880 ; Set to 5mb for a large number of files.`

- **short preserve case (G)**

This boolean parameter controls if new files which conform to 8.3 syntax, that is all in upper case and of suitable length, are created upper case, or if they are forced to be the `"default"` case. This option can be use with **"preserve case =yes"** to permit long filenames to retain their case, while short names are lowered. Default *Yes*.

See the section on **NAME MANGLING**.

Default: `short preserve case = yes`

- **smb passwd file (G)**

This option sets the path to the encrypted smbpasswd file. By default the path to the smbpasswd file is compiled into Samba.

Default: `smb passwd file= <compiled default>`

Example: `smb passwd file = /usr/samba/private/smbpasswd`

- **smbrun (G)**

This sets the full path to the **smbrun** binary. This defaults to the value in the Makefile.

You must get this path right for many services to work correctly.

You should not need to change this parameter so long as Samba is installed correctly.

Default: `smbrun=<compiled default>`

Example: `smbrun = /usr/local/samba/bin/smbrun`

- **socket address (G)**

This option allows you to control what address Samba will listen for connections on. This is used to support multiple virtual interfaces on the one server, each with a different configuration.

By default samba will accept connections on any address.

Example: `socket address = 192.168.2.20`

- **socket options (G)**

This option allows you to set socket options to be used when talking with the client.

Socket options are controls on the networking layer of the operating systems which allow the connection to be tuned.

This option will typically be used to tune your Samba server for optimal performance for your local network. There is no way that Samba can know what the optimal parameters are for your net, so you must experiment and choose them yourself. We strongly suggest you read the appropriate documentation for your operating system first (perhaps **"man setsockopt"** will help).

You may find that on some systems Samba will say "Unknown socket option" when you supply an option. This means you either incorrectly typed it or you need to add an include file to includes.h for your OS. If the latter is the case please send the patch to *samba-bugs@samba.org*.

Any of the supported socket options may be combined in any way you like, as long as your OS allows it.

This is the list of socket options currently settable using this option:

- SO_KEEPALIVE
- SO_REUSEADDR
- SO_BROADCAST
- TCP_NODELAY
- IPTOS_LOWDELAY
- IPTOS_THROUGHPUT
- SO_SNDBUF *
- SO_RCVBUF *
- SO_SNDLOWAT *
- SO_RCVLOWAT *

Those marked with a `*` take an integer argument. The others can optionally take a 1 or 0 argument to enable or disable the option, by default they will be enabled if you don't specify 1 or 0.

To specify an argument use the syntax SOME_OPTION=VALUE for example `SO_SNDBUF=8192`. Note that you must not have any spaces before or after the = sign.

If you are on a local network then a sensible option might be

```
socket options = IPTOS_LOWDELAY
```

If you have a local network then you could try:

```
socket options = IPTOS_LOWDELAY TCP_NODELAY
```

If you are on a wide area network then perhaps try setting IPTOS_ THROUGHPUT.

Note that several of the options may cause your Samba server to fail completely. Use these options with caution!

Default: `socket options = TCP_NODELAY`

Example: `socket options = IPTOS_LOWDELAY`

- **ssl (G)**

This variable is part of SSL-enabled Samba. This is only available if the SSL libraries have been compiled on your system and the configure option `"–with-ssl"` was given at configure time.

Note that for export control reasons this code is ***NOT*** enabled by default in any current binary version of Samba.

This variable enables or disables the entire SSL mode. If it is set to "no", the SSL enabled samba behaves exactly like the non-SSL samba. If set to "yes", it depends on the variables **"ssl hosts"** and **"ssl hosts resign"** whether an SSL connection will be required.

Default: `ssl=no` **Example:** `ssl=yes`

- **ssl CA certDir (G)**

This variable is part of SSL-enabled Samba. This is only available if the SSL libraries have been compiled on your system and the configure option `"–with-ssl"` was given at configure time.

Note that for export control reasons this code is ***NOT*** enabled by default in any current binary version of Samba.

This variable defines where to look up the Certification Authorities. The given directory should contain one file for each CA that samba will trust. The file name must be the hash value over the "Distinguished Name" of the CA. How this directory is set up is explained later in this document. All files within the directory that don't fit into this naming scheme are ignored. You don't need this variable if you don't verify client certificates.

Default: `ssl CA certDir = /usr/local/ssl/certs`

- **ssl CA certFile (G)**

This variable is part of SSL-enabled Samba. This is only available if the SSL libraries have been compiled on your system and the configure option `"–with-ssl"` was given at configure time.

Note that for export control reasons this code is ***NOT*** enabled by default in any current binary version of Samba.

This variable is a second way to define the trusted CAs. The certificates of the trusted CAs are collected in one big file and this variable points to the file. You will probably only use one of the two ways to define your CAs. The first choice is preferable if you have many CAs or want to be flexible, the second is preferable if you only have one CA and want to keep things simple (you won't need to create the hashed file names). You don't need this variable if you don't verify client certificates.

Default: `ssl CA certFile = /usr/local/ssl/certs/trustedCAs.pem`

- **ssl ciphers (G)**

This variable is part of SSL-enabled Samba. This is only available if the SSL libraries have been compiled on your system and the configure option `"–with-ssl"` was given at configure time.

Note that for export control reasons this code is ***NOT*** enabled by default in any current binary version of Samba.

This variable defines the ciphers that should be offered during SSL negotiation. You should not set this variable unless you know what you are doing.

- **ssl client cert (G)**

This variable is part of SSL-enabled Samba. This is only available if the SSL libraries have been compiled on your system and the configure option `"–with-ssl"` was given at configure time.

Note that for export control reasons this code is ***NOT*** enabled by default in any current binary version of Samba.

The certificate in this file is used by **smbclient** if it exists. It's needed if the server requires a client certificate.

Default: `ssl client cert = /usr/local/ssl/certs/smbclient.pem`

- **ssl client key (G)**

This variable is part of SSL-enabled Samba. This is only available if the SSL libraries have been compiled on your system and the configure option `"–with-ssl"` was given at configure time.

Note that for export control reasons this code is ***NOT*** enabled by default in any current binary version of Samba.

This is the private key for **smbclient**. It's only needed if the client should have a certificate.

Default: `ssl client key = /usr/local/ssl/private/smbclient.pem`

- **ssl compatibility (G)**

This variable is part of SSL-enabled Samba. This is only available if the SSL libraries have been compiled on your system and the configure option `"–with-ssl"` was given at configure time.

Note that for export control reasons this code is ***NOT*** enabled by default in any current binary version of Samba.

This variable defines whether SSLeay should be configured for bug compatibility with other SSL implementations. This is probably not desirable because currently no clients with SSL implementations other than SSLeay exist.

Default: `ssl compatibility = no`

- **ssl hosts (G)**

See **"ssl hosts resign"**.

- **ssl hosts resign (G)**

This variable is part of SSL-enabled Samba. This is only available if the SSL libraries have been compiled on your system and the configure option `"–with-ssl"` was given at configure time.

Note that for export control reasons this code is ***NOT*** enabled by default in any current binary version of Samba.

These two variables define whether samba will go into SSL mode or not. If none of them is defined, samba will allow only SSL connections. If the **"ssl hosts"** variable lists hosts (by IP-address, IP-address range, net group or name), only these hosts will be forced into SSL mode. If the **"ssl hosts resign"** variable lists hosts, only these hosts will NOT be forced into SSL mode. The syntax for these two variables is the same as for the **"hosts allow"** and **"hosts deny"** pair of variables, only that the subject of the decision is different: It's not the access right but whether SSL is used or not. See the **"allow hosts"** parameter for details. The example below requires SSL connections from all hosts outside the local net (which is 192.168.*.*).

Default: `ssl hosts = <empty string> ssl hosts resign = <empty string>`

Example: `ssl hosts resign = 192.168.`

- **ssl require clientcert (G)**

This variable is part of SSL-enabled Samba. This is only available if the SSL libraries have been compiled on your system and the configure option `"—with-ssl"` was given at configure time.

Note that for export control reasons this code is ***NOT*** enabled by default in any current binary version of Samba.

If this variable is set to `"yes"`, the server will not tolerate connections from clients that don't have a valid certificate. The directory/file given in **"ssl CA certDir"** and **"ssl CA certFile"** will be used to look up the CAs that issued the client's certificate. If the certificate can't be verified positively, the connection will be terminated. If this variable is set to `"no"`, clients don't need certificates. Contrary to web applications you really **should** require client certificates. In the web environment the client's data is sensitive (credit card numbers) and the server must prove to be trustworthy. In a file server environment the server's data will be sensitive and the clients must prove to be trustworthy.

Default: `ssl require clientcert = no`

- **ssl require servercert (G)**

This variable is part of SSL-enabled Samba. This is only available if the SSL libraries have been compiled on your system and the configure option `"—with-ssl"` was given at configure time.

Note that for export control reasons this code is ***NOT*** enabled by default in any current binary version of Samba.

If this variable is set to `"yes"`, the **smbclient** will request a certificate from the server. Same as **"ssl require clientcert"** for the server.

Default: `ssl require servercert = no`

- **ssl server cert (G)**

This variable is part of SSL-enabled Samba. This is only available if the SSL libraries have been compiled on your system and the configure option `"–with-ssl"` was given at configure time.

Note that for export control reasons this code is ***NOT*** enabled by default in any current binary version of Samba.

This is the file containing the server's certificate. The server _must_ have a certificate. The file may also contain the server's private key. See later for how certificates and private keys are created.

Default: `ssl server cert = <empty string>`

- **ssl server key (G)**

This variable is part of SSL-enabled Samba. This is only available if the SSL libraries have been compiled on your system and the configure option `"–with-ssl"` was given at configure time.

Note that for export control reasons this code is ***NOT*** enabled by default in any current binary version of Samba.

This file contains the private key of the server. If this variable is not defined, the key is looked up in the certificate file (it may be appended to the certificate). The server **must** have a private key and the certificate **must** match this private key.

Default: `ssl server key = <empty string>`

- **ssl version (G)**

This variable is part of SSL-enabled Samba. This is only available if the SSL libraries have been compiled on your system and the configure option `"–with-ssl"` was given at configure time.

Note that for export control reasons this code is ***NOT*** enabled by default in any current binary version of Samba.

This enumeration variable defines the versions of the SSL protocol that will be used. `"ssl2or3"`allows dynamic negotiation of SSL v2 or v3, `"ssl2"` results in SSL v2, `"ssl3"` results in SSL v3 and `"tls1"` results in

TLS v1. TLS (Transport Layer Security) is the (proposed?) new standard for SSL.

Default: `ssl version = "ssl2or3"`

- **stat cache (G)**

This parameter determines if **smbd** will use a cache in order to speed up case insensitive name mappings. You should never need to change this parameter.

Default: `stat cache = yes`

- **stat cache size (G)**

This parameter determines the number of entries in the **stat cache**. You should never need to change this parameter.

Default: `stat cache size = 50`

- **status (G)**

This enables or disables logging of connections to a status file that **smbstatus** can read.

With this disabled **smbstatus** won't be able to tell you what connections are active. You should never need to change this parameter.

Default: status = yes

- **strict locking (S)**

This is a boolean that controls the handling of file locking in the server. When this is set to `"yes"` the server will check every read and write access for file locks, and deny access if locks exist. This can be slow on some systems.

When strict locking is `"no"` the server does file lock checks only when the client explicitly asks for them.

Well behaved clients always ask for lock checks when it is important, so in the vast majority of cases **"strict locking = no"** is preferable.

Default: `strict locking = no`

Example: `strict locking = yes`

- **strict sync (S)**

Many Windows applications (including the Windows 98 explorer shell) seem to confuse flushing buffer contents to disk with doing a sync to disk. Under UNIX, a sync call forces the process to be suspended until the kernel has ensured that all outstanding data in kernel disk buffers has been safely stored onto stable storage. This is very slow and should only be done rarely. Setting this parameter to "no" (the default) means that smbd ignores the Windows applications requests for a sync call. There is only a possibility of losing data if the operating system itself that Samba is running on crashes, so there is little danger in this default setting. In addition, this fixes many performance problems that people have reported with the new Windows98 explorer shell file copies.

See also the **"sync always"** parameter.

Default: `strict sync = no`

Example: `strict sync = yes`

- **strip dot (G)**

This is a boolean that controls whether to strip trailing dots off UNIX filenames. This helps with some CDROMs that have filenames ending in a single dot.

Default: `strip dot = no`

Example: `strip dot = yes`

- **sync always (S)**

This is a boolean parameter that controls whether writes will always be written to stable storage before the write call returns. If this is false then the server will be guided by the client's request in each write call (clients can set a bit indicating that a particular write should be synchronous). If this is true then every write will be followed by a fsync() call to ensure the data is written to disk. Note that the **"strict sync"** parameter must be set to `"yes"` in order for this parameter to have any affect.

See also the **"strict sync"** parameter.

Default: `sync always = no`

Example: `sync always = yes`

- **syslog (G)**

This parameter maps how Samba debug messages are logged onto the system syslog logging levels. Samba debug level zero maps onto syslog LOG_ERR, debug level one maps onto LOG_WARNING, debug level two maps to LOG_NOTICE, debug level three maps onto LOG_INFO. The parameter sets the threshold for doing the mapping, all Samba debug messages above this threshold are mapped to syslog LOG_DEBUG messages.

Default: `syslog = 1`

- **syslog only (G)**

If this parameter is set then Samba debug messages are logged into the system syslog only, and not to the debug log files.

Default: `syslog only = no`

- **time offset (G)**

This parameter is a setting in minutes to add to the normal GMT to local time conversion. This is useful if you are serving a lot of PCs that have incorrect daylight saving time handling.

Default: `time offset = 0`

Example: `time offset = 60`

- **time server (G)**

This parameter determines if **nmbd** advertises itself as a time server to Windows clients. The default is False.

Default: `time server = False`

Example: `time server = True`

- **timestamp logs (G)**

Samba2.0 will a timestamps to all log entries by default. This can be distracting if you are attempting to debug a problem. This parameter allows the timestamping to be turned off.

Default: `timestamp logs = True`

Example: `timestamp logs = False`

- **unix password sync (G)**

This boolean parameter controls whether Samba attempts to synchronize the UNIX password with the SMB password when the encrypted SMB password in the smbpasswd file is changed. If this is set to true the program specified in the **"passwd program"** parameter is called **AS ROOT**—to allow the new UNIX password to be set without access to the old UNIX password (as the SMB password has change code has no access to the old password cleartext, only the new). By default this is set to `"false"`.

See also **"passwd program"**, **"passwd chat"**.

Default: `unix password sync = False`

Example: `unix password sync = True`

- **unix realname (G)**

This boolean parameter when set causes samba to supply the real name field from the unix password file to the client. This is useful for setting up mail clients and WWW browsers on systems used by more than one person.

Default: `unix realname = no`

Example: `unix realname = yes`

- **update encrypted (G)**

This boolean parameter allows a user logging on with a plaintext password to have their encrypted (hashed) password in the smbpasswd file to be updated automatically as they log on. This option allows a site to migrate from plaintext password authentication (users authenticate with plaintext password over the wire, and are checked against a UNIX account database) to encrypted password authentication (the SMB challenge/response authentication mechanism) without forcing all users to re-enter their passwords via smbpasswd at the time the change is made. This is a convenience option to allow the change over to encrypted passwords to be made over a longer period. Once all users have encrypted representations of their passwords in the smbpasswd file this parameter should be set to `"off"`.

In order for this parameter to work correctly the **"encrypt passwords"** parameter must be set to `"no"` when this parameter is set to `"yes"`.

Note that even when this parameter is set a user authenticating to smbd must still enter a valid password in order to connect correctly, and to update their hashed (smbpasswd) passwords.

Default: `update encrypted = no`

Example: `update encrypted = yes`

- **use rhosts (G)**

If this global parameter is a true, it specifies that the UNIX users `".rhosts"` file in their home directory will be read to find the names of hosts and users who will be allowed access without specifying a password.

NOTE: The use of **use rhosts** can be a major security hole. This is because you are trusting the PC to supply the correct username. It is very easy to get a PC to supply a false username. I recommend that the **use rhosts** option be only used if you really know what you are doing.

Default: `use rhosts = no`

Example: `use rhosts = yes`

- **user (S)**

Synonym for **"username"**.

- **users (S)**

Synonym for **"username"**.

- **username (S)**

Multiple users may be specified in a comma-delimited list, in which case the supplied password will be tested against each username in turn (left to right).

The **username=** line is needed only when the PC is unable to supply its own username. This is the case for the COREPLUS protocol or where your users have different WfWg usernames to UNIX usernames. In both these cases you may also be better using the `\\server\share%user` syntax instead.

The **username=** line is not a great solution in many cases as it means Samba will try to validate the supplied password against each of the usernames in the username= line in turn. This is slow and a bad idea for lots of users in case of duplicate passwords. You may get timeouts or security breaches using this parameter unwisely.

Samba relies on the underlying UNIX security. This parameter does not restrict who can login, it just offers hints to the Samba server as to what usernames might correspond to the supplied password. Users can login as whoever they please and they will be able to do no more damage than if they started a telnet session. The daemon runs as the user that they log in as, so they cannot do anything that user cannot do.

To restrict a service to a particular set of users you can use the **"valid users="** parameter.

If any of the usernames begin with a `'@'` then the name will be looked up first in the yp netgroups list (if Samba is compiled with netgroup support), followed by a lookup in the UNIX groups database and will expand to a list of all users in the group of that name.

If any of the usernames begin with a `'+'` then the name will be looked up only in the UNIX groups database and will expand to a list of all users in the group of that name.

If any of the usernames begin with a `'&'` then the name will be looked up only in the yp netgroups database (if Samba is compiled with netgroup support) and will expand to a list of all users in the netgroup group of that name.

Note that searching though a groups database can take quite some time, and some clients may time out during the search.

See the section **"NOTE ABOUT USERNAME/PASSWORD VALIDATION"** for more information on how this parameter determines access to the services.

Default: `The guest account if a guest service, else the name of the service.`

Examples:

```
username = fred

username = fred, mary, jack, jane, @users, @pcgroup
```

- **username level (G)**

This option helps Samba to try and 'guess' at the real UNIX username, as many DOS clients send an all-uppercase username. By default Samba tries all lowercase, followed by the username with the first letter capitalized, and fails if the username is not found on the UNIX machine.

If this parameter is set to non-zero the behavior changes. This parameter is a number that specifies the number of uppercase combinations to try whilst trying to determine the UNIX user name. The higher the number the more combinations will be tried, but the slower the discovery of usernames will be. Use this parameter when you have strange usernames on your UNIX machine, such as `"AstrangeUser"`.

Default: `username level = 0`

Example: `username level = 5`

- **username map (G)**

This option allows you to specify a file containing a mapping of usernames from the clients to the server. This can be used for several purposes. The most common is to map usernames that users use on DOS or Windows machines to those that the UNIX box uses. The other is to map multiple users to a single username so that they can more easily share files.

The use of this option, therefore, relates to UNIX usernames and not Windows (specifically NT Domain) usernames. In other words, once a name has been mapped using this option, the Samba server uses the mapped name for internal *AND* external purposes.

This option is *DIFFERENT* from the **"domain user map"** parameter, which maintains a one-to-one mapping between UNIX usernames and NT Domain Usernames: more specifically, the Samba server maintains a link between *BOTH* usernames, presenting the NT username to the external NT world, and using the UNIX username internally.

The map file is parsed line by line. Each line should contain a single UNIX username on the left then a `'='` followed by a list of usernames on the right. The list of usernames on the right may contain names of the form @group in which case they will match any UNIX username in that group. The special client name `'*'` is a wildcard and matches any name. Each line of the map file may be up to 1023 characters long.

The file is processed on each line by taking the supplied username and comparing it with each username on the right hand side of the `'='` signs. If the supplied name matches any of the names on the right hand side then it is replaced with the name on the left. Processing then continues with the next line.

If any line begins with a `'#'` or a `';'` then it is ignored

If any line begins with an `'!'` then the processing will stop after that line if a mapping was done by the line. Otherwise mapping continues with every line being processed. Using `'!'` is most useful when you have a wildcard mapping line later in the file.

For example to map from the name `"admin"` or `"administrator"` to the UNIX name `"root"` you would use:

```
root = admin administrator
```

Or to map anyone in the UNIX group `"system"` to the UNIX name `"sys"` you would use:

```
sys = @system
```

You can have as many mappings as you like in a username map file.

If your system supports the NIS NETGROUP option then the netgroup database is checked before the `/etc/group` database for matching groups.

You can map Windows usernames that have spaces in them by using double quotes around the name. For example:

```
tridge = "Andrew Tridgell"
```

would map the windows username `"Andrew Tridgell"` to the unix username tridge.

The following example would map mary and fred to the unix user sys, and map the rest to guest. Note the use of the `'!'` to tell Samba to stop processing if it gets a match on that line.

```
!sys = mary fred
guest = *
```

Note that the remapping is applied to all occurrences of usernames. Thus if you connect to `"\\server\fred"` and `"fred"` is remapped to `"mary"` then you will actually be connecting to `"\\server\mary"` and will need to supply a password suitable for `"mary"` not `"fred"`. The only exception to this is the username passed to the **"password server"** (if you have one). The password server will receive whatever username the client supplies without modification.

Also note that no reverse mapping is done. The main effect this has is with printing. Users who have been mapped may have trouble deleting print jobs as PrintManager under WfWg will think they don't own the print job.

Default: `no username map`

Example: `username map = /usr/local/samba/lib/users.map`

- **valid chars (S)**

The option allows you to specify additional characters that should be considered valid by the server in filenames. This is particularly useful for national character sets, such as adding u-umlaut or a-ring.

The option takes a list of characters in either integer or character form with spaces between them. If you give two characters with a colon between them then it will be taken as an lowercase:uppercase pair.

If you have an editor capable of entering the characters into the config file then it is probably easiest to use this method. Otherwise you can specify the characters in octal, decimal or hexadecimal form using the usual C notation.

For example to add the single character `'Z'` to the charset (which is a pointless thing to do as it's already there) you could do one of the following

```
valid chars = Z
valid chars = z:Z
valid chars = 0132:0172
```

The last two examples above actually add two characters, and alter the uppercase and lowercase mappings appropriately.

Note that you MUST specify this parameter after the **"client code page"** parameter if you have both set. If **"client code page"** is set after the **"valid chars"** parameter the **"valid chars"** settings will be overwritten.

See also the **"client code page"** parameter.

Default:

`Samba defaults to using a reasonable set of valid characters for English systems`

Example `valid chars = 0345:0305 0366:0326 0344:0304`

The above example allows filenames to have the Swedish characters in them.

NOTE: It is actually quite difficult to correctly produce a **"valid chars"** line for a particular system. To automate the process *tino@augsburg.net* has written a package called **"validchars"** which will automatically produce a complete **"valid chars"** line for a given client system. Look in the examples/validchars/ subdirectory of your Samba source code distribution for this package.

- **valid users (S)**

This is a list of users that should be allowed to login to this service. Names starting with `'@'`, `'+'` and `'&'` are interpreted using the same rules as described in the **"invalid users"** parameter.

If this is empty (the default) then any user can login. If a username is in both this list and the **"invalid users"** list then access is denied for that user.

The current servicename is substituted for **"%S"**. This is useful in the **[homes]** section.

See also **"invalid users"**.

Default: `No valid users list. (anyone can login)`

Example: `valid users = greg, @pcusers`

- **veto files(S)**

This is a list of files and directories that are neither visible nor accessible. Each entry in the list must be separated by a `'/'`, which allows spaces to be included in the entry. `'*'` and `'?'` can be used to specify multiple files or directories as in DOS wildcards.

Each entry must be a unix path, not a DOS path and must **not** include the unix directory separator `'/'`.

Note that the **"case sensitive"** option is applicable in vetoing files.

One feature of the veto files parameter that it is important to be aware of, is that if a directory contains nothing but files that match the veto files parameter (which means that Windows/DOS clients cannot ever see them) is deleted, the veto files within that directory *are automatically deleted* along with it, if the user has UNIX permissions to do so.

Setting this parameter will affect the performance of Samba, as it will be forced to check all files and directories for a match as they are scanned.

See also **"hide files"** and **"case sensitive"**.

Default: `No files or directories are vetoed.`

Examples:

Example 1.

```
Veto any files containing the word Security,
any ending in .tmp, and any directory containing the
word root.
veto files = /*Security*/*.tmp/*root*/
```

Example 2.

```
Veto the Apple specific files that a NetAtalk server
creates.
veto files = /.AppleDouble/.bin/.AppleDesktop/Network
Trash Folder/
```

- **veto oplock files (S)**

This parameter is only valid when the "**oplocks**" parameter is turned on for a share. It allows the Samba administrator to selectively turn off the granting of oplocks on selected files that match a wildcarded list, similar to the wildcarded list used in the "**veto files**" parameter.

Default: `No files are vetoed for oplock grants.`

Examples:

You might want to do this on files that you know will be heavily contended for by clients. A good example of this is in the NetBench SMB benchmark program, which causes heavy client contention for files ending in `".SEM"`. To cause Samba not to grant oplocks on these files you would use the line (either in the **[global]** section or in the section for the particular NetBench share:

```
veto oplock files = /*.SEM/
```

- **volume (S)**

This allows you to override the volume label returned for a share. Useful for CDROMs with installation programs that insist on a particular volume label.

The default is the name of the share.

- **wide links (S)**

This parameter controls whether or not links in the UNIX file system may be followed by the server. Links that point to areas within the directory tree exported by the server are always allowed; this parameter controls access only to areas that are outside the directory tree being exported.

Default: `wide links = yes`

Example: `wide links = no`

- **wins proxy (G)**

This is a boolean that controls if **nmbd** will respond to broadcast name queries on behalf of other hosts. You may need to set this to `"yes"` for some older clients.

Default: `wins proxy = no`

- **wins server (G)**

This specifies the IP address (or DNS name: IP address for preference) of the WINS server that **nmbd** should register with. If you have a WINS server on your network then you should set this to the WINS server's IP.

You should point this at your WINS server if you have a multi-subnetted network.

NOTE. You need to set up Samba to point to a WINS server if you have multiple subnets and wish cross-subnet browsing to work correctly.

See the documentation file BROWSING.txt in the docs/ directory of your Samba source distribution.

Default: `wins server =`

Example: `wins server = 192.9.200.1`

- **wins support (G)**

This boolean controls if the **nmbd** process in Samba will act as a WINS server. You should not set this to true unless you have a multi-subnetted network and you wish a particular **nmbd** to be your WINS server. Note that you should **NEVER** set this to true on more than one machine in your network.

Default: `wins support = no`

- **workgroup (G)**

This controls what workgroup your server will appear to be in when queried by clients. Note that this parameter also controls the Domain name used with the **"security=domain"** setting.

Default: `set at compile time to WORKGROUP`

Example: workgroup = MYGROUP

- **writable (S)**

Synonym for **"writeable"** for people who can't spell :-). Pronounced "ritter-bull".

- **write list (S)**

This is a list of users that are given read-write access to a service. If the connecting user is in this list then they will be given write access, no matter what the **"read only"** option is set to. The list can include group names using the @group syntax.

Note that if a user is in both the read list and the write list then they will be given write access.

See also the **"read list"** option.

Default: `write list = <empty string>`

Example: `write list = admin, root, @staff`

- **write ok (S)**

Synonym for **writeable**.

- **write raw (G)**

This parameter controls whether or not the server will support raw writes SMB's when transferring data from clients. You should never need to change this parameter.

Default: `write raw = yes`

- **writeable**

An inverted synonym is **"read only"**.

If this parameter is `"no"`, then users of a service may not create or modify files in the service's directory.

Note that a printable service **("printable = yes")** will **ALWAYS** allow writing to the directory (user privileges permitting), but only via spooling operations.

Default: `writeable = no`

Examples:

```
read only = no
writeable = yes
write ok = yes
```

WARNINGS

Although the configuration file permits service names to contain spaces, your client software may not. Spaces will be ignored in comparisons anyway, so it shouldn't be a problem—but be aware of the possibility.

On a similar note, many clients—especially DOS clients—limit service names to eight characters. **Smbd** has no such limitation, but attempts to connect from such clients will fail if they truncate the service names. For this reason you should probably keep your service names down to eight characters in length.

Use of the **[homes]** and **[printers]** special sections make life for an administrator easy, but the various combinations of default attributes can be tricky. Take extreme care when designing these sections. In particular, ensure that the permissions on spool directories are correct.

VERSION

This man page is correct for version 2.0 of the Samba suite.

SEE ALSO

smbd (8), **smbclient (1)**, **nmbd (8)**, **testparm (1)**, **testprns (1)**, **Samba**, **nmblookup (1)**, **smbpasswd (5)**, **smbpasswd (8)**.

AUTHOR

The original Samba software and related utilities were created by Andrew Tridgell *samba-bugs@samba.org*. Samba is now developed by the Samba Team as an Open Source project similar to the way the Linux kernel is developed.

The original Samba man pages were written by Karl Auer. The man page sources were converted to YODL format (another excellent piece of Open Source software, available at **ftp://ftp.icce.rug.nl/pub/unix/**) and updated for the Samba2.0 release by Jeremy Allison. *samba-bugs@amba.org*.

See **samba (7)** to find out how to get a full list of contributors and details on how to submit bug reports, comments etc.

APPENDIX E.5 SMBCLIENT(1)

SMBCLIENT (1)

SAMBA

23 OCT 1998

NAME

SMBCLIENT—FTP-LIKE CLIENT TO ACCESS SMB/CIFS RESOURCES ON SERVERS

SYNOPSIS

smbclient servicename [password] [-s smb.conf] [-B IP addr] [-O socket options][-R name resolve order] [-M NetBIOS name] [-i scope] [-N] [-n NetBIOS name] [-d debuglevel] [-P] [-p port] [-l log basename] [-h] [-I dest IP] [-E] [-U username] [-L NetBIOS name] [-t terminal code] [-m max protocol] [-W workgroup] [-T<c|x>IXFqgbNan] [-D directory] [-c command string]

DESCRIPTION

This program is part of the **Samba** suite.

smbclient is a client that can 'talk' to an SMB/CIFS server. It offers an interface similar to that of the ftp program (see **ftp (1)**). Operations include things like getting files from the server to the local machine, putting files from the local machine to the server, retrieving directory information from the server and so on.

OPTIONS

- **servicename** servicename is the name of the service you want to use on the server. A service name takes the form `//server/service` where *server* is the NetBIOS name of the SMB/CIFS server offering the desired service and *service* is the name of the service offered. Thus to connect to the service *printer* on the SMB/CIFS server *smbserver*, you would use the servicename

```
//smbserver/printer
```

Note that the server name required is NOT necessarily the IP (DNS) host name of the server! The name required is a NetBIOS server name, which may or may not be the same as the IP hostname of the machine running the server.

The server name is looked up according to either the **-R** parameter to **smbclient** or using the **name resolve order** parameter in the smb.conf file, allowing an administrator to change the order and methods by which server names are looked up.

- **password** password is the password required to access the specified service on the specified server. If this parameter is supplied, the **-N** option (suppress password prompt) is assumed.

There is no default password. If no password is supplied on the command line (either by using this parameter or adding a password to the **-U** option (see below)) and the **-N** option is not specified, the client will prompt for a password, even if the desired service does not require one. (If no password is required, simply press ENTER to provide a null password.)

Note: Some servers (including OS/2 and Windows for Workgroups) insist on an uppercase password. Lowercase or mixed case passwords may be rejected by these servers.

Be cautious about including passwords in scripts.

- **-s smb.conf** This parameter specifies the pathname to the Samba configuration file, smb.conf. This file controls all aspects of the Samba setup on the machine and smbclient also needs to read this file.
- **-B IP addr** The IP address to use when sending a broadcast packet.
- **-O socket options** TCP socket options to set on the client socket. See the socket options parameter in the **smb.conf (5)** manpage for the list of valid options.
- **-R name resolve order** This option allows the user of smbclient to determine what name resolution services to use when looking up the NetBIOS name of the host being connected to.

The options are :"lmhosts", "host", "wins" and "bcast". They cause names to be resolved as follows:

- **lmhosts**: Lookup an IP address in the Samba lmhosts file. The lmhosts file is stored in the same directory as the **smb.conf** file.
- **host**: Do a standard host name to IP address resolution, using the system /etc/hosts, NIS, or DNS lookups. This method of name resolution is operating system depended for instance on IRIX or Solaris this may be controlled by the */etc/nsswitch.conf* file).
- **wins**: Query a name with the IP address listed in the **wins server** parameter in the smb.conf file. If no WINS server has been specified this method will be ignored.
- **bcast**: Do a broadcast on each of the known local interfaces listed in the **interfaces** parameter in the smb.conf file. This is the least reliable of the name resolution methods as it depends on the target host being on a locally connected subnet. To specify a particular broadcast address the **-B** option may be used.

If this parameter is not set then the name resolve order defined in the **smb.conf** file parameter (**name resolve order**) will be used.

The default order is lmhosts, host, wins, bcast and without this parameter or any entry in the **"name resolve order"** parameter of the **smb.conf** file the name resolution methods will be attempted in this order.

- **-M NetBIOS name** This options allows you to send messages, using the "WinPopup" protocol, to another computer. Once a connection is established you then type your message, pressing ^D (control-D) to end.

If the receiving computer is running WinPopup the user will receive the message and probably a beep. If they are not running WinPopup the message will be lost, and no error message will occur.

The message is also automatically truncated if the message is over 1600 bytes, as this is the limit of the protocol.

One useful trick is to cat the message through **smbclient**. For example:

```
cat mymessage.txt | smbclient -M FRED
```

will send the message in the file *mymessage.txt* to the machine FRED.

You may also find the **-U** and **-I** options useful, as they allow you to control the FROM and TO parts of the message.

See the **message command** parameter in the **smb.conf (5)** for a description of how to handle incoming WinPopup messages in Samba.

Note: Copy WinPopup into the startup group on your WfWg PCs if you want them to always be able to receive messages.

- **-i scope** This specifies a NetBIOS scope that smbclient will use to communicate with when generating NetBIOS names. For details on the use of NetBIOS scopes, see rfc1001.txt and rfc1002.txt. NetBIOS scopes are *very* rarely used, only set this parameter if you are the system administrator in charge of all the NetBIOS systems you communicate with.
- **-N** If specified, this parameter suppresses the normal password prompt from the client to the user. This is useful when accessing a service that does not require a password.

Unless a password is specified on the command line or this parameter is specified, the client will request a password.

- **-n NetBIOS name** By default, the client will use the local machine's hostname (in uppercase) as its NetBIOS name. This parameter allows you to override the host name and use whatever NetBIOS name you wish.
- **-d debuglevel** debuglevel is an integer from 0 to 10, or the letter 'A'.

The default value if this parameter is not specified is zero.

The higher this value, the more detail will be logged to the log files about the activities of the client. At level 0, only critical errors and serious warnings will be logged. Level 1 is a reasonable level for day to day running—it generates a small amount of information about operations carried out.

Levels above 1 will generate considerable amounts of log data, and should only be used when investigating a problem. Levels above 3 are designed for use only by developers and generate HUGE amounts of log data, most of which is extremely cryptic. If debuglevel is set to the letter

'A', then *all* debug messages will be printed. This setting is for developers only (and people who *really* want to know how the code works internally).

Note that specifying this parameter here will override the **log level** parameter in the **smb.conf (5)** file.

- **-P** This option is no longer used. The code in Samba2.0 now lets the server decide the device type, so no printer specific flag is needed.
- **-p port** This number is the TCP port number that will be used when making connections to the server. The standard (well-known) TCP port number for an SMB/CIFS server is 139, which is the default.
- **-l logfilename** If specified, logfilename specifies a base filename into which operational data from the running client will be logged.

The default base name is specified at compile time.

The base name is used to generate actual log file names. For example, if the name specified was "log", the debug file would be `log.client`.

The log file generated is never removed by the client.

- **-h** Print the usage message for the client.
- **-I IP address** IP address is the address of the server to connect to. It should be specified in standard "a.b.c.d" notation.

Normally the client would attempt to locate a named SMB/CIFS server by looking it up via the NetBIOS name resolution mechanism described above in the **name resolve order** parameter above. Using this parameter will force the client to assume that the server is on the machine with the specified IP address and the NetBIOS name component of the resource being connected to will be ignored.

There is no default for this parameter. If not supplied, it will be determined automatically by the client as described above.

- **-E** This parameter causes the client to write messages to the standard error stream (stderr) rather than to the standard output stream.

By default, the client writes messages to standard output—typically the user's tty.

- **-U username** This specifies the user name that will be used by the client to make a connection, assuming your server is not a downlevel server that is running a protocol level that uses passwords on shares, not on usernames.

Some servers are fussy about the case of this name, and some insist that it must be a valid NetBIOS name.

If no username is supplied, it will default to an uppercase version of the environment variable `USER` or `LOGNAME` in that order. If no username is supplied and neither environment variable exists the username "GUEST" will be used.

If the `USER` environment variable contains a '%' character, everything after that will be treated as a password. This allows you to set the environment variable to be `USER=username%password` so that a password is not passed on the command line (where it may be seen by the ps command).

If the service you are connecting to requires a password, it can be supplied using the **-U** option, by appending a percent symbol ("%") then the password to username. For example, to attach to a service as user `"fred"` with password `"secret"`, you would specify.

```
-U fred%secret
```

on the command line. Note that there are no spaces around the percent symbol.

If you specify the password as part of username then the **-N** option (suppress password prompt) is assumed.

If you specify the password as a parameter *AND* as part of username then the password as part of username will take precedence. Putting nothing before or nothing after the percent symbol will cause an empty username or an empty password to be used, respectively.

The password may also be specified by setting up an environment variable called `PASSWORD` that contains the users password. Note that this may be very insecure on some systems but on others allows users to script smbclient commands without having a password appear in the command line of a process listing.

Note: Some servers (including OS/2 and Windows for Workgroups) insist on an uppercase password. Lowercase or mixed case passwords may be rejected by these servers.

Be cautious about including passwords in scripts or in the `PASSWORD` environment variable. Also, on many systems the command line of a running process may be seen via the `ps` command to be safe always allow smbclient to prompt for a password and type it in directly.

- **-L** This option allows you to look at what services are available on a server. You use it as `"smbclient -L host"` and a list should appear. The **-I** option may be useful if your NetBIOS names don't match your tcp/ip dns host names or if you are trying to reach a host on another network.
- **-t terminal code** This option tells smbclient how to interpret filenames coming from the remote server. Usually Asian language multibyte UNIX implementations use different character sets than SMB/CIFS servers (*EUC* instead of *SJIS* for example). Setting this parameter will let smbclient convert between the UNIX filenames and the SMB filenames correctly. This option has not been seriously tested and may have some problems.

The terminal codes include `sjis`, `euc`, `jis7`, `jis8`, `junet`, `hex`, `cap`. This is not a complete list, check the Samba source code for the complete list.

- **-m max protocol level** With the new code in Samba2.0, **smbclient** always attempts to connect at the maximum protocols level the server supports. This parameter is preserved for backwards compatibility, but any string following the **-m** will be ignored.
- **-W WORKGROUP** Override the default workgroup specified in the **workgroup** parameter of the **smb.conf** file for this connection. This may be needed to connect to some servers.
- **-T tar options** smbclient may be used to create **tar (1)** compatible backups of all the files on an SMB/CIFS share. The secondary tar flags that can be given to this option are :
- **c** Create a tar file on UNIX. Must be followed by the name of a tar file, tape device or `"-"` for standard output. If using standard output you must turn the log level to its lowest value `-d0` to avoid corrupting your tar file. This flag is mutually exclusive with the **x** flag.
- **x** Extract (restore) a local tar file back to a share. Unless the **-D** option is given, the tar files will be restored from the top level

of the share. Must be followed by the name of the tar file, device or "-" for standard input. Mutually exclusive with the **c** flag. Restored files have their creation times (mtime) set to the date saved in the tar file. Directories currently do not get their creation dates restored properly.

- **I** Include files and directories. Is the default behavior when filenames are specified above. Causes tar files to be included in an extract or create (and therefore everything else to be excluded). See example below. Filename globbing works in one of two ways. See **r** below.
- **X** Exclude files and directories. Causes tar files to be excluded from an extract or create. See example below. Filename globbing works in one of two ways now. See **r** below.
- **b** Blocksize. Must be followed by a valid (greater than zero) blocksize. Causes tar file to be written out in blocksize*TBLOCK (usually 512 byte) blocks.
- **g** Incremental. Only back up files that have the archive bit set. Useful only with the **c** flag.
- **q** Quiet. Keeps tar from printing diagnostics as it works. This is the same as tarmode quiet.
- **r** Regular expression include or exclude. Uses regular regular expression matching for excluding or excluding files if compiled with HAVE_REGEX_H. However this mode can be very slow. If not compiled with HAVE_REGEX_H, does a limited wildcard match on * and ?.
- **N** Newer than. Must be followed by the name of a file whose date is compared against files found on the share during a create. Only files newer than the file specified are backed up to the tar file. Useful only with the **c** flag.
- **a** Set archive bit. Causes the archive bit to be reset when a file is backed up. Useful with the **g** and **c** flags.

Tar Long File Names

smbclient's tar option now supports long file names both on backup and restore. However, the full path name of the file must be less than 1024 bytes. Also, when a tar archive is created, smbclient's tar option places all files in the archive with relative names, not absolute names.

Tar Filenames

All file names can be given as DOS path names (with \ as the component separator) or as UNIX path names (with / as the component separator).

Examples

- Restore from tar file backup.tar into myshare on mypc (no password on share).

  smbclient //mypc/myshare "" -N -Tx backup.tar

- Restore everything except users/docs

  smbclient //mypc/myshare "" -N -TXx backup.tar users/docs

- Create a tar file of the files beneath users/docs.

  smbclient //mypc/myshare "" -N -Tc backup.tar users/docs

- Create the same tar file as above, but now use a DOS path name.

  smbclient //mypc/myshare "" -N -tc backup.tar users\edocs

- Create a tar file of all the files and directories in the share.

  smbclient //mypc/myshare "" -N -Tc backup.tar *

- **-D initial directory** Change to initial directory before starting. Probably only of any use with the tar **-T** option.
- **-c command string** command string is a semicolon separated list of commands to be executed instead of prompting from stdin. **-N** is implied by **-c**.

This is particularly useful in scripts and for printing stdin to the server, e.g. `-c 'print -'`.

OPERATIONS

Once the client is running, the user is presented with a prompt :

smb:\>

The backslash ("\") indicates the current working directory on the server, and will change if the current working directory is changed.

The prompt indicates that the client is ready and waiting to carry out a user command. Each command is a single word, optionally followed by parameters specific to that command. Command and parameters are space-delimited unless these notes specifically state otherwise. All commands are case-insensitive. Parameters to commands may or may not be case sensitive, depending on the command.

You can specify file names which have spaces in them by quoting the name with double quotes, for example "a long file name".

Parameters shown in square brackets (e.g., "[parameter]") are optional. If not given, the command will use suitable defaults. Parameters shown in angle brackets (e.g., "<parameter>") are required.

Note that all commands operating on the server are actually performed by issuing a request to the server. Thus the behavior may vary from server to server, depending on how the server was implemented.

THE COMMANDS AVAILABLE ARE GIVEN HERE IN ALPHABETICAL ORDER.

- **? [command]** If "command" is specified, the **?** command will display a brief informative message about the specified command. If no command is specified, a list of available commands will be displayed.
- **! [shell command]** If "shell command" is specified, the **!** command will execute a shell locally and run the specified shell command. If no command is specified, a local shell will be run.
- **cd [directory name]** If "directory name" is specified, the current working directory on the server will be changed to the directory specified. This operation will fail if for any reason the specified directory is inaccessible.

If no directory name is specified, the current working directory on the server will be reported.

- **del <mask>** The client will request that the server attempt to delete all files matching "mask" from the current working directory on the server.
- **dir <mask>** A list of the files matching "mask" in the current working directory on the server will be retrieved from the server and displayed.

- **exit** Terminate the connection with the server and exit from the program.
- **get <remote file name> [local file name]** Copy the file called "remote file name" from the server to the machine running the client. If specified, name the local copy "local file name". Note that all transfers in smbclient are binary. See also the **lowercase** command.
- **help [command]** See the **?** command above.
- **lcd [directory name]** If "directory name" is specified, the current working directory on the local machine will be changed to the directory specified. This operation will fail if for any reason the specified directory is inaccessible.

If no directory name is specified, the name of the current working directory on the local machine will be reported.

- **lowercase** Toggle lowercasing of filenames for the **get** and **mget** commands.

When lowercasing is toggled ON, local filenames are converted to lowercase when using the **get** and **mget** commands. This is often useful when copying (say) MSDOS files from a server, because lowercase filenames are the norm on UNIX systems.

- **ls <mask>** See the **dir** command above.
- **mask <mask>** This command allows the user to set up a mask which will be used during recursive operation of the **mget** and **mput** commands.

The masks specified to the **mget** and **mput** commands act as filters for directories rather than files when recursion is toggled ON.

The mask specified with the .B mask command is necessary to filter files within those directories. For example, if the mask specified in an **mget** command is "source*" and the mask specified with the mask command is "*.c" and recursion is toggled ON, the **mget** command will retrieve all files matching "*.c" in all directories below and including all directories matching "source*" in the current working directory.

Note that the value for mask defaults to blank (equivalent to "*") and remains so until the mask command is used to change it. It retains the most recently specified value indefinitely. To avoid unexpected results it would be wise to change the value of .I mask back to "*" after using the **mget** or **mput** commands.

- **md <directory name>** See the **mkdir** command.
- **mget <mask>** Copy all files matching mask from the server to the machine running the client.

Note that mask is interpreted differently during recursive operation and non-recursive operation—refer to the **recurse** and **mask** commands for more information. Note that all transfers in .B smbclient are binary. See also the **lowercase** command.

- **mkdir <directory name>** Create a new directory on the server (user access privileges permitting) with the specified name.
- **mput <mask>** Copy all files matching mask in the current working directory on the local machine to the current working directory on the server.

Note that mask is interpreted differently during recursive operation and non-recursive operation—refer to the **recurse** and **mask** commands for more information. Note that all transfers in .B smbclient are binary.

- **print <file name>** Print the specified file from the local machine through a printable service on the server.

See also the **printmode** command.

- **printmode <graphics or text>** Set the print mode to suit either binary data (such as graphical information) or text. Subsequent print commands will use the currently set print mode.
- **prompt** Toggle prompting for filenames during operation of the **mget** and **mput** commands.

When toggled ON, the user will be prompted to confirm the transfer of each file during these commands. When toggled OFF, all specified files will be transferred without prompting.

- **put <local file name> [remote file name]** Copy the file called "local file name" from the machine running the client to the server. If specified, name the remote copy "remote file name". Note that all transfers in smbclient are binary. See also the **lowercase** command.
- **queue** Displays the print queue, showing the job id, name, size and current status.
- **quit** See the **exit** command.

- **rd <directory name>** See the **rmdir** command.
- **recurse** Toggle directory recursion for the commands **mget** and **mput**.

When toggled ON, these commands will process all directories in the source directory (i.e., the directory they are copying .IR from) and will recurse into any that match the mask specified to the command. Only files that match the mask specified using the **mask** command will be retrieved. See also the **mask** command.

When recursion is toggled OFF, only files from the current working directory on the source machine that match the mask specified to the **mget** or **mput** commands will be copied, and any mask specified using the **mask** command will be ignored.

- **rm <mask>** Remove all files matching mask from the current working directory on the server.
- **rmdir <directory name>** Remove the specified directory (user access privileges permitting) from the server.
- **tar <c|x>[IXbgNa]** Performs a tar operation—see the **-T** command line option above. Behavior may be affected by the **tarmode** command (see below). Using g (incremental) and N (newer) will affect tarmode settings. Note that using the "-" option with tar x may not work—use the command line option instead.
- **blocksize <blocksize>** Blocksize. Must be followed by a valid (greater than zero) blocksize. Causes tar file to be written out in blocksize*TBLOCK (usually 512 byte) blocks.
- **tarmode <full|inc|reset|noreset>** Changes tar's behavior with regard to archive bits. In full mode, tar will back up everything regardless of the archive bit setting (this is the default mode). In incremental mode, tar will only back up files with the archive bit set. In reset mode, tar will reset the archive bit on all files it backs up (implies read/write share).
- **setmode <filename> <perm=[+|\-]rsha>** A version of the DOS attrib command to set file permissions. For example:

  ```
  setmode myfile +r
  ```

  would make myfile read only.

NOTES

Some servers are fussy about the case of supplied usernames, passwords, share names (AKA service names) and machine names. If you fail to connect try giving all parameters in uppercase.

It is often necessary to use the **-n** option when connecting to some types of servers. For example OS/2 LanManager insists on a valid NetBIOS name being used, so you need to supply a valid name that would be known to the server.

smbclient supports long file names where the server supports the LANMAN2 protocol or above.

ENVIRONMENT VARIABLES

The variable **USER** may contain the username of the person using the client. This information is used only if the protocol level is high enough to support session-level passwords.

The variable **PASSWORD** may contain the password of the person using the client. This information is used only if the protocol level is high enough to support session-level passwords.

INSTALLATION

The location of the client program is a matter for individual system administrators. The following are thus suggestions only.

It is recommended that the smbclient software be installed in the /usr/local/samba/bin or /usr/samba/bin directory, this directory readable by all, writeable only by root. The client program itself should be executable by all. The client should *NOT* be setuid or setgid!

The client log files should be put in a directory readable and writeable only by the user.

To test the client, you will need to know the name of a running SMB/CIFS server. It is possible to run **smbd (8)** an ordinary user—running that server as a daemon on a user-accessible port (typically any port number over 1024) would provide a suitable test server.

DIAGNOSTICS

Most diagnostics issued by the client are logged in a specified log file. The log file name is specified at compile time, but may be overridden on the command line.

The number and nature of diagnostics available depends on the debug level used by the client. If you have problems, set the debug level to 3 and peruse the log files.

VERSION

This man page is correct for version 2.0 of the Samba suite.

AUTHOR

The original Samba software and related utilities were created by Andrew Tridgell *samba-bugs@samba.org*. Samba is now developed by the Samba Team as an Open Source project similar to the way the Linux kernel is developed.

The original Samba man pages were written by Karl Auer. The man page sources were converted to YODL format (another excellent piece of Open Source software, available at **ftp://ftp.icce.rug.nl/pub/unix/**) and updated for the Samba2.0 release by Jeremy Allison. *samba-bugs@samba.org*.

See **samba (7)** to find out how to get a full list of contributors and details on how to submit bug reports, comments etc.

APPENDIX E.6 SMBD(8)

SMBD (8)

SAMBA

23 OCT 1998

NAME

SMBD—SERVER TO PROVIDE SMB/CIFS SERVICES TO CLIENTS

SYNOPSIS

smbd [-D] [-a] [-o] [-d debuglevel] [-l log file] [-p port number] [-O socket options] [-s configuration file] [-i scope] [-P] [-h]

DESCRIPTION

This program is part of the **Samba** suite.

smbd is the server daemon that provides filesharing and printing services to Windows clients. The server provides filespace and printer services to clients using the SMB (or CIFS) protocol. This is compatible with the LanManager protocol, and can service LanManager clients. These include MSCLIENT 3.0 for DOS, Windows for Workgroups, Windows 95, Windows NT, OS/2, DAVE for Macintosh, and smbfs for Linux.

An extensive description of the services that the server can provide is given in the man page for the configuration file controlling the attributes of those services (see **smb.conf (5)**. This man page will not describe the services, but will concentrate on the administrative aspects of running the server.

Please note that there are significant security implications to running this server, and the **smb.conf (5)** manpage should be regarded as mandatory reading before proceeding with installation.

A session is created whenever a client requests one. Each client gets a copy of the server for each session. This copy then services all connections made by the client during that session. When all connections from its client are closed, the copy of the server for that client terminates.

The configuration file, and any files that it includes, are automatically reloaded every minute, if they change. You can force a reload by sending a SIGHUP to the server. Reloading the configuration file will not affect connections to any service that is already established. Either the user will have to disconnect from the service, or smbd killed and restarted.

OPTIONS

- **-D** If specified, this parameter causes the server to operate as a daemon. That is, it detaches itself and runs in the background, fielding requests on the appropriate port. Operating the server as a daemon is the recommended way of running smbd for servers that provide more than casual use file and print services.

By default, the server will NOT operate as a daemon.

- **-a** If this parameter is specified, each new connection will append log messages to the log file. This is the default.
- **-o** If this parameter is specified, the log files will be overwritten when opened. By default, the log files will be appended to.
- **-d debuglevel** debuglevel is an integer from 0 to 10.

The default value if this parameter is not specified is zero.

The higher this value, the more detail will be logged to the log files about the activities of the server. At level 0, only critical errors and serious warnings will be logged. Level 1 is a reasonable level for day to day running—it generates a small amount of information about operations carried out.

Levels above 1 will generate considerable amounts of log data, and should only be used when investigating a problem. Levels above 3 are designed for use only by developers and generate HUGE amounts of log data, most of which is extremely cryptic.

Note that specifying this parameter here will override the **log level** parameter in the **smb.conf (5)** file.

- **-l log file** If specified, *log file* specifies a log filename into which informational and debug messages from the running server will be logged. The log file generated is never removed by the server although its size may be controlled by the **max log size** option in the **smb.conf (5)** file. The default log file name is specified at compile time.
- **-O socket options** See the **socket options** parameter in the **smb.conf (5)** file for details.
- **-p port number** port number is a positive integer value. The default value if this parameter is not specified is 139.

This number is the port number that will be used when making connections to the server from client software. The standard (well-known) port number for the SMB over TCP is 139, hence the default. If you wish to run the server as an ordinary user rather than as root, most systems will require you to use a port number greater than 1024—ask your system administrator for help if you are in this situation.

In order for the server to be useful by most clients, should you configure it on a port other than 139, you will require port redirection services on port 139, details of which are outlined in rfc1002.txt section 4.3.5.

This parameter is not normally specified except in the above situation.

- **-s configuration file** The file specified contains the configuration details required by the server. The information in this file includes server-specific information such as what printcap file to use, as well as descriptions of all the services that the server is to provide. See **smb.conf (5)** for more information. The default configuration file name is determined at compile time.
- **-i scope** This specifies a NetBIOS scope that the server will use to communicate with when generating NetBIOS names. For details on the use of NetBIOS scopes, see rfc1001.txt and rfc1002.txt. NetBIOS scopes are *very* rarely used, only set this parameter if you are the system administrator in charge of all the NetBIOS systems you communicate with.
- **-h** Prints the help information (usage) for smbd.
- **-P** Passive option. Causes smbd not to send any network traffic out. Used for debugging by the developers only.

FILES

/ETC/INETD.CONF

If the server is to be run by the inetd meta-daemon, this file must contain suitable startup information for the meta-daemon. See the section INSTALLATION below.

/ETC/RC

(or whatever initialization script your system uses).

If running the server as a daemon at startup, this file will need to contain an appropriate startup sequence for the server. See the section INSTALLATION below.

/ETC/SERVICES

If running the server via the meta-daemon inetd, this file must contain a mapping of service name (e.g., netbios-ssn) to service port (e.g., 139) and protocol type (e.g., tcp). See the section INSTALLATION below.

/USR/LOCAL/SAMBA/LIB/SMB.CONF

This is the default location of the *smb.conf* server configuration file. Other common places that systems install this file are */usr/samba/lib/smb.conf* and */etc/smb.conf*.

This file describes all the services the server is to make available to clients. See **smb.conf (5)** for more information.

LIMITATIONS

On some systems **smbd** cannot change uid back to root after a setuid() call. Such systems are called "trapdoor" uid systems. If you have such a system, you will be unable to connect from a client (such as a PC) as two different users at once. Attempts to connect the second user will result in "access denied" or similar.

ENVIRONMENT VARIABLES

PRINTER

If no printer name is specified to printable services, most systems will use the value of this variable (or "lp" if this variable is not defined) as the name of the printer to use. This is not specific to the server, however.

INSTALLATION

The location of the server and its support files is a matter for individual system administrators. The following are thus suggestions only.

It is recommended that the server software be installed under the /usr/local/samba hierarchy, in a directory readable by all, writeable only by root. The server program itself should be executable by all, as users may wish to run the server themselves (in which case it will of course run with their privileges). The server should NOT be setuid. On some systems it may be worthwhile to make smbd setgid to an empty group. This is because some systems may have a security hole where daemon processes that become a user can be attached to with a debugger. Making the smbd file setgid to an empty group may prevent this hole from being exploited. This security hole and the suggested fix has only been confirmed on old versions (pre-kernel 2.0) of Linux at the time this was written. It is possible that this hole only exists in Linux, as testing on other systems has thus far shown them to be immune.

The server log files should be put in a directory readable and writeable only by root, as the log files may contain sensitive information.

The configuration file should be placed in a directory readable and writeable only by root, as the configuration file controls security for the services offered by the server. The configuration file can be made readable by all if desired, but this is not necessary for correct operation of the server and is not recommended. A sample configuration file "smb. conf.sample" is supplied with the source to the server—this may be renamed to "smb.conf" and modified to suit your needs.

The remaining notes will assume the following:

- **smbd** (the server program) installed in /usr/local/samba/bin
- **smb.conf** (the configuration file) installed in /usr/local/samba/lib
- log files stored in /var/adm/smblogs

The server may be run either as a daemon by users or at startup, or it may be run from a meta-daemon such as inetd upon request. If run as a daemon, the server will always be ready, so starting sessions will be faster. If run from a meta-daemon some memory will be saved and utilities such as the tcpd TCP-wrapper may be used for extra security. For serious use as file server it is recommended that **smbd** be run as a daemon.

When you've decided, continue with either RUNNING THE SERVER AS A DAEMON or RUNNING THE SERVER ON REQUEST.

RUNNING THE SERVER AS A DAEMON

To run the server as a daemon from the command line, simply put the **-D** option on the command line. There is no need to place an ampersand at the end of the command line—the **-D** option causes the server to detach itself from the tty anyway.

Any user can run the server as a daemon (execute permissions permitting, of course). This is useful for testing purposes, and may even be useful as a temporary substitute for something like ftp. When run this way, however, the server will only have the privileges of the user who ran it.

To ensure that the server is run as a daemon whenever the machine is started, and to ensure that it runs as root so that it can serve multiple clients, you will need to modify the system startup files. Wherever appropriate (for example, in /etc/rc), insert the following line, substituting port number, log file location, configuration file location and debug level as desired:

/usr/local/samba/bin/smbd -D -L /VAR/ADM/SMBLOGS/LOG -S /USR/LOCAL/SAMBA/LIB/SMB.CONF

(The above should appear in your initialization script as a single line. Depending on your terminal characteristics, it may not appear that way in this man page. If the above appears as more than one line, please treat any newlines or indentation as a single space or TAB character.)

If the options used at compile time are appropriate for your system, all parameters except **-D** may be omitted. See the section OPTIONS above.

RUNNING THE SERVER ON REQUEST

If your system uses a meta-daemon such as **inetd**, you can arrange to have the smbd server started whenever a process attempts to connect to it. This requires several changes to the startup files on the host machine. If you are experimenting as an ordinary user rather than as root, you will need the assistance of your system administrator to modify the system files.

You will probably want to set up the NetBIOS name server **nmbd** at the same time as **smbd**. To do this refer to the man page for **nmbd (8)**.

First, ensure that a port is configured in the file `/etc/services`. The well-known port 139 should be used if possible, though any port may be used.

Ensure that a line similar to the following is in `/etc/services`:

```
netbios-ssn 139/tcp
```

Note for NIS/YP users—you may need to rebuild the NIS service maps rather than alter your local `/etc/services file`.

Next, put a suitable line in the file `/etc/inetd.conf` (in the unlikely event that you are using a meta-daemon other than inetd, you are on your own). Note that the first item in this line matches the service name in `/etc/services`. Substitute appropriate values for your system in this line (see **inetd (8)**):

```
netbios-ssn stream tcp nowait root
/usr/local/samba/bin/smbd -d1 -l/var/adm/smblogs/log
-s/usr/local/samba/lib/smb.conf
```

(The above should appear in `/etc/inetd.conf` as a single line. Depending on your terminal characteristics, it may not appear that way in this man page. If the above appears as more than one line, please treat any newlines or indentation as a single space or TAB character.)

Note that there is no need to specify a port number here, even if you are using a non-standard port number.

Lastly, edit the configuration file to provide suitable services. To start with, the following two services should be all you need:

```
[homes]
  writeable = yes
[printers]
 writeable = no
 printable = yes
 path = /tmp
 public = yes
```

This will allow you to connect to your home directory and print to any printer supported by the host (user privileges permitting).

TESTING THE INSTALLATION

If running the server as a daemon, execute it before proceeding. If using a meta-daemon, either restart the system or kill and restart the meta-daemon. Some versions of inetd will reread their configuration tables if they receive a HUP signal.

If your machine's name is "fred" and your name is "mary", you should now be able to connect to the service `\\fred\mary`.

To properly test and experiment with the server, we recommend using the smbclient program (see **smbclient (1)**) and also going through the steps outlined in the file *DIAGNOSIS.txt* in the *docs/* directory of your Samba installation.

VERSION

This man page is correct for version 2.0 of the Samba suite.

DIAGNOSTICS

Most diagnostics issued by the server are logged in a specified log file. The log file name is specified at compile time, but may be overridden on the command line.

The number and nature of diagnostics available depends on the debug level used by the server. If you have problems, set the debug level to 3 and peruse the log files.

Most messages are reasonably self-explanatory. Unfortunately, at the time this man page was created, there are too many diagnostics available in the source code to warrant describing each and every diagnostic. At this stage your best bet is still to grep the source code and inspect the conditions that gave rise to the diagnostics you are seeing.

SIGNALS

Sending the smbd a SIGHUP will cause it to re-load its smb.conf configuration file within a short period of time.

To shut down a users smbd process it is recommended that SIGKILL (-9) *NOT* be used, except as a last resort, as this may leave the shared memory area in an inconsistent state. The safe way to terminate an smbd is to send it a SIGTERM (-15) signal and wait for it to die on its own.

The debug log level of smbd may be raised by sending it a SIGUSR1 `(kill -USR1 <smbd-pid>)` and lowered by sending it a SIGUSR2 `(kill -USR2 <smbd-pid>)`. This is to allow transient problems to be diagnosed, whilst still running at a normally low log level.

Note that as the signal handlers send a debug write, they are not re-entrant in smbd. This you should wait until smbd is in a state of waiting for an incoming smb before issuing them. It is possible to make the signal handlers safe by un-blocking the signals before the select call and re-blocking them after, however this would affect performance.

SEE ALSO

hosts_access (5), **inetd (8)**, **nmbd (8)**, **smb.conf (5)**, **smbclient (1)**, **testparm (1)**, **testprns (1)**, and the Internet RFC's **rfc1001.txt**, **rfc1002.txt**. In addition the CIFS (formerly SMB) specification is available as a link from the Web page : http://samba.org/cifs/.

AUTHOR

The original Samba software and related utilities were created by Andrew Tridgell *samba-bugs@samba.org*. Samba is now developed by the Samba Team as an Open Source project similar to the way the Linux kernel is developed.

The original Samba man pages were written by Karl Auer. The man page sources were converted to YODL format (another excellent piece of Open Source software, available at **ftp://ftp.icce.rug.nl/pub/unix/**) and updated for the Samba2.0 release by Jeremy Allison. *samba-bugs@samba.org*.

See **samba (7)** to find out how to get a full list of contributors and details on how to submit bug reports, comments etc.

APPENDIX E.7 SMBPASSWD(5)

SMBPASSWD (5)

SAMBA

23 OCT 1998

NAME

smbpasswd—The Samba encrypted password file

SYNOPSIS

smbpasswd is the **Samba** encrypted password file.

DESCRIPTION

This file is part of the **Samba** suite.

smbpasswd is the **Samba** encrypted password file. It contains the username, Unix user id and the SMB hashed passwords of the user, as well as account flag information and the time the password was last changed. This file format has been evolving with Samba and has had several different formats in the past.

FILE FORMAT

The format of the smbpasswd file used by Samba 2.0 is very similar to the familiar Unix **passwd (5)** file. It is an ASCII file containing one line for each user. Each field within each line is separated from the next by a colon. Any entry beginning with # is ignored. The smbpasswd file contains the following information for each user:

- **name**
  This is the user name. It must be a name that already exists in the standard UNIX passwd file.
- **uid**
  This is the UNIX uid. It must match the uid field for the same user entry in the standard UNIX passwd file. If this does not match then Samba will refuse to recognize this **smbpasswd** file entry as being valid for a user.
- **Lanman Password Hash**
  This is the *LANMAN* hash of the users password, encoded as 32 hex digits. The *LANMAN* hash is created by DES encrypting a well known string with the users password as the DES key. This is the same password used by Windows 95/98 machines. Note that this password hash is regarded as weak as it is vulnerable to dictionary attacks and if two users choose the same password this entry will be identical (i.e. the password is not *"salted"* as the UNIX password is). If the user has a null password this field will contain the characters `"NO PASSWORD"` as the start of the hex string. If the hex string is equal to 32 `'X'` characters then the users account is marked as *disabled* and the user will not be able to log onto the Samba server.

WARNING !!. Note that, due to the challenge-response nature of the SMB/CIFS authentication protocol, anyone with a knowledge of this password hash will be able to impersonate the user on the network. For this reason these hashes are known as *"plain text equivalent"* and must *NOT* be made available to anyone but the root user. To protect these passwords the **smbpasswd** file is placed in a directory with read and traverse access only to the root user and the **smbpasswd** file itself must be set to be read/write only by root, with no other access.

- **NT Password Hash**
  This is the *Windows NT* hash of the users password, encoded as 32 hex digits. The *Windows NT* hash is created by taking the users password as represented in 16-bit, little-endian UNICODE and then applying the *MD4* (internet rfc1321) hashing algorithm to it.

This password hash is considered more secure than the **Lanman Password Hash** as it preserves the case of the password and uses a much higher quality hashing algorithm. However, it is still the case that if two users choose the same password this entry will be identical (i.e. the password is not *"salted"* as the UNIX password is).

WARNING !!. Note that, due to the challenge-response nature of the SMB/CIFS authentication protocol, anyone with a knowledge of this password hash will be able to impersonate the user on the network. For this reason these hashes are known as *"plain text equivalent"* and must *NOT* be made available to anyone but the root user. To protect these passwords the **smbpasswd** file is placed in a directory with read and traverse access only to the root user and the **smbpasswd** file tself must be set to be read/write only by root, with no other access.

- **Account Flags**
  This section contains flags that describe the attributes of the users account. In the **Samba2.0** release this field is bracketed by `'['` and `']'` characters and is always 13 characters in length (including the `'['` and `']'` characters). The contents of this field may be any of the characters.
- **'U'** This means this is a *"User"* account, i.e. an ordinary user. Only **User** and **Workstation Trust** accounts are currently supported in the **smbpasswd** file.
- **'N'** This means the account has *no* password (the passwords in the fields **Lanman Password Hash** and **NT Password Hash** are ignored). Note that this will only allow users to log on with no password if the **null passwords** parameter is set in the **smb.conf (5)** config file.
- **'D'** This means the account is disabled and no SMB/CIFS logins will be allowed for this user.
- **'W'** This means this account is a *"Workstation Trust"* account. This kind of account is used in the Samba PDC code stream to allow Windows NT Workstations and Servers to join a Domain hosted by a Samba PDC.

Other flags may be added as the code is extended in future. The rest of this field space is filled in with spaces.

- **Last Change Time**
  This field consists of the time the account was last modified. It consists of the characters `LCT-` (standing for *"Last Change Time"*) followed by a numeric encoding of the UNIX time in seconds since the epoch (1970) that the last change was made.
- **Following fields**
  All other colon separated fields are ignored at this time.

NOTES

In previous versions of Samba (notably the 1.9.18 series) this file did not contain the **Account Flags** or **Last Change Time** fields. The Samba 2.0

code will read and write these older password files but will not be able to modify the old entries to add the new fields. New entries added with **smbpasswd (8)** will contain the new fields in the added accounts however. Thus an older **smbpasswd** file used with Samba 2.0 may end up with some accounts containing the new fields and some not.

In order to convert from an old-style **smbpasswd** file to a new style, run the script **convert_smbpasswd**, installed in the Samba `bin/` directory (the same place that the **smbd** and **nmbd** binaries are installed) as follows:

```
cat old_smbpasswd_file | convert_smbpasswd > new_
smbpasswd_file
```

The `convert_smbpasswd` script reads from stdin and writes to stdout so as not to overwrite any files by accident.

Once this script has been run, check the contents of the new smbpasswd file to ensure that it has not been damaged by the conversion script (which uses awk), and then replace the <old smbpasswd file> with the <new smbpasswd file>.

VERSION

This man page is correct for version 2.0 of the Samba suite.

SEE ALSO

smbpasswd (8), **samba (7)**, and the Internet RFC1321 for details on the MD4 algorithm.

AUTHOR

The original Samba software and related utilities were created by Andrew Tridgell *samba-bugs@samba.org*. Samba is now developed by the Samba Team as an Open Source project similar to the way the Linux kernel is developed.

The original Samba man pages were written by Karl Auer. The man page sources were converted to YODL format (another excellent piece of Open Source software, available at **ftp://ftp.icce.rug.nl/pub/unix/**) and updated for the Samba2.0 release by Jeremy Allison, *samba-bugs@samba.org*.

See **samba (7)** to find out how to get a full list of contributors and details on how to submit bug reports, comments etc.

APPENDIX E.8 SMBPASSWD(8)

SMBPASSWD (8)

SAMBA

23 OCT 1998

NAME

smbpasswd—change a users SMB password

SYNOPSIS

smbpasswd [-a] [-d] [-e] [-D debug level] [-n] [-r remote_machine] [-R name resolve order] [-m] [-j DOMAIN] [-U username] [-h] [-s] username

DESCRIPTION

This program is part of the **Samba** suite.

The **smbpasswd** program has several different functions, depending on whether it is run by the *root* user or not. When run as a normal user it allows the user to change the password used for their SMB sessions on any machines that store SMB passwords.

By default (when run with no arguments) it will attempt to change the current users SMB password on the local machine. This is similar to the way the **passwd (1)** program works. **smbpasswd** differs from how the **passwd** program works however in that it is not *setuid root* but works in a client-server mode and communicates with a locally running **smbd**. As a consequence in order for this to succeed the **smbd** daemon must be running on the local machine. On a UNIX machine the encrypted SMB passwords are usually stored in the **smbpasswd (5)** file.

When run by an ordinary user with no options. **smbpasswd** will prompt them for their old smb password and then ask them for their new password twice, to ensure that the new password was typed correctly. No passwords will be echoed on the screen whilst being typed. If you have a blank smb password (specified by the string "NO PASSWORD" in the

smbpasswd file) then just press the <Enter> key when asked for your old password.

smbpasswd can also be used by a normal user to change their SMB password on remote machines, such as Windows NT Primary Domain Controllers. See the (**-r**) and **-U** options below.

When run by root, **smbpasswd** allows new users to be added and deleted in the **smbpasswd** file, as well as allows changes to the attributes of the user in this file to be made. When run by root, **smbpasswd** accesses the local **smbpasswd** file directly, thus enabling changes to be made even if **smbd** is not running.

OPTIONS

- **-a** This option specifies that the username following should be added to the local **smbpasswd** file, with the new password typed (type <Enter> for the old password). This option is ignored if the username following already exists in the **smbpasswd** file and it is treated like a regular change password command. Note that the user to be added **must** already exist in the system password file (usually /etc/passwd) else the request to add the user will fail.

This option is only available when running **smbpasswd** as root.

- **-d** This option specifies that the username following should be *disabled* in the local **smbpasswd** file. This is done by writing a *'D'* flag into the account control space in the **smbpasswd** file. Once this is done all attempts to authenticate via SMB using this username will fail.

If the **smbpasswd** file is in the 'old' format (pre-Samba 2.0 format) there is no space in the users password entry to write this information and so the user is disabled by writing 'X' characters into the password space in the **smbpasswd** file. See **smbpasswd (5)** for details on the 'old' and new password file formats.

This option is only available when running **smbpasswd** as root.

- **-e** This option specifies that the username following should be *enabled* in the local **smbpasswd** file, if the account was previously disabled. If the account was not disabled this option has no effect. Once the account is enabled then the user will be able to authenticate via SMB once again.

If the smbpasswd file is in the 'old' format then **smbpasswd** will prompt for a new password for this user, otherwise the account will be enabled by removing the *'D'* flag from account control space in the **smbpasswd** file. See **smbpasswd (5)** for details on the 'old' and new password file formats.

This option is only available when running **smbpasswd** as root.

- **-D debuglevel** debuglevel is an integer from 0 to 10. The default value if this parameter is not specified is zero.

The higher this value, the more detail will be logged to the log files about the activities of smbpasswd. At level 0, only critical errors and serious warnings will be logged.

Levels above 1 will generate considerable amounts of log data, and should only be used when investigating a problem. Levels above 3 are designed for use only by developers and generate HUGE amounts of log data, most of which is extremely cryptic.

- **-n** This option specifies that the username following should have their password set to null (i.e. a blank password) in the local **smbpasswd** file. This is done by writing the string "NO PASSWORD" as the first part of the first password stored in the **smbpasswd** file.

Note that to allow users to logon to a Samba server once the password has been set to "NO PASSWORD" in the **smbpasswd** file the administrator must set the following parameter in the [global] section of the **smb.conf** file :

null passwords = true

This option is only available when running **smbpasswd** as root.

- **-r remote machine name** This option allows a user to specify what machine they wish to change their password on. Without this parameter **smbpasswd** defaults to the local host. The *"remote machine name"* is the NetBIOS name of the SMB/CIFS server to contact to attempt the password change. This name is resolved into an IP address using the standard name resolution mechanism in all programs of the **Samba** suite. See the **-R name resolve order** parameter for details on changing this resolving mechanism.

The username whose password is changed is that of the current UNIX logged on user. See the **-U username** parameter for details on changing the password for a different username.

Note that if changing a Windows NT Domain password the remote machine specified must be the Primary Domain Controller for the domain (Backup Domain Controllers only have a read-only copy of the user account database and will not allow the password change).

Note that Windows 95/98 do not have a real password database so it is not possible to change passwords specifying a Win95/98 machine as remote machine target.

- **-R name resolve order** This option allows the user of smbclient to determine what name resolution services to use when looking up the NetBIOS name of the host being connected to.

The options are :"lmhosts", "host", "wins" and "bcast". They cause names to be resolved as follows:

- **lmhosts**: Lookup an IP address in the Samba lmhosts file.
- **host**: Do a standard host name to IP address resolution, using the system /etc/hosts, NIS, or DNS lookups. This method of name resolution is operating system dependent. For instance on IRIX or Solaris, this may be controlled by the */etc/nsswitch.conf* file).
- **wins**: Query a name with the IP address listed in the **wins server** parameter in the **smb.conf file**. If no WINS server has been specified this method will be ignored.
- **bcast**: Do a broadcast on each of the known local interfaces listed in the **interfaces** parameter in the smb.conf file. This is the least reliable of the name resolution methods as it depends on the target host being on a locally connected subnet.

If this parameter is not set then the name resolve order defined in the **smb.conf** file parameter **name resolve order** will be used.

The default order is lmhosts, host, wins, bcast and without this parameter or any entry in the **smb.conf** file the name resolution methods will be attempted in this order.

- **-m** This option tells **smbpasswd** that the account being changed is a *MACHINE* account. Currently this is used when Samba is being used as an NT Primary Domain Controller. PDC support is not a supported feature in Samba2.0 but will become supported in a later release. If you wish to know more about using Samba as an NT PDC then please subscribe to the mailing list *samba-ntdom@samba.org*.

This option is only available when running **smbpasswd** as root.

- **-j DOMAIN** This option is used to add a Samba server into a Windows NT Domain, as a Domain member capable of authenticating user accounts to any Domain Controller in the same way as a Windows NT Server. See the **security=domain** option in the **smb.conf (5)** man page.

In order to be used in this way, the Administrator for the Windows NT Domain must have used the program *"Server Manager for Domains"* to add the primary NetBIOS name of the Samba server as a member of the Domain.

After this has been done, to join the Domain invoke **smbpasswd** with this parameter. **smbpasswd** will then look up the Primary Domain Controller for the Domain (found in the **smb.conf** file in the parameter **password server** and change the machine account password used to create the secure Domain communication. This password is then stored by **smbpasswd** in a file, read only by root, called `<Domain>.<Machine>.mac` where `<Domain>` is the name of the Domain we are joining and `<Machine>` is the primary NetBIOS name of the machine we are running on.

Once this operation has been performed the **smb.conf** file may be updated to set the **security=domain** option and all future logins to the Samba server will be authenticated to the Windows NT PDC.

Note that even though the authentication is being done to the PDC all users accessing the Samba server must still have a valid UNIX account on that machine.

This option is only available when running **smbpasswd** as root.

- **-U username** This option may only be used in conjunction with the **-r** option. When changing a password on a remote machine it allows the user to specify the user name on that machine whose password will be changed. It is present to allow users who have different user names on different systems to change these passwords.

- **-h** This option prints the help string for **smbpasswd**, selecting the correct one for running as root or as an ordinary user.
- **-s** This option causes **smbpasswd** to be silent (i.e. not issue prompts) and to read it's old and new passwords from standard input, rather than from `/dev/tty` (like the **passwd (1)** program does). This option is to aid people writing scripts to drive **smbpasswd**
- **username** This specifies the username for all of the *root only* options to operate on. Only root can specify this parameter as only root has the permission needed to modify attributes directly in the local **smbpasswd** file.

NOTES

Since **smbpasswd** works in client-server mode communicating with a local **smbd** for a non-root user then the **smbd** daemon must be running for this to work. A common problem is to add a restriction to the hosts that may access the **smbd** running on the local machine by specifying a **"allow hosts"** or **"deny hosts"** entry in the **smb.conf** file and neglecting to allow *"localhost"* access to the **smbd**.

In addition, the **smbpasswd** command is only useful if **Samba** has been set up to use encrypted passwords. See the file **ENCRYPTION.txt** in the docs directory for details on how to do this.

VERSION

This man page is correct for version 2.0 of the Samba suite.

AUTHOR

The original Samba software and related utilities were created by Andrew Tridgell *samba-bugs@samba.org*. Samba is now developed by the Samba Team as an Open Source project similar to the way the Linux kernel is developed.

The original Samba man pages were written by Karl Auer. The man page sources were converted to YODL format (another excellent piece of Open Source software, available at **ftp://ftp.icce.rug.nl/pub/unix/**) and updated for the Samba2.0 release by Jeremy Allison. *samba-bugs@samba.org*.

See **samba (7)** to find out how to get a full list of contributors and details on how to submit bug reports, comments etc.

APPENDIX E.9 SMBSTATUS(1)

SMBSTATUS (1)

SAMBA

23 OCT 1998

NAME

smbstatus—report on current Samba connections

SYNOPSIS

smbstatus [-b] [-d] [-L] [-p] [-S] [-s configuration file] [-u username]

DESCRIPTION

This program is part of the **Samba** suite.

smbstatus is a very simple program to list the current Samba connections.

OPTIONS

- **-b** gives brief output.
- **-d** gives verbose output.
- **-L** causes smbstatus to only list locks.
- **-p** print a list of **smbd** processes and exit. Useful for scripting.
- **-S** causes smbstatus to only list shares.
- **-s configuration file** The default configuration file name is determined at compile time. The file specified contains the configuration details required by the server. See **smb.conf (5)** for more information.
- **-u username** selects information relevant to *username* only.

VERSION

This man page is correct for version 2.0 of the Samba suite.

SEE ALSO

SMB.CONF (5), SMBD (8)

AUTHOR

The original Samba software and related utilities were created by Andrew Tridgell *samba-bugs@samba.org*. Samba is now developed by the Samba Team as an Open Source project similar to the way the Linux kernel is developed.

The original Samba man pages were written by Karl Auer. The man page sources were converted to YODL format (another excellent piece of Open Source software, available at **ftp://ftp.icce.rug.nl/pub/unix/**) and updated for the Samba2.0 release by Jeremy Allison. *samba-bugs@samba.org*.

See **samba (7)** to find out how to get a full list of contributors and details on how to submit bug reports, comments etc.

APPENDIX F

TCP/IP DOCUMENTATION

APPENDIX OBJECTIVES

- ✔ TCP/IP Network Resources List
- ✔ Private IP Network addresses

Author's Note: In this Appendix I have chosen those manual pages that I feel will be most useful to you in working with Samba. There are other commands that you will find useful as you progress in learning Samba.

APPENDIX F.1 TCP/IP NETWORK RESOURCES LIST

The following list is an excellent reference for Internet TCP/IP Resources. It is used with the Uri's permission. For an uptodate list you will want to access the main URL listed below. If you are not very familiar with what kind of resources there are, you will want to look at the breadth of material listed below.

Uri's TCP/IP Resources List
FAQS, TUTORIALS, GUIDES, WEB PAGES & SITES, AND BOOKS ABOUT TCP/IP

BY URI RAZ

This posting contains a list of various resources (books, web sites, FAQS, newsgroups, and useful net techniques) intended to help a newbie to learn about the TCP/IP suite of protocols.

I have written this document over the last few years. Yet, I could not have made this document without the assistance of other people. I would, therefore, like to thank to Andrew Gierth, Trevor Jenkins, Mark Daugherty, Michael Hunter, David Peter, Erick Engelke, Jose Carrilho, Jose Carrilho, Al Vonkeman, Zia R. Siddiqui, Jarle Aase, Daryl Banttari, Daniel K. Kim, Brian Schwarz, James Marshall, Diane Boling and Gisle Vanem who helped me in many ways, and to all the people who worked to produce all the materials listed in this document.

This article is available as a web page at :

http://www.private.org.il/tcpip_rl.html
http://t2.technion.ac.il/~s2845543/tcpip_rl.html
http://www.best.com/~mphunter/tcpip_resources.html

This article is available via FTP at :

ftp://rtfm.mit.edu/pub/usenet-by-group/news.answers/internet/tcp-ip/resource-list
ftp://rtfm.mit.edu/pub/usenet-by-hierarchy/comp/protocols/tcp-ip/TCP_IP_Resources_List

```
***************************************************************************
*                                                                         *
*  If you have any comments, addition suggestions, corrections, etc,      *
*  to the article itself, please send them to me at the technion.         *
*            My email address is mailto:s2845543@t2.technion.ac.il        *
*                                                                         *
*  There are plenty of copies of this article on the web. Please do not   *
*  create another one, as when the copies go out of date all the          *
*  requests to remove dead links, add new links, fix typos, etc which I   *
*  already did in the latest version go to me.                            *
*                                                                         *
*  If you have any questions about TCP/IP in general, which are not       *
*  directly related to this article, please post them to an appropriate   *
*  newsgroup, as my time is limited, and as it will serve you better.     *
*                                                                         *
*  WARNING : job offers from outside Israel will be treated as spam.      *
*                                                                         *
***************************************************************************
```

1. Books About TCP/IP
__________-

Richard Stevens' TCP/IP illustrated.

```
Published by Addison-Wesley.
 Volume 1 - describes the TCP/IP protocols.
            ISBN 0201633469
 Volume 2 - describes the TCP/IP stack as implemented in 4.4BSD-Lite,
           at the source code level.
            ISBN 020163354X
 Volume 3 - describes HTTP, NNTP, and more.
            ISBN 0201634953

Richard Steven's UNIX Network Programming.
Published by Prentice Hall.
 Described here is the 2nd edition of the book.
 The 1st edition (ISBN 0139498761) will be sold until the third
 volume of of the 2nd edition will be out.
  Volume 1 - "Networking APIs: Sockets and XTI".
             Describes UNIX network programming in & out, including
             a lot of code examples, covering IPv4 & IPv6, sockets
             and XTI, TCP & UDP, raw sockets, programming techniques,
             multicasting & broadcasting, and what not. The best
             TCP/IP programming book around, IMHO.
              ISBN 013490012X
  Volume 2 - "Interprocess Communications".
              ISBN 0130810819
  Volume 3 - "Applications"
              Name is probable, to be published.

Douglas Comer's Internetworking with TCP/IP.
Published by Prentice-Hall.
 Volume 1 - describes the TCP/IP protocols, architecture and principles.
            ISBN 0132169878
 Volume 2 - describes a TCP/IP implementation (with C code),
            implemented on the XINU operating system.
            ISBN 0131255274
 Volume 3 - describes network programming, and has a sockets version
            (ISBN 013260969X), a TLI version (ISBN 0132609770),
            and a winsock version (ISBN 0138487146)

TCP/IP Explained
 By Philip Miller
 Published by Digital Press
 ISBN 1555581668
  A fine book about TCP/IP, covering all the layers, starting with an
  overview of the lowest 2 OSI layers, through IP(+ICMP), UDP, TCP,
  routing (RIP + OSPF + EGP + BGP), broadcasting and multicasting,
  DNS, SNMP, several apps (FTP, Telnet, SMTP, ...), with chapters
  about IPv6 and Internet Security. The book is readable, with lots
  of diagrams and packet trace decodes. Some points missing, such
  as TCP congestion avoidance.

Troubleshooting TCP/IP - Analyzing the Protocols of the Internet
 By Mark A. Miller
```

Published by M & T Books
ISBN 1558514503
A good troubleshooting guide, with good explanations of most protocols, starting from network layer, through ARP, DNS, routing, and up to the applications, including SMTP, FTP, and TELNET. Coverage includes SNMP, ATM, IPv6. Case studies, included for every subject, include sniffer output and explanations.

High-Speed Networks: TCP/IP and ATM Design Principles
By William Stallings
Published by Prentice-Hall
ISBN 0135259657
This book explains how to design high-speed networks (ATM, 100 Mbps & Gbps ethernet) intended to carry high volume data (WWW, still images, video on demand, etc). Coverage includes explanation of ATM and Fast & Gigabit Ethernet, the mathematical background needed for performance analysis, traffic management (IP & ATM), routing, and compression.

TCP/IP: Architecture, Protocols, and Implementation with IPv6 and IP Security
By Sidnie Feit
Published by McGraw-Hill
ISBN 0070213895
This book covers TCP/IP in one volume, starting from the physical layer, through IP, UDP & TCP, the various applications (WWW, mail, etc) to network management.

SNMP, SNMPv2, SNMPv3, and RMON1 and RMON2
By William Stallings
Published by Addison-Wesley
ISBN 0201485346
An encyclopedic book about SNMP & RMON. Covers the material in depth and clarity, giving good background of the subject.

Networking with Microsoft TCP/IP
By Drew Heywood
Published by New Riders
ISBN 1562057138
An excellent book about management of Microsoft Windows TCP/IP networks, starting from the basics of explaining networking technologies, through installation of TCP/IP on DOS and all MS Windows versions, routing, managing (DHCP, WINS, DNS), troubleshooting, IIS & FrontPage.

TCP/IP Network Administration
By Craig Hunt.
Published by O'Reilly
ISBN 093717582X
An excellent book about management of TCP/IP networks, covering every subject that needed, including DNS, routing, sendmail, configuring, and trouble-shooting. This book is UNIX oriented.

Networking Personal Computers with TCP/IP - Building TCP/IP Networks
By Craig Hunt
Published by O'Reilly
ISBN 1565921232
A good book about management of TCP/IP networks, which is PC oriented, covering DOS, Windows, Windows-95, and Windows-NT.

Teach Yourself TCP/IP in 14 days.
By Timothy Parker
Published by SAM'S Publishing.
ISBN 0672305496
This book is intended for network managers, and gives an overview of TCP/IP from ground up, in a short schedule.

PPP Design and Debugging
By James Carlson
Published by Addison-Wesley
ISBN 0201185393
An excellent book about PPP. This compact book is packed with info about PPP, covering it in both depth and width, covering LCP, negotiation & authentication, network layer protocols, bandwidth management, etc, including trace interpretation, C code & pseudo code, and lots of resources and references.

NOSintro – TCP/IP over Packet Radio
(An Introduction to the KA9Q Network Operating System)
By Ian Wade
Published by Dowermain
ISBN 1897649002
NOSintro describes in detail how to use Phil Karn's KA9Q Network Operating System, and is a classic reference work in this area. It includes full information on how to install & configure KA9Q, and how to make it work in a packet radio environment. The book is very well illustrated, with many diagrams & hands-on examples of keyboard commands.
Extracts from the book are available at http://www.netro.co.uk/nosintro.html

IPv6: The New Internet Protocol
By Christian Huitema
Published by Prentice-Hall.
ISBN 0138505055
This book, written by Christian Huitema - a member of the Internet Architecture Board, gives an excellent description of IPv6, how it differs from IPv4, and the hows and whys of it's development.

Unix Network Programming
By W. Richard Stevens
Published by Prentice-Hall
ISBN 0139498761
Obsoleted by the second edition, to be covered soon.

```
Unix System V. Network Programming
 By Steven A. Rago
 Published by Addison-Wesley
 ISBN 0201563185
  This books gives a good coverage of UNIX network programming.
  Though it is centered around SVR4, it covers many subjects,
  including STREAMS, TLI, sockets, RPC, and kernel level
  communications, including ethernet & SLIP drivers.

The Design and Implementation of the 4.4 BSD Operating System.
 By Marshall Kirk McKusick, Keith Bostic, Michael J. Karels
  and John S. Quarterman.
 Published by Addison-Wesley.
 ISBN 0201549794
  This book describes the internals of the 4.4 BSD operating system,
  including the Net/2 TCP/IP stack implementation. A good explanation
  of the most commonly used implementation of TCP/IP.

Linux Kernel Internals
 By M. Beck, H. Bohme, M. Dziadzka, U. Kunitz, R. Magnus,
  and D. Verworner.
 Published by Addison-Wesley
 ISBN 0201331438
  This book describes the internals of the Linux operating system,
  version 2.0, with a chapter devoted to the TCP/IP stack.

Windows Sockets Network Programming
 By Bob Quinn and Dave Shute
 Published by Addison-Wesley
 ISBN 0201633728
 An excellent book about winsock programming, with chapters about porting
  apps from BSD Unix & sockets, DLLs, debugging, and nice appendice.

  The two following books are not directly related to TCP/IP, but are
  recommended as good books for windows programmer who write TCP/IP
  clients & servers, and are complementary to the above book :

   1. Win32 Network Programming
      By Ralph Davis
      Published by Addison-Wesley
      ISBN 0201489309
       This book shows programmers how to build networked apps
       using the 32-bit features of Win95 and NT, and includes
       a floppy with all the examples' code.

   2. Multithreading Applications in Win32
      By Jim Beveridge and Robert Wiener
      Published by Addison-Wesley
      ISBN 0201442345
       This book shows developers how, when and where to use
       multi-threading in Win32 applications, and includes a CD-ROM.
```

Interconnections
By Radia Perlman
Published by Addison-Wesley
ISBN 0201563320
This is a good book about bridging and routing, which has both a wide coverage and a technical depth. The book covers TCP/IP routing in only one chapter, which is extensive, but gives a much wider perspective on bridging, brouting, and routing in general.

Routing in the Internet
By Christian Huitema
Published by Prentice Hall
ISBN 0131321927
A clear and thorough, though a bit dated, book about routing. Covers all major routing protocols (RIP, OSPF, IGRP & EIGRP, IS-IS, EGP, BGP3, BGP4 & CIDR), and covers multicast, mobility, and resource reservation.

Internet Routing Architectures
By Bassam Halabi
Published by Cisco Press
ISBN 1562056522
A clear and through book about interdomain routing network design, with many clear examples with diagrams. Focuses on BGP4 and is, naturally, oriented toward Cisco's way of doing it (which is not much of a limit, considering Cisco's dominance of the routers market).

OSPF, Anatomy of an Internet Routing Protocol
By John T. Moy
Published by Addison-Wesley
ISBN 0201634724
A great book about OSPF, including it's history, multicast routing, management, debugging, comparisons to other routing protocols, and the companion book (OSPF Complete Implementation) goes through a complete implementation of OSPF (included on a CD), with a port to FreeBSD 2.1 and a Windows-95 simulator.

BGP4
By John W. Stewart III
Published by Addison-Wesley
ISBN 0201379511
A small (<150 pages) book, covering BGP4 in full using clear language and drawings. The four chapters include an introduction, the protocol, operations, and extensions (scaling, route flap dampening, authentication, negotiation, etc).

Data and Computer Communications
By William Stallings
Published by Prentice-Hall.
ISBN 0024154253
A very good book about computer communications basics. Includes information about TCP/IP and IPv6.

```
Computer Networks
 By Andrew S. Tanenbaum
 Published by Prentice-Hall.
 ISBN 0133499456
  A very good book about computer communications basics.
  Describes communications according to the OSI seven layers model,
  but includes information about TCP/IP and IPv6.

Information Warfare and Security
 By Dorothy E. Denning
 Published by Addison-Wesley
 ISBN 0201433036
  A book covering all aspects of information warfare with clear
  explanations and many references. Gives an excellent framework
  to Internet security.


2. Major On-Line Resources
_____________

 1. The IETF's home page is http://www.ietf.org/
    This is _the_ authorative source for RFCs (which include all
    the standards for TCP/IP), FYIs, drafts, and other infos about
    the internet and TCP/IP.

    A good place to look for RFCs is the Kashpureff Family's site,
    at http://www.kashpureff.org/nic/, which has a copy of all
    RFCs and drafts, as well as a search engine to search for
    keywords through either RFCs or drafts.

    Cabletron has a repository of RFCs and drafts. Drafts are indexed
    by subject, while STDs & RFCs by title & number. A search engine
    is supplied to search through titles or bodies.

    Another source for RFCs is rfc-info@isi.edu - to get further info,
    send a message with any subject, and with the body having
    one line, containing either "help", or "help: ways_to_get_rfcs".

    Note : the RFCs are the documents giving the official documentation
           to the various internet protocols. For specs / description /
           details / info about any internet protocol, first look at
           the Kashpureff Family site or get the RFCs index via email.

   An excellent index of RFCs is available in an appendix in Comer's first
    volume, but it is current as of the publishing date only.

    Comment : as many people seem to look for RFCs on CD-ROMs,
              I list here two titles I know of :
               1. Infomagic has a 2 CDs set titled "STANDARDS" which
                  contains, among other things, all the RFCs & IENs.
```

```
          2. Walnut-Creek has a CD-ROM titled "Internet Info" which
             contains some of the RFCs & IENs, among other stuff.

    Network Research Group home page - http://www-nrg.ee.lbl.gov/nrg.html
    Internet Assigned Numbers Authority home page - http://www.iana.org/
    Internet Engineering Task Force home page     - http://www.ietf.org/
    Internet Research Task Force home page        - http://www.irtf.org/
   Internet Societal Task Force home page      - http://www.istf.isoc.org/
    Internet SOCiety home page                    - http://www.isoc.org/
    Internet Architecture Board home page         - http://www.iab.org/
    Internet Engineering Steering Group    - http://www.ietf.org/iesg.html
    Internet Engineering & Planning Group         - http://www.iepg.org/
    Internet Mail Consortium                      - http://www.imc.org/
    The Generic Top Level Domain
                  Memorandum of Understanding - http://www.gtld-mou.org/
    Internet Ad-Hoc Committee home page           - http://www.iahc.org/
    ICANN - The Internet Corporation for
                     Assigned Names and Numbers - http://www.icann.org/
    ICANN Watch                               - http://www.icannwatch.org/
    Open Root Server Confederation              - http://www.open-rsc.org/
    RFC editor's web page                     - http://www.rfc-editor.org/

    Overview of the DNS Controversy -
http://www.flywheel.com/ircw/overview.html
    Another article by Robert Shaw  - http://www.itu.int/intreg/dns.html

    The National Telecommunications and Information Administration's
    Proposals for Management of Internet Names and Addresses page.
                http://www.ntia.doc.gov/ntiahome/domainname/domainhome.htm

    The AlterNIC's home page is http://www.alternic.com/
    This site carries RFCs, internet drafts, and materials relating
    to freedom of speech, encryption, and more.

    The FAQs.org sites carries RFCs, STDs, and FYIs. Subject indices are
    available, and RFCs can be viewed by active/all basis, and with
    several levels of details. Page's URL is http://www.faqs.org/rfcs/

 2. The comp.answers & news.answers newsgroups contain (or at least should)
    all FAQ postings for the newsgroups dealing with computers.

    The following newsgroups contain discussion related to TCP/IP :
     - Newsgroups FAQs are posted periodically to their top-hierarchy
       answers newsgroup (e.g. comp.os.vms => comp.answers). Those
       groups, along with news.newusers.questions, are great places
       to look for FAQs & tips in.
     - the comp.protocols hierarchy, which covers various networking
       protocols, such as tcp/ip, kermit, and iso.
       notice that some TCP/IP related protocols have discussion
       groups of their own (e.g. NFS, SNMP, NTP, PPP).
     - the comp.dcom hierarchy, including groups that discuss lans,
```

```
      modems, and ethernet.
    - the comp.mail hierarchy, which covers various electronic
      mail programs (pine, elm, sendmail, etc).
    - The news hierarchy, which covers the various subjects related
      to usenet, including the NNTP protocol.

 3. All the newsgroups' FAQs, as well as other introductory documents are
    stored at ftp://rtfm.mit.edu/pub/. A good introductory to TCP/IP from
    the site is the file ftp://rtfm.mit.edu/pub/net/internet.text. The
FAQs
    can be accessed on the web at http://www.faqs.org/ as well.

    As the rtfm.mit.edu & faqs.org sites might be heavily loaded, and
    as many sites mirror the FAQs archive, it is advisable to search
    for FAQs at geographically nearer sites. A list of many mirror sites
    (allowing access via FTP, WWW, Gopher, mail, etc) is available at :
     ftp://rtfm.mit.edu/pub/faqs/news-answers/introduction

    The comp.protocols.tcp-ip group has a FAQ, previously maintained by
    George V. Neville-Neil, now by Mike Oliver, is located at :
     ftp://rtfm.mit.edu/pub/faqs/internet/tcp-ip/tcp-ip-faq/
     http://www.itprc.com/tcpipfaq/default.htm
     http://t2.technion.ac.il/~s2845543/tcpip-faq/default.htm

    The comp.protocols.tcp-ip.ibmpc newsgroup has a FAQ,
    written by Bernard D. Aboba, which can be found at at :
     ftp://ftp.netcom.com/pub/ma/mailcom/IBMTCP/ibmtcp.zip
     http://www.inetassist.com/faqs/tcpibmpc.htm

    The comp.protocols.tcp-ip.domains newsgroup has a FAQ,
    maintained by Chris Peckham, which can be found at :
     http://www.users.pfmc.net/~cdp/cptd-faq/
    ftp://rtfm.mit.edu/pub/usenet/news.answers/internet/tcp-ip/domains-faq/

    The sockets programming FAQ, by Vic Metcalfe, is located at :
     ftp://rtfm.mit.edu/pub/usenet/news.answers/unix-faq/socket
     http://www.faqs.org/faqs/unix-faq/socket/index.html

   The alt.winsock newsgroup has a FAQ, by Nancy Cedeno Alegria, located at :
     http://www.well.com/user/nac/alt-winsock-faq.html
     http://www.faqs.org/faqs/windows/winsock-faq/index.html
     ftp://rtfm.mit.edu/pub/usenet/news.answers/windows/winsock-faq

    The Winsock Programmer's FAQ, by Warren Young, is located at :
     http://www.cyberport.com/~tangent/programming/winsock/
     http://www.faqs.org/faqs/windows/winsock/programmer-faq/index.html
    ftp://rtfm.mit.edu/pub/usenet/news.answers/windows/winsock/programmer-faq

    The windows-sockets page, by Bob Quinn, is located at :
     http://www.sockets.com/
```

The sockaddr.com - Programming Resources for WinSock site, is located at :
http://www.sockaddr.com/

The Raw IP Networking FAQ, by Thamer Al-Herbish, is available at :
http://www.whitefang.com/rin/

Stardust has winsock pages, located at :
http://www.stardust.com/wsresource/wsresrce.html
http://www.winsock.com/

Wandel & Goltermann have brought up the decodes.com
The size lists is intended to be a "Resource for Network Protocol Analysis".
http://www.decodes.com/

The Secure Sockets Layer Discussion List FAQ is located at :
http://www.consensus.com/security/ssl-talk-faq.html
ftp://ftp.consensus.com/pub/security/ssl-talk-faq.txt

Info about Ssh (Secure Shell) may be found at :
http://www.ssh.org/
http://www.cs.hut.fi/ssh/
http://www.faqs.org/faqs/computer-security/ssh-faq/index.html
ftp://rtfm.mit.edu/pub/usenet-by-group/comp.security.ssh/

Info about SOCKS (secure sockets using proxies / firewalls) -
http://www.socks.nec.com/
ftp://coast.cs.purdue.edu/pub/doc/faq/faq_socks

The DNS Resources Directory, an excellent resource, may be found at -
http://www.dns.net/dnsrd/

Jarle Aase's FTP Protocol Resource Center site may be found at -
http://war.jgaa.com:8080/ftp/

Info about various TCP/IP protocols originating from UNIX utilities, such as r-* services, lpd, and talk, can be found in a page I've written up for the purpose of concentrating the info at a single point.
http://t2.technion.ac.il/~s2845543/mini-tcpip.faq.html

4. The comp.protocols.tcp-ip.ibmpc is gated to a mailing list as well, and it is served by listserv@list.nih.gov, under the name PCIP.

   The alt.winsock newsgroup is gated to a mailing list as well. The mailing list is named winsock@microdyne.com. The [un]subscribe address is, of course, winsock-request@microdyne.com

   There's an IPv6 mailing list. It's named ipng, and it is served served by Majordomo@sunroof.eng.sun.com

5. RFC #1180 (RFC1180), titled "A TCP/IP Tutorial", is a good tutorial, with a focus on how an IP packet travels from source to destination.

```
 RFC #2151 (FYI30), titled "A Primer On Internet and TCP/IP Tools" is a
good introductory to TCP/IP tools, such as ping, finger, and traceroute.


3. Misc Web Pages
__________


 1. The Unix Guru Universe's home page is http://www.ugu.com/
    You could find in this site references to all kinds of info relating
    to UNIX, including TCP/IP.

    There are three great sites for all of MS-Windows's versions, which
   cover a lot of info relating to connecting MS-Windows to TCP/IP networks.
    The sites are :
     http://www.windows.com/
     http://www.windows-95.com/
     http://www.windows98.org/
     http://support.microsoft.com/  [requires registration]

    The Network Professionals Resource Center contains links to
    many FAQs, computers & networking magazines' home pages, etc.
     http://www.inetassist.com/

    The Network Management Server carries FAQs, white papers,
    free software, etc related to network management.
     http://netman.cit.buffalo.edu/

   The Direct Cable Connection, Null-modem, Serial Ports site explains how
    to connect two windows machines to each other using serial or parallel
    ports to create a two nodes network.
     http://php.indiana.edu/~jrrricha/dcc1.html

 2. You can find many books on the web :
      1. Macmillan's Personal Bookshelf
          http://www.mcp.com/personal/
      2. McGraw-Hill's BetaBooks
          http://www.pbg.mcgraw-hill.com/betabooks/
      3. National Academy Press's Reading Room
          http://www.nap.edu/info/browse.htm
      4. The Network Administrators' Guide
         By Olaf Kirch
          http://sunsite.unc.edu/mdw/LDP/nag/nag.html
      5. Computer Networks and Internets
         By Douglas E. Comer
          http://www.netbook.cs.purdue.edu/

    Books related pages :
      1. The Xinu BUG Page at the University of Canberra, Australia.
          http://willow.canberra.edu.au/~chrisc/bugs.html
      2. List of enhancements to Comer's TCP code by Simon Ilyushchenko
          http://www.internasoft.com/simon/tcp/
```

```
  You can find on-line networking magazines :
   1. Network Magazine
       http://www.networkmagazine.com/
   2. Data Communications
       http://www.data.com/
   3. Network Computing
       http://www.networkcomputing.com/

  A copy of "Netizens: An Anthology" is available at
   1. http://www.columbia.edu/~rh120/                  - HTML
   2. ftp://wuarchive.wustl.edu/doc/misc/acn/netbook/ - ASCII

3. The following links would supply intro info on TCP/IP :
    1. gopher://gopher-chem.ucdavis.edu/11/Index/Internet_aw/
    2. Optimized Engineering Technical Compendium (LANs & IP)
        http://www.optimized.com/COMPENDI/
    3. Introduction to TCP/IP
        http://pclt.cis.yale.edu/pclt/COMM/TCPIP.HTM
    4. Introduction to the Internet Protocols
        http://oac3.hsc.uth.tmc.edu/staff/snewton/tcp-tutorial/
   5. Under the hood of the 'net: An overview of the TCP/IP Protocol Suite,
       By Jason Yanowitz.
        http://info.acm.org/crossroads/xrds1-1/tcpjmy.html
    6. IP overview, by Cisco.
        http://www.cisco.com/univercd/cc/td/doc/cisintwk/ito_doc/ip.htm
    7. Tech-NIC's technical page
        http://www.tech-nic.dk/html/technical.html
    8. Thomas's Technical Links
        http://www.psp.demon.co.uk/tfl/techlinks.htm
    9. Several nice tutorials from Scan Technologies
        http://www.scan-technologies.com/tutorials.htm
   10. The IP Address and Classes
        http://www.sangoma.com/fguide.htm
         (linked from http://www.sangoma.com/tutorial.htm)
   11. Subnetting :
        What's A Netmask?
         http://www.digitalmx.com/wires/subnet.html
        IP Address Subnetting Tutorial
         http://www.ziplink.net/~ralphb/IPSubnet/index.html
        IP Subnet Calculations
         http://www.swcp.com/~jgentry/topo/unit3.htm
        Daryl's TCP/IP Primer
        Addressing and Subnetting on the Near Side of the 'Net
         http://ipprimer.windsorcs.com/
        Breeze Through Subnet Masking, by John Lambert, MCSE
         http://support.wrq.com/tutorials/tcpip/tcpipfundamentals.html
        Al Vokeman's netmask calculator
        The calculator is implemented via JavaScript (not CGI),
        making it quick, but requires JavaScript supported and enabled.
         http://www.telusplanet.net/public/sparkman/netcalc.htm
        Another CIDR subnet mask calculator can be found at
```

http://minnie.cs.adfa.edu.au/Gateways/range_check.html

12. A CIDR FAQ
    http://www.rain.net/faqs/cidr.faq.html
13. Cisco's Internetworking Terms and Acronyms
    http://cio-sys.cisco.com/univercd/data/doc/cintrnet/ita.htm
14. "TCP/IP Tutorial and Technical Overview" from IBM
    http://publib.boulder.ibm.com/cgi-bin/bookmgr/BOOKS/GG243376/CCONTENTS
15. An Overview of TCP/IP Protocolsi and the Internet
    http://www.hill.com/library/staffpubs/tcpip.html
16. IP Addressing Fundamentals
    http://support.wrq.com/tutorials/tcpip/tcpipfundamentals.html
17. Understanding IP Addressing: Everything You Ever Wanted To Know
    http://www.3com.com/nsc/501302.html
18. Understanding IP Addressing
    http://noc.gate.net/doclib/faqs/help/net.html
19. hedrick-intro to the Internet Protocols
    http://www.duth.gr/InfoBase/intro.ip.toc.html
20. A short page about TCP/IP security by Chris Chambers, Justin Dolske, and Jayaraman Iyer.
    http://www.cis.ohio-state.edu/~dolske/gradwork/cis694q/
21. Von Welch has a network performance page at
    http://www.ncsa.uiuc.edu/People/vwelch/net_perf/
    One of the subpages explains TCP windows
    http://www.ncsa.uiuc.edu/People/vwelch/net_perf/tcp_windows.html
22. Marc Slemko' Path MTU Discovery and Filtering ICMP
    http://www.worldgate.com/~marcs/mtu/
23. Cliff Green's Introduction to Internet Protocols for Newbies
    http://www.halcyon.com/cliffg/uwteach/shared_info/internet_protocols.html
24. Catalyst's Introduction to TCP/IP Programming
    http://www.catalyst.com/tcpintro.html
25. Frank Dekervel's DNS Tutorial
    http://www.geocities.com/SiliconValley/Network/4504/dns_tut.txt
    Gary Kessler's Setting Up Your Own DNS
    http://www.hill.com/library/staffpubs/dns.html
    The DNS Security Extensions, by Cricket Liu.
    http://www.acmebw.com/papers/dnssec.pdf
26. RPC
    http://pandonia.canberra.edu.au/OS/l14_1.html
    http://www.ja.net/documents/NetworkNews/Issue44/RPC.html
    http://www.mmt.bme.hu/~kiss/docs/dce/rpc.html
    http://glacier.unl.edu/~samal/class/DIST/lectures/rpc.html
27. DHCP
    Ralph Droms' DHCP Resources site
    http://www.dhcp.org/
    Alan Dobkin's DHCP Resources
    http://nws.cc.emory.edu/webstaff/alan/net-man/computing/dhcp/
28. BSD socket programming tutorials
    Quick - http://ftp.std.com/homepages/jimf/sockets.html
    Intro - http://ccnga.uwaterloo.ca/~mvlioy/stuff/ipc_intro_tut.txt

```
         Advanced - http://ccnga.uwaterloo.ca/~mvlioy/stuff/ipc_adv_tut.txt
          Windows socket programming tutorials
           http://users.neca.com/vmis/wsockexp.htm
           http://users.neca.com/vmis/wsockprg.htm
          An Introduction to Socket Programming
           http://www.uwo.ca/its/doc/courses/notes/socket/index.html
          Beej's Guide to Network Programming
           http://www.ecst.csuchico.edu/~beej/guide/net/
          Vijay Mukhi's Winsock Programming page
           http://users.neca.com/vmis/wsockprg.htm
          Network Programmer's Guide
           http://www.ibr.cs.tu-bs.de/~harbaum/docs/netprog/contents.html
          Unix Network Programming
           http://gaia.cs.umass.edu/ntu_socket/
          Spencer's Socket Site
           http://www.lowtek.com/sockets/
      29. Xiaomu's WinSock page
           http://omni.cc.purdue.edu/~xniu/winsock.htm
      30. Routing protocols
           In general             - http://www.bind.com/
           http://www.cisco.com/univercd/cc/td/doc/cisintwk/ito_doc/rout-
ing.htm
            IGRP                  -
http://www.cisco.com/univercd/cc/td/doc/cisintwk/ito_doc/igrp.htm
           IGRP & Enhanced IGRP   -
http://www.cisco.com/warp/public/103/index.shtml
           IGRP & Enhanced IGRP   -
http://www.cisco.com/univercd/cc/td/doc/cisintwk/ito_doc/en_igrp.htm
           RIP                    -
http://www.cisco.com/univercd/cc/td/doc/cisintwk/ito_doc/rip.htm
           OSPF, BGP, IPv6, GateD - http://www.roedu.net/~cmatei/network/
           EGP                    -
http://www.cisco.com/univercd/cc/td/doc/cisintwk/ito_doc/55143.htm
           BGP4                   - http://www.cisco.com/warp/pub-
lic/459/18.html
           BGP                    -
http://www.cisco.com/univercd/cc/td/doc/cisintwk/ito_doc/bgp.htm
           OSPF                   - http://www.cisco.com/warp/pub-
lic/104/1.html
           OSPF                   -
http://www.cisco.com/univercd/cc/td/doc/cisintwk/ito_doc/ospf.htm
           OSPF                   - http://www.3com.com/nsc/501304.html
           NLSP (Novell)          - http://www.3com.com/nsc/501309.html
           Multi Layer Routing    - http://infonet.aist-
nara.ac.jp/member/nori-d/mlr/
      31. Merit GateD Consortium
           This site contains wealth of information about GateD, including
           source distributions, documentation, etc.
            http://www.gated.org/
          GNU Zebra site
           The GBU Zebra project is a router software implementing OSPFv2,
```

BGP4, RIPv1, and RIPv2. It has a special architecture that differs from GateD in that it allows to offloads the computation from the CPU to special ASICs and in it's modularity.
http://www.zebra.org/

32. Switching :
"Layer 3 and 4 Switching", article from Performance Computing.
http://www.performancecomputing.com/columns/packets/9812.shtml
"IP Switching: Issues and Alternatives,", by R. Jain.
http://www.cis.ohio-state.edu/~jain/talks/ipsw.htm
"IP Switching", course given by Shishir Agrawal.
http://www.cis.ohio-state.edu/~jain/cis788-97/ip_switching/index.htm
"L5: A Self Learning Layer 5 Switch", a report from IBM
<suddenly unavailable online>
33. Internet Performance Measurement and Analysis Project home page.
http://www.merit.edu/ipma/
34. Host Name to Latitude/Longitude
http://cello.cs.uiuc.edu/cgi-bin/slamm/ip2ll/
35. Internet Weather Report
http://www.internetweather.com/
http://www3.mids.org/weather/
http://www.internettrafficreport.com/
36. Connected: An Internet Encyclopedia
http://www.freesoft.org/CIE/index.htm
37. The Network Engineer's Toolkit Site
http://www.wanresources.com/
38. TCP/IP For Internet Administrators
http://techref.ezine.com/tc/
39. Roll Your Own Intranet page
http://users.neca.com/vmis/roll.htm
40. Materials on TCP/IP Networking
http://spectral.mscs.mu.edu/NetworksClass/Materials/
41. Windows and TCP/IP for Internet Access
http://learning.lib.vt.edu/wintcpip/wintcpip.html
42. Al's WinSock Tuning FAQ
http://www.cerberus-sys.com/~belleisl/mtu_mss_rwin.html
43. Henning Schulzrinne's RTP (Real Time Protocol) site
http://www.cs.columbia.edu/~hgs/rtp/
Queen's University Real - Time Transport Protocol (QRTP)
http://htm4.ee.queensu.ca:8000/ling/QRTP.html
44. My own IP -> Geographical Location Detective's page
http://t2.technion.ac.il/~s2845543/IP2geo.html
45. Computer Networking and Internet Protocols
By Keith W. Ross and James F. Kurose
http://www.seas.upenn.edu/~ross/book/Contents.htm
46. Shawn J. Rappaport's Internetworking page
http://www.futureone.com/~opeth/internetwork.html
47. Slow start & delayed ack explained
http://www.sun.com/sun-on-net/performance/tcp.slowstart.html
48. Information about NetBIOS and NetBEUI can be found at
http://www.s390.ibm.com/bookmgr-cgi/bookmgr.cmd/BOOKS/bk8p7001/CCONTENTS

http://ourworld.compuserve.com/homepages/timothydevans/nbf.htm

49. RGB's TCP/IP Whitepapers & Guides
    http://www.rgb.co.uk/support/guides/tcpip.htm
50. ADTRAN PPP Internetworking Primer
    http://www.alliancedatacom.com/dial-up-point-to-point-technology.htm
51. IP Masquerade for Linux
    http://ipmasq.cjb.net/

TCP/IP courses from universities :

0. The Cooperative Association for Internet Data Analysis maintains a list of pointers to Internet Engineering related university courses.
   http://www.caida.org/iec.evi/courses/index.html
1. Dr. Reuven Cohen
   Internet Networking
   Technion - Israel Institute of Science
   http://www.cs.technion.ac.il/Courses/cs236341/
2. Dr. Shlomi Dolev
   Computer Communications and Distributed Algorithms
   Ben-Gurion University
   http://www.cs.bgu.ac.il/~ccda982/ (slides are in hebrew)
3. Dr. Ofer Hadar
   Introduction To Computer Networks
   Technion - Israel Institute of Science
   http://www.cs.technion.ac.il/~cs236334/ (slides are in hebrew)
4. Prof. Deborah Estrin
   Computer Communications
   University of South California
   http://catarina.usc.edu/cs551/cs551.html
5. Dave Hollinger
   Network Programming
   http://www.cs.rpi.edu/courses/netprog/index.html
6. Prof. Jim Kurose
   Computer Networks
   http://gaia.cs.umass.edu:80/cs653/
7. David C. Blight
   Telecommunication Networks
   http://www.ee.umanitoba.ca/~blight/c24759-97/
8. Phil Scott
   Data Communications, Computer Networks
   http://ironbark.bendigo.latrobe.edu.au/staff/pscott/pscott.home.html
9. David Cyganski
   Telecommunications Transmission Technologies
   http://bugs.wpi.edu:8080/EE535/
10. S. Keshav
    Engineering Computer Networks
    http://www.cs.cornell.edu/cs519/
11. Prof. Ralph Droms
    Purdue University
    Computer Networks

http://www.netbook.cs.purdue.edu/cs363/index.html

12. Simon Cleary
    RMIT university
    Computer Networks and Protocols
    http://www.cse.rmit.edu.au/~rdssc/courses/ds454/
13. Phil Scott
    La Trobe university
    Computer Networks
    http://ironbark.bendigo.latrobe.edu.au/subjects/bitcne/

The following links would supply info about IPv6 :

1. IP Next Generation
   This is the first site to visit to get any information about IPv6, from overviews, through RFCs & drafts, to implementations (including availability of stacks on various platforms & source code for IPv6 stacks)
   http://playground.sun.com/pub/ipng/html/ipng-main.html
2. UK IPv6 Resource Centre
   http://www.cs-ipv6.lancs.ac.uk/
3. 6bone Home Page
   http://www.6bone.net/
4. IP Next Generation Overview
   http://info.isoc.org/HMP/PAPER/PT1/html/pt1.html.hinden
5. IPv6: The New Internet Protocol
   By William Stallings
   http://www.comsoc.org/pubs/surveys/stallings/stallings-orig.html
6. The New and Improved Internet Protocol
   By William Stallings
   http://www.byte.com/art/9609/sec5/art2.htm
7. The IPng Group's home page
   http://ganges.cs.tcd.ie/4ba2/ipng/
8. IPv6 RFCs & links collection
   http://www.aloni.com/IPv6.htm
9. IPv6: The New Version of the Internet Protocol
   By Steve Deering
   http://trail.isi.edu/deering/
10. The Future of the Internet: IPng and the TCP/IP Protocols
    http://ccnga.uwaterloo.ca/~dkidston/presentations/IPng/index.html
11. IPv6 specifications - Latest RFCs and Internet Drafts Collection
    http://seusa.sumitomo.com/htmls/randd/ipv6/doc.html
12. Process' IPv6 Resource Center.
    http://www.process.com/ipv6.htp
13. IPv6: The Next Generation Internet Protocol
    By Gary C. Kessler
    http://www.hill.com/library/staffpubs/ipv6_exp.html
14. IPv6: Next Generation Internet Protocol
    http://www.3com.com/nsc/ipv6.html
15. Literature Research IPv6 (IPng), by Mike Crawfurd.
    http://www.mediaport.org/~iamano/lr.zip
16. Existing Routing Protocols and IPv6
    http://www.pub.ro/~cmatei/network/ipv6/

```
 17. The IPv6 organization site.
      http://www.ipv6.org/

For information about the Internet's future :
 1. Internet ][ site.
     http://www.internet2.org/
 2. Next Generation Internet Initiative
     http://www.ngi.gov/
 3. The Quality of Service Forum site.
     http://www.qosforum.com/tech_resources.htm

The following links would supply info about IP multicasting :
 1. The IP Multicast Initiative home page
     http://www.ipmulticast.com/
 2. The Mbone (multicast bone) FAQ
     http://www.cs.columbia.edu/~hgs/internet/mbone-faq.html
 3. The multicast backbone home page
     http://www.mbone.com/
 4. An Introduction to IP Multicast
     http://ganges.cs.tcd.ie/4ba2/multicast/index.html
 5. Introduction to IP Multicast Routing
     http://www.3com.com/nsc/501303.html
 6. A collection of documents explaining multicast routing.
     ftp://ftpeng.cisco.com/ipmulticast/multicast_training.html

The following links would supply info about IP security :
 1. Internet Security Survey  - http://www.trouble.org/survey/
 2. Phrack Magazine's site    - http://www.phrack.com/
 3. The SKIP site             - http://www.skip.org/
    SKIP - Simple Key management for Internet Protocols - encrypts
    info at the IP layer, enabling all applications which communicate
    via IP (using either TCP or UDP) to benefit from security.
 4. Peter Gutmann's "Security and Encryption-related Resources and Links"
    contains a huge collection of links to security sites.
     http://www.cs.auckland.ac.nz/~pgut001/links.html
 5. COAST's Hotlist: Computer Security, Law & Privacy is another huge
    collection of links to security & privacy isses.
     http://www.cs.purdue.edu/homes/spaf/hotlists/csec-plain.html
 6. Telstra has a Security Papers & Documents page, most of them
    relating to network security.
     http://www.telstra.com.au/pub/docs/security/
 7. SunWorld has a good article about IPsec
     http://www.sun.com/sunworldonline/swol-06-1998/swol-06-ipsec.html

Pages about research into networking can be found at :
 1. Networking Research at the PSC
     http://www.psc.edu/networking/
 2. List of Publications by Raj Jain's Group
     http://www.cis.ohio-state.edu/~jain/papers.html
 3. Luigi Rizzo - Research work
     http://www.iet.unipi.it/~luigi/research.html
```

4. UCLA Internet Research Lab
   http://irl.cs.ucla.edu/
5. TCP Over Satellite work group
   http://tcpsat.lerc.nasa.gov/tcpsat/
6. Mobile Computing Paper Collection at NTHU
   http://piggy.cs.nthu.edu.tw/paper/Mobile/index.html
7. Rutgers university DataMan mobile computing laboratory
   http://www.cs.rutgers.edu/dataman/
8. Network Bibliography
   http://www.cs.columbia.edu/~hgs/netbib/
9. ValueRocket Consulting
   http://www.valuerocket.com/papers/

Mark Daugherty's TCP/IP page contains IPv4 Datagram Reference Chart in AutoCad format (.dxf) and as a 9 pages Word document, as well as lots of other links to such stuff as well known port numbers, FAQs, ethernet resources, etc, in his home-page.

http://mdaugherty.home.mindspring.com/index.html
http://mdaugherty.home.mindspring.com/tcpip.html [TCP/IP page]

The protocols.com site has posters of many protocols in both HTML and PDF formats, though the later requires (free) registration.

http://www.protocols.com/pbook/tcpip.htm [HTML posters]
http://www.protocols.com/pbook/pdf/index.html [PDF posters]

The Information Technology Professional's Resource Center contains plenty of links to networking subjects, including IP, Cisco, guides, magazines' home pages, networking security, and more.

http://www.itprc.com/

Randy Baker's Introduction to Data Communications page
http://www.georcoll.on.ca/staff/rbaker/idccbt.htm

TechFest's Networking page.
http://www.techfest.com/networking/

First Monday is a journal about the Internet which is published on the internet, with all it's articles peer-reviewed.
It's archives contain articles about TCP/IP, indexed at
http://www.firstmonday.dk/subjects/technical.html

The Institute for Global Communications (IGC) has an excellent page of TCP/IP resources, starting from some general background, through pointers to platform specific links and comm-hardware links.

http://www.igc.org/igc/help/tcpip.html

Cisco's site contains a couple of internetworking guides :

A. IP Protocols page
   http://cio.cisco.com/warp/public/732/IP/index.html
B. IP Technical Tips page
   http://www.cisco.com/warp/public/105/

```
     C. Internetworking Technology Overview
        http://www.cisco.com/univercd/cc/td/doc/cisintwk/ito_doc/index.htm
     D. Internetwork Design Guide
         http://www.cisco.com/univercd/cc/td/doc/cisintwk/idg4/index.htm

    IBM's Austin site contains a couple of TCP/IP guides :
     A. TCP/IP Tutorial and Technical Overview
       http://www.austin.ibm.com/resource/aix_resource/Pubs/redbooks/html-
books/gg243376.04/3376fm.html
     B. Using the Information Superhighway
       http://www.austin.ibm.com/resource/aix_resource/Pubs/redbooks/html-
books/gg242499.00/2499fm.html
     C. Accessing the Internet
       http://www.austin.ibm.com/resource/aix_resource/Pubs/redbooks/html-
books/sg242597.00/2597fm.html

  4. Richard Stevens' home page      http://www.kohala.com/~rstevens/
     Douglas Comer's home page       http://www.cs.purdue.edu/people/comer
     Andrew Tannenbaum's home page   http://www.cs.vu.nl/~ast/
     William Stallings's home page   http://www.shore.net/~ws
     James Carlson's home page
http://people.ne.mediaone.net/carlson/ppp
     Raj Jain's home page            http://www.cis.ohio-state.edu/~jain/

  5. O'Reilly          http://www.ora.com/
     Prentice Hall     http://www.prenhall.com/
     Addison Wesley    http://www.aw.com/
     MacMillan         http://www.mcp.com/
     McGraw-Hill       http://www.mcgraw-hill.com/
     MIS:Press         http://www.mispress.com/ (M & T Books)
     New Riders        http://www.newriders.com/

     InfoMagic        home page  http://www.infomagic.com/
                       ftp site  ftp://ftp.infomagic.com/
     Walnut Creek's   home page  http://www.cdrom.com/
                       ftp site  ftp://ftp.cdrom.com/

  6. GNU project             http://www.gnu.org/
     OpenBSD's home page     http://www.openbsd.org/
     FreeBSD's home page     http://www.freebsd.org/
     NetBSD's home page      http://www.netbsd.org/
     Linux's home page       http://www.linux.org/
     Trinux's home page      http://www.trinux.org/
     Linux Kernel Archive    http://www.kernel.org/

     The Internet Software Consortiumi, a non-profit organization, carries
     and supports BIND, DHCP, and INN. The software is supplied for free,
     as well as limited support via mailing list. A support contract comes,
     naturally, with a fee.
      http://www.isc.org/
```

```
Erick Engelke has a web page titled "WATTCP Locator", supplying lots
of info about WATTCP, a TCP/IP package for DOS. The latest version of
WATTCP is pointed to from this page.
 http://www.supro.com/wattcp/wattcp.html

Gisle Vanem has upgraded the WATTCP tcp/ip stack to include
DHCP, RARP, file-based lookup, BSD-compatibel API. Supports
several compilers and DOS-extenders. WATT-32 is found at
 http://www.bgnett.no/~giva/index.html

Phil Karn's KA9Q (DOS TCP/IP stack) is under Karn's home page.
 http://people.qualcomm.com/karn/code/ka9qnos/

Michael Bernardi's MS-DOS Applications for Internet Use FAQ, which
contains a list of TCP/IP stacks & applications for DOS.
 ftp://ftp.demon.co.uk/pub/doc/ibmpc/dos-apps.txt
 http://www.dendarii.demon.co.uk/FAQs/dos-apps.html

Dan Kegel has a page titled "MS-DOS TCP/IP Programming", which
is crammed with links & info about TCP/IP for DOS.
 http://www.alumni.caltech.edu/~dank/trumpet/

The Public Netperf Homepage is available, courtesy of HP, at
 http://www.netperf.org/

The Linux Router Project, making a floppy sized distribution of Linux
used to build and maintain routers, terminal servers, etc.
 http://www.linuxrouter.org/

7. A good search engine could supply further info.
   The Yahoo engine, at http://www.yahoo.com/, has a good index,
   including a page about TCP-IP.
   Some other good search engines are
    AltaVista at http://www.altavista.digital.com/
    InfoSeek  at http://www.infoseek.com/
    Hotbot    at http://www.hotbot.com/

   The Networked Computer Science Technical Reference Library site
   is an archive of computer science articles, which can be searched
   through using an impressive search engine.
    http://www.ncstrl.org/

   The DejaNews site archives all the posts to usenet.
   The site, at http://www.dejanews.com/, enables users to search through
   posts sent over the past few years using different methods, which
   may be combined, such as words from articles, authors, and newsgroups.
   The ability to find past posts discussing unfamiliar subjects is an
   endless source of information, and may supply immediate answers to
   questions asked on usenet in the past.

   If you wish to have a post of yours not archived in dejanews add
```

```
    the header "X-No-Archive: Yes" to your posting's header, or write
    it as your article's first line. Notice that this wouldnt prevent
    other people from quoting your article, thus causing the quoted
    material to be archived.

    Other useful features of DejaNews :
     - Get poster profiles.
       This gives a count of how many posts did a poster send to each
       newsgroup, with a poster identified by it's email address.
     - Search for newsgroups discussing given subjects.
       As the search is done by frequency of words in posts, the
       results should be taken with a grain of salt, e.g.
```

```
          NEWSGROUPS WHERE PEOPLE TALK ABOUT: christianity

All the newsgroups in the following list contain christianity in some article.
The confidence rating indicates how sure we are that people talk about your
query in the newsgroup. Clicking on the newsgroup name will show you all of
the articles within the group which match your query.

          Confidence   Newsgroup
             99%       alt.atheism
             63%       rec.games.frp.misc
             54%       rec.music.christian
             39%       alt.religion.christian
             38%       soc.religion.christian
             38%       soc.penpals
             33%       austin.general
```

```
    The Norwegian University of Science and Technology, located at Trondheim,
     has an FTP search engine on the web, located at
    http://ftpsearch.ntnu.no/ftpsearch, that can find files on anonymous FTP
     servers world wide.

     The search is similar to the one done by archie, and can be very
     useful for finding source code for utilities, FAQs, etc.

     A quick search for the word ping produced the following output :
```

```
ftp.cc.uec.ac.jp (Japan)
  1 ftp.cc.uec.ac.jp  /.0/4.4BSD-Lite/usr/src/sbin/ping
  2 ftp.cc.uec.ac.jp  /.0/4.4BSD-Lite/usr/src/sys/i386/floppy/ping
  3 ftp.cc.uec.ac.jp  /.0/Linux/redhat-
4.1/i386/RedHat/instimage/usr/bin/ping
  4 ftp.cc.uec.ac.jp  /.0/Linux/redhat-
devel/i386/RedHat/instimage/usr/bin/ping

ftp.dwc.edu (Educational)
  5 ftp.dwc.edu       /.03/redhat/i386/RedHat/instimage/usr/bin/ping
  6 ftp.dwc.edu       /.03/redhat/sparc/RedHat/instimage/usr/bin/ping
```

```
  7 ftp.dwc.edu       /.03/redhat/sparc/misc/src/trees/rescue/bin/ping

ftp.fujixerox.co.jp (Japan)
  8 ftp.fujixerox.co.jp  /.1/NetBSD-current/src/sbin/ping

 [more links snipped]
```

Other files search engine are located at http://www.filez.com/ and http://castor.acs.oakland.edu/cgi-bin/vsl-front/ which can find files for specific platforms (e.g. unix, windows, mac) or specific formats (e.g. wav, midi, fonts, source code).

4. Newsgroups Discussing Networking & TCP/IP

---

news:alt.comp.dcom.sys.xyplex
Discussions relating to Whittaker/Xyplex

news:alt.dcom.slip-emulators
Pseudo-SLIP/PPP with shell accounts. TIA, SLAP, etc.

news:alt.dcom.telecom
Unmoderated discussion of telecommunications technology.

news:alt.dcom.telecom.radius
Remote Authentication Dial-In User Service

news:alt.mbone
Global InterNet multicast network discussions

news:alt.winsock
Windows Sockets.

news:alt.winsock.programming
Programming Windows Sockets.

news:alt.winsock.trumpet
The Trumpet newsreader.

news:comp.dcom.cabling
Cabling selection, installation and use.

news:comp.dcom.cell-relay
Forum for discussion of Cell Relay-based products.

news:comp.dcom.frame-relay
Technology and issues regarding frame relay networks.

news:comp.dcom.isdn
The Integrated Services Digital Network (ISDN).

news:comp.dcom.lans.ethernet
Discussions of the Ethernet/IEEE 802.3 protocols.

news:comp.dcom.lans.fddi
Discussions of the FDDI protocol suite.

news:comp.dcom.lans.hyperchannel
Hyperchannel networks within an IP network.

news:comp.dcom.lans.misc
Local area network hardware and software.

news:comp.dcom.lans.token-ring
Installing and using token ring networks.

news:comp.dcom.modems
Data communications hardware and software.

news:comp.dcom.modems.cable
Cable modems and internet access via cable tv.

news:comp.dcom.net-analysis
Network Testing and Analysis Procedures and Results.

news:comp.dcom.net-management
Network management methods and applications.

news:comp.dcom.sys.bay-networks
Bay Networks hardware, software, other products.

news:comp.dcom.sys.cisco
Info on Cisco routers and bridges.

news:comp.dcom.sys.nortel
Nortel telecommunications products and systems.

news:comp.dcom.telecom
Telecommunications digest. (Moderated)

news:comp.dcom.telecom.tech
Discussion of technical aspects of telephony.

news:comp.dcom.wan
All topics concerned with wide area networking.

news:comp.dcom.xdsl
Discussion area for different DSL technologies.

```
news:comp.os.linux.networking
         Networking and communications under Linux.

news:comp.os.ms-windows.apps.winsock.mail
         Winsock email applications.

news:comp.os.ms-windows.apps.winsock.misc
         Other Winsock applications.

news:comp.os.ms-windows.apps.winsock.news
         Winsock news applications.

news:comp.os.ms-windows.networking.misc
         Windows and other networks.

news:comp.os.ms-windows.networking.ras
         Windows RAS networking.

news:comp.os.ms-windows.networking.tcp-ip
         Windows and TCP/IP networking.

news:comp.os.ms-windows.networking.win95
         Win95 to Novell, TCP/IP, other nets.

news:comp.os.ms-windows.networking.windows
         Windows' built-in networking.

news:comp.os.ms-windows.nt.admin.networking
         Windows NT network administration.

news:comp.os.ms-windows.programmer.networks
         Network programming.

news:comp.os.ms-windows.programmer.tools.winsock
         Winsock programming.

news:comp.os.os2.networking.tcp-ip
         TCP/IP under OS/2.

news:comp.protocols.dns.bind
         Berkeley Internet Name Domain (BIND). (Moderated)

news:comp.protocols.dns.ops
         DNS operations (where not BIND specific). (Moderated)

news:comp.protocols.dns.std
         DNS standards activities, including IETF. (Moderated)

news:comp.protocols.iso
         The ISO protocol stack.
```

```
news:comp.protocols.kerberos
        The Kerberos authentication server.

news:comp.protocols.misc
        Various forms and types of protocol.

news:comp.protocols.nfs
        Discussion about the Network File System protocol.

news:comp.protocols.ppp
        Discussion of the Internet Point to Point Protocol.

news:comp.protocols.smb
        SMB file sharing protocol and Samba SMB server/client.

news:comp.protocols.snmp
        The Simple Network Management Protocol.

news:comp.protocols.tcp-ip
        TCP and IP network protocols.

news:comp.protocols.tcp-ip.domains
        Topics related to Domain Style names.

news:comp.protocols.tcp-ip.ibmpc
        TCP/IP for IBM(-like) personal computers.

news:comp.protocols.time.ntp
        The network time protocol.

news:comp.security.firewalls
        Anything pertaining to network firewall security.

news:comp.security.misc
        Security issues of computers and networks.

news:comp.std.wireless
       Examining standards for wireless network technology. (Moderated)

news:comp.unix.large
        UNIX on mainframes and in large networks.

news:trumpet.questions
        Questions & general discussion of Trumpet Winsock.

news:trumpet.bugs
        Reporting & discussion of bugs or "features" in Trumpet
Winsock.

news:microsoft.public.win16.programmer.networks
```

news:microsoft.public.win32.programmer.networks

news:microsoft.public.win95.dialupnetwork

news:microsoft.public.win95.networking

news:microsoft.public.win98.comm.dun

news:microsoft.public.win98.comm.modem

news:microsoft.public.win98.networking

news:microsoft.public.windowsnt.protocol.routing

news:microsoft.public.windowsnt.protocol.tcpip

5. Misc Networking Pages

---

1. A networking terms dictionary is available
   http://www.ktek.com/ktek/Lans-Wans.html

2. The comp.protocols.ppp FAQ is available at
   http://www.faqs.org/faqs/ppp-faq/part1/index.html
   ftp://rtfm.mit.edu/pub/usenet-by-group/comp.protocols.ppp/

   The comp.protocols.snmp FAQ FAQ is available at
   http://www.pantherdig.com/snmpfaq/index.html
   ftp://ftp.cs.utwente.nl/pub/src/snmp/

   There is a DHCP FAQ, written by John Wobus, available at
   http://web.syr.edu/~jmwobus/comfaqs/dhcp.faq.html

   The Amiga TCP/IP FAQ, written by Mike Meyer, is available at
   http://www.phone.net/ATCPFAQ/amitcp.txt
   http://www.phone.net/ATCPFAQ/amitcp.html

   There's a site for the Kermit project at
   http://www.kermit-project.org/

3. The comp.dcom.lans.ethernet FAQ is available at
   http://www.faqs.org/faqs/LANs/ethernet-faq/index.html
   ftp://rtfm.mit.edu/pub/usenet-by-hierarchy/news/answers/LANs/ethernet-faq

   Charles Spurgeon's Ethernet Page is at
   http://wwwhost.ots.utexas.edu/ethernet/ethernet-home.html

   The comp.dcom.lans.token-ring FAQ is available at
   http://home.sprynet.com/sprynet/jtmesser/faq/contents.html

The comp.dcom.cabling FAQ is available at
http://www.faqs.org/faqs/LANs/cabling-faq/index.html
ftp://rtfm.mit.edu/pub/usenet-by-group/comp.dcom.cabling/

The comp.dcom.cell-relay FAQ is available at
http://cell-relay.indiana.edu/cell-relay/FAQ/ATM-FAQ/FAQ.html

4. The Daedalus project at Berkeley deals with wireless networking and mobile computing, and it's web page contains links to some articles.
http://daedalus.cs.berkeley.edu/

Two pages decribing T1 with technical details are
http://www.laruscorp.com/t1tut.htm
http://www.gsnetworks.com/ezvu/ezvu500/TUTORIAL/PROTOCOL/genT1.txt

5. The Big-LAN FAQ, created for the big-lan@listserv.syr.edu mailing list, which discusses "[the] issues in designing and operating Campus-Size Local Area Networks, ..." is available at
ftp://rtfm.mit.edu/pub/usenet-by-hierarchy/news/answers/LANs/big-lan-faq

The comp.security.firewalls newsgroup has a FAQ, available at
http://www.clark.net/pub/mjr
ftp://ftp.greatcircle.com/pub/firewalls/FAQ

There's also a firewalls mailing list,
served by mailto:Majordomo@GreatCircle.com
archived at ftp://ftp.greatcircle.com/pub/firewalls/archive/

Daniel K. Kim has built a Searchable Check Point FireWall-1 discussion archive site (other mailing lists archived as well).
http://msgs.securepoint.com/

6. A large collection of communication tutorials may be found at IOL's training page, which has links to materials on TCP/IP, LAN technologies, programming & administrations manuals, and more.
http://www.iol.unh.edu/training/index.html

Data Communications magazine has a collection of technical tutorials available at it's site, covering such subjects as ATM, IP, high speed networking, etc.
http://www.data.com/Tutorials/

The University of Leeds ATM MultiMedia group has a collection of articles, links, etc about ATM.
http://www.scs.leeds.ac.uk/atm-mm/links.html

3COM has a page containing links to a collection of networking articles.
http://www.3com.com/technology/tech_net/white_papers/index.html

7. The comp.unix.programmer FAQ can be found at :
   http://www.erlenstar.demon.co.uk/unix/
   http://www.whitefang.com/unix/
   ftp://rtfm.mit.edu/pub/usenet/comp.unix.programmer/faq

8. The windows 95 FAQ, which covers, among other subjects, subjects relating to TCP/IP, networking, and modems, can be found at :
   http://www.orca.bc.ca/win95/
   ftp://rtfm.mit.edu/pub/usenet/news.answers/windows/win95/faq/

9. Committee T1's World Wide Web Site
   http://www.t1.org/

   The ATM Forum's home page can be found at
   http://www.atmforum.com/

   The Frame Relay Forum's home page can be found at
   http://www.frforum.com/

   The Frame Relay Resource Center
   http://www.alliancedatacom.com/

   The cable modems home page
   http://www.cablemodems.com/

   The GigaBit Ethernet Alliance home page
   http://www.gigabit-ethernet.org/

10. Protocols for WAN, LAN, ATM data communications and telecommunications.
    http://www.protocols.com/

    Oceanwave Technical Resources.
    http://www.oceanwave.com/technical-resources/

    Rohit's Srivastava's High Speed Networking & Programming page.
    http://members.tripod.com/~srohit/compu.html

    Network Design Tutorials and Other Resources.
    http://www.alaska.net/~research/Net/tutorial.htm

    Networking Technologies - Software Toolkits and Documentation
    http://www.nsrc.org/lowcost_tools/net-tech.html

    Network Troubleshooting site.
    http://www.networktroubleshooting.com/

    Tomi Engdahl's Telecommunication Electronics Page.
    http://junitec.ist.utl.pt/einfo/telecom.html

    Edwin Kremer's Security References.

http://www.cs.ruu.nl/~edwin/hot-lst.html

Standards (and Cross References)
http://www.cmpcmm.com/cc/standards.html

Lynn Larrow's Modems, Networking and Communications Links page.
http://www.webcom.com/~llarrow/comfaqs.html

Randy's Home Page.
http://ic.net/~nunez/

Hill Associates IT Technology Training networking articles.
http://www.hill.com/library/staffpubs/index.html

Appendix F.2 Private IP Network addresses

Author's Note: The following document is an example of an RFC (Request for Comment) that was used at the main way of setting standards on the Internet. The RFC is produced by a small working group that may be affiliated with any of a number of companies or organizations. If an RFC passed the public review stage it would become a standard. Because the Internet and technology has become so complex the standards are usually set by standards groups that use a number of different numbering schemes such as IEEE, ISO, ASCII, etc.

The following RFC was used to define private address network ranges that can be used by anyone without having to get prior approval. These addresses are not routed across the Internet. You can use these addresses on an isolated network, an Intranet, or local LAN/WAN side of a firewall that is also connected to the Internet. Your network will also be inaccessible from the Internet when the local addresses are accessed from outside the firewall because they are not being routed. However, your router can be used to allow you to access the Internet from your local LAN/WAN.

```
Network Working Group                                         Y. Rekhter
Request for Comments: 1918                                 Cisco Systems
Obsoletes: 1627, 1597                                       B. Moskowitz
BCP: 5                                                   Chrysler Corp.
Category: Best Current Practice                            D. Karrenberg
                                                                RIPE NCC
                                                          G. J. de Groot
                                                                RIPE NCC
```

E. Lear
Silicon Graphics, Inc.
February 1996

Address Allocation for Private Internets

Status of this Memo

This document specifies an Internet Best Current Practices for the Internet Community, and requests discussion and suggestions for improvements. Distribution of this memo is unlimited.

1. Introduction

For the purposes of this document, an enterprise is an entity autonomously operating a network using TCP/IP and in particular determining the addressing plan and address assignments within that network.

This document describes address allocation for private internets. The allocation permits full network layer connectivity among all hosts inside an enterprise as well as among all public hosts of different enterprises. The cost of using private internet address space is the potentially costly effort to renumber hosts and networks between public and private.

2. Motivation

With the proliferation of TCP/IP technology worldwide, including outside the Internet itself, an increasing number of non-connected enterprises use this technology and its addressing capabilities for sole intra-enterprise communications, without any intention to ever directly connect to other enterprises or the Internet itself.

The Internet has grown beyond anyone's expectations. Sustained exponential growth continues to introduce new challenges. One challenge is a concern within the community that globally unique address space will be exhausted. A separate and far more pressing concern is that the amount of routing overhead will grow beyond the capabilities of Internet Service Providers. Efforts are in progress within the community to find long term solutions to both of these problems. Meanwhile it is necessary to revisit address allocation procedures, and their impact on the Internet routing system.

To contain growth of routing overhead, an Internet Provider obtains a block of address space from an address registry, and then assigns to its customers addresses from within that block based on each customer requirement. The result of this process is that routes to many customers will be aggregated together, and will appear to other providers as a single route [RFC1518], [RFC1519]. In order for route aggregation to be effective, Internet providers encourage customers joining their network to use the provider's block, and thus renumber their computers. Such encouragement may become a requirement in the future.

With the current size of the Internet and its growth rate it is no longer realistic to assume that by virtue of acquiring globally unique IP addresses out of an Internet registry an organization that acquires such addresses would have Internet-wide IP connectivity once the organization gets connected to the Internet. To the contrary, it is quite likely that when the organization would connect to the Internet to achieve Internet-wide IP connectivity the organization would need to change IP addresses (renumber) all of its public hosts (hosts that require Internet-wide IP connectivity), regardless of whether the addresses used by the organization initially were globally unique or not.

It has been typical to assign globally unique addresses to all hosts that use TCP/IP. In order to extend the life of the IPv4 address space, address registries are requiring more justification than ever before, making it harder for organizations to acquire additional address space [RFC1466].

Hosts within enterprises that use IP can be partitioned into three categories:

Category 1: hosts that do not require access to hosts in other enterprises or the Internet at large; hosts within this category may use IP addresses that are unambiguous within an enterprise, but may be ambiguous between enterprises.

Category 2: hosts that need access to a limited set of outside services (e.g., E-mail, FTP, netnews, remote login) which can be handled by mediating gateways (e.g., application layer gateways). For many hosts in this category an unrestricted external access (provided via IP connectivity) may be unnecessary and even undesirable for privacy/security reasons. Just like hosts within the first category, such hosts may use IP addresses that are unambiguous within an enterprise, but may be ambiguous between enterprises.

Category 3: hosts that need network layer access outside the enterprise (provided via IP connectivity); hosts in the last category require IP addresses that are globally unambiguous.

We will refer to the hosts in the first and second categories as "private". We will refer to the hosts in the third category as "public".

Many applications require connectivity only within one enterprise and do not need external (outside the enterprise) connectivity for the majority of internal hosts. In larger enterprises it is often easy to identify a substantial number of hosts using TCP/IP that do not need network layer connectivity outside the enterprise.

Some examples, where external connectivity might not be required, are:

- A large airport which has its arrival/departure displays individually addressable via TCP/IP. It is very unlikely that these displays need to be directly accessible from other networks.

- Large organizations like banks and retail chains are switching to TCP/IP for their internal communication. Large numbers of local workstations like cash registers, money machines, and equipment at clerical positions rarely need to have such connectivity.

- For security reasons, many enterprises use application layer gateways to connect their internal network to the Internet. The internal network usually does not have direct access to the Internet, thus only one or more gateways are visible from the Internet. In this case, the internal network can use non-unique IP network numbers.

- Interfaces of routers on an internal network usually do not need to be directly accessible from outside the enterprise.

3. Private Address Space

The Internet Assigned Numbers Authority (IANA) has reserved the following three blocks of the IP address space for private internets:

```
10.0.0.0        -   10.255.255.255  (10/8 prefix)
172.16.0.0      -   172.31.255.255  (172.16/12 prefix)
192.168.0.0     -   192.168.255.255 (192.168/16 prefix)
```

We will refer to the first block as "24-bit block", the second as "20-bit block", and to the third as "16-bit" block. Note that (in pre-CIDR notation) the first block is nothing but a single class A network number, while the second block is a set of 16 contiguous class B network numbers, and third block is a set of 256 contiguous class C network numbers.

An enterprise that decides to use IP addresses out of the address space defined in this document can do so without any coordination with IANA or an Internet registry. The address space can thus be used by many enterprises. Addresses within this private address space will only be unique within the enterprise, or the set of enterprises which choose to cooperate over this space so they may communicate with each other in their own private internet.

As before, any enterprise that needs globally unique address space is required to obtain such addresses from an Internet registry. An enterprise that requests IP addresses for its external connectivity will never be assigned addresses from the blocks defined above.

In order to use private address space, an enterprise needs to determine which hosts do not need to have network layer connectivity outside the enterprise in the foreseeable future and thus could be classified as private. Such hosts will use the private address space defined above. Private hosts can communicate with all other hosts inside the enterprise, both public and private. However, they cannot have IP connectivity to any host outside of the enterprise. While not having external (outside of the enterprise) IP connectivity private hosts can still have access to external services via mediating gateways (e.g., application layer gateways).

All other hosts will be public and will use globally unique address space assigned by an Internet Registry. Public hosts can communicate with other hosts inside the enterprise both public and private and can have IP connectivity to public hosts outside the enterprise. Public hosts do not have connectivity to private hosts of other enterprises.

Moving a host from private to public or vice versa involves a change of IP address, changes to the appropriate DNS entries, and changes to configuration files on other hosts that reference the host by IP address.

Because private addresses have no global meaning, routing information about private networks shall not be propagated on inter-enterprise links, and packets with private source or destination addresses should not be forwarded across such links. Routers in networks not using private address space, especially those of Internet service providers, are expected to be configured to reject (filter out) routing information about private networks. If such a router receives such information the rejection shall not be treated as a routing protocol error.

Indirect references to such addresses should be contained within the enterprise. Prominent examples of such references are DNS Resource Records and other information referring to internal private addresses. In particular, Internet service providers should take measures to prevent such leakage.

4. Advantages and Disadvantages of Using Private Address Space

The obvious advantage of using private address space for the Internet at large is to conserve the globally unique address space by not using it where global uniqueness is not required.

Enterprises themselves also enjoy a number of benefits from their usage of private address space: They gain a lot of flexibility in network design by having more address space at their disposal than they could obtain from the globally unique pool. This enables operationally and administratively convenient addressing schemes as well as easier growth paths.

For a variety of reasons the Internet has already encountered situations where an enterprise that has not been connected to the Internet had used IP address space for its hosts without getting this space assigned from the IANA. In some cases this address space had been already assigned to other enterprises. If such an enterprise would later connects to the Internet, this could potentially create very serious problems, as IP routing cannot provide correct operations in presence of ambiguous addressing. Although in principle Internet Service Providers should guard against such mistakes through the use of route filters, this does not always happen in practice. Using private address space provides a safe choice for such enterprises, avoiding clashes once outside connectivity is needed.
A major drawback to the use of private address space is that it may actually reduce an enterprise's flexibility to access the Internet. Once one commits to using a private address, one is committing to renumber part or all of an enterprise, should one decide to provide IP connectivity between that part (or all of the enterprise) and the Internet. Usually the cost of renumbering can be measured by counting the number of hosts that have to transition from private to public. As was discussed earlier, however, even if a network uses globally unique addresses, it may still have to renumber in order to acquire Internet-wide IP connectivity.

Another drawback to the use of private address space is that it may require renumbering when merging several private internets into a single private internet. If we review the examples we list in Section 2, we note that companies tend to merge. If such companies prior to the merge maintained their uncoordinated internets using private address space, then if after the merge these private internets would be combined into a single private internet, some addresses within the combined private internet may not be unique. As a result, hosts with these addresses would need to be renumbered.

The cost of renumbering may well be mitigated by development and deployment of tools that facilitate renumbering (e.g. Dynamic Host Configuration Protocol (DHCP)). When deciding whether to use private addresses, we recommend to inquire computer and software vendors about availability of such tools. A separate IETF effort (PIER Working Group) is pursuing full documentation of the requirements and procedures for renumbering.

5. Operational Considerations

One possible strategy is to design the private part of the network first and use private address space for all internal links. Then plan public subnets at the locations needed and design the external connectivity.

This design does not need to be fixed permanently. If a group of one or more hosts requires to change their status (from private to public or vice versa) later, this can be accomplished by renumbering only the hosts involved, and changing physical connectivity, if needed. In locations where such changes can be foreseen (machine rooms, etc.), it is advisable to configure separate physical media for public and private subnets to facilitate such changes. In order to avoid major network disruptions, it is advisable to group hosts with similar connectivity needs on their own subnets.

If a suitable subnetting scheme can be designed and is supported by the equipment concerned, it is advisable to use the 24-bit block (class A network) of private address space and make an addressing plan with a good growth path. If subnetting is a problem, the 16-bit block (class C networks), or the 20-bit block (class B networks) of private address space can be used.

One might be tempted to have both public and private addresses on the same physical medium. While this is possible, there are pitfalls to such a design (note that the pitfalls have nothing to do with the use of private addresses, but are due to the presence of multiple IP subnets on a common Data Link subnetwork). We advise caution when proceeding in this area.

It is strongly recommended that routers which connect enterprises to external networks are set up with appropriate packet and routing filters at both ends of the link in order to prevent packet and routing information leakage. An enterprise should also filter any private networks from inbound routing information in order to protect itself from ambiguous routing situations which can occur if routes to the private address space point outside the enterprise.

It is possible for two sites, who both coordinate their private address space, to communicate with each other over a public network. To do so they must use some method of encapsulation at their borders to a public network, thus keeping their private addresses private.

If two (or more) organizations follow the address allocation specified in this document and then later wish to establish IP connectivity with each other, then there is a risk that address uniqueness would be violated. To minimize the risk it is strongly recommended that an organization using private IP addresses choose randomly from the reserved pool of private addresses, when allocating sub-blocks for its internal allocation.

If an enterprise uses the private address space, or a mix of private and public address spaces, then DNS clients outside of the enterprise should not see addresses in the private address space used by the enterprise, since these addresses would be ambiguous. One way to ensure this is to run two authority servers for each DNS zone containing both publicly and privately addressed hosts. One server would be visible from the public address space and would contain only the subset of the enterprise's addresses which were reachable using public addresses. The other server would be reachable only from the private network and would contain the full set of data, including the private addresses and whatever public addresses are reachable the private network. In order to ensure consistency, both servers should be configured from the same data of which the publicly visible zone only contains a filtered version. There is certain degree of additional complexity associated with providing these capabilities.

6. Security Considerations

Security issues are not addressed in this memo.

7. Conclusion

With the described scheme many large enterprises will need only a relatively small block of addresses from the globally unique IP address space. The Internet at large benefits through conservation of globally unique address space which will effectively lengthen the lifetime of the IP address space. The enterprises benefit from the increased flexibility provided by a relatively large private address space. However, use of private addressing requires that an organization renumber part or all of its enterprise network, as its connectivity requirements change over time.

8. Acknowledgments

We would like to thank Tony Bates (MCI), Jordan Becker (ANS), Hans-Werner Braun (SDSC), Ross Callon (BayNetworks), John Curran (BBN Planet), Vince Fuller (BBN Planet), Tony Li (cisco Systems), Anne Lord (RIPE NCC), Milo Medin (NSI), Marten Terpstra (BayNetworks), Geza Turchanyi (RIPE NCC), Christophe Wolfhugel (Pasteur Institute), Andy Linton (connect.com.au), Brian Carpenter (CERN), Randy Bush (PSG), Erik Fair (Apple Computer), Dave Crocker (Brandenburg Consulting), Tom Kessler (SGI), Dave Piscitello (Core Competence), Matt Crawford (FNAL), Michael Patton (BBN), and Paul Vixie (Internet Software Consortium) for their review and constructive comments.

9. References

[RFC1466] Gerich, E., "Guidelines for Management of IP Address Space", RFC 1466, Merit Network, Inc., May 1993.

[RFC1518] Rekhter, Y., and T. Li, "An Architecture for IP Address Allocation with CIDR", RFC 1518, September 1993.

[RFC1519] Fuller, V., Li, T., Yu, J., and K. Varadhan, "Classless Inter-Domain Routing (CIDR): an Address Assignment and Aggregation Strategy", RFC 1519, September 1993.

10. Authors' Addresses

Yakov Rekhter
Cisco systems
170 West Tasman Drive
San Jose, CA, USA
Phone: +1 914 528 0090
Fax: +1 408 526-4952
EMail: yakov@cisco.com

Robert G Moskowitz
Chrysler Corporation
CIMS: 424-73-00
25999 Lawrence Ave
Center Line, MI 48015
Phone: +1 810 758 8212
Fax: +1 810 758 8173
EMail: rgm3@is.chrysler.com

Daniel Karrenberg
RIPE Network Coordination Centre
Kruislaan 409
1098 SJ Amsterdam, the Netherlands
Phone: +31 20 592 5065
Fax: +31 20 592 5090
EMail: Daniel.Karrenberg@ripe.net

Geert Jan de Groot
RIPE Network Coordination Centre
Kruislaan 409
1098 SJ Amsterdam, the Netherlands
Phone: +31 20 592 5065
Fax: +31 20 592 5090
EMail: GeertJan.deGroot@ripe.net

Eliot Lear
Mail Stop 15-730
Silicon Graphics, Inc.
2011 N. Shoreline Blvd.
Mountain View, CA 94043-1389
Phone: +1 415 960 1980
Fax: +1 415 961 9584
EMail: lear@sgi.com

APPENDIX G

NAMESERVER DOCUMENTATION

APPENDIX OBJECTIVES

 DNS How-To

Author's Note: This appendix goes into more detail on making your own nameserver. Once you feel confident about the discussions in the text you should examine the following to see how you can expand your nameserver's capabilities.

APPENDIX G.1 DNS HOW-TO

Author's Note: The following discussion talks about how to create a DNS nameserver from a technical aspect and covers some of the differences between DNS version 4 and version 8. It is available at http://metalab.unc.edu/pub/linux/docs/HOWTO/DNS-HOWTO

```
DNS HOWTO
```

Nicolai Langfeldt janl@math.uio.no

```
v2.2, 11 February 1999

HOWTO become a totally small time DNS admin.
```

Table of Contents

1. Preamble

  1.1 Legal stuff

1.2 Credits and request for help.
1.3 Dedication

2. Introduction.

3. A caching only name server.

3.1 Starting named
3.2 Making it even better
3.3 Congratulations

4. A

4.1 But first some dry theory
4.2 Our own domain
4.3 The reverse zone
4.4 Words of caution
4.5 Why reverse lookups don't work.
4.5.1 The reverse zone isn't delegated.
4.5.2 You've got a classless subnet

5. A real domain example

5.1 /etc/named.conf (or /var/named/named.conf)
5.2 /var/named/root.hints
5.3 /var/named/zone/127.0.0
5.4 /var/named/zone/land-5.com
5.5 /var/named/zone/206.6.177

6. Maintenance

7. Converting from version 4 to version 8

8. Questions and Answers

9. How to become a bigger time DNS admin.

---

1. Preamble

Keywords: DNS, bind, bind-4, bind-8, named, dialup, ppp, slip, isdn, Internet, domain, name, hosts, resolving, caching.

This document is part of the Linux Documentation Project.

1.1. Legal stuff

1.2. Credits and request for help.

I want to thank Arnt Gulbrandsen whom I cause to suffer through the drafts to this work and whom provided many useful suggestions. I also want to thank the numerous people that have e-mailed suggestions and notes.

This will never be a finished document, please send me mail about your problems and successes, it can make this a better HOWTO. So please send comments and/or questions or money to janl@math.uio.no. If you send e-mail and want an answer please show the simple courtesy of making sure that the return address is correct and working. Also, please read the "QnA" section before mailing me. Another thing, I can only understand Norwegian and English.

If you want to translate this HOWTO please notify me so I can keep track of what languages it has been published in, and also I can notify you when the HOWTO has been updated.

1.3. Dedication

This HOWTO is dedicated to Anne Line Norheim Langfeldt. Though she will probably never read it since she's not that kind of girl.

2. Introduction.

What this is and isn't.

DNS is is the Domain Name System. DNS converts machine names to the IP addresses that all machines on the net have. It maps from name to address and from address to name, and some other things. This HOWTO documents how to define such mappings using a Linux system. A mapping is simply a association between two things, in this case a machine name, like ftp.linux.org, and the machines IP number (or address) 199.249.150.4.

DNS is, to the uninitiated (you ;-), one of the more opaque areas of network administration. This HOWTO will try to make a few things clearer. It describes how to set up a simple DNS name server. Starting with a caching only server and going on to setting up a primary DNS server for a domain. For more complex setups you can check the "QnA" section of this document. If it's not described there you will need to read the Real Documentation. I'll get back to what this Real Documentation consists of in "the last chapter".

Before you start on this you should configure your machine so that you can telnet in and out of it, and successfully make all kinds of connections to the net, and you should especially be able to do telnet 127.0.0.1 and get your own machine (test it now!). You also need a good /etc/nsswitch.conf (or /etc/host.conf), /etc/resolv.conf and /etc/hosts files as a starting point, since I will not explain their function here. If you don't already have all this set up and working the NET-3-HOWTO and/or the PPP-HOWTO explains how to set it up. Read them.

When I say 'your machine' I mean the machine you are trying to set up DNS on. Not any other machine you might have that's involved in your networking effort.

I assume you're not behind any kind of firewall that blocks name queries. If you are you will need a special configuration, see the section on "QnA".

Name serving on Unix is done by a program called named. This is a part of the "bind" package which is coordinated by Paul Vixie for The Internet Software Consortium. Named is included in most Linux distributions and is usually installed as /usr/sbin/named. If you have a named you can probably use it; if you don't have one you can get a binary off a Linux ftp site, or get the latest and greatest source from ftp.isc.org:/isc/bind/src/cur/bind-8/. This HOWTO is about bind version 8. The old version of the HOWTO, about bind 4 is still available at http://www.math.uio.no/~janl/DNS/ in case you use bind 4. If the named man page talks about (at the very end, the FILES section) named.conf you have bind 8, if it talks about named.boot you have bind 4. If you have 4 and are security conscious you really ought to upgrade to a recent 8.

DNS is a net-wide database. Take care about what you put into it. If you put junk into it, you, and others will get junk out of it. Keep your DNS tidy and consistent and you will get good service from it. Learn to use it, admin it, debug it and you will be another good admin keeping the net from falling to it's knees by mismanagement.

In this document I state flatly a couple of things that are not completely true (they are at least half truths though). All in the interest of simplification. Things will (probably ;-) work if you believe what I say.

Tip: Make backup copies of all the files I instruct you to change if you already have them, so if after going through this nothing works you can get it back to your old, working state.

3. A caching only name server.

A first stab at DNS config, very useful for dialup users.

A caching only name server will find the answer to name queries and remember the answer the next time you need it. This will shorten the waiting time the next time significantly, especially if you're on a slow connection.

First you need a file called /etc/named.conf. This is read when named starts. For now it should simply contain:

```
// Config file for caching only name server

options {
    directory "/var/named";

    // Uncommenting this might help if you have to go through a
    // firewall and things are not working out:

    // query-source port 53;
};

zone "." {
    type hint;
    file "root.hints";
};

zone "0.0.127.in-addr.arpa" {
    type master;
    file "pz/127.0.0";
};
```

The 'directory' line tells named where to look for files. All files named subsequently will be relative to this. Thus pz is a directory under /var/named, i.e., /var/named/pz. /var/named is the right directory according to the Linux File system Standard.

The file named /var/named/root.hints is named in this. /var/named/root.hints should contain this:

```
;
; There might be opening comments here if you already have this file.
; If not don't worry.
;
.          6D IN NS    G.ROOT-SERVERS.NET.
.          6D IN NS    J.ROOT-SERVERS.NET.
.          6D IN NS    K.ROOT-SERVERS.NET.
.          6D IN NS    L.ROOT-SERVERS.NET.
.          6D IN NS    M.ROOT-SERVERS.NET.
.          6D IN NS    A.ROOT-SERVERS.NET.
.          6D IN NS    H.ROOT-SERVERS.NET.
.          6D IN NS    B.ROOT-SERVERS.NET.
.          6D IN NS    C.ROOT-SERVERS.NET.
.          6D IN NS    D.ROOT-SERVERS.NET.
.          6D IN NS    E.ROOT-SERVERS.NET.
.          6D IN NS    I.ROOT-SERVERS.NET.
.          6D IN NS    F.ROOT-SERVERS.NET.

G.ROOT-SERVERS.NET.   5w6d16h IN A  192.112.36.4
J.ROOT-SERVERS.NET.   5w6d16h IN A  198.41.0.10
K.ROOT-SERVERS.NET.   5w6d16h IN A  193.0.14.129
L.ROOT-SERVERS.NET.   5w6d16h IN A  198.32.64.12
M.ROOT-SERVERS.NET.   5w6d16h IN A  202.12.27.33
A.ROOT-SERVERS.NET.   5w6d16h IN A  198.41.0.4
H.ROOT-SERVERS.NET.   5w6d16h IN A  128.63.2.53
B.ROOT-SERVERS.NET.   5w6d16h IN A  128.9.0.107
C.ROOT-SERVERS.NET.   5w6d16h IN A  192.33.4.12
D.ROOT-SERVERS.NET.   5w6d16h IN A  128.8.10.90
E.ROOT-SERVERS.NET.   5w6d16h IN A  192.203.230.10
I.ROOT-SERVERS.NET.   5w6d16h IN A  192.36.148.17
F.ROOT-SERVERS.NET.   5w6d16h IN A  192.5.5.241
```

The file describes the root name servers in the world. This changes over time and must be maintained. See the "maintenance section" for how to keep it up to date.

The next section in named.conf is the last zone. I will explain its use in a later chapter, for now just make this a file named 127.0.0 in the subdirectory pz:

```
@         IN   SOA   ns.linux.bogus. hostmaster.linux.bogus. (
                 1     ; Serial
                 8H    ; Refresh
                 2H    ; Retry
                 1W    ; Expire
```

```
                1D)    ; Minimum TTL
            NS    ns.linux.bogus.
1            PTR    localhost.
```

Next, you need a /etc/resolv.conf looking something like this:

```
search subdomain.your-domain.edu your-domain.edu
nameserver 127.0.0.1
```

The 'search' line specifies what domains should be searched for any host names you want to connect to. The 'nameserver' line specifies the address of your nameserver, in this case your own machine since that is where your named runs (127.0.0.1 is right, no matter if your machine has an other address too). If you want to list several name servers put in one 'nameserver' line for each. (Note: Named never reads this file, the resolver that uses named does.)

To illustrate what this file does: If a client tries to look up foo, then foo.subdomain.your-domain.edu is tried first, then foo.your-fomain.edu, finally foo. If a client tries to look up sunsite.unc.edu, sunsite.unc.edu.subdomain.your-domain.edu is tried first (yes, it's silly, but that's the way it works), then sunsite.unc.edu.your-domain.edu, and finally sunsite.unc.edu. You may not want to put in too many domains in the search line, it takes time to search them all.

The example assumes you belong in the domain subdomain.your-domain.edu, your machine then, is probably called your-machine.subdomain.your-domain.edu. The search line should not contain your TLD (Top Level Domain, 'edu' in this case). If you frequently need to connect to hosts in another domain you can add that domain to the search line like this:

```
search subdomain.your-domain.edu your-domain.edu other-domain.com
```

---

and so on. Obviously you need to put real domain names in instead. Please note the lack of periods at the end of the domain names. This is important, please note the lack of periods at the end of the domain names.

```
Next, depending on your libc version you either need to fix
/etc/nsswitch.conf or /etc/host.conf. If you already have
nsswitch.conf that's what we'll fix, if not, we'll fix host.conf.

/etc/nsswitch.conf

This is a long file specifying where to get different kinds of data
types, from what file or database. It usually contains helpful
comments at the top, which you should consider reading. After that
find the line starting with 'hosts:', it should read
```

```
hosts:   files dns
```

```
If there is no line starting with 'hosts:' then put in the one above.
It says that programs should first look in the /etc/hosts file, then
check DNS according to resolv.conf.

/etc/host.conf

It probably contains several lines, one should start with order and
it
should look like this:
```

```
order hosts,bind
```

```
If there is no 'order' line you should add one. It tells the host
name resolving routines to first look in /etc/hosts, then ask the name
server (which you in resolv.conf said is at 127.0.0.1).

3.1. Starting named

After all this it's time to start named. If you're using a dialup
connection connect first. Type 'ndc start', and press return, no
options. If that does not work try '/usr/sbin/ndc start' instead. If
that back-fires see the "QnA" section. If you view your syslog
message file (usually called /var/adm/messages, but another directory
to look in is /var/log and another file to look in is syslog) while
starting named (do tail -f /var/log/messages) you should see something
like:

(the lines ending in \ continue on the next line)

  Feb 15 01:26:17 roke named[6091]: starting. named 8.1.1 Sat Feb 14 \
```

```
     00:18:20 MET 1998 ^Ijanl@roke.uio.no:/var/tmp/bind-
8.1.1/src/bin/named
     Feb 15 01:26:17 roke named[6091]: cache zone "" (IN) loaded (ser-
ial 0)
     Feb 15 01:26:17 roke named[6091]: master zone "0.0.127.in-
addr.arpa" \
      (IN) loaded (serial 1)
     Feb 15 01:26:17 roke named[6091]: listening [127.0.0.1].53 (lo)
     Feb 15 01:26:17 roke named[6091]: listening [129.240.230.92].53
(ippp0)
     Feb 15 01:26:17 roke named[6091]: Forwarding source address is
[0.0.0.0].1040
     Feb 15 01:26:17 roke named[6092]: Ready to answer queries.
```

If there are any messages about errors then there is a mistake. Named will name the file it is in (one of named.conf and root.hints I hope :-) Kill named and go back and check the file.

Now you can test your setup. Start nslookup to examine your work.

```
$ nslookup
Default Server: localhost
Address: 127.0.0.1

>
```

If that's what you get it's working. We hope. Anything else, go back and check everything. Each time you change the named.conf file you need to restart named using the ndc restart command.

Now you can enter a query. Try looking up some machine close to you. pat.uio.no is close to me, at the University of Oslo:

```
> pat.uio.no
Server: localhost
Address: 127.0.0.1

Name:  pat.uio.no
Address: 129.240.130.16
```

nslookup now asked your named to look for the machine pat.uio.no. It then contacted one of the name server machines named in your root.hints file, and asked its way from there. It might take tiny while before you get the result as it may need to search all the domains you named in /etc/resolv.conf.

If you ask the same again you get this:

```
> pat.uio.no
Server: localhost
Address: 127.0.0.1

Non-authoritative answer:
Name:  pat.uio.no
Address: 129.240.2.50
```

Note the "Non-authoritative answer:" line we got this time around. That means that named did not go out on the network to ask this time, the information is in the cache now. But the cached information might be out of date (stale). So you are informed of this (very slight) possibility by it saying 'Non-authorative answer:'. When nslookup says this the second time you ask for a host it's a sure sign that named caches the information and that it's working. You exit nslookup by giving the command 'exit'.

3.2. Making it even better

In large, well organized, academic or ISP (Internet Service Provider) networks you will sometimes find that the network people has set up a forwarder hierarchy of DNS servers which helps lighten the internal network load and on the outside servers as well. It's not easy to know if you're inside such a network or not. It is however not important and by using the DNS server of your network provider as a "forwarder" you can make the responses to queries faster and less of a load on your network. If you use a modem this can be quite a win. For the sake of this example we assume that your network provider has two name servers they want you to use, with IP numbers 10.0.0.1 and 10.1.0.1. Then, in your named.conf file, inside the opening section called "options" insert these lines:

```
forward first;
forwarders {
  10.0.0.1;
  10.1.0.1;
};
```

Restart your nameserver and test it with nslookup. Should work fine.

3.3. Congratulations

Now you know how to set up a caching named. Take a beer, milk, or whatever you prefer to celebrate it.

4. A simple domain.

How to set up your own domain.

4.1. But first some dry theory

Before we really start this section I'm going to serve you some theory on and an example of how DNS works. And you're going to read it because it's good for you. If you don't want to you should at least skim it very quickly. Stop skimming when you get to what should go in your named.conf file.

DNS is a hierarchical, tree structured, system. The top is written '.' and pronounced 'root'. Under . there are a number of Top Level Domains (TLDs), the best known ones are ORG, COM, EDU and NET, but there are many more. Just like a tree it has a root and it branches out. If you have any computer science background you will recognize DNS as a search tree, and you will be able to find nodes, leaf nodes and edges.

When looking for a machine the query proceeds recursively into the hierarchy starting at the top. If you want to find out the address of prep.ai.mit.edu your name server has to find a name server that serves edu. It asks a . server (it already knows the . servers, that's what the root.hints file is for), the . server gives a list of edu servers:

```
$ nslookup
Default Server: localhost
Address: 127.0.0.1
```

Start asking a root server:

```
> server c.root-servers.net.
Default Server: c.root-servers.net
Address: 192.33.4.12
```

Set the Query type to NS (name server records):

```
> set q=ns
```

Ask about edu:

```
> edu.
```

The trailing . here is significant, it tells nslookup we're asking that edu is right under . (and not under any of our search domains, it speeds the search).

```
edu    nameserver = A.ROOT-SERVERS.NET
edu    nameserver = H.ROOT-SERVERS.NET
edu    nameserver = B.ROOT-SERVERS.NET
edu    nameserver = C.ROOT-SERVERS.NET
edu    nameserver = D.ROOT-SERVERS.NET
edu    nameserver = E.ROOT-SERVERS.NET
edu    nameserver = I.ROOT-SERVERS.NET
edu    nameserver = F.ROOT-SERVERS.NET
edu    nameserver = G.ROOT-SERVERS.NET
A.ROOT-SERVERS.NET   internet address = 198.41.0.4
H.ROOT-SERVERS.NET   internet address = 128.63.2.53
B.ROOT-SERVERS.NET   internet address = 128.9.0.107
C.ROOT-SERVERS.NET   internet address = 192.33.4.12
D.ROOT-SERVERS.NET   internet address = 128.8.10.90
E.ROOT-SERVERS.NET   internet address = 192.203.230.10
I.ROOT-SERVERS.NET   internet address = 192.36.148.17
F.ROOT-SERVERS.NET   internet address = 192.5.5.241
G.ROOT-SERVERS.NET   internet address = 192.112.36.4
```

This tells us that all ROOT-SERVERS.NET servers serves EDU., so we can go on asking any of them. We'll continue asking C. Now we want to know who serves the next level of the domain name: mit.edu.:

```
> mit.edu.
Server: c.root-servers.net
Address: 192.33.4.12

Non-authoritative answer:
mit.edu nameserver = W20NS.mit.edu
mit.edu nameserver = BITSY.mit.edu
mit.edu nameserver = STRAWB.mit.edu

Authoritative answers can be found from:
W20NS.mit.edu  internet address = 18.70.0.160
BITSY.mit.edu  internet address = 18.72.0.3
STRAWB.mit.edu internet address = 18.71.0.151
```

steawb, w20ns and bitsy all serves mit.edu, we select one and inquire about the name one more level up: ai.mit.edu:

```
> server W20NS.mit.edu.
```

Host names are not case sensitive, but I use my mouse to cut and paste so it gets copied as-is from the screen.

```
Server: W20NS.mit.edu
Address: 18.70.0.160
```

```
> ai.mit.edu.
Server: W20NS.mit.edu
Address: 18.70.0.160

Non-authoritative answer:
ai.mit.edu    nameserver = ALPHA-BITS.AI.MIT.EDU
ai.mit.edu    nameserver = GRAPE-NUTS.AI.MIT.EDU
ai.mit.edu    nameserver = TRIX.AI.MIT.EDU
ai.mit.edu    nameserver = MUESLI.AI.MIT.EDU
ai.mit.edu    nameserver = LIFE.AI.MIT.EDU
ai.mit.edu    nameserver = BEET-CHEX.AI.MIT.EDU
ai.mit.edu    nameserver = MINI-WHEATS.AI.MIT.EDU
ai.mit.edu    nameserver = COUNT-CHOCULA.AI.MIT.EDU
ai.mit.edu    nameserver = MINTAKA.LCS.MIT.EDU

Authoritative answers can be found from:
AI.MIT.EDU    nameserver = ALPHA-BITS.AI.MIT.EDU
AI.MIT.EDU    nameserver = GRAPE-NUTS.AI.MIT.EDU
AI.MIT.EDU    nameserver = TRIX.AI.MIT.EDU
AI.MIT.EDU    nameserver = MUESLI.AI.MIT.EDU
AI.MIT.EDU    nameserver = LIFE.AI.MIT.EDU
AI.MIT.EDU    nameserver = BEET-CHEX.AI.MIT.EDU
AI.MIT.EDU    nameserver = MINI-WHEATS.AI.MIT.EDU
AI.MIT.EDU    nameserver = COUNT-CHOCULA.AI.MIT.EDU
AI.MIT.EDU    nameserver = MINTAKA.LCS.MIT.EDU
ALPHA-BITS.AI.MIT.EDU  internet address = 128.52.32.5
GRAPE-NUTS.AI.MIT.EDU  internet address = 128.52.36.4
TRIX.AI.MIT.EDU internet address = 128.52.37.6
MUESLI.AI.MIT.EDU    internet address = 128.52.39.7
LIFE.AI.MIT.EDU internet address = 128.52.32.80
BEET-CHEX.AI.MIT.EDU  internet address = 128.52.32.22
MINI-WHEATS.AI.MIT.EDU internet address = 128.52.54.11
COUNT-CHOCULA.AI.MIT.EDU    internet address = 128.52.38.22
MINTAKA.LCS.MIT.EDU   internet address = 18.26.0.36
```

So museli.ai.mit.edu is a nameserver for ai.mit.edu:

```
   > server MUESLI.AI.MIT.EDU
   Default Server: MUESLI.AI.MIT.EDU
   Address: 128.52.39.7
```

Now I change query type, we've found the name server so now we're going to ask about everything wheaties knows about prep.ai.mit.edu.

```
> set q=any
> prep.ai.mit.edu.
```

```
Server: MUESLI.AI.MIT.EDU
Address: 128.52.39.7

prep.ai.mit.edu CPU = dec/decstation-5000.25  OS = unix
prep.ai.mit.edu
    inet address = 18.159.0.42, protocol = tcp
     ftp telnet smtp finger
prep.ai.mit.edu preference = 1, mail exchanger = gnu-life.ai.mit.edu
prep.ai.mit.edu internet address = 18.159.0.42
ai.mit.edu   nameserver = beet-chex.ai.mit.edu
ai.mit.edu   nameserver = alpha-bits.ai.mit.edu
ai.mit.edu   nameserver = mini-wheats.ai.mit.edu
ai.mit.edu   nameserver = trix.ai.mit.edu
ai.mit.edu   nameserver = muesli.ai.mit.edu
ai.mit.edu   nameserver = count-chocula.ai.mit.edu
ai.mit.edu   nameserver = mintaka.lcs.mit.edu
ai.mit.edu   nameserver = life.ai.mit.edu
gnu-life.ai.mit.edu   internet address = 128.52.32.60
beet-chex.ai.mit.edu  internet address = 128.52.32.22
alpha-bits.ai.mit.edu  internet address = 128.52.32.5
mini-wheats.ai.mit.edu internet address = 128.52.54.11
trix.ai.mit.edu internet address = 128.52.37.6
muesli.ai.mit.edu    internet address = 128.52.39.7
count-chocula.ai.mit.edu    internet address = 128.52.38.22
mintaka.lcs.mit.edu   internet address = 18.26.0.36
life.ai.mit.edu internet address = 128.52.32.80
```

So starting at . we found the successive name servers for the each level in the domain name. If you had used your own DNS server instead of using all those other servers, your named would of-course cache all the information it found while digging this out for you, and it would not have to ask again for a while.

In the tree analogue each "." in the name is a branching point. And each part between the "." s are the names of individual branches in the tree.

We climb the tree by taking the name we want (prep.ai.mit.edu) first finding the root (.) and then looking for the next branch to climb, in this case edu. Once we have found it we climb it by switching to the server that knows about that part of the name. Next we look for the mit branch over the edu branch (the combined name is mit.edu) and climb it by switching to a server that knows about mit.edu. Again we look for the next branch, it's ai.mit.edu and again we switch to the server that knows about it. Now we have arrived at the right server, at the right branching point. The last part is finding prep.ai.mit.edu, which is simple. In computer science we usually call prep a leaf on the tree.

A much less talked about, but just as important domain is in-addr.arpa. It too is nested like the 'normal' domains. in-addr.arpa allows us to get the hosts name when we have its address. A important thing here is to note that ip addresses are written in reverse order in the in-addr.arpa domain. If you have the address of a machine: 192.128.52.43 named proceeds just like for the prep.ai.mit.edu example: find arpa. servers. Find in-addr.arpa. servers, find 192.in-addr.arpa. servers, find 128.192.in-addr.arpa. servers, find 52.128.192.in-addr.arpa. servers. Find needed records for 43.52.128.192.in-addr.arpa. Clever huh? (Say 'yes'.) The reversion of the numbers can be confusing for years though.

I have just told a lie. DNS does not work precisely the way I just told you. But it's close enough.

4.2. Our own domain

Now to define our own domain. We're going to make the domain linux.bogus and define machines in it. I use a totally bogus domain name to make sure we disturb no-one Out There.

One more thing before we start: Not all characters are allowed in host names. We're restricted to the characters of the English alphabet: a-z, and numbers: 0-9 and the character '-' (dash). Keep to those characters. Upper and lower-case characters are the same for DNS, so pat.uio.no is identical to Pat.UiO.No.

We've already started this part with this line in named.conf:

```
zone "0.0.127.in-addr.arpa" {
    type master;
    file "pz/127.0.0";
};
```

Please note the lack of '.' at the end of the domain names in this file. This says that now we will define the zone 0.0.127.in-addr.arpa, that we're the master server for it and that it is stored in a file called pz/127.0.0. We've already set up this file, it reads:

```
@       IN   SOA   ns.linux.bogus. hostmaster.linux.bogus. (
                    1    ; Serial
                    8H   ; Refresh
                    2H   ; Retry
                    1W   ; Expire
                    1D)    ; Minimum TTL
                NS   ns.linux.bogus.
1                PTR   localhost.
```

Please note the '.' at the end of all the full domain names in this file, in contrast to the named.conf file above. Some people like to start each zone file with a $ORIGIN directive, but this is superfluous. The origin (where in the DNS hierarchy it belongs) of a zone file is specified in the zone section of the named.conf file, in this case it's 0.0.127.in-addr.arpa.

This 'zone file' contains 3 'resource records' (RRs): A SOA RR. A NS RR and a PTR RR. SOA is short for Start Of Authority. The '@' is a special notation meaning the origin, and since the 'domain' column for this file says 0.0.127.in-addr.arpa the first line really means

```
0.0.127.in-addr.arpa.  IN   SOA ...
```

NS is the Name Server RR. There is no '@' at the start of this line, it is implicit since the last line started with a '@'. Saves some typing that. So the NS line could also be written

```
0.0.127.in-addr.arpa.  IN   NS   ns.linux.bogus
```

It tells DNS what machine is the name server of the domain 0.0.127.in-addr.arpa, it is ns.linux.bogus. 'ns' is a customary name for name-servers, but as with web servers who are customarily named www.something the name may be anything.

And finally the PTR record says that the host at address 1 in the subnet 0.0.127.in-addr.arpa, i.e., 127.0.0.1 is named localhost.

The SOA record is the preamble to all zone files, and there should be exactly one in each zone file. It describes the zone, where it comes from (a machine called ns.linux.bogus), who is responsible for its contents (hostmaster@linux.bogus, you should insert your e-mail address here), what version of the zone file this is (serial: 1), and other things having to do with caching and secondary DNS servers. For the rest of the fields (refresh, retry, expire and minimum) use the numbers used in this HOWTO and you should be safe.

Now restart your named (the command is ndc restart) and use nslookup to examine what you've done:

```
$ nslookup

Default Server: localhost
Address: 127.0.0.1

> 127.0.0.1
Server: localhost
Address: 127.0.0.1

Name:  localhost
Address: 127.0.0.1
```

so it manages to get localhost from 127.0.0.1, good. Now for our main task, the linux.bogus domain, insert a new 'zone' section in named.conf:

```
zone "linux.bogus" {
    notify no;
    type master;
    file "pz/linux.bogus";
};
```

Note again the lack of ending '.' on the domain name in the named.conf file.

In the linux.bogus zone file we'll put some totally bogus data:

```
;
; Zone file for linux.bogus
;
; The full zone file
;
@     IN    SOA   ns.linux.bogus. hostmaster.linux.bogus. (
              199802151     ; serial, todays date + todays serial #
              8H       ; refresh, seconds
              2H       ; retry, seconds
              1W       ; expire, seconds
              1D )      ; minimum, seconds
```

```
;
        NS   ns       ; Inet Address of name server
        MX   10 mail.linux.bogus    ; Primary Mail Exchanger
        MX   20 mail.friend.bogus.  ; Secondary Mail Exchanger
;
localhost     A    127.0.0.1
ns       A    192.168.196.2
mail      A    192.168.196.4
```

Two things must be noted about the SOA record. ns.linux.bogus must be a actual machine with a A record. It is not legal to have a CNAME record for he machine mentioned in the SOA record. It's name need not be 'ns', it could be any legal host name. Next, hostmaster.linux.bogus should be read as hostmaster@linux.bogus, this should be a mail alias, or a mailbox, where the person(s) maintaining DNS should read mail frequently. Any mail regarding the domain will be sent to the address listed here. The name need not be 'hostmaster', it can be your normal e-mail address, but the e-mail address 'hostmaster' is often expected to work as well.

There is one new RR type in this file, the MX, or Mail eXchanger RR. It tells mail systems where to send mail that is addressed to someone@linux.bogus, namely too mail.linux.bogus or mail.friend.bogus. The number before each machine name is that MX RRs priority. The RR with the lowest number (10) is the one mail should be sent to if possible. If that fails the mail can be sent to one with a higher number, a secondary mail handler, i.e., mail.friend.bogus which has priority 20 here.
Restart named by running ndc restart. Examine the results with nslookup:

```
$ nslookup
> set q=any
> linux.bogus
Server: localhost
Address: 127.0.0.1

linux.bogus
    origin = ns.linux.bogus
    mail addr = hostmaster.linux.bogus
    serial = 199802151
    refresh = 28800 (8 hours)
    retry  = 7200 (2 hours)
    expire = 604800 (7 days)
    minimum ttl = 86400 (1 day)
linux.bogus   nameserver = ns.linux.bogus
linux.bogus   preference = 10, mail exchanger =
mail.linux.bogus.linux.bogus
```

```
linux.bogus   preference = 20, mail exchanger = mail.friend.bogus
linux.bogus   nameserver = ns.linux.bogus
ns.linux.bogus internet address = 192.168.196.2
mail.linux.bogus    internet address = 192.168.196.4
```

Upon careful examination you will discover a bug. The line

```
linux.bogus   preference = 10, mail exchanger =
mail.linux.bogus.linux.bogus
```

is all wrong. It should be

```
linux.bogus   preference = 10, mail exchanger = mail.linux.bogus
```

I deliberately made a mistake so you could learn from it :-) Looking in the zone file we find that the line

```
MX   10 mail.linux.bogus   ; Primary Mail Exchanger
```

is missing a period. Or has a 'linux.bogus' too many. If a machine name does not end in a period in a zone file the origin is added to its end causing the double linux.bogus.linux.bogus. So either

```
MX   10 mail.linux.bogus.  ; Primary Mail Exchanger
```

or

```
MX   10 mail          ; Primary Mail Exchanger
```

is correct. I prefer the latter form, it's less to type. There are some bind experts that disagree, and some that agree with this. In a zone file the domain should either be written out and ended with a '.' or it should not be included at all, in which case it defaults to the origin.

I must stress that in the named.conf file there should not be '.'s after the domain names. You have no idea how many times a '.' too many or few have fouled up things and confused the h*ll out of people.

So having made my point here is the new zone file, with some extra information in it as well:

```
;
; Zone file for linux.bogus
;
; The full zone file
;
@     IN    SOA   ns.linux.bogus. hostmaster.linux.bogus. (
                199802151    ; serial, todays date + todays serial #
                8H        ; refresh, seconds
                2H        ; retry, seconds
                1W        ; expire, seconds
                1D )       ; minimum, seconds
;
        TXT   "Linux.Bogus, your DNS consultants"
        NS   ns        ; Inet Address of name server
        NS   ns.friend.bogus.
        MX   10 mail      ; Primary Mail Exchanger
        MX   20 mail.friend.bogus. ; Secondary Mail Exchanger

localhost    A    127.0.0.1

gw       A    192.168.196.1
        HINFO  "Cisco" "IOS"
        TXT   "The router"

ns       A    192.168.196.2
        MX   10 mail
        MX   20 mail.friend.bogus.
        HINFO  "Pentium" "Linux 2.0"
www       CNAME  ns

donald     A    192.168.196.3
        MX   10 mail
        MX   20 mail.friend.bogus.
        HINFO  "i486"   "Linux 2.0"
        TXT   "DEK"

mail      A    192.168.196.4
        MX   10 mail
        MX   20 mail.friend.bogus.
        HINFO  "386sx" "Linux 1.2"

ftp       A    192.168.196.5
        MX   10 mail
        MX   20 mail.friend.bogus.
        HINFO  "P6" "Linux 2.1.86"
```

There are a number of new RRs here: HINFO (Host INFOrmation) has two parts, it's a good habit to quote each. The first part is the hardware or CPU on the machine, and the second part the software or OS on the machine. The machine called 'ns' has a Pentium CPU and runs Linux 2.0. CNAME (Canonical NAME) is a way to give each machine several names. So www is an alias for ns.

CNAME record usage is a bit controversial. But it's safe to follow the rule that a MX, CNAME or SOA record should never refer to a CNAME record, they should only refer to something with a A record, so it is inadvisable to have

```
foobar      CNAME   www             ; NO!
```

but correct to have

```
foobar      CNAME   ns              ; Yes!
```

It's also safe to assume that a CNAME is not a legal host name for a e-mail address: webmaster@www.linux.bogus is an illegal e-mail address given the setup above. You can expect quite a few mail admins Out There to enforce this rule even if it works for you. The way to avoid this is to use A records (and perhaps some others too, like a MX record) instead:

```
www        A     192.168.196.2
```

A number of the arch-bind-wizards, recommend not using CNAME at all. But the discussion of why or why not is beyond this HOWTO.

But as you see, this HOWTO and many sites does not follow this rule.

Load the new database by running ndc reload, this causes named to read its files again.

```
$ nslookup
```

```
Default Server: localhost
Address: 127.0.0.1

> ls -d linux.bogus
```

This means that all records should be listed. It results in this:

```
[localhost]
$ORIGIN linux.bogus.
@            1D IN SOA    ns hostmaster (
                   199802151     ; serial
                   8H        ; refresh
                   2H        ; retry
                   1W        ; expiry
                   1D )       ; minimum

            1D IN NS    ns
            1D IN NS    ns.friend.bogus.
            1D IN TXT    "Linux.Bogus, your DNS consultants"
            1D IN MX    10 mail
            1D IN MX    20 mail.friend.bogus.
gw           1D IN A     192.168.196.1
            1D IN HINFO   "Cisco" "IOS"
            1D IN TXT    "The router"
mail          1D IN A     192.168.196.4
            1D IN MX    10 mail
            1D IN MX    20 mail.friend.bogus.
            1D IN HINFO   "386sx" "Linux 1.0.9"
localhost        1D IN A     127.0.0.1
www          1D IN CNAME   ns
donald         1D IN A     192.168.196.3
            1D IN MX    10 mail
            1D IN MX    20 mail.friend.bogus.
            1D IN HINFO   "i486" "Linux 1.2"
            1D IN TXT    "DEK"
ftp           1D IN A     192.168.196.5
            1D IN MX    10 mail
            1D IN MX    20 mail.friend.bogus.
            1D IN HINFO   "P6" "Linux 1.3.59"
ns           1D IN A     192.168.196.2
            1D IN MX    10 mail
            1D IN MX    20 mail.friend.bogus.
            1D IN HINFO   "Pentium" "Linux 1.2"
```

That's good. As you see it looks a lot like the zone file itself. Let's check what it says for www alone:

```
> set q=any
> www.linux.bogus.
```

```
Server: localhost
Address: 127.0.0.1

www.linux.bogus canonical name = ns.linux.bogus
linux.bogus   nameserver = ns.linux.bogus
linux.bogus   nameserver = ns.friend.bogus
ns.linux.bogus internet address = 192.168.196.2
```

In other words, the real name of www.linux.bogus is ns.linux.bogus, and it gives you some of the information it has about ns as well, enough to connect to it if you were a program.

Now we're halfway.

4.3. The reverse zone

Now programs can convert the names in linux.bogus to addresses which they can connect to. But also required is a reverse zone, one making DNS able to convert from an address to a name. This name is used buy a lot of servers of different kinds (FTP, IRC, WWW and others) to decide if they want to talk to you or not, and if so, maybe even how much priority you should be given. For full access to all services on the Internet a reverse zone is required.

Put this in named.conf:

```
zone "196.168.192.in-addr.arpa" {
    notify no;
    type master;
    file "pz/192.168.196";
};
```

This is exactly as with the 0.0.127.in-addr.arpa, and the contents are similar:

```
@     IN    SOA    ns.linux.bogus. hostmaster.linux.bogus. (
              199802151 ; Serial, todays date + todays serial
              8H    ; Refresh
              2H    ; Retry
              1W    ; Expire
```

```
            1D)    ; Minimum TTL
        NS    ns.linux.bogus.

1        PTR    gw.linux.bogus.
2        PTR    ns.linux.bogus.
3        PTR    donald.linux.bogus.
4        PTR    mail.linux.bogus.
5        PTR    ftp.linux.bogus.
```

Now you restart your named (ndc restart) and examine your work with nslookup again:

```
> 192.168.196.4
Server: localhost
Address: 127.0.0.1

Name:  mail.linux.bogus
Address: 192.168.196.4
```

so, it looks OK, dump the whole thing to examine that too:

```
> ls -d 196.168.192.in-addr.arpa
[localhost]
$ORIGIN 196.168.192.in-addr.arpa.
@            1D IN SOA    ns.linux.bogus. hostmaster.linux.bogus. (
                   199802151    ; serial
                   8H       ; refresh
                   2H       ; retry
                   1W       ; expiry
                   1D )      ; minimum

            1D IN NS    ns.linux.bogus.
1            1D IN PTR    gw.linux.bogus.
2            1D IN PTR    ns.linux.bogus.
3            1D IN PTR    donald.linux.bogus.
4            1D IN PTR    mail.linux.bogus.
5            1D IN PTR    ftp.linux.bogus.
@            1D IN SOA    ns.linux.bogus. hostmaster.linux.bogus. (
                   199802151    ; serial
                   8H       ; refresh
                   2H       ; retry
                   1W       ; expiry
```

```
                  1D )       ; minimum
```

Looks good! If your output didn't look like that look for error-messages in your syslog, I explained how to do that at the very beginning of this chapter.

4.4. Words of caution

There are some things I should add here. The IP numbers used in the examples above are taken from one of the blocks of 'private nets', i.e., they are not allowed to be used publicly on the internet. So they are safe to use in an example in a HOWTO. The second thing is the notify no; line. It tells named not to notify its secondary (slave) servers when it has gotten a update to one of its zone files. In bind-8 the named can notify the other servers listed in NS records in the zone file when a zone is updated. This is handy for ordinary use, but for private experiments with zones this feature should be off, we don't want the experiment to pollute the Internet do we?

And, of course, this domain is highly bogus, and so are all the addresses in it. For a real example of a real-life domain see the next main-section.

4.5. Why reverse lookups don't work.

There are a couple of "gotchas" that normally are avoided with name lookups that are often seen when setting up reverse zones. Before you go on you need reverse lookups of your machines working on your own nameserver. If it isn’t go back and fix it before continuing.

I will discuss two failures of reverse lookups as seen from outside your network:

4.5.1. The reverse zone isn't delegated.

When you ask a service provider for a network-address range and a domain name the domain name is normally delegated as a matter of course. A delegation is the glue NS record that helps you get from one nameserver to another as explained in the dry theory section above. You read that, right? If your reverse zone dosn't work go back and read it. Now.

The reverse zone also needs to be delegated. If you got the 192.168.196 net with the linux.bogus domain from your provider they need to put NS records in for your reverse zone as well as for your forward zone. If you follow the chain from in-addr.arpa and up to your net you will probably find a break in the chain. Most probably at your service provider. Having found the break in the chain contact your service-provider and ask them to correct the error.

4.5.2. You've got a classless subnet

This is a somewhat advanced topic, but classless subnets are very common these days and you probably have one unless you're a medium sized company.

A classless subnet is what keeps the Internet going these days. Some years ago there was much ado about the shortage of ip numbers. The smart people in IETF (the Internet Engineering Task Force, they keep the Internet working) stuck their heads together and solved the problem. At a price. The price is that you'll get less than a "C" subnet and some things may break. Please see Ask Mr. DNS at http://www.acmebw.com/askmrdns/00007.htm for an good explanation of this and how to handle it.

Did you read it? I'm not going to explain it so please read it.

The first part of the problem is that your ISP must understand the technique described by Mr. DNS. Not all small ISPs have a working understanding of this. If so you might have to explain to them and be persistent. But be sure you understand it first ;-). They will then set up a nice reverse zone at their server which you can examine for correctness with nslookup.

The second and last part of the problem is that you must understand the technique. If you're unsure go back and read about it again. Then you can set up your own classless reverse zone as described by Mr. DNS.

There is another trap lurking here. Old resolvers will not be able to follow the CNAME trick in the resolving chain and will fail to reverse-resolve your machine. This can result in the service assigning it an incorrect access class, deny access or something along those lines. If you stumble into such a service the only solution (that I know of) is for your ISP to insert your PTR record directly into their trick classless zone file instead of the trick CNAME record.

Some ISPs will offer other ways to handle this, like Web based forms for you to input your reverse-mappings in or other automagical systems.

5. A real domain example

Where we list some real zone files

Users have suggested that I include a real example of a working domain as well as the tutorial example.

I use this example with permission from David Bullock of LAND-5. These files were current 24th of September 1996, and were then edited to fit bind 8 restrictions and use extensions by me. So, what you see here differs a bit from what you find if you query LAND-5's name servers now.

5.1. /etc/named.conf (or /var/named/named.conf)

Here we find master zone sections for the two reverse zones needed: the 127.0.0 net, as well as LAND-5's 206.6.177 subnet. And a primary line for land-5's forward zone land-5.com. Also note that instead of stuffing the files in a directory called pz, as I do in this HOWTO, he puts them in a directory called zone.

```
// Boot file for LAND-5 name server

options {
    directory "/var/named";
};

zone "." {
    type hint;
    file "root.hints";
};

zone "0.0.127.in-addr.arpa" {
    type master;
    file "zone/127.0.0";
};

zone "land-5.com" {
    type master;
    file "zone/land-5.com";
};
```

```
zone "177.6.206.in-addr.arpa" {
    type master;
    file "zone/206.6.177";
};
```

If you put this in your named.conf file to play with PLEASE put "notify no;" in the zone sections for the two land-5 zones so as to avoid accidents.

5.2. /var/named/root.hints

Keep in mind that this file is dynamic, and the one listed here is old. You're better off using one produced now, with dig, as explained earlier.

```
; <<>> DiG 8.1 <<>> @A.ROOT-SERVERS.NET.
; (1 server found)
;; res options: init recurs defnam dnsrch
;; got answer:
;; ->>HEADER<<- opcode: QUERY, status: NOERROR, id: 10
;; flags: qr aa rd; QUERY: 1, ANSWER: 13, AUTHORITY: 0, ADDITIONAL: 13
;; QUERY SECTION:
;;    ., type = NS, class = IN

;; ANSWER SECTION:
.           6D IN NS    G.ROOT-SERVERS.NET.
.           6D IN NS    J.ROOT-SERVERS.NET.
.           6D IN NS    K.ROOT-SERVERS.NET.
.           6D IN NS    L.ROOT-SERVERS.NET.
.           6D IN NS    M.ROOT-SERVERS.NET.
.           6D IN NS    A.ROOT-SERVERS.NET.
.           6D IN NS    H.ROOT-SERVERS.NET.
.           6D IN NS    B.ROOT-SERVERS.NET.
.           6D IN NS    C.ROOT-SERVERS.NET.
.           6D IN NS    D.ROOT-SERVERS.NET.
.           6D IN NS    E.ROOT-SERVERS.NET.
.           6D IN NS    I.ROOT-SERVERS.NET.
.           6D IN NS    F.ROOT-SERVERS.NET.

;; ADDITIONAL SECTION:
G.ROOT-SERVERS.NET.    5w6d16h IN A  192.112.36.4
J.ROOT-SERVERS.NET.    5w6d16h IN A  198.41.0.10
K.ROOT-SERVERS.NET.    5w6d16h IN A  193.0.14.129
L.ROOT-SERVERS.NET.    5w6d16h IN A  198.32.64.12
M.ROOT-SERVERS.NET.    5w6d16h IN A  202.12.27.33
```

```
A.ROOT-SERVERS.NET.    5w6d16h IN A  198.41.0.4
H.ROOT-SERVERS.NET.    5w6d16h IN A  128.63.2.53
B.ROOT-SERVERS.NET.    5w6d16h IN A  128.9.0.107
C.ROOT-SERVERS.NET.    5w6d16h IN A  192.33.4.12
D.ROOT-SERVERS.NET.    5w6d16h IN A  128.8.10.90
E.ROOT-SERVERS.NET.    5w6d16h IN A  192.203.230.10
I.ROOT-SERVERS.NET.    5w6d16h IN A  192.36.148.17
F.ROOT-SERVERS.NET.    5w6d16h IN A  192.5.5.241

;; Total query time: 215 msec
;; FROM: roke.uio.no to SERVER: A.ROOT-SERVERS.NET. 198.41.0.4
;; WHEN: Sun Feb 15 01:22:51 1998
;; MSG SIZE sent: 17 rcvd: 436
```

5.3. /var/named/zone/127.0.0

Just the basics, the obligatory SOA record, and a record that maps 127.0.0.1 to localhost. Both are required. No more should be in this file. It will probably never need to be updated, unless your nameserver or hostmaster address changes.

```
@        IN   SOA   land-5.com. root.land-5.com. (
                199609203     ; Serial
                28800  ; Refresh
                7200  ; Retry
                604800 ; Expire
                86400) ; Minimum TTL
             NS   land-5.com.

1             PTR   localhost.
```

5.4. /var/named/zone/land-5.com

Here we see the mandatory SOA record, the needed NS records. We can see that he has a secondary name server at ns2.psi.net. This is as it should be, always have a off site secondary server as backup. We can also see that he has a master host called land-5 which takes care of many of the different Internet services, and that he's done it with CNAMEs (a alternative is using A records).

As you see from the SOA record, the zone file originates at land-5.com, the contact person is root@land-5.com. hostmaster is

```
another oft used address for the contact person. The serial number is
in the customary yyyymmdd format with todays serial number appended;
this is probably the sixth version of zone file on the 20th of
September 1996. Remember that the serial number must increase
monotonically, here there is only one digit for todays serial#, so
after 9 edits he has to wait until tomorrow before he can edit the
file again. Consider using two digits.
```

```
@     IN    SOA    land-5.com. root.land-5.com. (
                199609206     ; serial, todays date + todays serial #
                8H        ; refresh, seconds
                2H        ; retry, seconds
                1W        ; expire, seconds
                1D )       ; minimum, seconds
        NS    land-5.com.
        NS    ns2.psi.net.
        MX    10 land-5.com. ; Primary Mail Exchanger
        TXT    "LAND-5 Corporation"

localhost     A     127.0.0.1

router      A     206.6.177.1

land-5.com.    A     206.6.177.2
ns        A     206.6.177.3
www        A     207.159.141.192

ftp        CNAME  land-5.com.
mail       CNAME  land-5.com.
news       CNAME  land-5.com.

funn       A     206.6.177.2

;
;     Workstations
;
ws-177200     A     206.6.177.200
        MX    10 land-5.com.  ; Primary Mail Host
ws-177201     A     206.6.177.201
        MX    10 land-5.com.  ; Primary Mail Host
ws-177202     A     206.6.177.202
        MX    10 land-5.com.  ; Primary Mail Host
ws-177203     A     206.6.177.203
        MX    10 land-5.com.  ; Primary Mail Host
ws-177204     A     206.6.177.204
        MX    10 land-5.com.  ; Primary Mail Host
ws-177205     A     206.6.177.205
        MX    10 land-5.com.  ; Primary Mail Host
```

```
; {Many repetitive definitions deleted - SNIP}
ws-177250     A    206.6.177.250
        MX    10 land-5.com.  ; Primary Mail Host
ws-177251     A    206.6.177.251
        MX    10 land-5.com.  ; Primary Mail Host
ws-177252     A    206.6.177.252
        MX    10 land-5.com.  ; Primary Mail Host
ws-177253     A    206.6.177.253
        MX    10 land-5.com.  ; Primary Mail Host
ws-177254     A    206.6.177.254
        MX    10 land-5.com.  ; Primary Mail Host
```

If you examine land-5s nameserver you will find that the host names are of the form ws_number. As of late bind 4 versions named started enforcing the restrictions on what characters may be used in host names. So that does not work with bind-8 at all, and I substituted '-' (dash) for '_' (underline) for use in this HOWTO.

Another thing to note is that the workstations don't have individual names, but rather a prefix followed by the two last parts of the IP numbers. Using such a convention can simplify maintenance significantly, but can be a bit impersonal, and, in fact, be a source of irritation among your customers.

We also see that funn.land-5.com is an alias for land-5.com, but using an A record, not a CNAME record. This is a good policy as noted earlier.

5.5. /var/named/zone/206.6.177

I'll comment on this file below

```
@        IN    SOA    land-5.com. root.land-5.com. (
                      199609206     ; Serial
                      28800  ; Refresh
                      7200   ; Retry
                      604800 ; Expire
                      86400) ; Minimum TTL
                 NS    land-5.com.
                 NS    ns2.psi.net.
;
;    Servers
;
1    PTR   router.land-5.com.
2    PTR   land-5.com.
```

```
2    PTR   funn.land-5.com.
;
;    Workstations
;
200    PTR    ws-177200.land-5.com.
201    PTR    ws-177201.land-5.com.
202    PTR    ws-177202.land-5.com.
203    PTR    ws-177203.land-5.com.
204    PTR    ws-177204.land-5.com.
205    PTR    ws-177205.land-5.com.
; {Many repetitive definitions deleted - SNIP}
250    PTR    ws-177250.land-5.com.
251    PTR    ws-177251.land-5.com.
252    PTR    ws-177252.land-5.com.
253    PTR    ws-177253.land-5.com.
254    PTR    ws-177254.land-5.com.
```

The reverse zone is the bit of the setup that seems to cause the most grief. It is used to find the host name if you have the IP number of a machine. Example: you are an IRC server and accept connections from IRC clients. However you are a Norwegian IRC server and so you only want to accept connections from clients in Norway and other Scandinavian countries. When you get a connection from a client the C library is able to tell you the IP number of the connecting machine because the IP number of the client is contained in all the packets that are passed over the network. Now you can call a function called gethostbyaddr that looks up the name of a host given the IP number. Gethostbyaddr will ask a DNS server, which will then traverse the DNS looking for the machine. Supposing the client connection is from ws-177200.land-5.com. The IP number the C library provides to the IRC server is 206.6.177.200. To find out the name of that machine we need to find 200.177.6.206.in-addr.arpa. The DNS server will first find the arpa. servers, then find in-addr.arpa. servers, following the reverse trail through 206, then 6 and at last finding the server for the 177.6.206.in-addr.arpa zone at LAND-5. From which it will finally get the answer that for 200.177.6.206.in-addr.arpa we have a "PTR ws-177200.land-5.com" record, meaning that the name that goes with 206.6.177.200 is ws-177200.land-5.com. As with the explanation of how prep.ai.mit.edu is looked up, this is slightly fictitious.

Getting back to the IRC server example. The IRC server only accepts connections from the Scandinavian countries, i.e., *.no, *.se, *.dk, the name ws-177200.land-5.com clearly does not match any of those, and the server will deny the connection. If there was no reverse mapping of 206.2.177.200 through the in-addr.arpa zone the server would have been unable to find the name at all and would have to settle to comparing 206.2.177.200 with *.no, *.se and *.dk, none of which will match.

Some people will tell you that reverse lookup mappings are only important for servers, or not important at all. Not so: Many ftp, news, IRC and even some http (WWW) servers will not accept connections from machines of which they are not able to find the name. So reverse mappings for machines are in fact mandatory.

6. Maintenance

Keeping it working.

There is one maintenance task you have to do on nameds, other than keeping them running. That's keeping the root.hints file updated. The easiest way is using dig, first run dig with no arguments, you will get the root.hints according to your own server. Then ask one of the listed root servers with dig @rootserver. You will note that the output looks terribly like a root.hints file. Save it to a file (dig @e.root-servers.net . ns >root.hints.new) and replace the old root.hints with it.

Remember to reload named after replacing the cache file.

Al Longyear sent me this script, that can be run automatically to update root.hints, install a crontab entry to run it once a month and forget it. The script assumes you have mail working and that the mail-alias 'hostmaster' is defined. You must hack it to suit your setup.

```
#!/bin/sh
#
# Update the nameserver cache information file once per month.
# This is run automatically by a cron entry.
#
# Original by Al Longyear
# Updated for bind 8 by Nicolai Langfeldt
# Miscelanious error-conditions reported by David A. Ranch
# Ping test suggested by Martin Foster
#
(
 echo "To: hostmaster <hostmaster>"
 echo "From: system <root>"
 echo "Subject: Automatic update of the root.hints file"
 echo

 PATH=/sbin:/usr/sbin:/bin:/usr/bin:
 export PATH
 cd /var/named
```

```
# Are we online? Ping a server at your ISP
case 'ping -qnc some.machine.net' in
 *'100% packet loss'*)
   echo "The network is DOWN. root.hints NOT updated"
   echo
   exit 0
   ;;
esac

dig @rs.internic.net . ns >root.hints.new 2>&1

case 'cat root.hints.new' in
 *NOERROR*)
   # It worked
   :;;
 *)
   echo "The root.hints file update has FAILED."
   echo "This is the dig output reported:"
   echo
   cat root.hints.new
   exit 0
   ;;
esac

echo "The root.hints file has been updated to contain the following
information:"
echo
cat root.hints.new

chown root.root root.hints.new
chmod 444 root.hints.new
rm -f root.hints.old
mv root.hints root.hints.old
mv root.hints.new root.hints
ndc restart
echo
echo "The nameserver has been restarted to ensure that the update
is complete."
echo "The previous root.hints file is now called
/var/named/root.hints.old."
) 2>&1 | /usr/lib/sendmail -t
exit 0
```

Some of you might have picked up that the root.hints file is also available by ftp from Internic. Please don't use ftp to update root.hints, the above method is much more friendly to the net, and Internic.

7. Converting from version 4 to version 8

This was originally a section on using bind 8 written by David E. Smith (dave@bureau42.ml.org). I have edited it some to fit the new section name.

There's not much to it. Except for using named.conf instead of named.boot, everything is identical. And bind8 comes with a perl script that converts old-style files to new. Example named.boot (old style) for a cache-only name server:

```
directory /var/named
cache  .                      root.hints
primary 0.0.127.IN-ADDR.ARPA          127.0.0.zone
primary localhost                localhost.zone
```

On the command line, in the bind8/src/bin/named directory (this assumes you got a source distribution. If you got a binary package the script is probably around, I'm not sure where it would be though. -ed.), type:

```
./named-bootconf.pl < named.boot > named.conf
```

Which creates named.conf:

```
// generated by named-bootconf.pl

options {
    directory "/var/named";
};

zone "." {
    type hint;
    file "root.hints";
```

```
};

zone "0.0.127.IN-ADDR.ARPA" {
    type master;
    file "127.0.0.zone";
};

zone "localhost" {
    type master;
    file "localhost.zone";
};
```

It works for everything that can go into a named.boot file, although it doesn't add all of the new enhancements and configuration options that bind8 allows. Here's a more complete named.conf that does the same things, but a little more efficiently.

```
// This is a configuration file for named (from BIND 8.1 or later).
// It would normally be installed as /etc/named.conf.
// The only change made from the 'stock' named.conf (aside from this
// comment :) is that the directory line was uncommented, since I
// already had the zone files in /var/named.

options {
    directory "/var/named";
    datasize 20M;
};

zone "localhost" IN {
    type master;
    file "localhost.zone";
};

zone "0.0.127.in-addr.arpa" IN {
    type master;
    file "127.0.0.zone";
};

zone "." IN {
    type hint;
    file "root.hints";
};
```

In the bind 8 distributions directory bind8/src/bin/named/test you find this, and copies of the zone files, that many people can just drop in and use instantly.

The formats for zone files and root.hints files are identical, as are the commands for updating them.

8. Questions and Answers

Please read this section before mailing me.

1. My named wants a named.boot file

   You are reading the wrong HOWTO. Please see the old version of this HOWTO, which covers bind 4, at http://www.math.uio.no/~janl/DNS/

2. How do use DNS from inside a firewall?

   A hint: forward only;, You will probably also need

```
query-source port 53;
```

inside the "options" part of the named.conf file as suggested in the example "caching" section.

3. How do I make DNS rotate through the available addresses for a service, say www.busy.site to obtain a load balancing effect, or similar?

   Make several A records for www.busy.site and use bind 4.9.3 or later. Then bind will round-robin the answers. It will not work with earlier versions of bind.

4. I want to set up DNS on a (closed) intranet. What do I do?

   You drop the root.hints file and just do zone files. That also means you don't have to get new hint files all the time.

5. How do I set up a secondary (slave) name server?

   If the primary/master server has address 127.0.0.1 you put a line like this in the named.conf file of your secondary:

```
zone "linux.bogus" {
   type slave;
   file "sz/linux.bogus";
   masters { 127.0.0.1; };
};
```

You may list several alternate master servers the zone can be copied from inside the masters list, separated by ';' (semicolon).

6. I want bind running when I'm disconnected from the net.

   There are three items regarding this:

- I have received this mail from Ian Clark <ic@deakin.edu.au> where he explains his way of doing this:

I run named on my 'Masquerading' machine here. I have two root.hints files, one called root.hints.real which contains the real root server names and the other called root.hints.fake which contains...

```
—
; root.hints.fake
; this file contains no information
—
```

When I go off line I copy the root.hints.fake file to root.hints and restart named.

When I go online I copy root.hints.real to root.hints and restart named.

This is done from ip-down & ip-up respectively.

The first time I do a query off line on a domain name named doesn't have details for it puts an entry like this in messages..

Jan 28 20:10:11 hazchem named[10147]: No root nameserver for class IN

which I can live with.

It certainly seems to work for me. I can use the nameserver for local machines while off the 'net without the timeout delay for external domain names and I while on the 'net queries for external domains work normally

- I have also received information about how bind interacts with NFS and the portmapper on a mostly offline machine from Karl-Max Wanger:

I use to run my own named on all my machines which are only occasionally connected to the Internet by modem. The nameserver only acts as a cache, it has no area of authority and asks back for everything at the name servers in the root.cache file. As is usual with Slackware, it is started before nfsd and mountd.

With one of my machines (a Libretto 30 notebook) I had the problem that sometimes I could mount it from another system connected to my local LAN, but most of the time it didn't work. I had the same effect regardless of using PLIP, a PCMCIA ethernet card or PPP over a serial interface.

After some time of guessing and experimenting I found out that apparently named messed with the process of registration nfsd and mountd have to carry out with the portmapper upon startup (I start these daemons at boot time as usual). Starting named after nfsd and mountd eliminated this problem completely.

As there are no disadvantages to expect from such a modified boot sequence I'd advise everybody to do it that way to prevent potential trouble.

- Finally, there is HOWTO information about this at Ask Mr. DNS at http://www.acmebw.com/askmrdns/#linux-ns. It is about bind 4 though, so you have to adapt what he says to bind 8.

7. Where does the caching name server store its cache? Is there any way I can control the size of the cache?

The cache is completely stored in memory, it is not written to disk at any time. Every time you kill named the cache is lost. The cache is not controllable in any way. named manages it according to some simple rules and that is it. You cannot control the cache or the cache size in any way for any reason. If you want to you can "fix" this by hacking named. This is however not recommended.

8. Does named save the cache between restarts? Can I make it save it? No, named does not save the cache when it dies. That means that the cache must be built anew each time you kill and restart named. There is no way to make named save the cache in a file. If you want you can "fix" this by hacking named. This is however not recommended.

9. How can I get a domian? I want to set up my own domain called (for example) linux-rules.net. How can I get the domain I want assigned to me?

Please contact your network service provider. They will be able to help you with this. Please note that in most parts of the world you need to pay money to get a domain.

9. How to become a bigger time DNS admin.

Documentation and tools.

Real Documentation exists. Online and in print. The reading of several of these is required to make the step from small time DNS admin to a big time one. In print the standard book is DNS and BIND by C. Liu and P. Albitz from O'Reilly & Associates, Sebastopol, CA, ISBN 0-937175-82-X. I read this, it's excellent, though based on bind 4, this is not a real problem though. There is also a section in on DNS in TCP/IP Network Administration, by Craig Hunt from O'Reilly..., ISBN 0-937175-82-X. Another must for Good DNS administration (or good anything for that matter) is Zen and the Art of Motorcycle Maintenance by Robert M. Pirsig :-) Available as ISBN 0688052304 and others.

Online you will find stuff on <http://www.dns.net/dnsrd/> (DNS Resources Directory), <http://www.isc.org/bind.html>; A FAQ, a reference manual (BOG; Bind Operations Guide) as well as papers and protocol definitions and DNS hacks (these, and most, if not all, of the RFCs mentioned below, are also contained in the bind distribution). I have not read most of these, but then I'm not a big-time DNS admin either. Arnt Gulbrandsen on the other hand has read BOG and he's ecstatic about it :-). The newsgroup comp.protocols.tcp-ip.domains is about DNS. In addition there are a number of RFCs about DNS, the most important are probably these:

RFC 2052
A. Gulbrandsen, P. Vixie, A DNS RR for specifying the location of services (DNS SRV), October 1996

RFC 1918
Y. Rekhter, R. Moskowitz, D. Karrenberg, G. de Groot, E. Lear, Address Allocation for Private Internets, 02/29/1996.

RFC 1912
D. Barr, Common DNS Operational and Configuration Errors, 02/28/1996.

RFC 1912 Errors
B. Barr Errors in RFC 1912, this is available at <http://www.cis.ohio-state.edu/~barr/rfc1912-errors.html>

RFC 1713
A. Romao, Tools for DNS debugging, 11/03/1994.

RFC 1712
C. Farrell, M. Schulze, S. Pleitner, D. Baldoni, DNS Encoding of Geographical Location, 11/01/1994.

RFC 1183
R. Ullmann, P. Mockapetris, L. Mamakos, C. Everhart, New DNS RR Definitions, 10/08/1990.

RFC 1035
P. Mockapetris, Domain names - implementation and specification, 11/01/1987.

RFC 1034
P. Mockapetris, Domain names - concepts and facilities, 11/01/1987.

RFC 1033
M. Lottor, Domain administrators operations guide, 11/01/1987.

RFC 1032
M. Stahl, Domain administrators guide, 11/01/1987.

RFC 974
C. Partridge, Mail routing and the domain system, 01/01/1986.

APPENDIX H

NFS DOCUMENTATION

APPENDIX OBJECTIVES

 NFS How-To Page 125

APPENDIX H.1 NFS HOW-TO

Author's Note: The following discussion talks about how to create an NFS file It goes beyond the discussion in the text and is designed to supplement your learning experience. It is available at http://metalab.unc.edu/pub/linux/docs/HOWTO/NFS-HOWTO

NFS HOWTO
Nicolai Langfeldt janl@math.uio.no
v0.7, 3 November 1997

HOWTO set up NFS clients and servers.

1. Preamble

1.1. Legal stuff

(C)opyright 1997 Nicolai Langfeldt. Do not modify without amending copyright, distribute freely but retain this paragraph. The FAQ section is based on a NFS FAQ compiled by Alan Cox. The Checklist section is based on a mount problem checklist compiled by the IBM Corporation.

1.2. Other stuff

This will never be a finished document, please send me mail about your problems and successes, it can make this a better HOWTO. Please send money, comments and/or questions to janl@math.uio.no. If you send E-mail please make sure that the return address is correct and working, I get a lot of E-mail and figuring out your e-mail address can be a lot of work. Please.

If you want to translate this HOWTO please notify me so I can keep track of what languages I have been published in :-).

Curses and Thanks to Olaf Kirch who got me to write this and then gave good suggestions for it :-)

This HOWTO covers NFS in the 2.0 versions of the kernel. There are significant enhancements, and changes, of NFS in the 2.1 versions of the kernel.

1.3. Dedication

This HOWTO is dedicated to Anne Line Norheim Langfeldt. Though she will probably never read it since she's not that kind of girl.

2. README.first

NFS, the Network File System has three important characteristics:

It makes sharing of files over a network possible.

It mostly works well enough.

It opens a can of security risks that are well understood by crackers, and easily exploited to get access (read, write and delete) to all your files.

I'll say something on both issues in this HOWTO. Please make sure you read the security section of this HOWTO, and you will be vulnerable to fewer silly security risks. The passages about security will at times be pretty technical and require some knowledge about IP networking and the terms used. If you don't recognize the terms you can either go back and check the networking HOWTO, wing it, or get a book about

TCP/IP network administration to familiarize yourself with TCP/IP. That's a good idea anyway if you're administrating UNIX/Linux machines. A very good book on the subject is TCP/IP Network Administration by Craig Hunt, published by O'Reilly & Associates, Inc. And after you've read it and understood it you'll have higher value on the job market, you can't loose ;-)

There are two sections to help you troubleshoot NFS, called Mount Checklist and FAQs. Please refer to them if something dosn't work as advertized.

3. Setting up a NFS server

3.1. Prerequisites

Before you continue reading this HOWTO you will need to be able to telnet back and forth between the machine you're using as server and the client. If that does not work you need to check the networking/NET-2 HOWTO and set up networking properly.

3.2. First step

Before we can do anything else we need a NFS server set up. If you're part of a department or university network there are likely numerous NFS servers already set up. If they will let you get access to them, or indeed, if you're reading this HOWTO to get access to one of them you obviously don't need to read this section and can just skip ahead to the section on "setting up a NFS client"

If you need to set up a non-Linux box as server you will have to read the system manual(s) to discover how to enable NFS serving and export of file systems through NFS. There is a separate section in this HOWTO on how to do it on many different systems. After you have figured all that out you can continue reading the next section of this HOWTO. Or read more of this section since some of the things I will say are relevant no matter what kind of machine you use as server.

Those of you still reading will need to set up a number of programs.

3.3. The portmapper

The portmapper on Linux is called either portmap or rpc.portmap. The man page on my system says it is a "DARPA port to RPC program number mapper". It is the first security holes you'll open reading this

HOWTO. Description of how to close one of the holes is in the "security section". Which I, again, urge you to read.

Start the portmapper. It's either called portmap or rpc.portmap and it should live in the /usr/sbin directory (on some machines it's called rpcbind). You can start it by hand now, but it will need to be started every time you boot your machine so you need to make/edit the rc scripts. Your rc scripts are explained more closely in the init man page, they usually reside in /etc/rc.d, /etc/init.d or /etc/rc.d/init.d. If there is a script called something like inet it's probably the right script to edit. But, what to write or do is outside the scope of this HOWTO. Start portmap, and check that it lives by running ps aux. It does? Good.

3.4. Mountd and nfsd

The next programs we need running are mountd and nfsd. But first we'll edit another file. /etc/exports this time. Say I want the file system /mn/eris/local which lives on the machine eris to be available to the machine called apollon. Then I'd put this in /etc/exports on eris:

```
/mn/eris/local  apollon(rw)
```

The above line gives apollon read/write access to /mn/eris/local. Instead of rw it could say ro which means read only (if you put nothing it defaults to read only). There are other options you can give it, and I will discuss some security related ones later. They are all enumerated in the exports man page which you should have read at least once in your life. There are also better ways than listing all the hosts in the exports file. You can for example use net groups if you are running NIS (or NYS) (NIS was known as YP), and always specify domain wild cards and IP-subnets as hosts that are allowed to mount something. But you should consider who can get access to the server in unauthorized ways if you use such blanket authorizations.

Note: This exports file is not the same syntax that other Unixes use. There is a separate section in this HOWTO about other Unixes exports files.

Now we're set to start mountd (or maybe it's called rpc.mountd and then nfsd (which could be called rpc.nfsd). They will both read the exports file.

If you edit /etc/exports you will have to make sure nfsd and mountd knows that the files have changed. The traditonal way is to run exportfs. Many Linux distributions lack a exportfs program. If you're exportfs-less you can install this script on your machine:

```
#!/bin/sh
killall -HUP /usr/sbin/rpc.mountd
killall -HUP /usr/sbin/rpc.nfsd
echo re-exported file systems
```

Save it in, say, /usr/sbin/exportfs, and don't forget to chmod a+rx it. Now, whenever you change your exports file, you run exportfs after, as root.

Now you should check that mountd and nfsd are running properly. First with rpcinfo -p. It should show something like this:

```
   program vers proto   port
    100000    2   tcp    111  portmapper
    100000    2   udp    111  portmapper
    100005    1   udp    745  mountd
    100005    1   tcp    747  mountd
    100003    2   udp   2049  nfs
    100003    2   tcp   2049  nfs
```

As you see the portmapper has announced it's services, and so has mountd and nfsd.

If you get rpcinfo: can't contact portmapper: RPC: Remote system error - Connection refused or something similar instead then the portmapper isn't running. Fix it. If you get No remote programs registered. then either the portmapper doesn't want to talk to you, or something is broken. Kill nfsd, mountd, and the portmapper and try the ignition sequence again.

After checking that the portmapper reports the services you can check with ps too. The portmapper will continue to report the services even after the programs that extend them have crashed. So a ps check can be smart if something seems broken.

Of course, you will need to modify your system rc files to start mountd and nfsd as well as the portmapper when you boot. It is very likely that the scripts already exist on your machine, you just have to uncomment the critical section or activate it for the correct init run levels.

Man pages you should be familiar with now: portmap, mountd, nfsd, and exports.

Well, if you did everything exactly like I said you should you're all set to start on the NFS client.

4. Setting up a NFS client

First you will need a kernel with the NFS file system either compiled in or available as a module. This is configured before you compile the kernel. If you have never compiled a kernel before you might need to check the kernel HOWTO and figure it out. If you're using a very cool distribution (like Red Hat) and you've never fiddled with the kernel or modules on it (and thus ruined it ;-), nfs is likely automagicaly available to you.

You can now, at a root prompt, enter a appropriate mount command and the file system will appear. Continuing the example in the previous section we want to mount /mn/eris/local from eris. This is done with this command:

```
mount -o rsize=1024,wsize=1024 eris:/mn/eris/local /mnt
```

(We'll get back to the rsize and wsize options.) The file system is now available under /mnt and you can cd there, and ls in it, and look at the individual files. You will notice that it's not as fast as a local file system, but a lot more convenient than ftp. If, instead of mounting the file system, mount produces a error message like mount: eris:/mn/eris/local failed, reason given by server: Permission denied then the exports file is wrong, or you forgot to run exportfs after editing the exports file. If it says mount clntudp_create: RPC: Program not registered it means that nfsd or mountd is not running on the server.

To get rid of the file system you can say

```
umount /mnt
```

To make the system mount a nfs file system upon boot you edit /etc/fstab in the normal manner. For our example a line such as this is required:

```
# device          mountpoint  fs-type  options                dump fsckorder
eris:/mn/eris/local  /mnt     nfs      rsize=1024,wsize=1024 0    0
```

That's all there is too it, almost. Read on please.

4.1. Mount options

There are some options you should consider adding at once. They govern the way the NFS client handles a server crash or network outage. One of the cool things about NFS is that it can handle this gracefully. If you set up the clients right. There are two distinct failure modes:

soft
The NFS client will report and error to the process accessing a file on a NFS mounted file system. Some programs can handle this with composure, most won't. I cannot recommend using this setting.

hard
The program accessing a file on a NFS mounted file system will hang when the server crashes. The process cannot be interrupted or killed unless you also specify intr. When the NFS server is back online the program will continue undisturbed from where it were. This is probably what you want. I recommend using hard,intr on all NFS mounted file systems.

Picking up the previous example, this is now your fstab entry:

```
# device          mountpoint  fs-type  options                          dump fsckorder
eris:/mn/eris/local  /mnt     nfs      rsize=1024,wsize=1024,hard,intr 0 0
```

4.2. Optimizing NFS

Normally, if no rsize and wsize options are specified NFS will read and write in chunks of 4096 or 8192 bytes. Some combinations of Linux kernels and network cards cannot handle that large blocks, and it might not be optimal, anyway. So we'll want to experiment and find a rsize and wsize that works and is as fast as possible. You can test the speed of your options with some simple commands. Given the mount command above and that you have write access to the disk you can do this to test the sequential write performance:

```
time dd if=/dev/zero of=/mnt/testfile bs=16k count=4096
```

This creates a 64Mb file of zeroed bytes (which should be large enough that caching is no significant part of any performance perceived, use a larger file if you have a lot of memory). Do it a couple (5-10?) of times and average the times. It is the `elapsed' or `wall clock' time that's most interesting in this connection. Then you can test the read performance by reading back the file:

```
time dd if=/mnt/testfile of=/dev/null bs=16k
```

do that a couple of times and average. Then umount, and mount again with a larger rsize and wsize. They should probably be multiples of 1024, and not larger than 16384 bytes since that's the maximum size in NFS version 2. Directly after mounting with a larger size cd into the mounted file system and do things like ls, explore the fs a bit to make sure everything is as it should. If the rsize/wsize is too large the symptoms are very odd and not 100% obvious. A typical symptom is incomplete file lists when doing 'ls', and no error messages. Or reading files failing mysteriously with no error messages. After establishing that the given rsize/wsize works you can do the speed tests again. Different server platforms are likely to have different optimal sizes. SunOS and Solaris is reputedly a lot faster with 4096 byte blocks than with anything else.

Newer Linux kernels (since 1.3 sometime) perform read-ahead for rsizes larger or equal to the machine page size. On Intel CPUs the page size is 4096 bytes. Read ahead will significantly increase the NFS read performance. So on a Intel machine you will want 4096 byte rsize if at all possible.

Remember to edit /etc/fstab to reflect the rsize/wsize you found.

A trick to increase NFS write performance is to disable synchronous writes on the server. The NFS specification states that NFS write requests shall not be considered finished before the data written is on a non-volatile medium (normally the disk). This restricts the write performance somewhat, asynchronous writes will speed NFS writes up. The Linux nfsd has never done synchronous writes since the Linux file system implementation does not lend itself to this, but on non-Linux servers you can increase the performance this way with this in your exports file:

```
/dir    -async,access=linuxbox
```

or something similar. Please refer to the exports man page on the machine in question. Please note that this increases the risk of data loss.

5. NFS over slow lines

Slow lines include Modems, ISDN and quite possibly other long distance connections.

This section is based on knowledge about the used protocols but no actual experiments. My home computer has been down for 6 months (bad HD, low on cash) and so I have had no modem connection to test this with. Please let me hear from you if try this :-)

The first thing to remember is that NFS is a slow protocol. It has high overhead. Using NFS is almost like using kermit to transfer files. It's slow. Almost anything is faster than NFS. FTP is faster. HTTP is faster. rcp is faster. ssh is faster.

Still determined to try it out? OK.

NFS' default parameters are for quite fast, low latency, lines. If you use these default parameters over high latency lines it can cause NFS to report errors, abort operations, pretend that files are shorter than they really are, and act mysteriously in other ways.

The first thing to do is not to use the soft mount option. This will cause timeouts to return errors to the software, which will, most likely not handle the situation at all well. This is a good way to get for mysterious failures. Instead use the hard mount option. When hard is active timeouts causes infinite retries instead of aborting whatever it was the software wanted to do. This is what you want. Really.

The next thing to do is to tweak the timeo and retrans mount options. They are described in the nfs(5) man page, but here is a copy:

---

timeo=n The value in tenths of a second before sending the first retransmission after an RPC timeout. The default value is 7 tenths of a second. After the first timeout, the timeout is doubled after each successive timeout until a maximum timeout of 60 seconds is reached or the enough retransmissions have occured to cause a major timeout. Then, if the filesystem is hard mounted, each new timeout cascade restarts at twice the initial value of the previous cascade, again doubling at each retransmission. The maximum timeout is always 60 seconds. Better overall performance may be achieved by increasing the timeout when mounting on a busy network, to a slow server, or through several routers or gateways.

retrans=n The number of minor timeouts and retransmissions that must occur before a major timeout occurs. The default is 3 timeouts. When a major timeout occurs, the file operation is either aborted or a "server not responding" message is printed on the console.

In other words: If a reply is not received within the 0.7 second (700ms) timeout the NFS client will repeat the request and double the timeout to 1.4 seconds. If the reply does not appear within the 1.4 seconds the request is repeated again and the timeout doubled again, to 2.8 seconds.

A lines speed can be measured with ping with the same packet size as your rsize/wsize options.

```
$ ping -s 8192 lugulbanda
PING lugulbanda.uio.no (129.240.222.99): 8192 data bytes
8200 bytes from 129.240.222.99: icmp_seq=0 ttl=64 time=15.2 ms
8200 bytes from 129.240.222.99: icmp_seq=1 ttl=64 time=15.9 ms
8200 bytes from 129.240.222.99: icmp_seq=2 ttl=64 time=14.9 ms
8200 bytes from 129.240.222.99: icmp_seq=3 ttl=64 time=14.9 ms
8200 bytes from 129.240.222.99: icmp_seq=4 ttl=64 time=15.0 ms

—— lugulbanda.uio.no ping statistics ——
5 packets transmitted, 5 packets received, 0% packet loss
round-trip min/avg/max = 14.9/15.1/15.9 ms
```

The time here is how long the ping packet took to get back and forth to lugulbanda. 15ms is quite fast. Over a 28.000 bps line you can expect something like 4000-5000ms, and if the line is otherwise loaded this time will be even higher, easily double. When this time is high we say that there is 'high latency'. Generally, for larger packets and for more loaded lines the latency will tend to increase. Increase timeo suitably for your line and load. And since the latency increases when you use the line for other things: If you ever want to use FTP and NFS at the same time you should try measuring ping times while using FTP to transfer files.

6. Security and NFS

I am by no means a computer security expert. But I do have a little advice for the security conscious. But be warned: This is by no means a complete list of NFS related problems and if you think you're safe once you're read and implemented all this I have a bridge I want to sell you.

This section is probably of no concern if you are on a closed network where you trust all the users, and no-one you don't trust can get access to machines on the network. I.e., there should be no way to dial into the network, and it should in no way be connected to other networks where you don't trust everyone using it as well as the security. Do you think I sound paranoid? I'm not at all paranoid. This is just basic security advice. And remember, the things I say here is just the start of it. A secure site needs a diligent and knowledgeable admin that knows where to find information about current and potential security problems.

NFS has a basic problem in that the client, if not told otherwise, will trust the NFS server and vice versa. This can be bad. It means that if the server's root account is broken into it can be quite easy to break into the client's root account as well. And vice versa. There are a couple of coping strategies for this, which we'll get back to.

Something you should read is the CERT advisories on NFS, most of the text below deals with issues CERT has written advisories about. See ftp.cert.org/01-README for a up to date list of CERT advisories. Here are some NFS related advisories:

CA-91:21.SunOS.NFS.Jumbo.and.fsirand 12/06/91
Vulnerabilities concerning Sun Microsystems, Inc. (Sun) Network File System (NFS) and the fsirand program. These vulnerabilities affect SunOS versions 4.1.1, 4.1, and 4.0.3 on all architectures. Patches are available for SunOS 4.1.1. An initial patch for SunOS 4.1 NFS is also available. Sun will be providing complete patches for SunOS 4.1 and SunOS 4.0.3 at a later date.

CA-94:15.NFS.Vulnerabilities 12/19/94
This advisory describes security measures to guard against several vulnerabilities in the Network File System (NFS). The advisory was prompted by an increase in root compromises by intruders using tools to exploit the vulnerabilities.

CA-96.08.pcnfsd 04/18/96
This advisory describes a vulnerability in the pcnfsd program (also known as rpc.pcnfsd). A patch is included.

6.1. Client Security

On the client we can decide that we don't want to trust the server too much a couple of ways with options to mount. For example we can forbid suid programs to work off the NFS file system with the nosuid option. This is a good idea and you should consider using this with all NFS mounted disks. It means that the server's root user cannot make a suid-root program on the file system, log in to the client as a normal user and then use the suid-root program to become root on the client too. We could also forbid execution of files on the mounted file system altogether with the noexec option. But this is more likely to be impractical than nosuid since a file system is likely to at least contain some scripts or programs that needs to be executed. You enter these options in the options column, with the rsize and wsize, separated by commas.

6.2. Server security: nfsd

On the server we can decide that we don't want to trust the client's root account. We can do that by using the root_squash option in exports:

```
/mn/eris/local apollon(rw,root_squash)
```

Now, if a user with UID 0 on the client attempts to access (read, write, delete) the file system the server substitutes the UID of the servers `nobody' account. Which means that the root user on the client can't access or change files that only root on the server can access or change. That's good, and you should probably use root_squash on all the file systems you export. "But the root user on the client can still use 'su' to become any other user and access and change that users files!" say you. To which the answer is: Yes, and that's the way it is, and has to be with Unix and NFS. This has one important implication: All important binaries and files should be owned by root, and not bin or other non-root account, since the only account the clients root user cannot access is the servers root account. In the NFSd man page there are several other squash options listed so that you can decide to mistrust whomever you (don't) like on the clients. You also have options to squash any UID and GID range you want to. This is described in the Linux NFSd man page.

root_squash is in fact the default with the Linux NFSd, to grant root access to a filesystem use no_root_squash.

Another important thing is to ensure that nfsd checks that all it's requests comes from a privileged port. If it accepts requests from any old port on the client a user with no special privileges can run a program that's is easy to obtain over the Internet. It talks nfs protocol and will claim that the user is anyone the user wants to be. Spooky. The Linux nfsd does this check by default, on other OSes you have to enable this check yourself. This should be described in the nfsd man page for the OS.

Another thing. Never export a file system to 'localhost' or 127.0.0.1. Trust me.

6.3. Server security: the portmapper

The basic portmapper, in combination with nfsd has a design problem that makes it possible to get to files on NFS servers without any privileges. Fortunately the portmapper Linux uses is relatively secure against this attack, and can be made more secure by configuring up access lists in two files.

First we edit /etc/hosts.deny. It should contain the line

```
portmap: ALL
```

which will deny access to everyone. That's a bit drastic perhaps, so we open it again by editing /etc/hosts.allow. But first we need to figure out what to put in it. It should basically list all machines that should have access to your portmapper. On a run of the mill Linux system there are very few machines that need any access for any reason. The portmapper administrates nfsd, mountd, ypbind/ypserv, pcnfsd, and 'r' services like ruptime and rusers. Of these only nfsd, mountd, ypbind/ypserv and perhaps pcnfsd are of any consequence. All machines that needs to access services on your machine should be allowed to do that. Let's say that your machines address is 129.240.223.254 and that it lives on the subnet 129.240.223.0 should have access to it (those are terms introduced by the networking HOWTO, go back and refresh your memory if you need to). Then we write

```
portmap: 129.240.223.0/255.255.255.0
```

in hosts.allow. This is the same as the network address you give to route and the subnet mask you give to ifconfig. For the device eth0 on this machine ifconfig should show

```
eth0    Link encap:10Mbps Ethernet  HWaddr 00:60:8C:96:D5:56
                     inet  addr:129.240.223.254     Bcast:129.240.223.255
Mask:255.255.255.0
          UP BROADCAST RUNNING MULTICAST  MTU:1500  Metric:1
```

```
RX packets:360315 errors:0 dropped:0 overruns:0
TX packets:179274 errors:0 dropped:0 overruns:0
Interrupt:10 Base address:0x320
```

and netstat -rn should show

```
Kernel routing table
Destination    Gateway    Genmask         Flags Metric Ref Use    Iface
129.240.223.0  0.0.0.0    255.255.255.0   U     0      0   174412 eth0
```

(Network address in first column).

The hosts.deny and hosts.allow files are described in the manual pages of the same names.

IMPORTANT: Do not put anything but IP NUMBERS in the portmap lines of
these files. Host name lookups can indirectly cause portmap activity which will trigger host name lookups which can indirectly cause portmap activity which will trigger...

The above things should make your server tighter. The only remaining problem (Yeah, right!) is someone breaking root (or boot MS-DOS) on a trusted machine and using that privilege to send requests from a secure port as any user they want to be.

6.4. NFS and firewalls

It's a very good idea to firewall the nfs and portmap ports in your router or firewall. The nfsd operates at port 2049, both udp and tcp protocols. The portmapper at port 111, tcp and udp, and mountd at port 745 and and 747, tcp and udp. Normally. You should check the ports with the rpcinfo -p command.

If on the other hand you want NFS to go through a firewall there are options for newer NFSds and mountds to make them use a specific (nonstandard) port which can be open in the firewall.

6.5. Summary

If you use the hosts.allow/deny, root_squash, nosuid and privileged port features in the portmapper/nfs software you avoid many of the presently known bugs in nfs and can almost feel secure about that at least. But still, after all that: When an intruder has access to your network, s/he can make strange commands appear in your /var/spool/ mail are mounted over NFS. For the same reason, you should never access your PGP private key over nfs. Or at least you should know the risk involved. And now you know a bit of it.

NFS and the portmapper makes up a complex subsystem and therefore it's not totally unlikely that new bugs will be discovered, either in the basic design or the implementation we use. There might even be holes known now, which someone is abusing. But that's life. To keep abreast of things like this you should at least read the newsgroups comp.os.linux.announce and comp.security.announce at a absolute minimum.

7. Mount Checklist

This section is based on IBM Corp. NFS mount problem checklist. My thanks to them for making it available for this HOWTO. If you experience a problem mounting a NFS filesystem please refer to this list before posting your problem. Each item describes a failure mode and the fix.

1. File system not exported, or not exported to the client in question.

Fix: Export it

2. Name resolution doesn't jibe with the exports list.

e.g.: export list says export to johnmad but johnmad's name is resolved as johnmad.austin.ibm.com. mount permission is denied.

Fix: Export to both forms of the name.

It can also happen if the client has 2 interfaces with different names for each of the two adapters and the export only specifies one.

Fix: export both interfaces.

This can also happen if the server can't do a lookuphostbyname or lookuphostbyaddr (these are library functions) on the client. Make sure the client can do host <name>; host <ip_addr>; and that both shows the same machine.

Fix: straighten out name resolution.

3. The file system was mounted after NFS was started (on that server). In that case the server is exporting underlying mount point, not the mounted filesystem.

Fix: Shut down NFSd and then restart it.

Note: The clients that had the underlying mount point mounted will get problems accessing it after the restart.

4. The date is wildly off on one or both machines (this can mess up make)

Fix: Get the date set right.

The HOWTO author recommends using NTP to synchronize clocks. Since there are export restrictions on NTP in the US you have to get NTP for debian, redhat or slackware from ftp://ftp.hacktic.nl/pub/replay/pub/linux or a mirror.

5. The server can not accept a mount from a user that is in more than 8 groups.

Fix: decrease the number of groups the user is in or mount via a different user.

8. FAQs

This is the FAQ section. Most of it was written by Alan Cox.

1. I get a lot of 'stale nfs handle' errors when using Linux as a nfs server.

This is caused by a bug in some oldish nfsd versions. It is fixed in nfs-server2.2beta16 and later.

2. When I try to mount a file system I get

can't register with portmap: system error on send

You are probably using a Caldera system. There is a bug in the rc scripts. Please contact Caldera to obtain a fix.

3. Why can't I execute a file after copying it to the NFS server?

The reason is that nfsd caches open file handles for performance reasons (remember, it runs in user space). While nfsd has a file open (as is the case after writing to it), the kernel won't allow you to execute it. Nfsds newer than spring 95 release open files after a few seconds, older ones would cling to them for days.

4. My NFS files are all read only

The Linux NFS server defaults to read only. RTFM the "exports" and nfsd manual pages. You will need to alter /etc/exports.

5. I mount from a linux nfs server and while ls works I can't read or write files.

On older versions of Linux you must mount a NFS servers with rsize=1024,wsize=1024.

6. I mount from a Linux NFS server with a block size of between 3500-4000 and it crashes the Linux box regularly

Basically don't do it then.

7. Can Linux do NFS over TCP

No, not at present.

8. I get loads of strange errors trying to mount a machine from a Linux box.

Make sure your users are in 8 groups or less. Older servers require this.

9. When I reboot my machine it sometimes hangs when trying to unmount a hung NFS server.

Do not unmount NFS servers when rebooting or halting, just ignore them, it will not hurt anything if you don't unmount them. The command is umount -avt nonfs.

10. Linux NFS clients are very slow when writing to Sun and BSD systems

NFS writes are normally synchronous (you can disable this if you don't mind risking losing data). Worse still BSD derived kernels tend to be unable to work in small blocks. Thus when you write 4K

read 4K page
alter 1K
write 4K back to physical disk
read 4K page
alter 1K
write 4K page back to physical disk
etc..

9. Exporting filesystems

The way to export filesytems with NFS is not completely consistent across platforms of course. In this case Linux and Solaris 2 are the deviants. This section lists, superficially the way to do it on most systems. If the kind of system you have is not covered you must check your OS man-pages. Keywords are: nfsd, system administration tool, rc scripts, boot scripts, boot sequence, /etc/exports, exportfs. I'll use one example throughout this section: How to export /mn/eris/local to apollon read/write.

9.1. IRIX, HP-UX, Digital-UNIX, Ultrix, SunOS 4 (Solaris 1), AIX

These OSes use the traditional Sun export format. In /etc/exports write:

```
/mn/eris/local -rw=apollon
```

The complete documentation is in the exports man page. After editing the file run exportfs -av to export the filesystems.

How strict the exportfs command is about the syntax varies. On some OSes you will find that previously entered lines reads:

```
/mn/eris/local apollon
```

or even something degenerate like:

```
/mn/eris/local rw=apollon
```

I recommend being formal. You risk that the next version of exportfs if much stricter and then suddenly everything will stop working.

9.2. Solaris 2

Sun completely re-invented the wheel when they did Solaris 2. So this is completely different from all other OSes. What you do is edit the file /etc/dfs/dfstab. In it you place share commands as documented in the share(1M) man page. Like this:

```
share -o rw=apollon -d "Eris Local" /mn/eris/local
```

After editing run the program shareall to export the filesystems.

10. PC-NFS

You should not run PC-NFS. You should run samba.

Sorry: I don't know anything about PC-NFS. If someone feels like writing something about it please do and I'll include it here.

INDEX

A

Access:
- cable internet, fee for, 232
- local and Internet, and Linux home network, 232–33
- Samba:
  - NT guest access, 249–50
  - Unix permissions control access, 260–61
  - user access control, 261
  - Win9X in user level access mode, 263–65

Address:
- broadcast, 4
- local, 4
- loopback, 4
- name-to-address resolution, 96–98
- TCP/IP, 3–4

`admin users` parameter, 307–9
`allow hosts` parameter, 308–9
`alternate permissions` parameter, 309
`announce as` parameter, 309
`announce version` parameter, 309–10
`auto services` parameter, 310
`available` parameter, 310

B

`bind`, 517–21
- converting from version 4 to version 8, 517–19

`bind interfaces only` parameter, 310–11
`blocking locks` parameter, 311
Broadband network, 230–32
Broadcast address, 4
`browsable` parameter, 311
`browseable` parameter, 312
`browse list` parameter, 312
Budget, for Linux home network, 224–25

C

Cable and broadband network, 230–32
Cable internet access, fee for, 232
Caching nameservers, 105
`case sensitive` parameter, 312
`change notify timeout` parameter, 312
`character set` parameter, 313
Classless subnet, dNS, 508–9
`client code page` parameter, 313–14
Client name resolution, enabling, 61–64
`codingsystem` parameter, 315
`comment` parameter, 315
Computer software, for Linux home network, 233–34
`config file` parameter, 316
Configuration, DNS, 487–90
`copy` parameter, 316
`create mask` parameter, 316–17
`create mode` parameter, 317
Current network characteristics, determining, 47–50
Current Windows network configuration, determining, 126–31

D

Data sharing:
- in Network File System (NFS), 191–212
- in Windows, 123–90

`deadtime` parameter, 317
`debug level` parameter, 318
`debug timestamp` parameter, 318
`default case` parameter, 318
`default service` parameter, 318–19
`delete readonly` parameter, 319
`delete veto files` parameter, 319
`deny hosts` parameter, 320
Device driver, 40–41
`dfree command` parameter, 320–21
DHCP (Dynamic Host Control Protocol), 231
`directory` parameter, 321
`directory mask` parameter, 321
`directory mode` parameter, 321
`dmesg` command, 41–42, 64–67
DNS, 483–524
DNS nameserver, 483–524
`dns proxy` parameter, 322
Documentation:
- nameservers, 483–524
- NFS, 525–44
- Samba, 235–86
- TCP/IP, 443–82

Domain controller, 126
`domain admin group` parameter, 322
`domain admin users` parameter, 322
`domain controller` parameter, 322
`domain group map` parameter, 322–24
`domain groups` parameter, 324
`domain guest users` parameter, 324–5
`domain logons` parameter, 325
`domain master` parameter, 325
Domain Name System, *See* DNS
Domains, 126
`domain user map` parameter, 326–27
`dont descend` parameter, 327
`dos filetime resolution` parameter, 328
`dos filetimes` parameter, 328

E

Electrical needs, for Linux home network, 226–27
`encrypt passwords` parameter, 326–27
`/etc/exports` file, 203
- sample, 193–94
- setting up to allow mounting, 193–96

Ethernet cabling, 227–28
`exec` parameter, 329

F

`fake directory create times` parameter, 329
`fake oplocks` parameter, 329–30
Family impact, Linux home network, 225
Firewalls, and NFS, 539

follow symlinks parameter, 330
force create mode parameter, 330
force directory mode parameter, 331
force group parameter, 331
force user parameter, 331–32
fstype parameter, 332

G

getwd cache parameter, 332
GNU General Public License, 235–43
group parameter, 332
guest account parameter, 332–33
guest ok parameter, 333
guest only parameter, 333

H

hide dot files parameter, 333
hide files parameter, 333–34
homedir map parameter, 334–35
Host table, setting up, 60–61
hosts allow parameter, 335
hosts deny parameter, 335
hosts equiv parameter, 335
HP-UX, and NFS, 543

I

ifconfig command, 9–10, 42, 67–68
importdir directory, 206
include parameter, 335
interfaces parameter, 335–36
Internet, 3
invalid users parameter, 336–37
IPv4, 3
IPv6, 3
IRIX, and NFS, 543

K

keepalive parameter, 337
kernel oplocks parameter, 337

L

LAN Manager and Lan Manager for UNIX (LM/X), 283
LAN Server for OS/2, 284
ldap bind as parameter, 337–38
ldap passwd file parameter, 338
ldap port parameter, 338
ldap server parameter, 338
ldap suffix parameter, 339
Linux, 219–21
  features, 219–21
  portmapper, 527–28, 538
Linux home network, 224–34
lm announce parameter, 339
lmhosts (5), 288–89
  description, 288
  file format, 288–89
  synopsis, 288
  version, 289
lm interval parameter, 339
load printers parameter, 340
Local address, 4
local group map parameter, 340–41
local master parameter, 341–42
lock dir parameter, 341–42
lock directory parameter, 342
locking parameter, 342
log file parameter, 342–43
log level parameter, 343
logon drive parameter, 343
logon home parameter, 343
logon path parameter, 343–44
logon script parameter, 344–45
Loopback address, 4
lppause command parameter, 345
lpq cache time parameter, 346
lpq command parameter, 346–47
lpresume command parameter, 347
lprm command parameter, 347–48
ls command, 200–203

M

machine password timeout parameter, 348
Maintenance, DNS, 515–16
magic output parameter, 348–49
mangle case parameter, 349
mangled map parameter, 349–50
mangled names parameter, 350–51
mangled stack parameter, 351
mangling char parameter, 351
map archive parameter, 351–52
map hidden parameter, 352
map system parameter, 352
map to guest parameter, 352–53
max connections parameter, 353–54
max disk size parameter, 354
max log size parameter, 354
max mux parameter, 354
maxopenfiles parameter, 355
max packet parameter, 355
max ttl parameter, 355
max wins ttl parameter, 355
max xmit parameter, 355–56
Mediaone, 230
message command parameter, 356–7
Microsoft Windows servers, 282–83
Minimal Linux, 219–21
  drawbacks of, 220–21
  Trinux, 221–22
min print space parameter, 357
min wins ttl parameter, 357
mount command, 196–99, 207, 209
mountd, 528–30
Mount problem checklist, NFS, 540–41

N

named.boot, 112–13
named.ca, 108
named.conf, 113–14
named.hosts, 110–11
named.local, 108–10
named.rev, 111–12
name resolve order parameter, 357–58
Nameservers:
  caching, 105
  current configuration, 95–103
  documentation, 483–524
  named.boot, 112–13
  named.ca, 108
  named.conf, 113–14
  named.hosts, 110–11
  named.local, 108–10
  named.rev, 111–12
  name-to-address resolution, 96–98
  primary, 104–20
  record types, 105–6
  resolv.conf, 106–7
  secondary, 105
  setting up, 93–121
  top-level domains, 95–98
  types of, 104–5
Name-to-address resolution, 96–98
netbios aliases parameter, 358
netbios name parameter, 358–59
NetBIOS names, 277

netmasks, 6–7
default binary representation of, 7
netscape command, 144, 154–55
netstat command, 10–11
netstat -nr command, 14, 69–70
netstat -r command, 14–15
Network address, 3–4
Network cabling, Linux home network, 227–28
Network classes, 4–6
Network File System (NFS):
and AIX, 543
data sharing, 191–212
and Digital-UNIX, 543
documentation, 525–44
/etc}/exports file:
sample, 194
setting up to allow mounting, 193–96
exporting filesystems, 543
FAQs, 541–43
and firewalls, 539
and HP-UX, 543
and IRIX, 543
mount options, 531
mount problem checklist, 540–41
nfsd, 357–58
optimizing, 532–33
over slow lines, 533–35
remote NFS mount, 196–200
mount command, 207–8
touch command, 207–9
security, 535–38
client, 536–37
server, 537–38
setting up, 192–210, 530–31
and SunOS 4 (Solaris 1), 543
and Ultrix, 543
Network hub, 229–30
Networking equipment, 228–30
network hub, 229–30
Network Interface Card (NIC), 228–29
Network interface:
bringing down, 51–53
bringing up, 53–60
Network Interface Card (NIC), 4, 228–29, 233
Ethernet values, 74
Newsgroups, TCP/IP, 466–70
NFS, *See* Network File System (NFS)
nfsd, 357–58, 528–30
nis homedir parameter, 359
nmbd, 290–94
description, 290–91
files, 293
options, 291–92
signals, 293
synopsis, 290
version, 294
nslookup command, 21–22, 25–27, 30–32, 46–47, 98–103
nt pipe support parameter, 359
nt smb support parameter, 359–60
null passwords parameter, 360

O

ole locking compatibility parameter, 360
only guest parameter, 360
only user parameter, 360–61
oplocks parameter, 361
Optimization, of NFS, 532–33
os level parameter, 361

P

packet size parameter, 362
panic action parameter, 362
passwd chat parameter, 362–63
passwd program parameter, 363–64
password level parameter, 364–65
password server parameter, 365–66
path parameter, 366
PATHWORKS, 283–84
Peer to peer, 126
ping command, 18–19, 23–25, 27–28
Portmapper, Linux, 527–28
postexec parameter, 367
postscript parameter, 367
PPP (Point-to-Point Protocol), 232–33
preexec parameter, 367–68
preferred master parameter, 368
Primary nameserver, setting up, 104–20
printable parameter, 370
print command parameter, 369–70
printcap parameter, 370
printcap name parameter, 370–71
printer driver file parameter, 372
printer driver location parameter, 372–73
printer driver parameter, 371–72
printer name parameter, 373
printer parameter, 371
printing parameter, 373
print ok parameter, 370
protocol, 373–74
Public address ranges, 6
public parameter, 374

Q

queuepause command parameter, 374
queueresume command parameter, 374–75

R

read bmpx parameter, 375
read list parameter, 375
read only parameter, 375
read prediction parameter, 376
read raw parameter, 376
read size parameter, 376–77
Record types, 105–6
Red Hat Package Manager, 160–61
remote announce parameter, 377
remote browse sync parameter, 377–78
Remote NFS mount, 196–200
mount command, 207–8
touch command, 207–9
resolv.conf, 106–7
revalidate parameter, 378
Reverse lookups, DNS, 507
Reverse zone, DNS, 505–8
RFCs, DNS, 523–24
RJ11, 227
RJ45, 227
root directory parameter, 379
root parameter, 378–79
root postexec parameter, 379
root preexec parameter, 379
route command, 45
Routing, 8–9, 42–45
rpm command, 174–77
RPM method of installation, 148, 160–61
RPMS directory, 149–50, 155
rs.internic.net, 23–24

S

samba (7), 289–90, 294–97
availability, 296
components, 295–96
contributions, 296

credits, 296–97
description, 295
version, 296
Samba, 143–59
connecting from Windows to, 170–73
connecting to Windows from, 171–73
determining your current version of, 161–62
documentation, 235–86
download page, 148
FAQ, 243–73
FTP screen for selecting version of, 149
getting, 143–54
GNU General Public License, 235–43
home page, 146
installing, 164–65
Linus, command-line screen for, 145
manual pages, 287–442
author, 289–90
lmhosts (5), 288–89
nmbd, 290–94
samba (7), 289–90, 294–97
smbclient (1), 289–90, 408–22
smb.conf (5), 289–90, 297–408
smbd (8), 422–31
smbpasswd (5), 431–34
smbpasswd (8), 289, 434–40
smbstatus (1), 441–42
`Netscape Download` screen, 157
Red Hat directory for Samba download, 150
removing, 162–64
RPM method of installation, 148, 160–61
setting times when not owner, 270
setting up, 167–69
SMB (Server Message Block), 274–86
testing, 167–69
upgrading, 166
versions of, for Red Hat 5.2, 151–54
Web page, 147
Secondary nameservers, 105
`security` parameter, 380–84
Server Message Block, *See* SMB
`set directory` parameter, 384
`share modes` parameter, 384–85
`shared mem size` parameter, 385
`short preserve case` parameter, 385
SLIP (Serial Line Interface Protocol), 233
Slow lines, NFS over, 533–35
SMB:
clients, 284–85
currently available clients and servers, 280–81
defined, 276–80
NetBIOS names, 277
protocol variants, 277–80
sample SMB exchange, 280
servers, 281–84
domains, 282
LAN Manager and Lan Manager for UNIX (LM/X), 283
LAN Server for OS/2, 284
Microsoft Windows servers, 282–83
PATHWORKS, 283–84
Samba, 282
TotalNET Advanced Server, 283
Vision FS, 283
workgroups, 282
smbclient (1), 289–90, 408–22
commands, 417–20
description, 408
diagnostics, 421–22
installation, 421
notes, 421
operations, 416–17
options, 408–16
synopsis, 408
version, 422
smb.conf (5), 289–90, 297–408
file format, 298
global parameters, 305–406
smbd (8), 422–31
description, 423
diagnostics, 429–30
files, 425–26
installation, 426–27
testing, 429
limitations, 426
options, 423–25
printer, 426
running the server:
as a daemon, 427–28
on request, 428–29
signals, 430
synopsis, 422
version, 429
SMB network, categorizing, 126
smbpasswd (5), 431–34
description, 431
file format, 431–33
notes, 433–34
synopsis, 431
version, 434
smbpasswd (8), 289, 434–40
description, 435–36
notes, 440
options, 436–40
synopsis, 435
version, 440
`smb passwd file` parameter, 385–86
`smbrun` parameter, 386
smbstatus (1), 441–42
description, 441
options, 441
synopsis, 441
version, 441
`socket address` parameter, 386
`socket options` parameter, 386–87
SRPMS directory, 149
`ssl` parameter, 388
`ssl CA certDir` parameter, 388
`ssl CA certFile` parameter, 388–89
`ssl ciphers` parameter, 389
`ssl client cert` parameter, 389
`ssl client key` parameter, 389–90
`ssl compatibility` parameter, 390
`ssl hosts` parameter, 390
`ssl hosts resign` parameter, 390–91
`ssl require clientcert` parameter, 391
`ssl require servercert` parameter, 391
`ssl server cert` parameter, 392
`ssl server key` parameter, 392
`ssl version` parameter, 392–93
`stat cache` parameter, 393
`stat cache size` parameter, 393
`status` parameter, 393
`strict locking` parameter, 393–94
`strip dot` parameter, 394
Subnet, 7–8
SunOS 4 (Solaris 1), and NFS, 543
`sync always` parameter, 394–95
`syslog` parameter, 395

T

TCP/IP:
address, 3–4
ranges/characteristics, 5
books about, 444–50
broadcast address, 4
defined, 3
documentation, 443–82
network resources list, 443–73
private IP network addresses, 473–82
ifconfig command, 9–10, 42, 67–68, 70–71
major on-line resources, 450–54
miscellaneous networking pages, 470–73
miscellaneous Web pages, 454–66
netmask, 6–7
netstat command, 10–11
network classes, 4–6
newsgroups, 466–70
nslookup command, 21–22, 25–27, 30–32, 46–47, 98–103
ping command, 18–19, 23–25, 27–28
public address ranges, 6
routing, 8–9
sample network characteristics, 6
subnet, 7–8
traceroute command, 18, 19–21, 23, 25, 29
TCP/IP network, 1–38
accessing other TCP/IP hosts, 18–38
client name resolution, enabling, 61–64
configuring, 39–87
current network characteristics, determining, 47–50
current system TCP/IP values, 2–17
host table, setting up, 60–61
network interface:
bringing down, 51–53
brining up, 53–60
setting up, 40–91
device driver, 40–41
dmesg command, 41–42, 64–67
hosts file, 46
ifconfig command, 42, 67–68, 70–71
nslookup command, 46–47
route command, 45
routing, 42–45
10Base5, 227–28
Thick ethernet, 227–28
Thin ethernet, 227
time offset parameter, 395
time server parameter, 395
timestamp logs parameter, 395–96
Tiny Linux, 219–21
Top-level domains, 95–98
TotalNET Advanced Server, 283
touch command, 207–9
traceroute command, 18, 19–21, 23, 25, 29
Trinux, 221–22
disadvantages of, 222
features of, 221–22

U

Ultrix, and NFS, 543
unix password sync parameter, 396
unix realname parameter, 396
update encrypted parameter, 396–97
use rhosts parameter, 397
username level parameter, 399
username map parameter, 399–401
username parameter, 397–99
user parameter, 397
users parameter, 397
/usr/local/exportdir, 209–10

V

valid chars parameter, 401–2
valid users parameter, 402–3
veto files parameter, 403
veto oplock files parameter, 404
Vision FS, 283
volume parameter, 404

W

wide links parameter, 404
Windows:
Control Panel, 136
Entire Network display, 184
File and Print Sharing window, 137
Network Access Control display, 139
network configuration:
determining, 125–42
Windows SMB-based network, 125–26
Network Configuration display, 136–37
network environment, verifying, 133–34
Network Identification display, 138, 181–82
Network Neighborhood screen, 183
Settings menu, 135
setting up/logging on as Windows network user, 131–33
Start menu, 135
winds server parameter, 405
wins proxy parameter, 404
wins support parameter, 405
workgroup parameter, 405
Workgroups, 126
writable parameter, 405
write list parameter, 406
write ok parameter, 406
write raw parameter, 406

LICENSE AGREEMENT AND LIMITED WARRANTY

READ THE FOLLOWING TERMS AND CONDITIONS CAREFULLY BEFORE OPENING THIS CD PACKAGE. THIS LEGAL DOCUMENT IS AN AGREEMENT BETWEEN YOU AND PRENTICE-HALL, INC. (THE "COMPANY"). BY OPENING THIS SEALED CD PACKAGE, YOU ARE AGREEING TO BE BOUND BY THESE TERMS AND CONDITIONS. IF YOU DO NOT AGREE WITH THESE TERMS AND CONDITIONS, DO NOT OPEN THE CD PACKAGE. PROMPTLY RETURN THE UNOPENED CD PACKAGE AND ALL ACCOMPANYING ITEMS TO THE PLACE YOU OBTAINED THEM FOR A FULL REFUND OF ANY SUMS YOU HAVE PAID.

1. **GRANT OF LICENSE:** In consideration of your purchase of this book, and your agreement to abide by the terms and conditions of this Agreement, the Company grants to you a nonexclusive right to use and display the copy of the enclosed software program (hereinafter the "SOFTWARE") on a single computer (i.e., with a single CPU) at a single location so long as you comply with the terms of this Agreement. The Company reserves all rights not expressly granted to you under this Agreement.

2. **OWNERSHIP OF SOFTWARE:** You own only the magnetic or physical media (the enclosed CD) on which the SOFTWARE is recorded or fixed, but the Company and the software developers retain all the rights, title, and ownership to the SOFTWARE recorded on the original CD copy(ies) and all subsequent copies of the SOFTWARE, regardless of the form or media on which the original or other copies may exist. This license is not a sale of the original SOFTWARE or any copy to you.

3. **COPY RESTRICTIONS:** This SOFTWARE and the accompanying printed materials and user manual (the "Documentation") are the subject of copyright. The individual programs on the CD are copyrighted by the authors of each program. Some of the programs on the CD include separate licensing agreements. If you intend to use one of these programs, you must read and follow its accompanying license agreement. You may not copy the Documentation or the SOFTWARE, except that you may make a single copy of the SOFTWARE for backup or archival purposes only. You may be held legally responsible for any copying or copyright infringement which is caused or encouraged by your failure to abide by the terms of this restriction.

4. **USE RESTRICTIONS:** You may not network the SOFTWARE or otherwise use it on more than one computer or computer terminal at the same time. You may physically transfer the SOFTWARE from one computer to another provided that the SOFTWARE is used on only one computer at a time. You may not distribute copies of the SOFTWARE or Documentation to others. You may not reverse engineer, disassemble, decompile, modify, adapt, translate, or create derivative works based on the SOFTWARE or the Documentation without the prior written consent of the Company.

5. **TRANSFER RESTRICTIONS:** The enclosed SOFTWARE is licensed only to you and may not be transferred to any one else without the prior written consent of the Company. Any unauthorized transfer of the SOFTWARE shall result in the immediate termination of this Agreement.

6. **TERMINATION:** This license is effective until terminated. This license will terminate automatically without notice from the Company and become null and void if you fail to comply with any provisions or limitations of this license. Upon termination, you shall destroy the Documentation and all copies of the SOFTWARE. All provisions of this Agreement as to warranties, limitation of liability, remedies or damages, and our ownership rights shall survive termination.

7. **MISCELLANEOUS:** This Agreement shall be construed in accordance with the laws of the United States of America and the State of New York and shall benefit the Company, its affiliates, and assignees.

8. **LIMITED WARRANTY AND DISCLAIMER OF WARRANTY:** The Company warrants that the SOFTWARE, when properly used in accordance with the Documentation, will operate in substantial conformity with the description of the SOFTWARE set forth in the Documentation. The Company does not warrant that the SOFTWARE will meet your requirements or that the operation

of the SOFTWARE will be uninterrupted or error-free. The Company warrants that the media on which the SOFTWARE is delivered shall be free from defects in materials and workmanship under normal use for a period of thirty (30) days from the date of your purchase. Your only remedy and the Company's only obligation under these limited warranties is, at the Company's option, return of the warranted item for a refund of any amounts paid by you or replacement of the item. Any replacement of SOFTWARE or media under the warranties shall not extend the original warranty period. The limited warranty set forth above shall not apply to any SOFTWARE which the Company determines in good faith has been subject to misuse, neglect, improper installation, repair, alteration, or damage by you. EXCEPT FOR THE EXPRESSED WARRANTIES SET FORTH ABOVE, THE COMPANY DISCLAIMS ALL WARRANTIES, EXPRESS OR IMPLIED, INCLUDING WITHOUT LIMITATION, THE IMPLIED WARRANTIES OF MERCHANTABILITY AND FITNESS FOR A PARTICULAR PURPOSE. EXCEPT FOR THE EXPRESS WARRANTY SET FORTH ABOVE, THE COMPANY DOES NOT WARRANT, GUARANTEE, OR MAKE ANY REPRESENTATION REGARDING THE USE OR THE RESULTS OF THE USE OF THE SOFTWARE IN TERMS OF ITS CORRECTNESS, ACCURACY, RELIABILITY, CURRENTNESS, OR OTHERWISE.

IN NO EVENT, SHALL THE COMPANY OR ITS EMPLOYEES, AGENTS, SUPPLIERS, OR CONTRACTORS BE LIABLE FOR ANY INCIDENTAL, INDIRECT, SPECIAL, OR CONSEQUENTIAL DAMAGES ARISING OUT OF OR IN CONNECTION WITH THE LICENSE GRANTED UNDER THIS AGREEMENT, OR FOR LOSS OF USE, LOSS OF DATA, LOSS OF INCOME OR PROFIT, OR OTHER LOSSES, SUSTAINED AS A RESULT OF INJURY TO ANY PERSON, OR LOSS OF OR DAMAGE TO PROPERTY, OR CLAIMS OF THIRD PARTIES, EVEN IF THE COMPANY OR AN AUTHORIZED REPRESENTATIVE OF THE COMPANY HAS BEEN ADVISED OF THE POSSIBILITY OF SUCH DAMAGES. IN NO EVENT SHALL LIABILITY OF THE COMPANY FOR DAMAGES WITH RESPECT TO THE SOFTWARE EXCEED THE AMOUNTS ACTUALLY PAID BY YOU, IF ANY, FOR THE SOFTWARE.

SOME JURISDICTIONS DO NOT ALLOW THE LIMITATION OF IMPLIED WARRANTIES OR LIABILITY FOR INCIDENTAL, INDIRECT, SPECIAL, OR CONSEQUENTIAL DAMAGES, SO THE ABOVE LIMITATIONS MAY NOT ALWAYS APPLY. THE WARRANTIES IN THIS AGREEMENT GIVE YOU SPECIFIC LEGAL RIGHTS AND YOU MAY ALSO HAVE OTHER RIGHTS WHICH VARY IN ACCORDANCE WITH LOCAL LAW.

ACKNOWLEDGMENT

YOU ACKNOWLEDGE THAT YOU HAVE READ THIS AGREEMENT, UNDERSTAND IT, AND AGREE TO BE BOUND BY ITS TERMS AND CONDITIONS. YOU ALSO AGREE THAT THIS AGREEMENT IS THE COMPLETE AND EXCLUSIVE STATEMENT OF THE AGREEMENT BETWEEN YOU AND THE COMPANY AND SUPERSEDES ALL PROPOSALS OR PRIOR AGREEMENTS, ORAL, OR WRITTEN, AND ANY OTHER COMMUNICATIONS BETWEEN YOU AND THE COMPANY OR ANY REPRESENTATIVE OF THE COMPANY RELATING TO THE SUBJECT MATTER OF THIS AGREEMENT.

Should you have any questions concerning this Agreement or if you wish to contact the Company for any reason, please contact in writing at the address below.

Robin Short

Prentice Hall PTR

One Lake Street

Upper Saddle River, New Jersey 07458

About the CD-ROM

Contents

The CD-ROM included with *Linux Network Administrator's Interactive Workbook* contains Stampede Linux and a number of TinyLinux versions. The TinyLinux versions, you should note, provide you with the ability the ability to:

- Run Linux without installing it on a hard disk. They can be run off diskette, Zip disk, or loaded into ROM or EEPROMs. This gives you the potential to reduce the cost, size, or complexity of your system.
- Easily make changes to Linux and test it without affecting a permanent install on your hard disk.
- Develop routers, firewalls, gateways, and web servers that can be run totally out of memory. Since memory access is much faster than disk access, you can increase considerably the performance of these systems.
- By running software out of memory, any security breaches or damage to the run-time image can be overwritten with a safe image.

The CD includes the following TinyLinux distributions: DLX Distribution; DOSLINUX; ELKS; FloppyX; LOAF; LODS; LRP; Monkey Linux; Small Linux; Trinux; hal91; and tomsrtbt.

The CD-ROM can be used on Linux and Microsoft Windows® 95/98/NT®.

Technical Support

For issues regarding bad media or replacement software, please contact Prentice Hall at `disc_exchange@prenhall.com`.